Post-Crisis Perspectives

Óscar García Agustín / Christian Ydesen (eds.)

Post-Crisis Perspectives

The Common and its Powers

PETER LANG
EDITION

Bibliographic Information published by the Deutsche Nationalbibliothek
The Deutsche Nationalbibliothek lists this publication in the Deutsche Nationalbibliografie; detailed bibliographic data is available in the internet at http://dnb.d-nb.de.

Library of Congress Cataloging-in-Publication Data

Post-crisis perspectives : the common and its powers / Óscar García Agustín, Christian Ydesen (eds.).
pagescm
Includes bibliographical references.
ISBN 978-3-631-64038-8 — ISBN 978-3-653-02416-6 (E-book) 1. Global Financial Crisis, 2008-2009. 2. Financial crises—Social aspects. 3. Economic policy. 4. Economics. I. García Agustín, Óscar, author, editor of compilation. II. Ydesen, Christian, author, editor of compilation.
HB37172008 .P66 2013
330—dc23

2013033386

ISBN 978-3-631-64038-8 (Print)
E-ISBN 978-3-653-02416-6 (E-Book)
DOI 10.3726/978-3-653-02416-6

Peter Lang Edition is an Imprint of Peter Lang GmbH.

Peter Lang – Frankfurt am Main · Bern · Bruxelles · New York · Oxford · Warszawa · Wien

www.peterlang.com

It is the crisis of crises, a crisis that has a long story, and, in all likelihood, a long future. It is a violent crisis, of a violent finance. [...] It is a systemic crisis that saw an entire economic, political, and cultural model collapse under the pressure of its own contradictions, a crisis in which anger, disenchantment, distrust, and protest are limited to questioning the very limits of capitalism.

Christian Marazzi, *The Violence of Financial Capitalism*

Sometimes the event comes in a moment of economic and political crisis when people are suffering. Other times, though, the event arrives in times of prosperity when hopes and aspirations are rising. It's possible, even in the near future, that the entire financial structure will come crashing down. Or that debtors will gain the conviction and courage not to pay their debts. Or that people will en masse refuse to obey those in power. What will we do then? What society will we construct?

Michael Hardt & Antonio Negri, *Declaration*

Preface and Acknowledgements

The idea for this book originated from an interest in critical and radical political philosophy and the contemporary economic crisis shared by the editors. The idea materialized in a private get-together where we exchanged experiences about being the fathers of twins. Fortunately, the two pairs of twins needed a nap and the older children ran off to play, which left us time to contemplate this anthology.

We decided to organize a symposium under the title "A world after the economic crisis? Readings of Michael Hardt and Antonio Negri's political philosophy." Christian Marazzi very kindly agreed to be the keynote speaker and the symposium was held at Aalborg University on February 7, 2013. We succeeded in gathering a group of scholars working in Denmark interested in the work of Hardt and Negri and in exploring post-crisis perspectives.

Most of the contributions were written in English but others were translated by Maria Angela Ferrari, who has been very engaged in the topic, from Italian, French, and Portuguese. Although some of the authors are well known in English, we find it very relevant to introduce some who, surprisingly, have not been extensively translated into English. To present the thoughts of these authors to English-speaking readers is one of the reasons why we are very proud to edit and present this anthology.

We would like to thank our respective departments at Aalborg University for their support and funding of the whole project, with special mention to the former and current heads of the Department of Culture and Global Studies, Henrik Halkier and Marianne Rostgaard, and the head of the Department of Learning and Philosophy, Annette Lorentzen. Ulla Langballe has been very helpful in the preparation of the symposium and Jesper Bergmann did great work in the last reading of the manuscript. The collaboration with Peter Lang has been very easy and positive thanks to the good work of Ute Winkelkötter. Christian Marazzi's willingness to come to Aalborg was much appreciated, as were the (academic and human) lessons that we learned from him. It has likewise been a pleasure to work with all the contributors in a very constructive and enriching process. Patricio Clarey kindly gave us the authorization to reproduce the fantastic picture on the front page. And last but not least, we would like to thank Lise Rolandsen Agustín, Óscar's wife, and Heidi Lindblad Nielsen, Christian's girlfriend, for their understanding during the whole journey and for their support.

Óscar García Agustín & Christian Ydesen, May 2013

Table of Contents

Part II. Post-Crisis Readings of Hardt and Negri

In Search of Post-Crisis Perspectives

Óscar García Agustín and Christian Ydesen

"There must be some way out of here." These are the opening lyrics of Bob Dylan's song "All Along the Watchtower" from 1967. The quote might be interpreted as discontent with the current situation and a longing for something else. This makes the quote very telling about the contemporary economic crisis that started in the summer of 2007 and which has been affecting the lives of billions through social instability and instillation of a pining for a different world among large groups of people (Wacquant 2009; Marazzi 2011; Standing 2011).

A number of explanations for the origins of the crisis and different paths for overcoming it have taken center stage in various settings at the international, national, and local levels. However, the full consequences of the crisis remain to be seen and the majority of economists and politicians seem unable to think beyond a very economistic paradigm, one that caused the economic crisis in the first place. In other words, they offer only more of the same, such as austerity measures, social welfare cutbacks, and recurring initiatives to boost the financial sector and private enterprise. Zygmunt Bauman pointed out the paradox that all the measures proposed and implemented are only trying to restore the situation prior to the crisis, as if that situation was not the very cause of the crisis (Bauman 2012). And we are still there!

In this respect, it is remarkable that in the autumn of 2012 the International Monetary Fund (IMF) began to change its fiscal policy recommendations, culminating with the publication on January 3, 2013, of the report "Growth Forecast Errors and Fiscal Multipliers" (Blanchard & Leigh 2013). Instead of subscribing to the mantra of austerity measures as the only way to create economic growth, the report stated that the austerity measures implemented in many European countries have had more devastating effects than anticipated. As such, the report concluded that "fiscal multipliers were substantially higher than implicitly assumed by forecasters." (Blanchard & Leigh 2013, 19). However, this historical confession by the IMF's chief economist. Olivier Blanchard, of the effects austerity measures will have on European economies received little or no attention from the media, the governments, or the European Union.

According to Eric Heyer, vice-director of the Analysis and Forecasting Department at the French Economic Observatory, this neglect can be explained partly by the internal division between economic researchers and the more ideologically oriented and politically appointed, members of the IMF and partly by the fact that economic decisions are made by the troika of the IMF, the European Central Bank and the European Union. Of these, the IMF is so far the only organization that has recognized the erroneous economic recipe of Spartan fiscal policies (Heyer 2013). Neoliberal ideology and the fact that Germany is held as an example for all other European countries to follow sustain the tragic economic path laid out in most European countries fighting the economic crisis. Analysts such as those of Morgan Stanley have announced that Spain will be the next Germany due to the increasing competitiveness of its exports; Morgan Stanley cynically considers high unemployment rates and low labour costs an advantage.

The one-eyed focus on austerity measures is clearly visible in the Danish political context, where a newly elected center-left government has implemented significant neoliberal policies—such as welfare cutbacks, the lowering of business taxes, economic support to financial institutions, and facilitation of the implementation of new public management initiatives—in stark contrast with the pre-election promises. The pressure from international competition in terms of attracting foreign investments and improving the competitive capability of businesses, the use of economistic models, and the subscription to neoliberal notions of how society and human beings operate permeate and severely limit the innovative thinking of the political processes. If there is a way out from the left, we can unfortunately claim that the Danish government has no interest in exploring it.

However, in this anthology we are not so much concerned with the historical developments leading up to the economic crisis. Instead, we seek to understand the economic crisis in general and the paths leading to a post-crisis scenario in particular. Joseph Stiglitz (2013) very accurately speaks of post-crisis crises to refer to how their current solutions can exacerbate our long-term problems. We talk about post-crisis perspectives to refer to scenarios after the crisis and how to deal with them (the possible options) as well as to underline the importance of defining these scenarios, starting with the academic work in this anthology and more concretely from there. Intellectual and academic contributions to prefigure the world after the crisis are essential. To achieve these it is necessary to consult alternative analyses providing both in-depth and general insights into the very workings of the capitalist system itself. Such an outsider's view, untainted by the ruling logic of capital accumulation and economic competitiveness, can provide the helicopter perspective necessary for doing away with the failed prescriptions for more of the same offered by the establishment.

Thus, the purpose and aim of the anthology is to analyse the potential and bearings of these concepts and transform them into a post-crisis context. In other words, the anthology contributions seek to identify paths and perspectives leading beyond the contemporary economic crisis. This is what we call a post-crisis perspective, to deduce how the world/society/economics/institutions should/could be set up/organized in a society/world on the other side of the economic crisis. What are the viable lines of continuation and stability? What constitutes useful debris? Which functions are beneficial and which are not? How should we think about money, debt, institutions, politics, and the common?

As such, the anthology displays a very interdisciplinary framework, with contributions from the academic fields of political philosophy, jurisprudence, sociology, and economics, with the purpose of digging new ground to adequately understand the transition from a crisis to a post-crisis perspective. In other words, the anthology offers concepts and frameworks for thinking about post-crisis society.

Theorizing the crisis: the post-workerist perspective

Our main source of inspiration has been the post-workerist perspective, the theoretical framework drawn up by the Autonomia Operaia group of critical thinkers, which counts among its members Christian Marazzi, Antonio Negri, Paolo Virno, Maurizzio Lazzarato, and Franco "Bifo" Berardi (Lotringer & Marazzi 2007). Their works about the crisis have been published and distributed on the UniNomade platform. This developed a framework that presents analyses of central concepts, from financialization and money in the role of debt, institutions, and social movements to the very social ontology and political potential of the common and the multitude.

The most debated authorship related to the Autonomia group is undoubtedly the joint work of Antonio Negri and Michael Hardt. In 2012, these authors published their latest work, *Declaration*, in which they provide an updated analysis based on their complex trilogy about the global political and economic system (*Empire, Multitude* and *Commonwealth*). This analysis, written with militant enthusiasm in light of the protests of 2011, takes the most recent turn of events into account. In fact, the theoretical framework presented in Hardt and Negri's authorship incorporates many crucial dimensions characteristic of the global society, fruitfully sparking further discussions on the development of a post-crisis perspective.

Hardt and Negri's vision of the crisis as expressed in *Declaration* is characterized by moving to the anthropological level of the crisis and identifying four figures of subjectivity: *the indebted, the mediatized, the securitized,* and *the represented.* Each figure pertains to specific developments in the neoliberal crisis, such as the transition from welfare to debtfare, stifling as a result of information and communication overflow, total surveillance as the general condition of society, and representation as an obstacle to the realization of democracy, respectively.

Apart from the numerous examples and references to recent world events that make *Declaration* more concrete than the works of their trilogy, Hardt and Negri emphasize that various modes of flight—or the search for an escape door—is what happens as a response to the crisis. The avoidance of debt, the media, and surveillance, as well as the stifling and false discourse of representative democracy is what points toward a post-crisis perspective, according to Hardt and Negri. The core of the ability to escape is, however, the recognition of one's own power, which is also the very foundation for the ability to create real freedom and security. But to understand this power and the very foundation for creating freedom and security, it is necessary to focus on the constitutive forces of the common.

However, before *Declaration* was published, various other books appeared to account for the "crisis of crises," in the words of Marazzi (2011), that will change the world completely. All these analyses share a common understanding of the intellectual work, which we consider crucial for the post-crisis perspectives: they criticize the capitalist model and show all its contradictions but, at the same time, there is room for alternatives and the articulation of social struggle. That combination of radical critique and seeking potential ways out is palpable in these books and something we also tried to adopt in this anthology.

Without any intention of being exhaustive in this review, the following books, only some of which have been translated into English, must be mentioned. Andrea Fumagalli and Sandro Mezzadra (2010) edited *Crisis in the Global Economy,* which reflects the collective effort of the UniNomade network. The authors consider this to be the first crisis of cognitive capitalism, or biocapitalism. They present a common framework that reflects upon financialization as the new face of capitalism, based on accumulation, debt, and the exploitation of knowledge and the appropriation of the common. Ten theses about the financial crisis are included and represent, in our opinion, the most systematic presentation of post-crisis perspectives so far.

It is not coincidental that one of the contributions takes on a life of its own, *The Violence of Financial Capitalism* by Christian Marazzi (2011). It is a brief but clear-thinking analysis of the crisis that, through a historic approach, questions the separation between real and financial economy and unveils its political consequences, that is, the impossibility of institutional governance managing the new capitalist logic of accumulation. The co-editors of the *Crisis* anthology themselves have also deepened their own visions. Andrea Fumagalli (2007) meticulously describes biocapitalism in *Bieconomia e capitalism cognitivo* to account for the attempt of capitalism's total subsumption of life (bios). This transformation of every social activity into productive economic relations reinforces the increasing precarity of human existence. In the 2013 work *Border as Method, or, the Multiplication of Labor*, Sandro Mezzadra, in collaboration with Brett Neilson, reflects about the role of borders in organizing space and time in capitalism. As in Mezzadra's previous work, migration is closely attached to the economic logic of capitalism (accumulation, exploitation, labor vulnerability), which turns into a new composition and the diversification of labor.

Maurizzio Lazzarato (2012) must be credited for explaining how the logic of financialization affects social life and creates a new subjectivity, also included in Hardt and Negri's *Declaration*: the indebted man, probably the main figure of the crisis. Concurrently with David Graeber in his book *Debt*, Lazzarato points to the debtor–creditor relationship as the mechanism of exploitation and domination at every level of society today. The indebted man is a man without control over his future. Since credit is a promise to pay a debt, it becomes a security-state technique of the government and not just an economic mechanism, reducing the uncertainty in the behaviour of the indebted man, whose future consists of paying the debt (and fulfilling the promise to pay it).

Other very original contributions offer unexpected views of the world under the crisis. Cristina Morini (2010) sets up a new framework, the feminization of labour, to understand the increasing precarity in cognitive capitalism. Based on Deleuze's concept of "becoming a woman of work," Morini notes how capitalism has appropriated the woman's experience, from the realm of reproduction and claims that the socially precarious figure today is the woman, meaning that all persons, disregarding their gender, share the mobility and fragmentation experienced by women in the labour market. In *MundoBraz* Giuseppe Cocco (2009) offers an alternative reading of globalization from the South, particularly from Brazil. Despite the disillusioning idea of the world becoming poorer and poorer, with greater social injustice, it is still possible to reverse this trend by what Cocco calls MundoBraz, the openness of democracy and hybridity. Finally, we want to stress the thesis presented by Franco 'Bifo' Berardi (2012) with his book *The Uprising*, which conceptualizes the crisis as not merely economic but also a crisis of social imagination. Financial powers produce a separation of the general intellect from the body and automate language (a form of parthenogenesis whereby signs produce signs without passing through the flesh). To overcome the fragmentation of the general intellect, Bifo proposes the mobilization of its erotic body by the poetic revitalization of language.

A new language: the common and its powers

Cocco (2009) alerts us of the risks of losing the fight to generate a new lexicon appropriated to develop critical thinking against power relations, Bifo (2012) appeals to language's excess of poetry against the mathematization of language, and Hardt and Negri (2012) consider the making of a new truth to be a collective linguistic act of creativity, an opening of ourselves to a common language. It seems quite clear that talking about post-crisis perspectives is needed to rethink language to understand post-crisis scenarios and, at the same time, to struggle against the impositions of other terms and vocabulary that constrain the creation of alternatives and attempt to perpetuate a reinforced version of the pre-crisis world.

We believe that this anthology is a contribution in that direction. Drawing on post-workerism, it is possible to find not only an academic project but also a political one that we have anchored around the central role of the common and a number of new concepts to articulate it: financialization, biocapitalism, debtfare, the cognitariat, the precariat, substance of value, basic income, indebted man, borders, poor, feminization, tolerance, love, human rights, and institutionalization. Our proposals of post-crisis perspectives can be summarized in the following points, as developed in this book and other post-workerist contributions:

- A new system of domination,
- New subjectivities,
- The common and its powers.

The new system of domination refers to how capitalism has changed toward a new paradigm and how it has fallen into crisis; new subjectivities reflect how capitalism has created new figures at the anthropological and social levels; finally, the common is identified as new potential to challenge domination and reconstitute social relations.

In our opinion, it is necessary to grasp the shift to post-Fordism to understand the current financial crisis, as well as to point toward post-crisis perspectives. The transition to the hegemony of immaterial labour under the age of Empire represents the introduction of knowledge, languages, codes, information, communication, affects, and so forth, in the labour market. With the crisis of Fordism, the processes of producing surplus value have changed and value is no longer produced in factories but, rather, in social life. This situation has entailed a cognitive capitalism, or biocapitalism, that extracts its value from every form of life. Consequently, accumulation has also changed with financial capitalism and, instead of depending on the production of material goods, it is now about extracting value from the circulation of money (i.e., the production of money via money). In this process of financialization, a new modality of accumulation, financial economy becomes central and cannot be considered a parasite in relation to the real (production-based) economy.

We have already stressed the appearance of new subjectivities, emphasizing the indebted (since financialization entails a privatization of the logic of debtfare) together with the mediatized, the securitized, and the represented. However, it is clear that the main subjectivity of post-Fordism, intensified by the crisis, consists of the precarious singularities, a perspective shared by other social scientists such as Guy Standing (2011) and Loïc Waquant (2009). These precarious singularities can be identified with the poor (Cocco) or with women (Morini). The term accounts for new methods of alienation and domination, based on the exploitation of human existence (affects, communication, knowledge). Therefore the precariat is also called the cognitariat (Bifo), a class information far from the creative class, however, to stress the importance of these immaterial dimensions and the dissemination of technolinguistic and technosocial interfaces. The cognitariat combines the cognitive dimension of work with the exploitation applied to the proletariat and reveals a new subjectivity characteristic of the net economy.

This situation (financialization and its subjectivities in the form of new modalities of alienation and domination) does not neutralize at all the emergence of alternatives or the development of new struggles by social forces and singularities. We want to emphasize this creative dimension against capitalism's reduction and appropriation of the value of social life. That is why we talk about the common and its powers, borrowing the concept widely developed by Hardt and Negri (2009) in *Commonwealth* and likewise developed by other post-workerist authors. Indeed, the common is a good example of a new language, referred to above, to denominate a new political project and shed light on the new social struggles taking place in the post-crisis framework. As Hardt (2009) points out, "We need to explore another possibility: neither the private property of capitalism nor the public property of socialism but the common in communism."

The idea of the common in communism underlines that the common, the ground for a redefined communist project, has become central in capitalist production (ideas, affects, social relations, and forms of life), so that a door for the affirmation of the common (autonomous biopolitical production and the self-governed creation of a new humanity) remains open and must be explored. Although multitude is still the subjectivity of the Empire in Hardt and Negri's eyes, the common acquires an essential role. Thus, *Declaration* concludes with the commoner as the figure who "commons." It is not difficult to perceive the common not just as complementary but also as a more political subjectivity than multitude. On the one hand, the commoner, as multitude, does not imply sameness but, instead, different singularities interacting with each other (without being noticed by people outside the struggle). On the other hand—and this is clearer than in the notion of multitude—the commoner is a constituent participant of a democratic society based on the open sharing of the common (by undoing the four subjective figures of the crisis).

The centrality of the common as an alternative project is formulated most convincingly by Fumagalli (2007), who claims that all welfare politics aimed at strengthening social cohesion must take the common (as social cooperation) as a starting point. Fumagalli names, as part of the common, goods linked to survival and primary consumption (water, wind, food, clothes, housing, etc.) and other goods that have to do with (geographic and virtual) territory and environment (language and knowledge). This leads us to a new political model constituted by three intertwined pillars: basic income, flexicurity, and commonfare (as the welfare of the common). These can be formulated in terms of rights (to an income, to a job, and to the common) and may contribute to overcoming precariousness.

In sum, our aim with this anthology is to explore the new scenarios drawn by financialization and its subjectivities and the potential of the common, its subjectivities, and its powers to challenge domination and create alternatives to neoliberalism.

Book structure

The anthology is divided into two main parts. The first part contains unique contributions by a number of leading scholars connected to the UniNomade group, including the article of Tim Murphy, whose research on the work of Toni Negri and the Autonomia group is well acknowledged. These scholars present different interpretations of the crisis and the changes that are happening, as well as those to come. The second part is more focused on the reading, although not exclusively, of the work of Hardt and Negri and its potential to develop post-crisis perspectives.

Christian Marazzi's contribution is titled "Heterogeneity and the currency of the commons." In this article Marazzi throws light on the relation between money and finance and reflects on the relation between workerism and post-workerism. The author concludes that what is possible and even necessary is a *subjective* measurement of value, which requires reporting on the subjectivity of the struggle's movements and of all forms of struggle and life that uphold it.

In his article "Debt economy and the indebted man," Maurizzio Lazzarato takes a starting point in the cultural hegemony that the theory of freedom of the market exerts over society. The author points out that debt in contemporary capitalism is unpayable, non-reimbursable, and infinite and concludes, among other things, that the repayment of debt imposed on the European population is a political weapon to facilitate and achieve a neoliberal project, since everyone knows, from both the quantitative point of view (the sums are enormous) and the qualitative point of view (in financial capitalism debt is in continuous variation), that it is unpayable. We should assume and reverse this system, give another sense to the impossibility of repayment, and simply not pay.

Andrea Fumagalli throws light on the concept of cognitive biocapitalism and introduces the concept of basic income. Using a post-workerist approach and methodology, Fumagalli discusses the failure of the liberal governance of cognitive capitalism and forms of economic governance and the concept of the precarity trap as a means of regulating the new capital–labour relation. In conclusion, Fumagalli presents a few alternatives to exit the current global economic crisis, paying special attention to the proposition of unconditional basic income and to the unfeasibility of a way out of the crisis through the definition of a new New Deal.

In her article "Social reproduction as a paradigm of the common: Reproduction antagonism, production crisis", Cristina Morini sets out to provide answers to the question of whether the concept of social reproduction still makes sense today or, rather, how the concept may be recast. Morini concludes among other things that the concept of social resproduction can never be completely deterred, guided, or twisted and that it is possible to envisage paths or processes that could help us leave behind the categories of social control and internalization.

Sandro Mezzadra, in the contribution titled "Seizing Europe. Crisis management, constitutional transformations, constituent movements," focuses on the consequences of the crisis on such important political and legal concepts as citizenship and constitution. Mezzadra sketches three levels of political action and theoretical intervention: the invention of a new political discourse for a new left in Europe, the organization of political campaigns for the definition of a program and the construction of a coalition of subjects and forces struggling for radical transformation, and the intensification, multiplication, and coordination of struggles and practices of resistance working toward the production of a counter-rupture.

Guiseppe Cocco's contribution throws light on the constitutive power of the poor and emphasizes that today the relations between anthropophagy (forms of social relations that absorb the other, that are inclusive) and anthropoemy (forms of social relations that banish the other from the body of society, that are selective) are modulated with exclusion and inclusion continuously intertwined. Using a very powerful theoretical framework consisting of the concepts of, among others, Levi-Strauss, Deleuze, Merleau-Ponty, and even liberation theology, Cocco concludes, among other things, that the body of immaterial labour, biopolitical production, finds in the body of the poor the image of productive discourse of the *beautiful bodies* against the power over the beautiful.

Timothy Murphy's contribution is titled "Hetero-autonomia: Pathogenesis, financialization and the politics of time." In this text Murphy proposes that the negativity theorized by "Bifo" in his work on the psychopathologies of cognitive labour and the econometric analyses of finance capital articulated by Christian Marazzi can usefully supplement Hardt and Negri's autonomist model of an affirmative multitude struggling within and against a global Empire that steals its productive powers. The synthesis of perspectives and methods that results suggests that struggle over the whole range of temporalities subjected to capital—from the infinitesimal time of digital labor to the interminable time of debt servitude—must serve as a cornerstone of contemporary autonomist militancy.

Lars Poulsen throws light on the concept of power in the work of Hardt and Negri. Poulsen argues that Hardt and Negri's Foucault-inspired approach to power allows them to make important and sophisticated analyses of the production of subjectivity at different nodal points in the present network of power. Poulsen's main purpose is to describe how, according to Hardt and Negri, the subjectivity of human beings in multiple and complex ways is influenced by diverse forms of power, some specific to the present age. The author's secondary purpose is to discuss the idea of a form of non-alienated, subjective, and social being that can be considered an alternative to the influence of this power.

Christian Ydesen, in his article "The creative democratic potential of the multitude – solidarity and love as transcendence in immanence," sets out to analyse the social ontology of the common—the very foundation of the multitude's democratic potential—using the interconnected philosophical frameworks of Martin Buber and Michael Theunissen, with a specific focus on the two concepts of love and solidarity. The article argues that love and solidarity are inevitable phenomena in human existence, thus claiming validity in a post-crisis scenario.

Óscar García Agustín focuses on institutionalization and social change. In the article titled "The art of non-playing chess: the institutionalization of the common," the authors explores the possibility of creating institutions (or developing processes of institutionalization) that challenge, change, or replace the current ones. Using the game of chess as a constructive metaphor, García Agustín concludes, among other things, that although chess is still played according to well-known rules, other unexpected players are appearing on the board who want to be part of the game—but their game and not that from which they have been (or still are) excluded.

Ben Dorfman has written "Mendicancy on the edge of crisis: the gift of rights in a time of global strife." In this contribution Dorfman poses human rights as the resolution of strife and emphasizes that the concept of human rights' mendicancy ties rights to the notion of gift, or the idea that maximum power emerges from those who give gifts they cannot afford to give. The author's argument is that human rights are a demonstration of power from a place that has none. From this perspective, Dorfman argues that in the context of crisis, rights are greater than we will ever be; they are the standard we can only hope to achieve.

Pil Christensen's article is titled "Private debt in the age of crisis – strategies of resistance." It reflects the findings of the author's master's thesis, in which she empirically explores the role of private debt under the reign of neoliberalism. Christensen argues that the crisis has triggered transformations that have become decisive in the role of private debt. She concludes that the individualization of both guilt and responsibility should be seen in the context of the political and economic shifts following neoliberalism, shifts that are part of the reason for steadily rising private debt.

Kurt Dauer Keller's contribution is titled "Political attitude in the age of globalization." Keller criticizes Hardt and Negri's key concepts of the common, singularity, and multitude, which he finds are impeded by a speculative vitalism and mechanistic notions of sociality. Therefore, Hardt and Negri's framework offers only a poor conception of how the historicity of freedom and institution is a vertical formation of the ethics and power that structure social life with generation and potentiality. The understanding of this vertical, generative dimension is a relatively neglected phenomenology in Hardt and Negri's works that could be unfolded in an ethicopolitical notion of attitude and points to democratic politics for the predominant forms of praxes.

Finally, it should be noted that all the contributions included are original and written specifically for this anthology, with the exception of the pieces by Christian Marazzi and Tim Murphy, who developed existing papers and adapted them for this occasion. Articles not written in English were translated by Maria Angela Ferrari from Italian (Christian Marazzi, Andrea Fumagalli, in part, and Cristina Morini), French (Maurizzio Lazzarato), and Portuguese (Giuseppe Cocco). It is our hope that the readers will enjoy having access, in English, to this collection of contributions and to thus participate in the common production (of the common).

References

Bauman, Zygmunt. 2012. "Entrevista en Radio Nederland." Available at *Youtube*: http://www.youtube.com/watch?v=SoYbddPWRbg

Berardi, Franco "Bifo". 2012. *The Uprising. On Poetry and Finance*. Los Angeles: Semiotext(e).

Blanchard, Olivier, and Leigh, Daniel: "Growth Forecast Errors and Fiscal Multipliers," *International Monetary Fund Working Paper* No. 13/1, 2013.

Cocco, Giuseppe. 2009. *MundoBraz*. Rio de Janeiro: Record.

Fumagalli, Andrea. 2007. *Bioeconomia e capitalismo cognitivo*. Rome: Carocci.

Fumagalli, Andrea, and Mezzadra, Sandro. 2010. *Crisis in the Global Economy*. Los Angeles: Semiotext(e).

Hardt, Michael. 2009. "Common in communism." Presentation at the European Graduate School. Available at *Youtube*: http://www.youtube.com/watch?v=Q_Ey5ioS4GU

Hardt, Michael, and Negri, Antonio. 2009. *Commonwealth*. Cambridge: Harvard University Press.

Hardt, Michael, and Negri, Antonio. 2012. *Declaration*. E-book, Argo Navis Author Services.

Heyer, Eric. 2013. "IMF var for optimistiske i sine prognoser for den vestlige økonomi." Radio interview, *Danish National Broadcasting Corporation, Channel 1*, February 18, 2013.

Lazzarato, Maurizzio. 2012. *The Indebted Man*. Los Angeles: Semiotext(e).

Lotringer, Sylvere, Marazzi, Christian (eds.). 2007. *Autonomia: Post-Political Politics*. Semiotext(e) Intervention Series 1. Los Angeles: Semiotext(e).

Marazzi, Christian. 2011. *The Violence of Financial Capitalism*. Los Angeles: Semiotext(e).

Mezzadra, Sandro, and Neilson, Brett. 2013. *Border as Method, or, the Multiplication of Labor*. Durham NC: Duke University Press.

Morini, Cristina. 2010. *Per amore o per forza. Femminilizzazione del lavoro e biopolitiche del corpo*. Verona: Ombre Corte.

Standing, Guy. 2011. *The Precariat – The New Dangerous Class*. London: Bloomsbury Academic.

Stiglitz, Joseph. 2013. "The post-crisis crises." *Project Syndicate*, January 7.

Wacquant, Loïc. 2009. *Punishing the Poor – The Neoliberal Government of Social Insecurity*. London: Duke University Press.

Part I. The Crisis and Beyond

1. Money and Financial Capital: The Return of the Substance of Value

Christian Marazzi

To address the issue of the relation between money and finance, I conduct a historical analysis and suggest reflections on the relation between workerism and "post-workerism" (or something in that line), starting with money and then continuing on to financialization. A paper by Stefano Lucarelli (2010), titled "Sentiere Interrotti" (published in a collection on the experience of *Primo Maggio*, the militant history periodical edited by Sergio Bologna), allows us to return to the origins of financialization as a way to understand how in the 1970s workerism took the first steps in that direction. As the experience of *Primo Maggio* and particularly of the so-called money group (*gruppo della moneta*), "Sentieri Interrotti" wanes toward the end of that same decade to again reemerge in the 1990s, although under different shapes and taking a different, more individual course. This reemergence was especially triggered by the 1997 crisis in Southeast Asia and then Russia, the Internet bubble, and the severe systemic crisis of financial capitalism in 2007.

The non-measurability of value

Allow me to retrace our steps to the 1970s and to the issues that were taken up and explored within the *Primo Maggio* group, of which I have been a member. As one reads Lucarelli's (2010) reconstruction, one understands the importance of the August 15, 1971, declaration on the inconvertibility of the dollar into gold. That memorable declaration was the end of the road of the project woven at Bretton Woods in 1944 by White and Keynes. The Americans had come out victorious from that long-drawn process because in the 1930s and all during World War II they accumulated two-thirds of all the monetary gold and, anchored on the power of that metal and on their military power, proposed to create a system based on parity between the dollar and an ounce of gold (the famous $35 per ounce). Thus, the parity was determined between the dollar and other currencies, which would then have an indirect relation with this gold standard. It was a hybrid system, that is, the gold–dollar exchange standard. In the 1970s, however, it became obvious that the gold standard was extremely "loose," as the English describe it: the Americans had substantially raised the amount of dollars in global circulation as a consequence of the investments of multinational companies and import payments. For years, France's president Charles de Gaulle had protested insistently against the enormous inflow of dollars as payment for goods and services from Europe and the rest of the world and tried to ascertain the amount of gold behind that currency. It was a means of payment that started to be seen by all more as a symbol than as a value, a general equivalent. De Gaulle referred specifically to one economist, Jacques Rueff, who had suggested a fourfold increase in the price of gold to restore some sense of proportion between the paper money in circulation and the gold standard.

This background helps us understand the specifics of the 1970s, when the French had significantly minimized their stiffness, particularly following the workers' struggle for higher wages in 1968: faced with the struggle, they would have been better off fostering the flexibility of the exchange rates (the rate of exchange between the French franc and the dollar was actually fixed, a condition cemented in the agreements signed at Bretton Woods). Giovanni Arrighi (2007) commented in his latest book, in a note in which he recalls something often ignored, that the French, the first in line to demand the solidity of the monetary backing, partially withdrew from that position, realizing that in such a system it would be more advisable to adopt flexible rather than fixed exchange rates. It would thus be possible, through devaluation of the French franc or the national currency, to recover what had been lost in terms of labor costs.

In the United States, the situation evolved in the 1960s and culminated with the declaration of the inconvertibility of the dollar into gold. The operation was described as a "revolution from above." After August 15, 1971, Toni Negri reacted characteristically quickly, in an article in *Potere Operaio* (a monthly journal also distributed in the factories), packed with quotes from *Grundrisse*, in which he interprets this major operation from the point of view of the famous "The Fragment on Machines" where Marx foresees the end of the rule of the value of labor in view of the development of the productive forces of science incorporated into machines. At this point labor represents the miserable base of the value and therefore lacks reference to a general equivalent, whether gold or any other type of fiduciary money functioning as a general equivalent. The idea of Negri's article was to link the value's inconvertibility to its non-measurability. Thus, according to classical Marxism, the very possibility of reasoning in terms of general equivalents—that is, money as sovereign merchandise to which other goods are linked by finding their monetary expression—has vanished. Negri's interpretation was founded, therefore, on the rupture of the nexus between the measurability of value and the monetary representation of that measurability, that is, a general equivalent.

The following year, Sergio Bologna (1974) wrote what is considered a founding article of *Primo Maggio*, created in 1973, and of the money group: "*Currency and Crisis. Marx as correspondent of the 'New York Daily Tribune.'*" In it, Bologna, a militant historian, reviews the articles Marx had written as a *New York Daily Review* correspondent on the mid-19th century crisis in France that broke out in the aftermath of the comprehensive socialization of credit by the Péreire brothers' Crédit Mobilier, which had allowed Napoleon III to successfully exit the crisis generated by the class struggle of 1848. Once again, in those writings Marx insists on the concept of revolution from above, which, 20 years later, Engels will draw on in connection with Bismarck. It is the revolution of a capital that has to face a class of workers willing to struggle and destabilize the system; in view of such a crisis and linked to a certain type of class composition and subjectivity, a wide-scale operation emerges that is simultaneously a state operation and a capitalistic one. It is capitalistic in the sense that the Péreire Brother's Crédit Mobilier starts to acquire shares all across France, thus multiplying funds for further acquisitions. In other words, it is an *ante litteram* subprime credit system, with the support of the state and of Napoleon III as suppliers of liquidity. This great socialization project, a sort of "capital communism" by means of bank credit, consists of the creation of a currency by the state and the central bank in cooptation with the working class and transferring it back to labor. Obviously, Marx does not refrain from analyzing this operation from the point of view of its intrinsic contradictions.

The third volume of *Capital* (Marx 1981) describes the capacity of capital, through socialization made possible by means of credit, to expand and promote growth. However, capital growth contains, in itself, its own contradictions, that is, crisis and overproduction, the fact that one must eventually face the impossibility of other ways of extracting surplus value because of the rigidity of the necessary labor. So, the rigidity of the necessary labor is behind crisis and overproduction: this is what characterizes the workerist theories of the crisis, identified by several other Marxists, such as Lenin and also Grossman, who, perhaps better than anyone, is responsible for bringing the dynamics into focus. It is the impossibility of pursuing accumulation for lack of capitalistic interest: what can be done if the rate of profit does not increase? This is a recurring question in all Marxist interpretations along the 20th century. As an alternative to investing in productive processes, claims Grossman (1992), two paths open up: one can invest part of the profits abroad, refueling the accumulation, as in the case of Africa or China, or one can buy stock and then produce money through money with that part of the profits that are not created in the strictly productive process precisely because accumulation is blocked.

This is, in essence, the focus of Bologna's essay, in which the idea of revolution from above, which permeated the debate at that time, is recalled from a historical point of view. The context created by the declaration of the inconvertibility of the dollar into gold made the debate extremely timely. Another very important element is the state and the monetary dimensions of the operation: the resort to money, in its creation and manipulation by the banking system, is highly institutional. There is, additionally, a reference to class composition, perhaps one of the aspects most scarcely reflected in the vast literature dedicated to the analysis of the current crisis. Suddenly, everyone becomes an expert providing explanations on the spread and interest rates. Many have taken short courses to understand how finance works, but in this effort to catch up, something was lost along the way; this is what we call, still today, class composition. This issue demands effort and dedication, because it is not easy to use this category to analyze a situation that is increasingly characterized by fragmentation of the subjects of the world of labor and non-labor.

After the first projects of the money group, Lapo Berti (1978) wrote the article "Denaro come capitale [Money as capital]," one of the best-written pieces in the period. He explicitly refers to the typically Marxist category of money as capital, money that commands living labor, money created ex nihilo to produce, extract, and absorb surplus value. Suzanne de Brunhoff (1973)—an advocate of the operaist current, well-known theorist on currency according to Marx, and supporter and member of the French Communist Party—offers an unequivocal, rigid, and orthodox interpretation: according to Marx, money, which is found under various forms (fiat money, means of payment, etc.) is the universal equivalent. The debate with de Brunhoff centers on the possibility of continuing to adopt that Marx, because the inconvertibility of the dollar was the inconvertibility into precisely that general equivalent according to that very theory. Berti claims that the moment currency loses its intrinsic value, that is, when it is detached from gold, Marx's theory fails, because that which has always been considered the essence of the money—that is, the capacity to function as the equivalent of goods in the exchange—is missing. Insisting on the category money as capital was tantamount to claiming that, even though detached from the general equivalent, in the capitalistic regime money continues to function as command over living labor or the lever of the production of surplus value.

The crisis: capital and the imposition of measure

On the other hand, during that time the theory of "economic circuit" began to take hold internationally, among the "circuitists," as their advocates became later known. The theory was fathered by Bernard Schmitt, until recently a professor in Fribourg, Switzerland (invited to Padua in 1977). Other theorists appeared in Italy: Augusto Graziani, Riccardo Bellofiore, Roberto Convenevole, and Marcello Messori. Their starting point was Marx's capital circulation, expressed in the formula M–C–M': money opens the economic cycle and then closes it with the realization of profit. This theory, at least in its purest form, is wholly based on the concept of money created *ex nihilo,* which must be integrated into the economic cycle as the payment of wages. The capitalists pay wages by borrowing money from banks, which, in turn, borrow from the central bank. Thus, the money that lubricates and monetarizes the economic circuit through the payment of wages is created *ex nihilo* because, by the time it is integrated, the product has already been produced. This is a fundamental point that is also found in Marx's Theories of Surplusvalue: it is not necessary for money to preexist before the payment of wages. It could also be fiat money because there is a time gap between the signing of a contract, that is, the moment when the wages are fixed, and payment; in this lapse of time the product is created that will back this money. Money, therefore, is not created from nothing but, rather, on the basis of the separation of capital from labor. However, this poses still another problem. One of the merits of economic circuit theory is that it allows a new reading of Marx in light of the functioning of the monetary system and the capitalistic production process. Marx was insistent: money does not, in fact, exist prior to the valorization process. One can very well make a payment by means of an IOU because, by the time the wage earners are paid, they will already have produced both the portion with which their labor is paid and the surplus value. Therefore, there is already a material support transforming money into a general equivalent, which is to say that there is no need for a gold standard. In fact, in the theory of money created *ex nihilo*, the relation between money as command and money as capital and substance is inverted: command comes first and then comes substance. When the capitalist remunerates living labor, the value can be identified in terms of substance because a product exists beforehand.

This reflection leads us to revisit the first volume of *Capital* (Marx 1976), particularly the first chapters, which have generated plenty of problems in the history of Marxism. Marx's starting point is the simple circulation C–M–C, which then becomes but a phase in the circulation of capital. The concept of money created ex nihilo reveals how the issue of substance follows command; that is, the wage-goods do not exist before the worker starts working. The goods may be found in supermarkets, but from a point of view of an analysis of value, what comes first is the labor force that transforms itself into living labor, which happens through the lever of money created ex nihilo. Thus, goods are put into circulation with money as a reference, a general equivalent, for the very reason that value has been created somewhere. Today we can afford to reinterpret all that in light of what has happened, particularly from the impressive uncoupling of scriptural from fiduciary money. The latter was somewhat like gold during Marx's time: today, instead of gold, we have monetary reserves. The fiduciary currency, as it is known, is the euro or any other currency we carry in our pockets and represents less than 10% of the currency in circulation. All the rest is scriptural currency or fiat money; it is debt money, by definition, which means that more than 90% of the currency in circulation signals debt, which, in Marx's words, however, will not pose a problem as long as goods continue to change hands and are measurable. A crisis is triggered when the dynamics halt and shift from commensurability to measurability, where all indications of value will have to be compared to the fiduciary currency. People continue to want to own real currency, money that truly represents value. How did this crisis manifest itself in the 19th century, in the 20th century, and even in 2008 London? Judging from bank queues, it seems that people want to recover, at any cost, that which is recoverable of fiduciary money; they want to take the money home, which leads to a solvency crisis.

We can revisit the debate by trying to do something already used in Marx's days: stop considering money as the universal equivalent. According to Marx, money is indeed the form value takes in the different phases of the capital cycle. The general equivalent is but one function among many, just as money is a measure of value, a means of exchange, a means of payment, and, as such, credit currency. These functions support and articulate themselves and together define the form that value historically assumes based on a certain organic composition of capital and class. There was a time when the function of general equivalent was the most important of all, whereas today there are other functions in which we are embedded, among which the pivotal function of money as a means of payment, scriptural currency, and debt currency. Those functions have to be considered jointly, as a relation that, historically, may change in favor of one function or another, though all reproduce the form of value. Scriptural currency, debt currency, is by far the prevailing function: in the form of value, this function has relinquished to a second tier the function of general equivalent, which at some point seemed to be the most important of all. When we discuss a general equivalent, we refer to the labor contained in the goods, that is, their substance. The monetary revolution, triggered by the inconvertibility of the dollar into gold, robbed the currency of its substance. But this does not mean that the situation is irreversible, which is an issue worth discussing.

Starting in the 1970s, and because of the uncoupling of money from its substantial reference, there have been approximately 160 financial crises and 50 monetary crises. During the "glorious 1930s" of Fordism and the worker mass, that is, the period of the worker "as substance," however, not one single crisis occurred. My interpretation of substance, based on Tronti's ideas, is as follows: class is the substance that opposes capital. When Tronti (1966) writes that the workers come before capital, he claims that the crises are determined by the workers' struggle. Today, in an age of financial capitalism, the use of Tronti's analysis creates many problems: we can explain the current crisis as a result of the struggle of the multitude, but it is a crisis that involves all and affects all profoundly. On the other hand, we could sustain that from the moment it rid itself from substance to embark on the destruction of the working class, capital has not had a moment of truce. It is a question of interpretation: financial capitalism has distanced itself from the category of substance, subjecting the working class to a break-up, insecurity, and growing precarity at the cost of having built a monetary system that has fallen back on itself and collapsed. We could also say that the substance and therefore measurability of the quantity of labor is represented by the very form of the crisis: the cycle—as a relation between expansion, growth, bubbles, and recession—has been severely disrupted. As a very recent example, we thought that the injection of 1 billion euros by the European Central Bank (by the end of 2011 and beginning of 2012), could guarantee a truce in the financial markets, but that was short-lived; in the meantime, France has gone into recession, Italy and Spain have been struggling with recession for some time already, the United States shows anemic growth, and even China's growth rates are slowing down. It is difficult to make projections over more than one and a half or two years. In the meantime, the crisis has resulted in the vampirization, privatization, and destruction of welfare. In short, in financial capitalism, the crisis brings back the ever-recurrent issue of measure, but does so in the negative sense. It is not class that imposes the measure with its growth and struggles but, rather, capital that imposes its measure, turning it upside down, in the form of austerity.

Real and financial economy? The accumulation of capital

There are problems linked to the issue of substance. I do not think that we can subscribe completely to what has been, since the first part of the 1980s, the most important contribution of a certain current of economic thought to the interpretation of financialization. My position on the origin of financialization is still classic Marxist: it is the symptom of a crisis in the accumulation of capital; the crisis is therefore in the real economy. It is not true that financialization is the cause of the economic crisis. That occurred in the 1970s, as the combined effect of the erosion of rates of profit, the crisis of overproduction, and the crumbling of investment rates in the Fordist economy. Financialization was therefore an attempt to escape the crumbling profit rates of the 1970s, which were so great that in the Fordist sector profit rates stabilized at around 13–14%, down from the 22% it had reached during the glorious 1930s. Financialization has therefore permitted the increase of falling profits by new returns on profit or through the increase of financial gains.

One should not forget that financialization has its origins in the real economy, in large American corporations: starting in the 1980s, General Electric, General Motors, and Fiat developed a financial sector that today is superior to the directly productive sector. In the automotive industry, it is the system of sales, or that of credit and leasing, that has fed the financial system and which has opened the way to the reduction of the surplus of otherwise unsalable automobiles. Thus, the origins of financialization are to be found at the very heart of the real economy. This has enabled capital to hit two birds with one stone: on the one hand, it destroyed the working class with the flexibilization, growing precarity, and freezing of wages (which, by not growing, have contained demand); on the other hand, it has blocked investment. For the past 20 years capitalism has failed to invest, in the Keynesian sense, that is, increase employment; if anything, there has been investment in the emerging countries and then, more precisely, in the stock exchange. The rate of accumulation (made from investment in equipment and in wages) has not increased in the past 30 years and, if we were to exclude China and the emerging countries at the level of the global economy, that rate would definitely be negative. During that same period, however, profits have skyrocketed.

One can indeed say that those profits are essentially financial, since the remainder of the profits continues at the levels to which they fell in the mid-1970s. But, we may ask, is it really possible to distinguish industrial profits from financial profits when the latter are part of the same logic? I do not believe so, because I think that it is necessary to break away from the famous dichotomy real economy/financial economy. In the third volume of *Capital*, in the sections on the falling trend of profit rates, Marx (1981) claims something that is never taken into account: from the point of view of the reasoning on profit rates, one cannot distinguish commercial (financial) profits from industrial profits. It is not necessary to insist on the idea that capitalism must always be industrial; it can be something different, something new, and this something new is financial capitalism, at least at it has developed in the Western world. The division can perhaps be explained in light of the creation of financial gains and of a new elite: the financial bourgeoisie. All the new rich come from areas of finance, from insurance, and they are managers: it makes one miss the old technical manager! Those individuals have absolutely no idea what a factory is all about: they think only in terms of value to the shareholder because they also are shareholders. It is a fact that profits have increased because of the outlay of enormously increased financial gains. It is worth noting that I speak of outlay because the problem is one of realization, of the sale of surplus value, of its conversion into money. Indeed, if profits have increased, it is because they were *monetarily* realized through the increase of financial gains and, to an increasing degree, of private debt of both companies and households. This happened, as well known, first in the United States and then in the rest of the world.

To think in terms of the creation of added demand by means of financialization is tantamount to supporting a series of statements: first, in the capitalistic cycle surplus value is only attainable through the creation of added demand. For Keynes, the added demand was public *deficit spending*, with which the state built public schools or highways. In finance, the state no longer carries out *deficit spending*. State debt has increased, but not through the creation of added demand by means of the creation of services or the redistribution of wealth. For the past 30 years the *welfare state* has been under attack and has suffered progressive erosion. I worked at a *welfare* department for 12 years and, as early as in the 1980s, all people talked about was savings; I did not see a single project that might have created added demand. On the contrary, in the beginning of the 1980s, debt had grown because the state had reduced taxes on capital and incomes. Those are the reasons behind the increase in public debt, as is the Italian case, way before the explosion in 2007, to which we obviously have to add relative interest rates. Who, then, takes over the functions of the state as the agent responsible for creating added demand through *deficit spending*? The private sector. When one talks about financial economy, it is precisely the *privatization of deficit spending* that is in question, as if each of us had become a center of allocation and creation of added demand, through our spending, by means of contracting debt. This situation has allowed, as in the case of the United States after the Internet bubble burst, overproduction to be circumvented in the real estate market. The extremely high supply of homes compared to demand was reduced through cooptation in the economy of the indebtedness of a growing proportion of the population drawn into this mechanism precisely to purchase the excess housing, including the "ninja," or "no income, no job, no assets."

Thus, according to the Marxist theory of capital circulation, surplus value recalls the theory of imperialism, that is, the theory of the creation of a market outlet through the debt trap. Today, however, imperialism is found within the very empire. I recently read that Portugal will need the help of Brazil and Angola to find a way out of the crisis: this is an astounding reversal of the relations between center and periphery! But the imperialistic logic is represented within the Empire, as an attempt to create an "outside" in an enclosed and increasingly confining space.

As to the current process of accumulation of capital, I suggest recalling the analysis made in the 1980s and 1990s on the post-Fordism transformations of productive processes, that is, forms of creation of value increasingly more detached from the direct production processes: we sell work through subcontracting, outsourcing, the use of linguistic capacity and relations to produce value, and, finally, crowd-sourcing. We only have to think of the Ikea model or even the Google model, which captures value through attention created through cooperation and network. The reference is that of cooperation, language, relations, and knowledge. It is true that accumulation has flattened but, because of this transformation of the modes of production, capital has the organizational and strategic capacity to capture value outside directly productive processes—and this has taken place without consistent investment. Incidentally, investment in fixed capital is insignificant, because investing in an assembly line is quite different from investing in network processes, which costs considerably less. At the same time, however, investments have been made in devices that capture or extract value from society: we work for free every moment of the day and there is a continuous transfer of unpaid labor to the consumer. An example is home banking and another is the postal service, not to speak of Ikea (which forces the buyer to assemble its products at home) or Google. The trend is that of the "prosumer," that is, the producer–consumer, a consumer who produces at least part of what he consumes. Against the background of the financial gains, which have allowed the downstream production of profits, is a value, which is unpaid labor, absolute surplus value. This is why the expression "becoming rent of profit" is so pertinent.

Toward a subjective measurement of value

But let us turn to the concept of desubstantiation. I said that in the 1980s, mostly in France but also in the United States, a new perspective emerged on the functioning of the financial markets. Ultimately, one had been able to advance, although not to one's utmost satisfaction, a description that is reasonably truthful to the functioning and behavior of investors. It is the theory formulated by the school of "behavioral finances" (of which Robert Schiller is one of its founders in the United States). In France, a more extreme version of this theory is that of "self-referential finances," formulated by Michel Aglietta and André Orléan (1982). In substance, this theory is based on the explanation of the behavior of the investors proposed by Keynes (1936) in *General Theory*. It is copycat behavior, in which rationality in the financial markets has nothing to do with the substance of value. The idea is this: I do not invest in Microsoft shares because I believe that there is substantially real value behind them. Behavioral finance theorists and even more so theorists of self-referential finances always refer to the "beauty contest" example. Cited in Chapter 12 of *General Theory*, to explain the functioning of the markets Keynes suggests thinking about a beauty contest, where the young woman who wins is the one who was awarded the most points. My choice will not be based on what I think is the young woman's real beauty but, rather, on what I think the others think. In this case, rationality has to do not with aesthetic judgment or a value judgment but, rather, with what I think the others think and will decide to do. The reference is therefore a *collective belief*, a rationality formed on the basis of that collective belief: in the end, the winners will be those who chose and gave points to the person who everyone would have chosen as most beautiful.

This is also true for decisions on financial markets. René Girard (1965) talked about a "lack of being": we refer to the other to bridge an information gap and to find a certain level of subjective unanimity in determining an object's value. I need the other; then that same other—after serving as my reference model—becomes my rival because we are both competing for the appropriation of what we chose as a representation of wealth. It is true that in the financial markets there are no references to an underlying value or substance, in terms of the classic Marxist analysis of value, whether based on a neoclassic interpretation of the markets or on universal access to all information related to the underlying so-called value of a certain financial asset. According to the latter, the price of the shares reflects their value, which in turn is determined by the relation between demand and supply; the reference is therefore to something that lies outside the dynamics of the financial markets, something objective. Neither does the law of value proposed by Marx apply, since it is anchored in a certain amount of labor incorporated into products. In his remarkable *L'Empire de la valeur*, André Orléan (2011) sums up over 20 years of reflections on that approach to analyzing the functioning of the financial economy. This theory completely desubstantiates value, which in turn provokes a certain degree of perplexity.

It allows us, for example, to explain the generation of debt in a Minsky-like scheme or the fact that in the financial economy the relation between an asset's price and demand is completely different from that in any other market of ordinary goods. If, on par with purchasing power in the market of ordinary goods, prices increase, demand will drop. In the case of the financial markets, however, the opposite occurs: the higher the price of an asset, the more investors will seek it, also because access to credit makes it possible. A spiral is thus created that leads to an increase in prices until the mechanism becomes completely self-referential, that is, detached from any possible substantial value.

Having stated that, I somewhat doubt one can avoid the issue of substance completely. Perhaps substance will return, although in a different form. We previously noted that it would manifest itself in a negative form, in the form of a crisis, of a compulsion to measure; a crisis allows us to measure ourselves against our poverty. But there could be another way of interpreting substance. We can think of the movements against illegitimate debt: in Greece and other countries audits and assessments of the origin of public debt are forcefully demanded. However, what is actually being asked is an examination of the balance sheets and debt to determine what is right and wrong. It is not easy to distinguish between good and bad debt, but it is certainly true that there is a clear difference between becoming indebted for having imported weapons from Germany or France, as is the case in Greece, or becoming indebted for having built childcare facilities or useful social services. But before one can distinguish between the two, it is necessary to address the challenge of measurement. The objective measurement of value is probably no longer feasible. What is possible and even necessary is a *subjective* measurement of value and this requires reporting to the subjectivity of the struggle movements and of all forms of struggle and life that uphold it.

References

Aglietta, Michel, and Orléan, André. 1982. *La Violence de la monnaie.* Paris: PUF.

Arrighi, Giovanni. 2007. *Adam Smith in Beijing. Lineages of the Twenty-First Century*. London: Verso.

Berti, Lapo. 1978. "Denaro come capitale," in *Moneta, Crisi e Stato Capitalistico,* edited by Berti Lapo. Milan: Feltrinelli.

Bologna, Sergio. 1974. "Moneta e crisi: Marx corrispondente della 'New York Daily Tribune,' 1856–57." In *Crisi e Organizzazione Operaia*, edited by Sergio Bologna et al. 9–72. Milano: Feltrinelli.

De Brunhoff, Suzanne. 1973. *Marx on Money.* New York: Urizen Books.

Girard, René. 1965. *Deceit, Desire and the Novel: Self and Other in Literary Structure*. Baltimore: Johns Hopkins University Press.

Grossman, Henryk. 1992. *The Law of Accumulation and Breakdown of the Capitalist System.* London: Pluto Press.

Keynes, John Maynard. 1936. *The General Theory of Employment, Interest and*

Money. London: Macmillan.

Lucarelli Stefano. 2010. "Sentieri interrotti: il lavoro del gruppo sulla moneta di 'Primo Maggio.'" In *La Rivista "Primo Maggio" (1973–1989)*, edited by Cesare Bermani, 111-137. Rome: Derive Approdi.

Marx, Karl. 1976. *Capital. A Critique of Political Economy, vol. 1*. London: Penguin Books.

Marx, Karl. 1981. *Capital. A Critique of Political Economy, vol. 3*, London: Penguin Books.

Orléan, André. 2011. *L'Empire de la valeur. Refonder l'économie*. Paris: Seuil.

Tronti, Mario. 1966. *Operai e Capitale*. Turin: Einaudi.

2. Debt Economy and the Indebted Man

Maurizio Lazzarato

'Man is no longer the sick man, but rather the indebted man.'
Gilles Deleuze (1990)

One of the major outcomes of the liberal counter-revolution is the cultural hegemony that the theory of freedom of the market exerts over society. The driver of this hegemony is the triptych consisting of the scholar, the expert, and the journalist. The power relations between journalists, academics, and experts tend to favor the former, since the media have less and less need to report exterior analyses (those of scholars and experts). Rather, scholars and experts "are called to become journalists if they wish to conform to the norms of contemporary communication" (Deleuze 2003, 131).

These reflections are based on three quotes from scholars who, either directly or indirectly, have been part of this apparatus of enunciation, although they are not necessarily liberal. Philosophers, anthropologists, and economists make a statement that conveys significant meaning (or nonsense) to us: currency, exchange, and the market have finally released us from the servitude of personal relations, of which debt is a paradigm. The liberal and neoliberal freedom produced by the market and currency is freedom from debt. If we are free, it is because we are no longer and will never again be indebted. Let us hear what the scholars have to say, starting, as one should, with the economists, because the economy is the origin and model of all social sciences.

Where does mankind's economic freedom, that is, market freedom, come from? From the possibility that men have freed themselves from the debt they incurred with the federal powers, personal debt that existed between the vassal and the suzerain or the serf and the master. The abstraction of the debt made possible by the generalization of currency releases mankind from personal relations. Debt becomes transferable, it can circulate, and it is the very essence of the monetary economy. Capitalism invents an egalitarian system where individuals increasingly owe nothing to anyone. The market is thus an extraordinary system of debt abstraction, transferability, and liquidation.

Currency releases relations from personal subordination, as debt expressed in currency renders relations impersonal, anonymous, and transferable. Let us not forget the expressions *anonymous* and *transferable*, because, as we shall see, they played a role in the so-called subprime crisis.

Let us continue on to the next scholar: the anthropologist. Anthropologists study archaic societies. Anthropologists are well aware that, historically, debt existed long before exchange:

> One could ask whether the enormous movements of the modern economy … is not the definite and the final as well as the most radical way of doing away with the gods, of doing away with the gift, and doing away with debt.

The economy liberates us not only from economic debt, but also from the original debt, that primordial debt, the debt of life to the gods and supernatural forces.

To end the citations, we refer to the philosopher, a true apologist of the market and currency, who provides an outstanding definition of the modern individual as a sovereign individual free from all bonds and all attachments:

> In a non-monetary society, I have no claims except against the closest individuals to which I have rendered services for free. When, on the other hand, I supply a commercial (monetary) service, the individual who benefits from it, by paying for the service, is immediately released from any debt towards me. The money I receive from him represents, indeed, a claim, but a claim against someone completely anonymous and abstract, to whom I am in no way bound to in terms of gratitude, of recognition of the debt. Relieved from all psychological and moral weight, the exchange can conclude, rationally, efficiently and freely.

We are free, from not only an economic and religious point of view, but also the moral and psychological. With all those freedoms, we are fulfilled individuals.

The three scholars articulate a counterintuitive truth, because we, contrariwise, have the impression that debt, instead of disappearing, is everywhere, that the discourse on private debt, the sovereign debt, the repayment of debt, and the guilt of debtors have been obsessively polluting our existence for the past six years.

The knowledge factory is a financial enterprise

Before we examine the theoretical and political reasons that lead those scholars to such contrasting conclusions regarding reality, I would like to reflect on the American university where at least two of those scholars teach.

Why universities in the United States? Because those temples of conservation and production of Western knowledge are a paradigm of the financial enterprise and the debt economy in several ways. They represent, first and foremost, the ideal realization of the creditor–debtor relation and the predation of the latter by the former. In addition, because the American student is the perfect incarnation of the condition of the indebted man expressing, in a paradigmatic manner and for the entire society, the conditions of the subjectification of the debt economy.

A few months ago, a quarterly report on the debt of U.S. households broadcast on the Federal Reserve, or Fed, channel in New York revealed data on student debt. On March 31, 2012, the loans to pay tuition that had to be paid back amounted to $904 billion, $30 billion more than three months earlier. To get a better idea of this figure, it is roughly more than half the public debt of Italy and France combined, France being a country of 60 million inhabitants. Because of their much lower debt, Europe and the International Monetary Fund did not hesitate to destroy Greece (in its sixth year of recession) and has now set out against Spain, Italy, Portugal, and so forth. For comparable or even lower amounts, they have imposed austerity, sacrifices, unemployment, poverty, and recession upon millions of persons.

In the United States, two-thirds of all college graduates are indebted. The number of people who incurred debt to finish college amounts to 37 million today, while their prospects of repayment are increasingly reduced. This trend is confirmed in a study conducted by the Fed, which reveals that 32% of all debtors are over 40 years of age and 5% are over 60. One becomes a debtor before entering the labor market and one remains indebted for the rest of one's life. In the United States, one out of five households (19%) was expected to pay back a student loan in 2010, double the number of similar households 20 years ago and 15% more than in 2007. The Fed notes that student loans ranked second in overall U.S. household debt in 2010, surpassing credit card debt (home mortgages are in first place).

With the economic crisis, many young graduates are having a hard time finding a job. Graduate unemployment under 24 years of age exceeds 15%. The Fed points out that the percentage of defaulting student loans (8.69% in the first quarter) is higher than that for home mortgages and automobile loans and that the figure is probably underestimated.

Is there any better way to be initiated into the world of work and its rules of profitability, productivity, and culpability than to enter indebted?

Creditors and debtors

The makeup of American students represents the ideal of the financialized society, since it is composed of a majority of indebted individuals and of the wealthy, the children of the creditors. Here, in the knowledge factory, the class divide does not materialize as an opposition between capitalists and wage earners but, rather, between debtors and creditors. This is a reality that the capitalist elites would like to see reproduced throughout the rest of society: a limited number of rich creditors and a large mass of debtors.

Completely blind, the scholars cited in my introduction teach a public comprising the indebted and the children of creditors that debt is finally disappearing thanks to currency, exchange, and the market. I would love to attend one of these surreal classes. The situation must be both hilarious and tragic. It gives a good idea of the state of social sciences under the hegemony of neoliberalism in Western universities.

Student indebtedness is a clear example of the neoliberal strategies applied since the 1970s: the replacement of social rights (right to an education, to health, to a pension, etc.) by the right to incur debt. Gone is the mutualization of pension contributions, replaced by individual pensions funds; gone are the salary increases, replaced by consumer credit; gone is "social" sickness compensation, replaced by individual insurance; gone is the right to housing, replaced by the possibility of securing a loan to buy a home—a home that, in the words of Greenspan, ex-chairman of the Fed, becomes your bank because, since home prices increase constantly, it entitles you to open additional credit lines, to continue borrowing, endlessly.

This individualization of social policies entails a radical change of the welfare state. Because educational expenses are fully borne by the students, the state can free up resources that it can hurriedly transfer to companies and the wealthiest households through tax reduction and subsidies. The real beneficiaries of assistance are no longer the poor, the unemployed, the sick, and single parents but, rather, the companies and the wealthy, and all thanks to debt.

The student loan bubble

To try to understand the functioning of contemporary capitalism, we could pursue our exploitation of this factory of indebted men, which is the university. The university produces the same impasse and the same harm for society as financialization.

There is talk of a bubble in the United States similar to that of the subprime loans, those risky mortgage loans that crumbled, drawing the United States and the world into a serious recession in 2008. Over one-third of U.S. student debt is securitized, in other words, regrouped and then passed on to investors under the form of derivatives.

To promote the constant expansion of the financial economy and its gains, everyone must be granted access to credit, even those with modest incomes. However, as credit access is broadened, debtors become poorer as a consequence of the reduction or freezing of their salaries and the reduction of social transfers and social spending; eventually, they are no longer able to make the interest payments on their debt.

This is where the instruments of release from debt, ensuring transferability and anonymity through currency, prove to be, contrary to what our scholars claim, no longer the cause of the disappearance of debt but, rather, its diffusion and multiplication. Loans obtained to buy homes in the United States, the infamous subprime loans, transformed into negotiable securities, were effectively transferred to a number of banks and financial institutions. Those transfers, however, are the very vehicles of the infection and multiplication of debt. Furthermore, anonymity has proven to be yet another cause of the crisis, because nobody knew which banks held rotten securities and in what amounts.

In reality, if financial transactions can be made anonymous, commercial transactions are less and less so. The number of purchases made using credit cards and that constitute a financial transaction exponentially increases the number of operations that require electronic identification before completion. The bank can follow, at any instant, your purchases, while marketing companies can plot your lifestyle, and so forth. It is the very image of the transaction (and of credit itself) between two free and equal individuals, based on trust, that is at stake, for the transaction is mediatized by the enormous technical and institutional system of, for example, banks and their payment systems.

Control, subjectivity, time

Debt as a relation of power between the creditor and the debtor implies a particular subjectification of the debtor. The power of control and constraint is not external, as in a disciplinary society but, rather, internal to the debt subject himself. The student is his own master, his own controller.

The worker is controlled within an enclosed space, consisting of the factory walls, for a limited period (eight working hours) and is controlled by persons and apparatus outside of himself that are easily recognizable. To resist, he can support himself not only on individual resources, but also on the work collective and its solidarity.

Control through the apparatus of debt is carried out differently. Its space is not enclosed and the time during which control and constraint are exerted is not limited. The space and time are those of one's life, since the duration of a repayment can extend over 20–30 years and, during that period, the debtor must organize his life to repay the debt.

The issue of time and of duration is at the heart of the debt issue. It is not a question of working time, but of lifetime. Debt establishes a bridge between the present and the future, anticipating and exerting an appropriation of the future.

Through one's current debt one attempts to determine, to "hypothesize," and to control future behavior.

Debt is a technique to individualize and destroy all solidarity and all possibility of collective action. The indebted man is alone and is individually responsible before the credit system. He cannot count on any form of solidarity except that of the family (which risks becoming indebted as well). He feels shame and guilt. The only time American students began to show a sort of coming out was during the Occupy Wall Street demonstrations.

Debt is the apparatus of production of subjectivity adequate for the fabrication of human capital and for the entrepreneur himself. The graduating student must not only consider himself as capital, which needs to be valued by its own investments (the loans secured for tuition payment); he must also act, think, and behave as if he were an individual enterprise. Debt demands that persons yet to enter the labor market learn the rules, accounting, and organizational principles.

Students enjoy all the inconveniences and none of the advantages of being transformed into "individual enterprises." In spite of the fact that the students are obliged to behave as an enterprise, the law does not provide for the possibility of bankruptcy in their case. A legislative project of the U.S. Senate is currently contemplating extending the right to go bankrupt to those who have incurred debt to pay their way through school, as for any other debtor.

The credit relation inscribed into an electronic chip

Students are also a good example when discussing another trait of Americans in general and their relationship with credit–debt. In 2008, 84% of all U.S. students had at least one credit card, compared to a total of 76% in 2004. Even more surprising is the fact that each student carries, on average, 4.6 credit cards. This is a consequence of the explosion of the cost of a university degree.

Instead of disappearing, credit–debt is carried in the pockets of Americans, as well as the English, to be sure. The creditor–debtor relationship is engraved into the electronic chips of their credit cards. Each purchase is a financial act that mobilizes credit and debt.

Debt not only accompanies us in the wondrous world of consumption, but also becomes infinite debt:

> Consumer credit used to be granted upon explicit request, whereas the card system renders credit automatic; the inversion of the initiative is obvious: with the cards, the credit relation is always established beforehand; all one has to do is to use the card to make it effective.... We are no longer credit applicants, but rather card recipients. Thus, the card payment system creates a permanent debt structure. (Haesler 1995, 225)

Debt as a capture scheme

Debt works as a scheme that captures social wealth. The capture of the surplus value produced by society does only entail "profits" alone. On the contrary: profits are but a part of income. Debt is the incarnation of the "vampire," referred to by Marx when evoking the functioning of capital, in financial capitalism. It sucks the surplus value of every segment of society! The capacity to act on a purely social dimension has rendered finances a strategic apparatus of capitalism.

Who profits from the capture, in the form of interest on the debt paid by the students? First, the banks, which hold the bulk of the billions of debt, by fixing interest rates at their discretion. Next, the federal government, because the interest rates on the student loans are much higher than the rates at which they lend money. And the college chairmen and its administration. As far as the faculty (to which our scholars belong) is concerned, their salaries depend on the ever-increasing debt of their students, who mortgage their future salaries to be able to attend their courses.

The same exact thing occurs within society. We are paying, through our taxes, through cuts in social spending and through salary reductions, for the damage created by the creditors. Not only do we pay for their mistakes, but we also continue to make them wealthier during the crisis and because of it. To conclude this section, I would like to cite Aristotle, amply contradicted by the reality of our economies: "Knowledge and money have no common measure." Finances, contradicting this statement, have established a measure of knowledge that, though arbitrary, is accepted and effective. The loans granted and their repayment periods represent the price of access to science and truth and determine the income on which live the banks, the state, and university chairmen and their administrators and faculty.

Money and debt

I would now like to touch upon the theoretical reasons that led our scholars to such unlikely conclusions. I limit myself to raising the issue of money: after having lost its relation to gold, has money become solely and finally debt? I would like to recall Nietzsche in examining the nature of debt, concentrating particularly on the following question: in contemporary capitalism, is debt infinite?

Our scholars express the view generally shared by the social sciences that the market, exchange, and money liberate us from debt. Let us concentrate on money, which poses formidable problems for economic science, which is incapable of inserting money into its system of balance and development, causing one to seriously doubt the capacity of its theories on capitalism. After all, our economy is not only a monetary economy, but first and foremost a credit–debt economy.

Money to which our scholars assign the capacity to liberate us from debt is exchange money, money as a means of payment, of measure, of treasurization, and so forth. Trade money, as it should also be called, is a type of money in circulation but, in capitalist societies, it does not play a strategic role, since it does not incarnate the power of capital. The specifically capitalist money is capital money, credit money, debt money.

Exchange money presupposes and creates a symmetrical (and contractual) relationship between producers/traders, whereas capital money creates an asymmetric relationship (of exploitation, class differentiation, privative appropriation). Marx claimed that on exchange money one can read the slogan of the French Revolution: liberty, equality. On the face of capital money, however, what can be read are the words *domination, exploitation, power to destroy/create, debt, desire, predation, the capacity to determine what should be produced and how, uneven distributions of jobs and functions.*

Opposed to the rationality of exchange money,[1] which favors the "*doux commerce,*" the expulsion of violence, by the facilitation of liberty, equality, fraternity, is the "irrational rationality" of capital money. The definition proposed by Gilles Deleuze is clear when confronting the effects of finances on the contemporary crisis:

> Money, capital-money, is in such an advanced stage of dementia that finds no parallel in psychiatry: it is what we could call the terminal-stage patient. Capital-money reaches this terminal stage in the stock-exchange mechanism which is absolutely rational, we can understand it, learn it, the capitalists know how to use it and, yet, it is completely delirious, it suffers from dementia.

---

1 Simmel (1987, 356) offers the best description of the nature of exchange money: "Before the simple forms of plunder or theft, where purely subjective impulses allow free rein, the exchange presupposes an objective assessment, reflection, mutual recognition, and immediate subjective restraint of greed." By eliminating the personal element, money augments the individual's freedom, "because it creates relations between human beings, but keeps them outside them" (Simmel 1987, 373). Bakhtin (2003) observed that Simmel was incapable of overcoming the rift between subject and object, subjective culture and objective culture, that stems from his exchange money theory. On the other hand, credit and its functions and thus capital money are completely absent, at least as the practice of "distinguished men": "It is not necessary to be a gentleman in order to obtain credit, but rather that whoever demands credit is a gentleman" (Bakhtin 2003, 616). This chivalrous concept of credit completely backfires for not only capitalist credit, but capitalism itself.

In their book *Anti-Oedipus*, Deleuze & Guattari show that there is a difference in the nature of the two types of money, which is expressed as a difference of power, since exchange money is subjected to capital money. Mixing the two or considering them equivalent would be "cosmic fraud." Even worse, considering exchange money alone while ignoring capital money, as scholars do, is the perpetuation of fraud.

Debt theory in heterodox economics

But let us distance ourselves from the three scholars committed to their dead-end and let us analyze the monetary theory of the French regulation school, which introduces remarkable new concepts to standard economics. According to that school, currency is not, as in classic and neoclassic political economy, deducted first from the barter economy and then from commercial exchange but, rather, from debt. This important shift is immediately neutralized by a debt concept that is transcendent, holistic, and complete, as a lifelong debt, which imposes collective constraints on individuals.

With human nature defined as a "lack of being," debt is confused with deficit, incompleteness, which only the gods, the state, or society are able to combat and in whose regard we become debtors. Hence, they neutralize debt as original debt and universalize it by transforming it into a feature of all archaic societies. Debt is first and foremost primordial debt, original debt, lifelong debt; in other words, "recognition of a dependence of the living to sovereign powers, gods and ancestors who have granted part of the cosmic force of which they are the source" (Aglietta & Orléan 1998, 21).

The living, as the counterpart having received the gift from the vital power, are obliged to repay this debt, a repayment that has no end, since, in reality, this lifelong debt is infinite debt. If you ever hear someone mention lifelong debt, original debt, and so forth, you are certainly listening to a priest, a statesman, or a psychoanalyst. Surely.

Lifelong debt has another function of interest to everyone, particularly regulation economists, since it carries and represents sovereignty and its obligation toward the individual: "It builds the sovereignty and cements the community in its work and its life, particularly through sacrifices, rituals and gifts" (Aglietta & Orléan 1998, 21).

What heterodox economists search for is not at all the truth about the functioning of archaic societies; rather, they see in original debt, in primordial debt, the same holistic, transcendent, binding dynamics that they assign to the state or the collective. The concept of lifelong debt for Deleuze and Guattari (and for

Nietzsche) is totally different, since it refers neither to nature nor to the universal.

Original debt is not an expression of the link attaching individuals to the community nor is it the sign of original indebtedness transmitted by birth or the inaugural debt, which will never be repaid. On the contrary: it is produced by a political context in which it is possible to trace its genealogy and the history, because hierarchically organized, state-based, monotheist societies are the ones that introduce debt for the duration of one's existence, lifelong debt, primordial debt.

For scholars and the school of regulation, the debt of archaic societies is a debt that cannot be paid back, it is inexhaustible, whereas in capitalism one can always free oneself from debt through a monetary payment. Deleuze and Guattari claim exactly the opposite: archaic societies are characterized by "finite and mobile debt" and, with the emergence of empires, states, and monotheist religions, debt became infinite debt[2]:

> The abolition of debt and its accounting transformation trigger an unending task for the State which conditions all primitive alliances (the debt issue). The perennial debtor and the infinite debt replace all mobile and finite debt. There will always be monotheism at the despotism's horizon: debt becomes debt for life, debt linked to the individual's very existence. (Deleuze and Guattari 1972, 234)

By introducing the concept of the infinite into the economy and into production, capitalism continues and prolongs both the infinite debt of state imperial societies and the guilt, which also becomes infinite, that monotheist religions link to debt.

Financial capitalism has also intensified that trend, because it has instilled finance and credit money at the very heart of capitalist accumulation, turning debt into its driver. Financial capitalism turns debt into a promise one can keep, but only by incurring new debt, without ever being able to interrupt this infinite negative cycle. The crisis is there to remind us precisely of that.

---

2 The association of reactive forces is also followed by a transformation of debt, which becomes debt to "divinity," toward "society," "toward the State," toward the reactive bodies. Debt loses its active character, which made it participate in the liberation of men: under its new form, debt is repulsive, unpayable. Debt becomes the relation between a debtor who will never be able to pay back debt and a creditor who will never cease to claim interest on the debt: "Dette envers la divinité" (Deleuze 1962, 162–163).

The genealogy of morals and debt

Nietzsche and the "Genealogy of Morals" are, directly or indirectly, through the work of Deleuze and Guattari, at the origin of my work on debt. Anthropologists are very selective about the second dissertation, because they do not consider its content to reflect what their discipline establishes about archaic societies. Take, for example, David Graeber (2011), who recently wrote a thick volume on debt. According to the author, Nietzsche accepted Adam Smith's premises according to which life is an exchange and man is a "rational being" but, in opposition to Smith, he construes his idea of what the world would become as he interprets it in "commercial terms." Taking Adam Smith's thesis as a starting point, Nietzsche subscribes to the theory of original debt, primordial debt, lifelong debt that we have seen inserted in the work of those heterodox economists.

Concurring with the German philosopher, Graeber (2011) claims that "debt is uniquely an exchange which has not yet closed," presupposing the equality of the contracting parties, an equality that is overridden during the length of repayment but which can be re-established (and with it, reciprocity[3]) once the debt has been honored.

The anarchist thinks along the same lines as our scholars and the political economy: debt is always repayable. Debt is a relation that develops under the "shadow of a possible equality" and can always be paid; consequently, one can always "atone" for the sin that is attached to it. In our hypothesis, we suggest the complete opposite: in capitalism and particularly financial capitalism, debt is infinite, unpayable, unatonable, except in the case of a political repayment, as Benjamin puts it, and never in the form of a monetary repayment. How can it be that we arrive at such completely opposed conclusions? Nietzsche can help us determine whether debt is infinite and unrepayable in capitalism.

Let us concentrate exclusively on a few concepts that are more pertinent to our current reality: First and foremost, the "Genealogy of Morals" has no intentions of establishing a new anthropology. It is open to polemics, on the one hand, with the introduction of the utilitarian (What is the use of utilitarianism?) and contractual (What is the use of a contract?) exchange, of the political economy, and, on the other hand, its theory of value and of the rational man pro-

3 Reciprocity, even in archaic societies, does not mean balance, equity, symmetry. "Gifts may be reciprocal; but this does not make them any the less violent: the whole point of the gift-act is to make the other act, to extract an act from the other, to provoke a response. And in this sense there is no social action that is not an exchange of 'gifts,' insofar as all action is 'social' by being an action upon another action, a reaction to a reaction. Reciprocity means only recursivity; no society intended. Not to mention altruism. Life is robbery" (Viveiros 2009, 139).

duced by the exchange. Graeber claims something that even a first-year student would be hesitant to claim: Adam Smith's *homo economicus* and his rationality are at the basis of Nietzsche's philosophy, thus light-heartedly reducing the question of value to that of the market and that of the political economy.

Indeed, the Nietzschean man is the "being that measures the values, who assesses the evaluating animal par excellence." But those values have nothing to do with the market or with homo economicus. It is not the market or homo economicus that creates values and assesses them. Values entail evaluations, "appreciation points of view," from which their value derives, and the evaluations are ways of life and modes of existence.

Nietzsche opposes the political economy that has appropriated the "category of 'value'" making it derive from the exchange, to the future task of the philosopher: "resolving the issue of the value, determining the hierarchy of the values", "identifying what the different tables of values *are worth,*" inquiring on "the value of the evaluations." Criticizing economic and moral values requires "starting by questioning the very value of those values" (Nietzsche 1971, 14). We could not be farther away from Adam Smith's theory.

Second, for Nietzsche, debt does not imply equality or reciprocity but, rather their opposite. If the archetype of social organization is credit–debt and not exchange, it is because the forces that are at work are not equal but, rather, asymmetric. Credit mobilizes both active and reactive forces (both on the relations between humans and within every human being); it is the realm of confrontation of superior and inferior forces, whose objective is the construction of subjectivity, which is "capable of promising," and the promise presupposes a memory, the memory of words, which debt construes.

The creditor–debtor relation expresses the activity of breaking in and forming subjectivity before it takes on an economic meaning in the modern sense of the term. For Deleuze and Guattari (1972, 217), the logic of the debt in archaic society has nothing to do with exchange, because "the socius is the broker, it is up to him to inscribe upon the body, the circulation is but a secondary activity."

Third, there is the question of time, which, according to Bergson, if not creation, is nothing at all. The exchange is instantaneous, because the peculiarity of debt is to include, control, and exploit time by actualizing the future. Debt is a promise of repayment and it therefore relates to the future as open and undetermined time, as a radical uncertainty that we cannot anticipate or control by the logic of probabilities. Debt is a capitalist apparatus to enclose and preempt time, removing from it all forms of creation and innovation by normalizing it.

It is not enough to say that debt is an inconclusive exchange, because the duration, time, and uncertainty constitute the specific difference with regard to the exchange. "Breeding an animal that can promise" means "to be able to have access to the future in advance," "taking responsibility for the future." The asymmetry does not only concern active and reactive forces; it also concerns time (its control, appropriation, and expropriation) and thus also subjectivity.

Fourth, Nietzsche clarifies very well the transformation of finite and repayable debt to infinite and unpayable debt. Lifelong debt, original debt, primordial debt is a relatively late production imposed first by the constraint of society, then by the state, and finally by monotheist religions. "This change has been neither progressive nor voluntary"; it has been the consequence of a "rupture, of a leap, of a constraint, of an inescapable fatality" (Nietzsche 1971, 96).

From that leap on, mankind became indebted to society, to the state, to the gods, and the active forces that finite debt should have tamed to act upon the reactive forces, have recoiled into the inner man who remains forever guilty: "Now the perspective of a definite repayment disappears once and for all on a pessimistic note" and "the impossibility of releasing oneself from debt generates the idea of the impossibility of atonement, the impossibility of repayment" (Nietzsche 1971, 103).

The creditor–debtor relation as one of active and reactive forces, as the domain of time in terms of infinite debt, is invested in and continued by means of capital, which, together with financial capital, transforms it into a dominant relationship. In financial capitalism, it is impossible to release oneself from debt, because capital money—in other words, credit—is, by definition, debt.

If you consider credit money—debt, that is—the alpha and omega of the valorization of capital, repayment will never occur, because that would mean the extinction of the relation of capital. The creditor–debtor relation can never be extinguished, since it constitutes the relation of the policy of domination, as well as that of economic exploitation. Honoring one's debt means releasing oneself from the creditor–debtor relation and hence abandoning capitalism.

One could honor one's debts, but if one honors all one's debts at once, there will no longer be asymmetry, there will no longer be the power differential, there will no longer be superior and inferior forces, there will no longer be capital. The definitive repayment is, logically, the death of capitalism, because the class differential is expressed precisely by the credit–debt relation.

As the driver of social production, credit must be systematically reimbursed, but also immediately and necessarily renewed, *ad infinitum*. Capitalism does not release us from debt, it chains us to it. It is not by bowing to the injunctions of debt that we can be released from it. It is not through an act of payment but, rather, through a political act, through rupture, that one can break away from the relation of domination of debt.

In conclusion, and contrary to the opinion shared by all, from anarchists to neoliberals, debt in contemporary capitalism is unpayable, non-reimbursable, infinite. But we can express the functioning of credit in an even more precise manner by resorting no longer to economic categories, but to literary categories introduced by Franz Kafka; they are particularly suitable to our debtor condition because, precisely as K, we are all presumed guilty, even when having committed no fault.

The form of contemporary debt is less like apparent acquittal (we move from one debt to another, we subscribe to a loan and repay it, etc.) than unlimited procrastination,[4] where we are indebted continuously and debt is never (and shall never be) repaid because credit has not been granted to be reimbursed but, rather, to be in continuous variation.

This is the situation of the American consumer, as well as ours. Sovereign debt is in continuous variation and the spread gives us an idea of the amplitude of the oscillations in real time. The variations of public debt, in turn, set our salaries, our income, and our social services in continuous variation, but always in the same direction, toward the low end, whereas our taxes are set in continuous variation, but toward the high end.

Consequently, the repayment of debt imposed on the European population is a political weapon to intensify and achieve a neoliberal project, since everyone knows that both from the quantitative point of view (the sums are enormous) and the qualitative point of view (in financial capitalism debt is in continuous variation) it is unpayable. We should assume and reverse this apparatus, give another sense to the impossibility of repayment and simply "not pay."

I am often criticized for providing a rather somber picture of the situation. I will finish where I started, by answering with a phrase by Deleuze: "There is no need to fear or hope, but only to look for new weapons."

References

Aglietta, Michel, and Orléan, André. 1998. *La Monnaie souveraine.* Paris: Odile Jacob.

Bakhtin, Mikhail. 2003. *Pour une philosophie de l'acte.* Lausanne: L'Age d'Homme.

Deleuze, Gilles. 1962. *Nietzsche et la philosophie.* Paris: PUF.

Deleuze, Gilles. 2003. *Deux régimes de fous et autres textes (1975–1995).* Paris: Éditions de Minuit.

4 The German term adopted by Kafka, Verschleppung, has, as in the case of the term atermoiement in French, a legal connotation. However, in French it refers to the creditor–debtor relation, specifically, attermoyemens, "delay granted to a debtor by the creditor" (Isambert & Taillandier 1829, 15).

Deleuze, Gilles, and Guattari, Félix. 1972. *L'Anti-Oedipe: capitalisme et schizophrénie.* Paris: Éditions de Minuit.

Graeber, David. 2011. *Debt: The First 5,000 Years*. Brooklyn: Melville House Publishing.

Haesler, Aldo J. 1995. *Sociologie de l'argent et post-modernité*. Geneva: Droz.

Isambert, François André, and Taillandier, A. H. 1829. *Recueil général des anciennes lois françaises: depuis l'an 420 jusqu'à la révolution de 1789*. Paris: Belin-le-Prieur.

Nietzche, Friedrich. 1971. *Généalogie de la morale*. Paris: Gallimard.

Simmel, George. 1987. *Philosophie de l'argent.* Paris: PUF.

Viveiros de Castro, Eduardo. 2009. *Métaphysiques cannibales*. Paris: PUF.

3. Cognitive Biocapitalism, the Precarity Trap, and Basic Income: Post-Crisis Perspectives

Andrea Fumagalli[1]

Introduction

One of the fundamental features of the workerist approach in the past and of the post-workerist approach today is the analysis of the dynamics of the valorization processes based on the social subjectivity that underlines them. Over the past 30 years, the current process of capitalistic accumulation and valorization has received different names, among which *post-Fordism* is both the most common and the oldest. The concept spread in the course of the 1990s, particularly associated with the French *école de la regulation*.[2] However, like many other concepts that bear in their very essence a denial, it is not devoid of ambiguity and is prone to different interpretations. Post-Fordism today can be assigned to a period starting with the 1975 economic crisis and closing with that crisis in the early 1990s, at which point the process of accumulation and valorization ceased to be characterized by the centrality of Fordist material production in large and vertically integrated factories. At the same time, however, no alternative paradigm exists. Hence, it is no coincidence that the prefix *post-* imbues the idea of that which no longer is without revealing what occupies its place today. The post-Fordist phase is indeed characterized by the simultaneous co-existence of different productive models: from the Taylorist-inspired *just-in-time*[3] Japanese Toyota model to the industrial district model of the small enterprise[4] and including the

---

1 Psychedelic musical support by the Grateful Dead, Jimi Hendrix, and Phish is acknowledged. I would like to thank Cristina Morini for her seminal studies on these topics.

2 As well formulated by Turchetto (1999, 1), "the paternity of the concept of post-Fordism, however, does not stem from either the orthodox Marxism nor from workerism. Those two lines of thought have imported the concept and its definition from elsewhere, adapting it to their own conceptual framework. The copyright on post-Fordism stems from the so-called French Ecole de la Régulation." One of the first texts that adopts the post-Fordism concept is by the English geographer Amin (1994) and, under the French school, Jessop (1995), Lipietz (1997), and Boyer and Durand (1998). As for the Italian debate, the first text to adopt the concept of post-Fordism is by Bologna and Fumagalli (1997)—see also Rullani and Romano (1998) and the critical text already cited, "Oltre il Fordismo. Continuità e trasformazioni nel capitalismo contemporaneo" (Turchetto 1999)

3 See, for example, Ohno (1995), Bonazzi (1993), Revelli (1995), and Coriat (1991).

4 See Priore and Sabel (1984), Brusco (1989), and Becattini (2000). For a more critical analysis, see Lazzarato et al. (1993) and Fumagalli (1996–1997).

development of productive sectors that tend to become internationalized on a hierarchical basis.[5] At that point it is not yet possible to envisage a homogeneous paradigm.

Following the Gulf War in 1991, innovation in the fields of transportation and of language and communication began to consolidate around a single new paradigm of accumulation and valorization. The new capitalistic configuration identifies the new references on which the dynamic capacity of accumulation is based in "knowledge" as a product and in "space" (both geographic and virtual). Two new dynamics of scale economies are thus identified at the base of productivity growth (and, as such, as source of surplus value): the learning economy and the network economy. The former is associated with the process of generating and creating new knowledge (supported by new communication and information technologies); the latter derives from district-level organizational models (territorial networks or air systems), no longer applied solely for the production and distribution of goods but increasingly used as vehicles of the diffusion (and control) of knowledge and technological advancement.

This accumulation paradigm can be referred to as *cognitive capitalism*[6]:

> The term *capitalism* refers to the permanence, in metamorphosis, of the fundamental variables of the capitalist system: in particular, the leading role of profit and the salary relation or, more precisely, the different forms of labor from which surplus value is extracted; the terms cognitive refers to the new nature of labor, of the sources of valorization and structure of property, on which the process of accumulation is founded, and the contradictions derived thereof. (Lebert & Vercellone 2006, 22)

The centrality of the learning and network economies, typical of cognitive capitalism, is put to debate at the outset of the new millennium, following the bursting of the speculative net economy bubble in March 2000. The new cognitive paradigm is incapable of rescuing by itself the socio-economic system from the structural instability that characterizes it. New liquidity needs to be introduced into the financial markets. The capacity of the financial markets to generate val-

5 See Palloix (1979, 1982) and Bertin (1985).

6 Those terms appeared in France in the early 2000s, linked to the research activity of the Laboratoire Isys-Matisse, the Maison des Sciences Economique, the University of Paris, Sorbonne, under the coordination of B. Paulré, and were spread by the Multitudes journal, which published vary varied articles by Corsani, Lazzarato, Moulier-Boutang, Negri, Rullani, and Vercellone, among others. In this regard, see Paulré (2000), Azais, Corsani, and Dieuaide (2001), Moulier-Boutang (2002), Vercellone (2003), and Corsani et al. (2004). For more recent analysis, see Vercellone (2006a), Fumagalli (2007), and Moulier-Boutang (2007). See also the monograph "Le Capitalisme cognitif. Apports et perspectives" (Fumagalli & Vercellone 2007), with contributions, beyond those of the editors, by Arvidsson, Cassi, Corsani, Dieuaide, Lucarelli, Monnier, and Paulré.

ue is, in fact, linked to the development of "conventions" (speculation bubbles) able to create generally homogeneous expectations that induce the major financial operators to focus on certain types of financial activities (Orléan 2010). In the 1990s it was the net economy; during the first decade of 2000, the attraction was the development of markets in the Far East—with China's entry into the World Trade Organization in December 2001—as well as real estate property. Today, it tends to focus on maintenance of the European welfare system. Since it distances itself from prevailing conventions, contemporary capitalism is in permanent search of new social and vital terrain to absorb and commercialize, attracting growing interest in these vital faculties of human beings. It is for this reason that in the last few years one has begun to hear concepts such as *bioeconomics* and *biocapitalism.*[7]

At this point the reader should be able to understand that the concept we adopt is nothing but the expression of the syneresis between *cognitive capitalism* and contemporary capitalism, cognitive capitalism being a definition of contemporary capitalism.

This article will, supported on the post-workerist approach and methodology, attempt to discuss the failure of the liberal governance of cognitive capitalism. For that purpose, after analyzing its main features (Section 2), I discuss forms of economic governance and the concept of the precarity trap as a means of regulating the new capital–labor relation (or better yet, the relations of exploitation) that has been consolidated in the last two decades (Section 3). In conclusion, I present a few alternatives to exit the current global economic crisis, paying special attention to the proposition of unconditional basic income (Section 4) and to the unfeasibility of a way out of the crisis through the definition of a new *New Deal* (Section 5).

Characteristics of cognitive biocapitalism

In cognitive biocapitalism, finance, knowledge, and relations are the motor of accumulation. Finance is the pulsating heart; knowledge is the brain; relational activities are the nervous system. Cognitive biocapitalism is a single body, inside of which the "real" sphere cannot be separated from the financial, nor can

---

7 The terms bioeconomics and biocapitalism are recent creations. The concept of bioeconomics was introduced by Fumagalli as early as 2004 (Fumagalli 2004, 2005) and in addition to the previously cited Fumagalli (2007). An interesting analysis of the concept of bioeconomics can be found in cf. and also in Chicchi (2008) and Bazzigaluppo (2006). The term biocapitalism, on the other hand, was coined by Codeluppi (2008). See also the more recent work by Morini (2010).

the productive sphere be separated from the unproductive, or work time from life time, or production from reproduction and consumption….

We can say that in cognitive biocapitalism, financial markets directly influence and condition the process of accumulation and valorization.[8] In a broader sense, financialization marks the definitive passage from commodity money to sign money.[9] With the complete dematerialization of money (after the Bretton Woods collapse in 1971, marking the end of the convertibility of the dollar to gold), financial markets now define the social and hierarchic conventions that are able to secure short-term monetary value. At the same time, they leave open the relations of debit and credit, provided sufficient trust is generated in the operators. From this viewpoint, financial markets lubricate the process of accumulation. In the capitalistic system there is no accumulation without debt.

First, it is no coincidence that, from the 1990s onward, financial markets have taken care of financing accumulation activities: the liquidity drawn by financial markets rewards the restructuring of production aimed at exploiting knowledge and the control of spaces external to the firms.

Second, in the presence of capital gains, financial markets have the same role in the current economic system that the Keynesian multiplier (activated by deficit spending) had in industrial Fordist capitalism. But, unlike the classic Keynesian multiplier, the new financial multiplier leads to a distorted redistribution of income. For such a multiplier to be operative (Fumagalli & Lucarelli 2011), the financial basis (i.e., the extension of financial markets) must be constantly growing and the capital gain must be, on average, higher than the median salary loss. On the other hand, the polarization of incomes increases the risk of debt insolvency, which is the basis of the growth of the very financial foundation, and reduces the median salary.

Third, financial markets, forcibly channeling growing portions of labor income (such as severance indemnity and social security, as well as earnings that, through the social state, turn into institutions for health and public education), substitute in this way the state as a social provider. From this point of view, financial markets represent the privatization of the reproductive sphere of life.

Finally, financial markets are where capitalistic valorization is established today, that is, the place where the exploitation of social cooperation and of general intellect is measured by the dynamics of stock market values. As a consequence, profit transforms into rent and financial markets become the place

8 See Fumagalli and Mezzadra (2010, 237–39). For an in-depth analysis of the evolution of financial markets and the role of the monetary and credit markets, see Fumagalli (2007, Chapter 1).

9 For an in-depth analysis of this passage, see Amato and Fantacci (2012, 65–90).

where labor value is determined and transformed into finance value. The latter is nothing other than the subjective expression of the expectation of future profits articulated by the financial markets, which in this way secure a rent.

Financial markets thus exercise biopower (Lucarelli 2010, 119–138). Hence, in cognitive biocapitalism, we observe the "becoming-rent" of profit.[10] Rent is the main capture tool of both surplus value and the de-socialization/privatization of what is common. The meaning and key role of this becoming-rent of profit can be appreciated at two levels. On the one hand, this process is evident at the level of the social organization of production and of the distribution of revenues: the criteria underlying the traditional distinction between profit and rent become less and less pertinent. The confusion of the frontiers between rent and profit finds one of its expressions in the way in which financial power remodels the very criteria of company governance with the sole aim of creating value for the shareholder. In cognitive biocapitalism, not only do we witness the final decline of the Weberian entrepreneur (the figure combining the functions of firm ownership and direction, who had already partly disappeared in industrial-Fordist capitalism since the marginalist revolution of the 1930s), but we also see the irreversible crisis of the Galbraithian techno-structure, legitimized in its role by the planning of innovation and the organization of labor. The new governance of today's companies is increasingly founded on a type of management whose principal competence is exercising financial and speculative functions while delegating to employed labor the real functions of the organization of production. On the other hand, the competitiveness of a company is largely dependent not on internal economies but on external ones, that is, on the ability to capture productive surpluses that result from a territory's cognitive resources.

Capital, then, benefits freely from the collective knowledge of society, as if it were a gift of nature. From this point of view, the becoming-rent of profit takes the form of privatizing what is common,[11] gaining revenues from the creation of a scarcity of resources that is only artificial. It is the common that links together, in a single logic, the rent coming from real estate speculation and financial rent—which, since the beginning of the 1980s, has played a major role in the fiscal crisis and the dismantling of welfare state institutions due to the privatization of currency and public debt. The becoming-rent of profit derives, then, from the attempt to privatize knowledge and life (bios). This is achieved thanks to a politics promoting the reinforcement of intellectual property rights so

10 See Negri and Vercellone (2007); Vercellone (2010). See also Marazzi (2010), especially Chapter 3.

11 For a discussion of the concept of the common, see Hardt and Negri (2009).

that the cost of numerous commodities is kept artificially high, although their reproduction costs are extremely low or even close to zero.

In cognitive biocapitalism, value production is no longer founded on material production alone. Productive activity is increasingly based on immaterial elements, that is to say, on intangible raw materials, which are very hard to measure and quantify and that come directly from the utilization of the relational, sentimental, and cerebral faculties of human beings. The process of valorization loses, in this way, the measuring unit usually connected to material production. With the advent of cognitive biocapitalism, valorization tends to graft itself onto different forms of labor, which go beyond the official work time and coincides more and more with one's whole lifetime. Today, the value of labor at the basis of biocapitalistic accumulation is also the value of knowledge, of affects and relationships; it is the value of the imaginary and the symbolic.

It follows that value production is no longer founded on a homogeneous, standardized scheme for the organization of labor, independent of the type of goods produced. The activity of production is carried out in different organizational ways, which are characterized by a network structure, thanks to the development of technologies for linguistic communication and transportation. The result is a disruption of the traditional and unilateral hierarchic form typical of the factory. This is substituted by hierarchic structures activated in the territory along subcontractor production chains and characterized by relations of cooperation and/or control.

The division of labor itself takes on cognitive characteristics and therefore is based on the differential access and use of different forms of knowledge. Knowledge can be divided into four levels: information, codified knowledge, tacit knowledge, and culture (or systemic knowledge), characterized by unilateral relations of dependence. Information is the basic level of knowledge that is increasingly incorporated into the machine element. Codified knowledge is a specialized knowledge (knowhow) that derives from tacit knowledge but which is transmitted through standardized procedures, with machines as the intermediary, where its bearer can be substituted at any moment, having no contractual power. Tacit knowledge can derive from personal learning processes or from specific investments in research and development (R&D), thanks to intellectual property rights; furthermore, at least until codified, it can only be transmitted through a human being, thus possibly generating forms of enclosures. Those who possess tacit knowledge, which is relevant for the productive process, therefore have high contractual power and define the hierarchical structure of labor and production.

However, tacit knowledge, if relevant, is destined to transform into codified knowledge sooner or later and thus lose value. Culture is the set of knowledge that allows one to hold the intellectual function, that is to say, the ability to act critically and creatively, not immediately subsumed to the logic of biocapitalist valorization. As a consequence, culture is dangerous for the reproducibility of the socioeconomic system and also constitutes a surplus that exceeds control.

In cognitive biocapitalism, the condition of the labor force goes hand in hand with mobility and the predominance of individual contracting (precarity). This derives from the fact that nomadic individualities are put to work and the primacy of private rights over workers' rights brings about a transformation of the contribution of individualities—especially if characterized by cognitive, relational, and affective activities—into contractual individualism. Labor relations based on precarious conditions, that is to say, the temporal limit and spatial mobility of labor, are the basic paradigm in which the relationship between capital and labor takes place. Precarity then becomes a structural, existential, and generalized condition. An essential character of cognitive biocapitalism is the dematerialization of fixed capital and the transfer of its productive and organizational functions to the living body of labor force.

This process lies at the origin of one of the paradoxes of new capitalism: the contradiction between the rise in importance of cognitive labor as a lever for the production of wealth and, at the same time, the devaluation of that labor as far as salary and the profession are concerned. This paradox is inherent in Marazzi's definition of the "anthropogenetic character of contemporary capitalistic production," underlined in one of his essays.[12] In cognitive biocapitalism, the living being contains within itself the functions of both fixed and variable capital, that is, of both the material and machinery forms of labor belonging to the past and of the living labor of the present: bios.

Nowadays the separation between abstract labor and concrete labor is not as clear as it was in industrial-Fordist capitalism. First, what Marx used to call concrete labor, or labor producing use value, can today be renamed creative labor.[13]

12 See Marazzi (2000, 107–26). Marazzi's (2000, 109) complete quotation that defines the concept of the anthropogenetic model of production is as follows: "A model of production of man through man, in which the possibility of cumulative and endogenous growth is due, above all, to the development of the education sector (investment in human capital), the health sector (demographic evolution, biotechnologies) and the cultural sector (innovation, communication, creativity)."

13 Holloway (2006) writes the following: "The center of class struggle is located here: it is a struggle between creative action and abstract labor. In the past, we always thought of class struggle as a struggle between labor and capital, thus understanding labor as abstract, wage-earning labor. As a consequence, the working class was defined as the class of wage-earners. This is wrong. Wage-earning labor and capital are twenty theses mutually completing, the former being a stage of the latter. Doubtlessly, there is a conflict be-

This term allows us to better understand the cerebral contribution inherent in such activity, while the term *concrete labor*, though conceptually its synonym, refers more to the realm of *making* than to that of *thinking*, with a closer allusion to craftsmanship proper (Fumagalli 2013).

In cognitive biocapitalism, life itself is put to labor and produces value. The labor theory of value becomes a life theory of value (Fumagalli & Morini 2009). This happens through the valorization of the differences that individuals possess. These differences, in their uniqueness, make possible the relational activities that are the basis of the social cooperation producing general intellect. In addition to general differences based on race, gender, and so on, we need to add up differences *tout court*, which are valorized without any relation to the anthropological characteristics that define them. Now starting to be segmented and divided are cerebral differences, that is to say, individualities. Spatial and biological differences, gender and race in particular, can at most be instruments for the immediate disciplining of the social body. The preoccupying emerging tendency, however, is the constitution of a human subjectivity characterized by the contradictory conflict between creative actions and cerebral standardization: the creation of a sort of bionic being, capable of managing the anthropogenetic process of production. These elements suggest a world where individuality is erased but individualism is exalted. Cognitive biocapitalism is bioeconomic production: it is bioeconomy.

Since life itself becomes value, differences become value (Morini 2010). The traditional binary dichotomies inherited from industrial-Fordist capitalism are no longer topical. We are witnessing the overcoming of the separation between lifetime and labor time. As soon as labor activities use the existential faculties of individuals, it becomes impossible to define a temporal barrier between labor and non-labor time. Even if this distinction can nominally continue to exist on a formal juridical level, the difference between life, labor, and work no longer exists, which is also due to new language and communication technologies. Life appears completely subsumed into work and labor.

We are also witnessing the overcoming of the separation between workplace and life-space. The multiple forms of biolabor are nomadic labor, where mobility is a primary requisite. This phenomenon leads to the definition of non-

tween wage-earning labor and capital, but it is rather superficial: a conflict on salary levels, on work conditions, on the length of the work day. All these things are important, but they presuppose the existence of capital. The real threat to capital does not come from abstract labor, but from useful labor or creative action, because it is the latter that is radically opposed to capital, that is, to its own abstraction. Creative action says 'No, we will not let capital control us; we need to do what we think is necessary or desirable.'" (Holloway 2006) places of labor, as opposed to classic forms of domestication. In this case, indeed, we should not talk about a convergence of labor-place and life-space but, rather, about the expropriation of the workplace and of all possible consequences that this process might have on work identity. We are witnessing the overcoming of the separation between production and reproduction. This is the first consequence of life becoming work. When we talk about life, we do not only mean it as directly finalized to productive activity, but also to the social reproduction of life itself, a clear example of which is the almost exclusively female caretaking work. Having said this, we can state that the erasure of this distinction implies the partial overcoming of specific gender differences and poses the question of differences *tout court* (Morini 2010). In conclusion, we are witnessing the overcoming of the separation between production, circulation, and consumption. The act of consumption is, at the same time, a participation of public opinion, an act of communication, and self-marketing. In this sense, it allows the further valorization of commodities.

In cognitive biocapitalism, value creation is based preeminently on the process of expropriation of the general intellect for private accumulation. The general intellect is the outcome of basic social cooperation: it allows the passage from tacit knowledge to codified knowledge as social knowledge.

This passage is regulated by the evolution of the juridical forms of intellectual property rights. Such property is thereby added to that of the means of production, giving private property the control of the process of generating (intellectual property) and diffusing knowledge (ownership of the means of production). Since exploitation of the general intellect implies the valorization of the very existence of individuals, the process of value creation is no longer limited to the workday but extends to include the entire human existence. This means that the measure of exploitation is not really the time of the workday generating surplus work but, rather, that part of the life span that is necessary to generate tacit knowledge—and hence social knowledge—which is then expropriated by the process of accumulation.

The effective and direct forms with which the expropriation of general intellect creates value can vary. Among these, the valorization of commodities through the branding process is particularly significant. The value of commodities increases together with the increase of their symbolic meaning and of their ability to create an imaginary that is shared by consumers. Even in this case, surplus value originates from totally immaterial elements created by behavioral conventions and shared relational activities, just as for the financial markets. If private ownership of the means of production implies partly stealing the workday and allowing for the generation of surplus work, private intellectual property is then the theft of social knowledge understood as *commons*. In cognitive biocapitalism, the creation of value happens through the expropriation of the common.[14]

In cognitive biocapitalism, basic income is the compensation for work and active life, just as wages are the remuneration of labor. The idea of basic income is based on the concept of compensation or remuneration and not of support or assistance (subsidies, transfer payments, etc.). The logic that justifies its existence is then completely opposed to the doxastic interpretation of the current situation, that is, to measures that would guarantee a continuity of revenue in a temporary, conditioned way.[15] In the present context of cognitive biocapitalism, wealth is divided between those whose life becomes value (all residents, regardless of citizenship, etc.), on the one hand, and all those (much fewer) who create value from the private appropriation of common goods (the exploitation of intellectual property rights, of the territory, of financial flux, etc.) or who profit from productive and service activities. As a consequence, basic income is, by definition, unconditioned and perpetual (for the duration of one's life). In other words, basic income is nothing other, today, than the equivalent of salary in Fordist times (Fumagalli 2009).

It follows that in cognitive biocapitalism, the most adequate structure of welfare is the commonfare, or welfare of the common (Fumagalli 2007, 2008). The commonfare is based on two important concepts: on the one hand, we have the guarantee of continuity of unconditioned revenue, regardless of working conditions and professional, social, and citizenship status. This concept is complementary to any other form of direct revenue, as compensation for the productive social cooperation that forms the basis of value creation, currently expropriated for private rent and profit. On the other hand, we have access to common material and immaterial goods that allows full participation in social life by way of the free fruition of common natural/environmental goods (water, air, the environment) and immaterial common goods (knowledge, mobility, socialization, currency, primary social services).

In cognitive biocapitalism, the trade unions' slogan "right to work" should be changed to "right to choose work." We are witnessing an ethical overturning of how we conceive of actual work activity. If in industrial-Fordist capitalism the right to work is the foundation of many national constitutions (the Italian one, first of all) as well as the first objective of union struggle as a passage to

14 I cannot develop here an in-depth analysis of the theme of the common, but see Hardt and Negri (2000, 2009).

15 Such as, for instance, the French Revenu minimum d'activité (RMA) and analogous apparatuses, which simply function as social shock absorbers and promote the return to work.

revenue stability and the enjoyment of civil rights, in cognitive biocapitalism, insofar as life itself is productive, the necessity of work has largely taken up the function of blackmail and controlling actual work activity and is increasingly less relevant to accumulation. From this point of view, capital tends to reach autonomy, even though it still depends on the social connections that are inherent in the relation between labor and capital. In contrast, the right to choose one's work opens the path to autonomous work and thus this objective is not compatible with the current capitalistic valorization or subsumed by it. In other words, if in industrial-Fordist capitalism the right to work was, on the one hand, functional to the process of accumulation while, on the other hand, it represented the basic condition for the right to struggle, in cognitive biocapitalism the right to choose one's work is uniquely the right of subversion.

The socioeconomic governance of cognitive biocapitalism behind financialization: the precarity trap and the new industrial reserve army

In cognitive biocapitalism the labor market structure and labor composition are strongly modified. New elements have appeared that render obsolete the rigid separation between occupation and joblessness, production and unproductive labor, and labor and work. Today, as we have seen, being jobless is no longer tantamount to being unproductive and those who hold a formal occupation (with fixed working hours) are no longer the only ones considered productive from a capitalistic point of view. Other actions and life activities (e.g., reproduction and consumption, such as *work*, leisure, and play) have become productive. A distinction must be established between the concepts of labor and work and between those of play and leisure. Without pretending to go much deeper into this discussion,[16] let us limit ourselves to the idea that while *work*, leisure, and play (i.e., life) have a value, those individuals classified as jobless because they do not produce labor (but only *work*, leisure, and play) are not paid, even though, in real terms, they are "producers." There emerges, therefore, a gray area between jobs and joblessness, which statistics in the last few years have start to classify as "discouraged workers" or "neets" (i.e., not in education, employment, or training). In more general terms, this can be considered the area of subjective precarity.

Therefore, we face four different situations that correspond to three different subjectivities: precarious workers who are unable to reach a stable and certain labor activity; *discouraged* inactive but potentially active people; neets, who are

16 See Standing (2011) and Fumagalli (2013).

neither unemployed nor discouraged but live a precarious existence; and certifiably unemployed workers.

To complete the labor market, the traditional category of permanent employed workers should be added, but it is possible to consider them potentially precarious workers, just because of the generalized nature of today's precarity (Morini 2012).

Starting from these premises, we can now introduce the concept of *precarity trap*. This concept already exists in the economic and sociological literature, especially in Anglo-Saxon research. We are confronted with differing meanings for the term. One definition of precarity trap has to with a sort of vicious circle that prevents individuals from leaving precarity conditions because of the high costs of finding a stable job. To live in precarious conditions means to have a lot of expenses that will keep one there. What in theory are called high transaction costs (Standing 2011)—such as time spent applying for benefits, temporary job loss and the search for a new one, the time and cost of learning the new job, and the adjustment of all other activities, such as child care, around that new job—may very well gobble up a greater share of income. This can lead to a sort of precarity trap.

Another broader definition has to do with the fact that living in the precariat means experiencing the full force of *the risk society*. From this point of view, the precarity trap is the result of the lack of a social security policy and is seen as a conjunctural phenomenon. Recent research (Murraya & Gollmitzer 2012) based on the observation that precarious flexible labor is more diffuse in advanced and creative industries, argues that creative economy policies could be a panacea for revitalizing economies and allow for overcoming precarity. Existing policy instruments are mostly uncoordinated but can be divided into four categories, namely, education and training, awards and contests, business support, and social security policies, with the greatest emphasis on the first three. Escaping the precarity trap—existence without security—typical of much cultural work requires a rehabilitated notion of "flexicurity" that includes exceptional, subsectoral, and generalist strategies to support cultural workers. Therefore, a more holistic policy framework that uses a rights-based perspective and emphasizes social security measures could be valid.

In these two interpretations, precarity traps can be solved if adequate policies are implemented. But, according to our analysis, precarity is a structural and generalized phenomenon. It follows that it could be eliminated only if labor market dynamics change drastically. Hence, the precarity trap is physiological, overall, in the short term. It is constantly fueled by the peculiarities of existing labor activity, based on the exploitation of life faculties and the subjectivities of human beings.

My opinion is that the precarity trap is the result of a new type of industrial reserve army. The traditional definition of the industrial reserve army is based on the idea that the presence of unemployment acts as pressure on employees by reducing their bargaining power. The Polish economist Kalecki's (1943) famous essay on the political origins of unemployment argues that in a system of industrial relations it is quite convenient for the entrepreneurial class to give up to the optimization of profit (which will lead to full employment) to artificially create a pool of unemployment, which reduces the bargaining power of trade unions. This assumption makes sense if the distinction between labor and non-labor time (i.e., between employed and unemployed) is clear and precise, as it was during the Fordist period. But today, in the era of biocognitive capitalism, this distinction tends to vanish and the modality of labor control increasingly tends to be based on income blackmail and on the individualization of the same labor relationship. As we have already argued, that is the main reason why the precarious condition is generalized and structural. It is precisely this precarious condition, albeit perceived in different ways, that nourishes and defines the new industrial reserve army: an industrial reserve army no longer outside the labor market, but inside it instead.

It follows that there are good political reasons, despite any public and official declaration, to keep a certain degree of precarity, since in the Fordist free market it was not convenient to reach full employment (partially achieved only with the implementation of public policies). Today, the precarity trap plays the same role as the unemployment trap played in the last century, with a difference that makes the current situation even worse. Today, precarity is added to unemployment with anti-cyclical dynamics. In the recovery stage, in the first half of the last decade, before the deep financial/economic crisis of 2007, the number of unemployed could decrease and their state transformed into precarity, whereas in the current recession phase, the opposite is occurring: precarious workers are the first to become unemployed, giving rise to the group of the discouraged or neets. In any case, the biopolitical device that manages to subsume the labor force is guaranteed, together with the crisis of traditional trade unions and the fall of social claims and conflict.

Perspectives on the post-crisis: basic income and the precariat

Basic income is the provision of a certain amount of money to adjust deadlines and maintain a decent life, regardless of the labor performance. Basic income must have two fundamental characteristics: it must be universal and unconditional, that is, it must join the circle of human rights. In other words, it should be given to all human beings in a non-discriminatory way (gender, race, religion, or income). The mere existence is a guarantee of this right. Hence, basic income is not attached to any form of constraint or condition (i.e., it does not require from the recipient any particular responsibility and/or behavior). The two attributes, universality and unconditionality, should eliminate any misunderstandings. The concept of basic income falls exclusively within the sphere of redistribution, given the level of total wealth: it is an instrument of welfare. All redistributional proposals that reference either employment status (unemployment or precarity, insufficient to guarantee a minimum income) or the obligation to make contractual commitments, even if detached from labor performance (as in the case of the Roma in France), are discriminatory and do not conform to the status of "inalienable individual rights."

Basic income is the most suitable distribution (not redistribution) variable of cognitive biocapitalism. In a context in which life is not only enslaved to labor but is put to work, it becomes clear that basic income is the remuneration of a productive existence: thus, it is "primary" income.[17]

It is no coincidence that real labor time tends to "overflow" the labor contract, thereby eliminating the distinction between labor and non-labor or between income and wages. We have to start from here. Basic income is therefore defined by two components: the first component is wages, on the basis of the performance of life that immediately translates into labor performance (labor time, certified and remunerated, but also the lifetime used for the formation of the activity report and reproductive activity). The latter is a component of income (in addition to the first) due to the distribution of social wealth to each individual, resulting from social cooperation and the productivity of the territory. The latter aspects are today entirely the prerogative of profits and financial and real estate rent.

From that perspective, basic income is not only a handout, a subsistence allowance or a tool against poverty: of course, it can also reduce poverty but, in the production environment, basic income is, above all, the remuneration for a previously productive activity.

In the context of cognitive biocapitalism, therefore, basic income simply contributes to the remuneration of the entire and effective labor/work/leisure social activity. As such, it is part of that system of fair social cooperation proposed by Rawls (1999), toward the implementation of that contract of mutual

17 Primary income is the direct income derived from income distribution among productive inputs. Secondary or indirect income, in turn, results from public intervention in terms of welfare or fiscal policy, after income distribution. It is a second-level distribution, defined as a redistribution level, which distinguishes it from first-level distribution or the first-level distribution level (Vercellone 2006b).

solidarity that can be made possible by the introduction of the same basic income for all.[18]

From this point of view, basic income appears as a purely reformist measure but it can also be useful in the process of accumulation. It is not only the remuneration of a labor activity already carried out, but also a stimulus for the growth of those cognitive brain activities that are increasingly more central to the production structure and to levels of competitiveness. If the aim is to increase R&D expenditures and innovation activity with higher knowledge content and thus avoid competition from emerging countries and to be able to intervene in the definition of dominant technological trajectories and paradigms, it becomes increasingly necessary to develop human capital and encourage the production of general intellect.

Basic income, in theory, can play a function of income stabilization, reduce uncertainty, enhance the learning process, and ultimately foster capital accumulation according to the following formula:

Basic income → general intellect ↑ → productivity ↑ → accumulation ↑

However, most social partners are opposed to the introduction of basic income. Trade unions—because they have not yet fully understood the current transformation of labor and the new mode of valorization—fear the loss of their base; additionally, trade unions see wage labor as fundamentally ethical (labor ethics).[19] Entrepreneurial associations, distancing themselves from the conservative

18 Regarding the political and philosophical reasons in favor of the basic income hypothesis, see Van Parijs and Vanderborght (2006) and, for the English, see Van Parijs (1995). See also Del Bò (2004).

19 Numerous statements are common to several European trade unions, leftist parties, and even relevant newspapers. It is enough to analyze the congress of the European Trade Union Confederation or the French and German trade unions to have a confirmation. Even in Italy the situation has not changed. The same applies to the area of the radical left, personified by the Trotskyist parties, by Attac and Le Monde Diplomatique in France and the left CGIL, the Communist Refoundation and Il Manifesto in Italy. With a few exceptions, however remarkable, even antagonistic unions and the most antagonistic groups in principle opposed to basic income consider it a reformist tool, unable to undermine the essence of the capitalistic exploitation ratio. In favor of basic income, instead, are groups operating in the Social Centers' movement in Italy or in some European magazines, such as Multitudes in France, Posse and Infoxoa in Italy, and, more recently, UniNomade 2.0 Network (www.uninomade.org). Only recently, for example, have the slogans "right to income" and "reclaim the money" been fully accepted within Euro-May Day, the most visible manifestation of the precariat in Europe, which takes place in Milan on May 1 of each year. In this context, it is of fundamental importance to the birth in

stance of most unions, consider the introduction of basic income as potentially dangerous for the maintenance of labor discipline. Indeed, from that point of view, they are right. The introduction of basic income, in fact, can be considered a potential counterpower that undermines the current system of the subordination and blackmail of the precarious multitude.[20] To ensure stable and continuous income regardless of labor activity means reducing the degree of worker blackmail: blackmail imposed by contractual individualism and by the need to work for a living. Basic income can lead to the exercise of the right to choose one's own work (instead of the traditional right to work, whatever that may be), an element that could shake the foundations of hierarchical and social control in cognitive biocapitalism.

At the same time, the partial or total removal of income blackmail can potentially foster the process of recomposition of the precarious multitude. I say *potentially* because such a recomposition is not automatic but depends on the subjectivity of individuals involved.[21] The outcome of any event is linked, in any case, to less availability of a supine acceptance of any labor conditions. Second, and this is even a more important factor, although mostly misunderstood—basic income presupposes that a (greater or lesser) proportion of the social wealth produced by the general intellect and by the structure of cooperative production should return to the same producers. This means a reduction in profit margins, which are due to the exploitation of social cooperation and common goods, unless immaterial productivity gains, generated by more stable and satisfying income conditions, are unable to compensate for this reduction.

In cognitive biocapitalism, basic income can therefore be considered analogous to the claim for higher wages in the era of industrial Fordist capitalism. In Fordism, a wage increase or a policy of high wages, according to the happy expression by Keynes, could have two effects: the undermining of the productive system if this increase cannot be borne by the existing cost structure and technological conditions and thus lay the foundation for going beyond the capitalist system itself or, conversely, ensuring full employment growth with the increase in revenues and profits. The Fordist social pact had indeed intended to promote the second alternative in a disciplinary mechanism and control guaranteed by the

---

2009 of the associations Basic Income Network – Italy (www.bin-italy.org) and the Saint Precarious Icon (see www.precaria.org) and the review Quaderni di San Precario (http://quaderni.sanprecario.info).

20 For a deeper analysis, see Fumagalli (2005).

21 We agree with Standing's reflections on the risk that the precarious condition can lead to dangerous results if the individualistic and corporative ideology becomes the majority, with a risk of social dumping and racist political positions. The only antidote is a "politics of paradise" (Standing 2011)!

nation-state. Unlike wage increases, the introduction of basic income, however, does not bear only partially on firm costs, since it would be disbursed to local, national, or supranational public authorities. In other words, the financing of the income of existence depends on the existing tax structure.

In cognitive biocapitalism, a new social pact could therefore consist of basic income as being compatible with a tax constraint yet to be defined and would not result in a change of control over the relationship and hierarchy in the labor market.[22] But nothing can ensure this compatibility: the potential role of monetary counterpower (i.e., independence from income blackmail) and of countercultural production (the chance to choose and to reappropriate part of socially created production) depends on the perception and subjectivity that constitute the precarious multitude, which are, by definition, not controllable. From this point of view, basic income can become subversive and affect the exploitation ratio and the production of surplus value of cognitive biocapitalism.

On that basis, it is clear that the introduction of a basic income can be a valuable tool for escaping the precarity trap. The following are various reasons that lead to this conclusion.

1. The dominant economic policy has always argued that economic growth requires the increased competitiveness of enterprises, especially in the context of globalization. This would entail reducing production costs and increasing the flexibility and mobility of labor. Until that is achieved (the first time), it will not be possible to adapt to new labor conditions or social security or to improve living conditions and well-being (the second time). It is the same approach according to which the imposition of austerity policies is seen as an unavoidable measure to exit the European debt crisis. Only by enduring sacrifices today can we ensure tomorrow's benefits. But we know that this second time (the benefits) will never come. We also know that austerity policies create economic recession, so, in the last 25 years, flexible labor market policies have created increasing precarity, with negative effects on the competitiveness of the economic system itself. This originates the precarity trap and the Italian case (and those of other countries, particularly Spain) is a clear confirmation. It is necessary to reverse this policy by switching the two times. First, measures must be taken to support social security and only afterward should action be taken in the area of labor flexibility. Given the current characteristics of precarity as an industrial reserve army inside the labor market,

22 For a more detailed discussion, see thesis no. 9 in "Nothing will ever be the same" in Fumagalli and Mezzadra (2010, 254–59). For the Italian, see Fumagalli and Negri (2008).

the introduction of basic income becomes an appropriate means to promote economic growth and a measure of social equality that can allow escape from the precarity trap.

2. Basic income reduces uncertainty and allows greater freedom in choosing one's desired labor. Is it possible that no one will ever want to do any hard or less desirable work again? Not necessarily. Every job has its specificity and its remuneration to make it more or less acceptable. The guarantee of income, reducing the supply of people willing to accept low-paying, alienating, and exhausting jobs, puts enterprises at a crossroads: the choice between paying better wages to those who perform those tasks or adopting more complex technologies and organizational solutions to replace them. There were similar objections at the time of the debates on the reduction of working hours to eight hours per day and the result was not only an improvement in labor conditions but also relevant growth, since production systems were modernized.

3. A poverty trap is "any self-reinforcing mechanism which causes poverty to persist" (Azariadis & Stachurski 2005, 326). If it persists from generation to generation, the trap begins to reinforce itself unless steps are taken to break the cycle. The traditional literature describes the poverty trap as a structural condition from which people cannot free themselves despite their best efforts. A poverty trap is different from a welfare trap or an unemployment trap (Petrongolo 2008). The latter traps refer to the barrier created by means-tested social grants that—it is said—have built-in perverse incentives. One of the most common criticisms of the basic income concept has to do with the persistence of the poverty trap. The reasoning is as follows: the payment of a grant to the unemployed may lead them to prefer to remain unemployed over entering the labor market, with a consequent lack of efficiency in the economic system. Therefore, the mainstream literature seeks to underline how an increase in welfare benefits, especially when unconditional (which defines basic income), is one of the causes of voluntary unemployment that affect the optimal natural equilibrium.[23] But the empirical results are controversial. In the current situation, facing precarity as a structural condition, this kind of reasoning is almost irrelevant. The mismatch, is not between the choice to work or not to work but, rather, between precarious work and desired work. If, in cognitive biocapitalism, life is put to work and then to value, either directly or indirectly, the concept of unemployment changes radically. The unemployed today are no longer inactive, in the sense of being unproductive

23 For a survey of the literature, see, among others, Gwartney et al. (2011).

(from a capitalistic point of view); instead, they carry out productive activities that are not certified and, as such, unpaid.

Precarity is blackmail and the induction of self-control by the labor force itself. The precarity trap is the consequence. We are in a situation opposite that of the welfare trap, whose existence could make sense (if it were) in the Fordist era. If at that time the welfare trap could arise from the introduction of social security policies, today the precarity trap is the result of the absence of social security policies.

A post-crisis perspective: the impossibility of a new New Deal

To promote a way out of the current crisis of cognitive biocapitalism, it is essential—at least from the purely theoretical point of view—to reconsider the definition of redistributive variables so that they become more aligned with the production of value and accumulation.

Indeed, the likely superposition of labor and life and hence of salary and income is not yet admitted in the realm of institutional regulation (and neither by any other institutions that define themselves as antagonistic). We have suggested how basic income can represent an element of institutional regulation adapted to the new trends of our capitalism. Basic income is defined according to two components: the first is decidedly salary based, in the form of life contributions that translate immediately into labor contributions (certified and compensated working hours, but also the period of life dedicated to education and the time dedicated to relations and to reproduction). The second component is income (added to the first component) and represents the share of social wealth to which every individual is entitled. This social wealth depends on the cooperation and social productivity that occurs in a given territory (which today is the prerogative of profits and income from bonds and real estate). Thus, for the definition of *basic income,* salary and income appear to be complementary.

Furthermore, in cognitive biocapitalism, the accumulation process has broadened the very base of accumulation, encompassing in its core activities of the human being that in the Fordist-industrial capitalism were neither surplus value producing nor translated into abstract work. New inputs have thus been added or reinforced to the point of becoming strategic, such as the realization that they are goods in themselves (and not merely incorporated in the machine) and in space, in its physical-territorial as well as virtual sense. What follows is that the property of such factors no longer generates income but, when put into production, generates true profits. This is especially true of land property and the flow of communication, as well as the management of monetary and financial flows.

From that point of view, the indications of economic policy suggested by Keynes following the emergence of Fordism and which have been the basis of the American New Deal and of the development of the "30 glorious years" (1945–1975) could be rewritten, taking into account the novelty inherent to the transition into cognitive biocapitalism.

The measure of *basic income* replaces the policy of other salaries, while the euthanasia of Keynes' *rentier* could be declined in the euthanasia of intellectual property rights, accompanied by fiscal policies that could redefine the base taxable income, taking into account productive inputs, starting with space, knowledge, and financial flows.

With regard to Keynes' third proposal on the socialization of investments, cognitive biocapitalism is characterized by the socialization of production before the ever-increasing concentration of technological and financial flows, the levers that nowadays allow the control and command of flexible and outsourced productive activity. Any policy that could undermine such concentration at the base of investment flows has a direct impact on the structure of property and erodes very capitalist production relations at its root.

Possible "reformist" proposals, which could define a social pact in cognitive capitalism, are therefore limited to the introduction of a new salary regulation based on basic income and on a lower weight of intellectual property, which could end up by developing into a sort of euthanasia of income/profit derived from intellectual property.

Yet, in the present reality, there are no economic and political premises according to which this social pact could materialize. This is therefore a mere illusion. The Fordist New Deal was the success of an institutional intervention based on the presence of three assumptions:

- A national state that, independently although perhaps in coordination with other states, is able to develop national economic policy,
- The possibility of measuring productivity gains and thus ensuring their redistribution between profit and salaries,
- Industrial relations that are reciprocally recognized by the parties involved and legitimized at the institutional level, therefore representing, unequivocally, the interests of both entrepreneurs and the working class.

Today, all of those assumptions are absent from cognitive biocapitalism. The nation-state has suffered a crisis derived from the internationalization of production and financial globalization, which today represent—because of their declinations in terms of technology and knowledge, information, and military equipment—the underlying elements of the definition of a supranational imperial power.

In cognitive biocapitalism, it is possible to envisage the limit of a supranational geographic space entity. The European community could represent, from this perspective, a new definition of a socioeconomic public space where the new *New Deal* could be implemented. However, as things stand today, the European construction pursues monetary and neoliberal lines that translate into the negation of the possibility of creating an autonomous and independent public space, not conditioned by the dynamics of financial markets.

The dynamics of productivity tend to depend increasingly on the immaterial production and involvement of cognitive human faculties, which are difficult to measure with the traditional quantitative criteria adopted during Fordism. The current difficulty in measuring social productivity does not allow for the regulation of salaries on the basis of a relation between salary and productivity.[24] The *basic income* proposal could thus represent a solution. As we have suggested, this idea is considered *politically* unacceptable by the business community and also finds some resistance from the trade unions. The former consider it a *subversive* measure, since it could reduce the blackmail of the necessity of work and the dependence on labor. The latter claim it contradicts the labor ethics on which part of the trade unions continue to base their very identity and existence.

Last, but not least, the crisis pertains to the forms of social representation, in both the entrepreneurial and the labor union areas. The lack of a single organizational model leads to the fragmentation of both capital and labor. The former is segmented between the interests of small enterprises, often associated with the relations of hierarchical subcontracting, the interests of large multinational companies, and the speculative activity in financial and currency markets, and the appropriation of profits and earnings from the monopoly in the fields of distribution, transportation, energy, military equipment, and R&D. In particular, the contradiction between industrial capital, commercial capital, and financial capital in terms of strategies and different time frames and the contraction between national and supranational capital in terms of geoeconomic, geopolitical influence make it impossible to achieve a common of level of intent of the capitalist class or the definition of shared objectives. We could venture to say that it is the mixture of profit and income itself that prevents the capitalist class from being homogeneous. The main element that pulls together the interests of capital is the

24 Which does not mean that in a relatively near future such difficulties may be overcome.

pursuit of short-term profits (with different origins), which renders the formulation of progressive political reforms practically impossible, contrary to what was seen Fordist capitalism.

Conversely, the labor world appears increasingly fragmented, not only from a legal point of view but also and most importantly from the qualitative point of view. While the concept of industrial wage earners emerges in large parts of the globe, it is declining almost irreversibly in the Western countries, where it is being replaced by a series of concepts—atypical, precarious, dependent, para-subordinated, and autonomous workers—whose capacity of organization and representation is increasingly linked to the prevalence of individual contradictions and the incapacity of adapting Fordist trade union structures.

The result is that in cognitive capitalism there is no room for an institutional policy of reforms that could reduce the structural instability which characterizes it. No new New Deal is possible. That becomes even truer as one recognizes the measures aiming at favoring the recovery of a balance of the accumulation process. However, those measures—which we have identified as a regulation of salaries based on the proposal of basic income and productivity capacity founded on the free and productive circulation of knowledge—undermine the basis of the very nature of the capitalist system, that is, the necessity of labor and the blackmail of income as an instrument of domination of one class over the other and the violation of the principle of private property as the means of production (machines in the past and knowledge today).

In other words, we can conclude that in cognitive biocapitalism, a possible social compromise according to Keynesian models, adapted to the characteristics of the new accumulation process, is but a theoretical illusion, unworkable from a political point of view. We therefore find ourselves in a historical context where social dynamics do not allow room for the development of practices or, even more importantly, theories of reform. Hence, the consequence is that praxis will lead the way to theory and only conflict and the capacity to create wide-scale movements are able to, as always, drive mankind's social advancement.

References

Amato, M., and Fantacci, L. 2012. *The End of Finance*. Cambridge: Polity Press.

Amin, A. 1994. *Post-Fordism: A Reader*. Oxford: Blackwell Publishing.

Azais, C.; Corsani, A.; and Dieuaide, P. (eds.). 2001. *Vers un Capitalisme Cognitif*. Paris: L'Harmattan.

Azariadis, C., and Stachurski, J. 2005. "Poverty traps." In *Handbook of Economic Growth*, London: Elgar.

Bazzigaluppo, L. 2006. "Il Governo delle Vite." In Biopolitica ed Economia. Rome-Bari: La Terza.

Becattini, G. 2000. *Distretti Industriali e Sviluppo Locale.* Turin: Bollati Boringhieri.

Bertin, G. 1985. *Multinationales et Propriété Industrielle: Le Contrôle de la Technologie Mondiale.* Paris: Presse Universitaire du France.

Bologna, S., and Fumagalli, A. (eds.). 1997. *Il Lavoro Autonomo di Seconda Generazione. Scenari del post-Fordismo in Italia.* Milan: Feltrinelli.

Bonazzi, G. 1993. *Il Tubo di Cristallo. Modello Giapponese e Fabbrica Integrata alla Fiat.* Bologna: Il Mulino.

Boyer, R., and Durand, J. P. 1998. *L'Aprés-Fordisme.* Paris: Syros Edition.

Brusco, S. 1989. *Piccole Imprese e Distretti Industriali.* Turin: Rosenberg & Seller.

Chicchi, F. 2008. "Bioeconomia: ambienti e forme della mercificazione el vivente." In *Biopolitica, Bioeconomia e Processi di Soggettivazione*, edited by A. Amendola, L. Bazzigalupo, F. Chicchi, and A. Tucci, 143–158. Macerata: Quodlibet.

Codeluppi, V. 2008. *Il Biocapitalismo. Verso lo Sfruttamento Integrale di Corpi, Cervelli ed Emozioni.* Bollati Boringhieri.

Coriat, B. 1991. *Penser à l'Invers.* Paris: C. Bourgois.

Corsani, A.; Dieuaide, P.; Lazzarato, M.; Monnier, J. M.; Moulier-Boutang, Y.; Paulré, B.; and Vercellone, C. 2004. *Le Capitalism Cognitif Comme Sortie de la Crise du Capitalism Industriel. Un Programme de Recherche.* Paris: Matisse.

Del Bò, C. 2004. *Un'Introduzione al Basic Income.* Como: Ateneo.

Fumagalli, A. 1996-97. "Lavoro e piccola impresa nell'accumulazione flessibile in Italia. Part I and Part II." *Altreragioni* 1996–97, (5–6).

Fumagalli, A. 2004. "Conoscenza e bioeconomia." *Filosofia e Questioni Pubbliche* 9(1): 141–161.

Fumagalli, A. 2005. "Bioeconomics, labour flexibility and cognitive work: why not basic income?" In *Promoting Income Security as a Right. Europe and North America,* edited by G. Standing, 337-350. London: Anthem Press.

Fumagalli, A. 2007. *Bioeconomia e Capitalismo Cognitivo. Verso un Nuovo Paradigma di Accumulazione.* Rome: Carocci.

Fumagalli, A. 2008. "Trasformazione del lavoro e trasformazioni del welfare: precarietá e welfare del comune (commonfare) in Europa." In *L'Economia della Precarietà*, edited by P. Leon and R. Realfonso, 159-174. Rome: Manifestolibri.

Fumagalli, A. 2009. "Per una nuova interpretazione della teoria del basic income." In *Reddito per Tutti. Un'Utopia Concreta per l'Era Globale*, 125-140. Rome: Basic Income Network, Manifestolibri.

Fumagalli, A. 2013. *Lavoro male Comune*. Milano: B. Mondadori.

Fumagalli, A., and Lucarelli, S. 2011. "A macroeconomic policy in cognitive capitalism paradigm." In *Credit, Money and Macroeconomic Policy. A Post-Keynesian Approach*, edited by P. Gnos and L. F. Rochon, 313-334. London: Elgar Publisher.

Fumagalli, A., and Morini, C. 2011. "La vita messa a lavoro: verso una teoria del valore-vita. Il caso del lavoro affettivo." *Sociologia del Lavoro* 115(3): 94–116, 2009; in English, "Life put to work: towards a life theory of value." *Ephemera* 10: 234–252, 2011.

Fumagalli, A., and Mezzadra, S. (eds.). 2010. *Crisis in the Global Economy: Financial Markets, Social Struggles and New Political Scenarios*. Cambridge: Semiotext(e).

Fumagalli, A., and Negri, A. 2008. "John Maynard Keynes, capitalismo cognitivo, basic income, no copyright: e' possibile un nuovo "New Deal?" In *Quaderni di Economia Politica.* Dipartimento di Economia Politica e M.Q., Università di Pavia, gennaio, www.eco.unipv.it

Fumagalli, A., and Vercellone, C. (eds.). "Le Capitalisme cognitif. Apports et perspectives." *European Journal of Economic and Social Systems* 20(1).

Gwartney, J. D.; Stroup, R. L.; Sobel, R. S.; and MacPherson, D. A. (eds.). 2011. *Economics: Private and Public Choice*. Thomson South-Western.

Holloway, J. 2006. "*Noi siamo la crisi del lavoro astratto*." Intervention at the UniNomade seminar, Bologna, March 11–12.

Hardt, M., and Negri, T. 2000. *Empire*. Cambridge: Harvard University Press.

Hardt, M., and Negri, T. 2009. *Commonwealth*. Cambridge: Harvard University Press.

Jessop, B. 1995. *The Regulation Approach, Governance and Post-Fordism, Economy and Society*. Blackwell.

Kalecki, M. 1943. "Political aspects of full employment." *Political Quarterly* 14(4): 322–330.

Lazzarato, M.; Moulier-Boutang, Y.; Negri, A.; and Santilli, G. 1993. *Des Entreprises pas Comme le Autres*. Paris: Publisud.

Lebert, D., and Vercellone, C. 2006. "Il ruolo della conoscenza nella dinamica di lungo periodo del capitalismo: l'ipotesi del capitalismo cognitivo." In *Capitalismo cognitive,* edited by C. Vercellone. Rome: Manifestolibri.

Lipietz, A. 1997. "The Post Fordist World: Labor Relations, International Hierarchy and Global Ecology." *Review of International Political Economy,* Spring: 1–41.

Lucarelli, S. 2010. "Financialization as biopower." In *Crisis in the Global Economy,* edited by Fumagalli, Andrea & Mezzadra, Sandro. Cambridge: Semiotext(e).

Marazzi, C. 2000. "Capitalismo digitale e modello antropogenetico del lavoro. L'ammortamento del corpo-macchina." In *Reinventare il Lavoro,* edited by J. L. Laville, C. Marazzi, M. La Rosa, and F. Chicchi. Rome: Sapere.

Marazzi, C. 2010. *The Violence of Financial Capitalism.* Cambridge: Semiotext(e).

Morini, C. 2010. *Per Amore o per Forza. Femminilizzazione del Lavoro e Biopolitiche del Corpo*. Verona: Ombre Corte.

Morini, C. 2012. "La cognizione dell'impermanenza: il lavoro a tempo indeterminate paradigma della precarietà contemporanea." *Quaderni di San Precario*, March 3: 175–198.

Moulier-Boutang, Y. 2002. *L'Età del capitalismo cognitive*. Verona: Ombre Corte.

Moulier-Boutang, Y. 2007. *Le Capitalism cognitif. Comprendre la nouvelle grande trasformation et ses enjeux*. Paris: Editions Amsterdam.

Murraya, C., and Gollmitzer, M. 2012. "Escaping the precarity trap: a call for creative labour policy." *International Journal of Cultural Policy* 18(4): 419–438.

Negri, A., and Vercellone, C. 2007. "Il rapporto capitale/lavoro nel capitalismo cognitive." *Posse* November.

Ohno, T. 1995. *Toyota Production System: Beyond Large-scale Production.* New York: Productivity Press.

Orléan, A. 2010. *Dall'Euforia al panico. Pensare la crisi finanziaria e altri saggi*. Ombre Corte.

Palloix, C. 1979 & 1982. *L'Economia mondiale e le multinazionali*. Milan: Jaca Book.

Paulré, B. 2000. "De la New Economy au capitalisme cognitif ." *Multitudes* 2: 25–42.

Petrongolo, B. 2008. "The unemployment trap." Paper No. CEPCP249, *CentrePiece* 13(1), Spring. Available at http://cep.lse.ac.uk/CentrePiece/browse.asp?vol=13&issue=1

Priore, M., and Sabel, C. 1984. *The second industrial divide. Possibilities for prosperity*. New York: Basic Books.

Rawls, J. 1999. *A Theory of Justice*. Cambridge: Harvard University Press.

Revelli, M. 1995. "Economia e modello sociale nel passaggio tra Fordismo e toyotismo." In *Appuntamenti di fine secolo,* edited by P. Ingrao and R. Rossanda, 161–224. Rome: Manifestolibri.

Rullani, E., and Romano, L. 1998. *Il PostFordismo. Idee per il capitalismo prossimo venturo*, Milan: Etas Libri.

Standing, G. 2011. *The precariat: the dangerous class*. London: Bloomsbury.

Turchetto, M. 1999. "Fordismo e post-Fordismo. Qualche dubbio su un'analisi un po' troppo consolidata." In *Oltre il Fordismo. Continuità e trasformazioni nel capitalismo contemporaneo,* edited by Marchi, Edoardo De; Grassa, Gianfranco La; Turchetto, Maria Milan: Unicopli.

Van Parijs, P. 1995. *Real Freedom for All. What (If Anything) Can Justify Capitalism*. Oxford: Clarendon Press.

Van Parijs, P., and Vanderborght, Y. 2006. *Reddito minimo universal.* Milan: Egea.

Vercellone, C. (ed.). 2003. *Sommes-nous sortis du capitalisme industriel?* Paris: La Dispute.

Vercellone, C. (ed.). 2006a. *Capitalismo Cognitivo*. Rome: Manifestolibri.

Vercellone, C.. 2006b. "Il giusto prezzo di una vita produttiva." *Il Manifesto* November 22, 2006. Available at http://archive. globalproject.info/art-10097.html

Vercellone, C. 2010. "The new articulation of wages, rent and profit in cognitive capitalism," paper presented at Queen Mary University, London, February 29.

4. Social reproduction as a paradigm of the common: Reproduction antagonism, production crisis

Cristina Morini

The purpose of this article is to provide answers to the question of whether the concept of social reproduction still makes sense today or, rather, how the concept may be recast. This notion, I believe, is the most suitable when trying to define the type of contemporary diffuse social production. Better yet, one should speak of comprehensive social reproduction, the realm of the unpaid labor of reproduction (Dalla Costa & James 1972) as well as of the social factory (Tronti 1973) and the informal economy (Latouche 1993).

I think that the notion of production, undermining every ranking precedent or hierarchical scale, is unfit today to reflect the comprehensive amplitude of the productive activity of human beings. Mankind has always acted upon the world by transforming it and today we find ourselves surrounded by the utmost complexity, within which we identify, more and more clearly, the significant alterity vis-à-vis the market as traditionally understood. Our reflection takes a starting point in Marx: "The wealth of society where capitalist production prevails consists of a dreadful gathering of goods." (Marx 1964: 67). George Caffentzis noted that the way wealth takes shape (e.g., the profits of a telephone company in an average-sized European or American city) "does not reveal the wealth of information, of social order, of stories or of struggle carried through the telephone wires." (Caffentzis 1996: 175).

Furthermore, in labor, forces and means applied by men are partially applied but are then included in the results of labor itself: In order to continue producing, it is necessary to constantly reproduce these results. In this process of assimilation and dissimilation, speaking of comprehensive social reproduction does not only mean referring to the production and reproduction of values in the use of goods, but also calls attention to a fundamental albeit unknown aspect of economic science, which is the biological reproduction of oneself through a finalistic activity incorporated into labor. At the end of each social process, what is produced and reproduced is more than the material conditions for an individual's existence: the relationships among such individuals are also reproduced. Each production process reproduces, therefore, not only material realities but also social realities. Hence, the reproduction relationships reveal not only different ways of production, but also different forms of society. The contemporary production process is thus, above all, a process of self-production understood as a fundamental activity of a living organism.[1] This underlying idea is common to all forms of life in society.[2]

Defining social reproduction

My starting point is a science fiction narrative that may support our attempt to bring reality to light: the drama surrounding 18 years of total experimental infertility of the insane and violent dystopian society depicted in Alfonso Cuarón's film *The Children of Men.* The year is 2027 and Diego Ricardo, the youngest person on the planet, is killed outside a Buenos Aires bar, stabbed by a fan who wanted his autograph. "Born in 2009 to a proletarian couple living in Mendoza, Baby Diego was aged 18 years, 4 months, 20 days, 16 hours, and eight minutes," we are told in one of the first scenes of the film:

> He had always had trouble dealing with his celebrity status deriving from the fact that he was the last baby born on Earth. For mankind, every single instant of Baby Diego's life represented a tragic reminder. With his death, the first place goes to a woman: she is aged 18 years, five months and 11 days.

The fantastic representation of the universe suggested in the film, concocted in a space and time based on logical-scientific consequentiality, awakens a sense of estrangement that allows us to finally recognize the profound meaning of a situation that borders the limits of the usual vision, which is normally generated within a condition perceived as ordinary, normal, given. By dislodging an ordinary object of our daily life from its usual place, we notice it or, rather, recognize it. This tale introduced leads us to the immediate recognition of the foremost and decisive role of *reproduction*, namely, its biological role: the survival of the species, the reproduction of life, having life to be able to give life. This fundamental starting point serves also as the most obvious conclusion to our definition of social reproduction today: being alive, having life, existing in life, acquires meaning that surpasses the natural function because *existence* today is also the most immediate and most explicit source of creation of economic value. It all

1 "The capitalist production process, seen as a comprehensive process, that is, as a process of reproduction, produces not only goods and surplus; it also produces and reproduces the capitalist relation itself: "On the one side, the capitalist; on the other, the wage earner" (Marx 1964: 634).

2 "I call corpus collectivum hominum et rerum the (abstract) idea of any human community able to reproduce itself biotically (sexual reproduction) and through labor; that is, a society equipped with its own typical biotopic system in a natural environment" (Mazzone 1999: 1).

stems from a mandatory and yet surprisingly overlooked perception: without life, without *madame la Terre*, we would all be dead, including *monsieur le Capital*. What becomes immediately clear is the social rather than the merely natural character of the biological reproduction itself, which can be defined as labor, inasmuch as it implies a creative process of mediation where feelings, choices, energy, and effort are invested and whose end result is a baby boy or girl, hence a specific social value (O'Brien 1981).

Throughout the centuries, nevertheless, reproduction has been neglected and construed solely as the antithesis of productive labor. Productive labor occurs outside, in the market, in the public space of a city, in the factory; reproductive labor is developed inside, within a room, away from the streets: it is therefore the *shadow* of productive labor, the realm where production represents the content. Marxist feminism in the 1970s and 1980s already provided explanations on the origin of this shadiness. Alisa del Re and Maria Rosa Dalla Costa, Lucia Chisté, and Silvia Federici, among others, around that time denounced the existence of this unbalanced binomial, originating in the sexual division of labor and in the sexual contract that establishes a crystallized hierarchy, that is, the fact that only productive labor can grant the right to citizenship (Dalla Costa & James 1972, Chisté et al 1979, Federici 1980, Fortunati 1981).

This productive labor finds its support in a broadly multidisciplinary ideological construction that cuts across the classes and is shared by both religious and lay ethics. From the protestant, Calvinist ethics the notion was transposed to political economy, to become common sense, a norm of behavior, a pivotal piece of our society's imaginary. Since Adam Smith (2008), "external" labor—that directed to the market—together with capital (as the fruits of the labor activity) have been considered the productive factors par excellence. All *the rest of labor* becomes eclipsed, since it does not generate value—one claims—and therefore has no value. We are well aware of that, since, in summary, according to Marx's theory of value, productive labor is that which lends its labor to the production of goods and tangible merchandise that have an exchange value (Marx 1969). Conversely, non-productive labor, because it is not attached or incorporated into any physical object, adds no value to anything: it is the labor of domestic workers and that is women's reproductive labor.

But even Marx realized that the desire for surplus at the base of the capitalist cycle maintains in itself a possibility of crisis and dissolution. This is so because the superficial balance of the process of value appreciation, the triumph of the metamorphosis of goods is constructed upon the eternal suppression of human needs and on a contradiction that is continuously dissimulated, albeit fundamental: "once the weave the ties that ties together goods and money is temporarily loosened, the result is a rupture from which the fundamental contradictions of capitalist life emerge." (Caffentzis 1996: 183). As Georges Bataille claims, the capitalist accumulation is based on portions of unlived desire, in other words, on the rupture of the social ties that must be torn apart to become linked to the intrinsic contradictions of goods (Bataille 2003).

The enigma of reproduction lies in its being a " hidden phase of the capitalist accumulation," as well as in the fact that it is always inseparably linked to the cycles of the exchange process that bind goods and money, revealing the deep and inescapable truth of the social reproduction process.

More recently, Dalla Costa cast some more light on the issue by adding, "We find the enigma but not the secret." (Dalla Costa 2002). Unearthing the secret of reproduction is indeed no easy task. We could resort to empirical approximations and, as Ferruccio Rossi Landi suggests, we could write a *catalog,* which would mean ordering in a single file all the infinite acts, gestures, exchanges, signs, actions that constitute the essence of existence, an extremely vast and highly variable process, dependent upon tastes and needs, fashions and postures (Rossi Landi 2002). It would require, before all else, deepening the concept of *fundamental need*—for whom? Where? It would also require admitting that each *need* brings with it the creation of tools adequate to its fulfillment (flint for hunting, a bowl for containing grain, etc.) - a process that is not directly associated with what we are describing - and then the need for an organization coherent with the development of various actions (searching for food, cooking, preserving food, taking care of the newborn and the sick) with their hierarchical consequences. In short, a complex catalog prone to grow infinitely as, notwithstanding the precautions taken, "any instance of social reproduction ... shall encompass the majority of the needs and desires, but will never be able to please everyone." (Ibid. 12).

Alisa del Re suggests an arrangement into three fields: *domestic or elementary labor,* the simplest of all, transferable, measurable, which can be immediately transformed into a merchandise and replaced by machines; *reproductive labor* or, rather, the reproduction of the species, the rearing of children; and *care*, understood as the realm in which human relationships, contacts, affection, and sex are deployed. These three fields may be intertwined: the reproductive field encompasses, for example, elementary labor and includes the entire sphere of care for dependents (including the elderly and the handicapped) (del Re 2012).

Rossi Landi, taking a distance from the catalog concept in an attempt to provide a definition, suggests resorting to three models sufficiently ample and formal to be applied to very different instances of social reproduction. Hence, the author suggests that the human animal is socially produced, reproduced, and conditioned at three levels (Rossi Landi 2002: 11):

> At the structural level (in the production-exchange-consumption cycle); at the level of the signal systems, starting with the most important, that of the language spoken in a certain community; to the post-linguistic level, more complex, which is that of the super-structures.

In other words, these three levels are where ideologies and consensus, life styles, and behavioral norms are produced: biopolitics, in short.

Welcome to the present

Felix Baumgartner, a 41-year-old Austrian parachutist, jumped from a space capsule 39,000 meters from the Earth. He fell as a missile at 1,342 kilometers per hour, breaking the speed of sound. The American beverage producer "Red Bull" financed the team's project and installed 30 cameras inside the capsule to allow spectators to follow every single moment of the mission.

In the United Kingdom, each ovulation cycle is compensated for by £750. The economic crisis has seen the number of donors increase. Heterologous in vitro insemination (the use of ovules or semen not belonging to the couple) in Great Britain was legalized in 1990 and donations can occur for payment. In the United Kingdom, the launching of the so-called IVF lottery (which never materialized), whose prize was an in vitro fertilization treatment ("Buy a ticket you could win a baby!"), created an uproar: "The winner of the jackpot gets a package worth £25,000 including stay at a luxury hotel, treatment in a specialized and recognized fertility clinic, and a private driver to take the patient between the hotel and the clinic." The idea of infertility as the object of a lottery confirms the disproportionate costs surrounding the process, the limitations in insurance coverage for overweight individuals and smokers, and the difficulty of access for those who already have children or who are single.

In the United States, the compensation for a single ovulation cycle is $8,000. University bulletin boards are filled with ads from centers recruiting donors. Since one year's tuition in law or medical school can cost $50,000, more and more university students have been forced to take out loans and to consider such an alternative to make ends meet.

Benetton Spa launched a new advertising campaign "Unemployee of the year": A contest dedicated to the unemployed youth between 18 and 30 years of age, seeking to "spread a positive message of hope and celebrate young people's ingenuity, creativity, and their ability. And their capacity to cope brilliantly with the problem of unemployment." One hundred winners of this competition - which will reward activities carried out outside of work and the individuals referred to as ***NEET****, that is* Not in Education, Employment or Training - *will get €5000 to finance their own idea:* "To lose, even in part, the contribution, the vision, the energy of those young people is one of the biggest risks," explained Alessandro Benetton.

Recent research carried out by the MIT and the Semel Institute of Neuroscience and Human Behavior at the University of California in Los Angeles refers to the computer as a modern "form of cocaine." Studies conducted in 15 different countries have focused on the problem of addiction to the Internet, electronic games, and social networks. Facebook stimulates compulsive use by bringing the visionary image of total interaction between man and machine increasingly closer: today, the paranoia of a constant presence in Facebook figures as a problem in various manuals and statistics on mental disorders. According to research conducted in 2008 in California, the brain of Internet dependent individuals undergoes changes and produces more neural connections in the areas corresponding to attention, control, and executive functions.

To identify useful frameworks and to produce an updated definition of social reproduction, I feel that some suggestions may be useful. I have mentioned a few, although different ideas could be added. They are useful to stress all that we do to give life and remain living, to guarantee the life of the community (to prepare meals and eat, to raise children, to care for the elderly) and to keep on living (to take a bus to work, to ask the driver for information, to study, to find a solution to a problem, to interact with a colleague, to write a project or an e-mail, to learn to play the piano). And there is something else: the reproductive activities are placed vertically in relation to all others; that is, they allow, in substance, all other activities to be carried out. They are at the base, a precondition to the eternal turning of the world. And, in addition to the labor force, they provide a background to human relations, emotions, and feelings; they also produce a sense of identity and belonging. At this level, ideologies, legality, and rules are also created.

The centrality of social reproduction was made evident by Michel Foucault when he cast light on capitalism as a system that develops life, that is, biopower (Foucault 1991: 124):

> This biopower has, without any doubt, been one of the indispensable factors in the development of capitalism, which could only be consolidated through the controlled introduction of the bodies in the production apparatus, thanks to an adaptation of the phenomena of populations to the economic processes. But it has asked more than that: it demanded the promotion of the growth of both, their reinforcement and their utility and ductility. It also demanded the introduction of methods of power susceptible to greater forces, attitudes, life in general without turning more difficult their subjection.

The entry of "life into history" (ibid. 125) that Foucault discusses helps us identify a theory of social reproduction that questions once and for all the alleged subordination of spheres of life external to the market. From this perspective, the possible links between the theories inherent to relational-cognitive biocapitalism and the issue of social reproduction must be stressed. It is an interesting, dramatically contemporary passage, heavy in tension that *becomes concrete in the overt becoming of the social aspect of production,* which must be analyzed resorting not only to economic laws but also to psychoanalysis and current events. In this context, Dalla Costa, Fortunati, Federici, and other feminists—who, from the mid-1970s, focused on the issue of the invisibility of labor, recognizing that the most important source of social surplus is unpaid labor—provide some powerful insights (Dalla Costa 1974, Federici & Fortunati 1984).

Obviously, this vision is confirmed today in the generalization of the free character of labor made explicit by the generalization of the precarization of labor. Symbolically, those processes transfer the entirety of current economic processes to a sort of economy of work at home, a comprehensive restructuring of work that acquires many of the features typical of female work, except that it can now be equally carried out by men and women. This transfer is translated into the concrete possibility of being used as a reserve labor force, more as servants than as workers, subject to paid and unpaid labor time, regardless of agreed work schedules. This supposes the large-scale downgrading of jobs. A domestic work economy means that (Haraway 1995: 63):

> The factory, the home and the market are integrated in a completely novel relationship, and that the women's positions are crucial and must be analyzed with regard to the differences between the women and with regard to the meaning the relations between men and women take in different contexts.

We can say that reproduction is a weave, a net formed by *cultural factors* stemming from the mere act of living. And, today, those cultural factors take on a special meaning at the level of exchange, contaminating use value. In the exchange, *use value* (that is, the utility a certain product has to an individual), is transformed into *exchange value* (the value a product has when exchanged in the market). Whereas use value is directly associated to the relation of men with that which they shall use, the capitalist value of the goods is realized in the *exchange*, that is, in that social process that is at the base of its production and that allows different types of products of human labor to be valued comparatively. The crucial issue lies precisely here, in this transition, in the transformation of linguistic-relational productions into *goods,* in the shifting of relations into *commodities*. This is where the epochal change of the productive paradigm that we are experiencing lies: what becomes obvious is that the entire economic process nowadays is founded on the product-becoming of the human, confirming the thesis of operaist feminism with regard to the generalization of the production of surplus. And as the becoming-production of reproduction is established, we require an update of the value–labor theory as well. It must be stressed how *concrete labor* (labor qualitatively defined, which produces some sort of use value), which constitutes the sole property of the free worker, becomes fully embedded in the productive process to be transformed into surplus. And because the productive process excludes the capitalist's ownership of the means of production (we, ourselves, are the means of production), we may venture to say that the transformation of produced goods (linguistic-relational) into money takes the shape of income rather than profit. And perhaps one should add that if we do not become collectively aware of the amplitude and seriousness of those processes and dispositives, capital will end up by taking over us completely, by maximizing its interest for living matter and the way of living.

Words and messages, just like physical objects, do not exist in nature but are, rather, produced by men. The concept that permeates simultaneously all of those elements that seem to be separate (material production versus linguistic or immaterial production) is the notion of *labor*. If material goods are quite different from linguistic or relational products, the *labor* from which they result is in essence the same, since the notion of labor refers to men and women, in their complexity and unity, at the same time. If anything, so far, the concept of labor has excluded so-called reproductive labor. As already pointed out, the scope of industrial capitalism was the production of *manufactured goods* and the type of organization associated with it required the formal marginalization of reproduction. Today, however, this exclusion is all but functional. The scheme has collapsed; nothing remains the way we remember from the old days. Recalling Rossi Landi once more, "man is a working and talking animal who sets himself apart from all others by *producing* tools and words." (Rossi Landi 2003: 63).

Tools and words, therefore... The attention is geared toward *manufacture*, toward *brainfacture* (Forti 1999). The only farsightedness in following this suggestion that helps us come forward is that one must be aware that the changes produced by *labor* are intentional and therefore differ from those produced by *activity*. All that changes my being and social relations is work: "the idea of social awareness ascribed to the Marxist concept of *general intellect*, the set of knowledge and competences resulting from the relational activity of individuals inside the organized social contexts." Whereas in industrial capitalism the propaedeutic precondition to accumulation was the control of the machines that tended to incorporate technical knowledge, "in cognitive capitalism accumulation is based on the appropriation and the control of knowledge and social awareness." (Fummagalli 2007: 65).

This is the secret of social reproduction. Reproduction is no longer only the premise or the cornerstone, the foundation, the unknown principle of original accumulation, the concealed portion of the salary that contributes to the creation of surplus: today, it is the very core of the process of value creation generated by the metropolitan social woman worker, a potential driver of today's social subversion, the prototypical subject of our times. It is the precarious female worker, the sex worker, the woman immigrant who puts her body and individuality to work, who manifests the productive depth that *we do, live, and are.*

Fordism's orderly pace is no more: the roles, the places, the materiality, and the measurability are gone. Obviously, the scope of today's capitalism is that of "absorbing and subjugating, in a parasite-like world, the collective conditions of production of knowledge, suffocating the potential for emancipation inscribed in the society of the *general intellect,*" as Carlo Vercellone puts it (2012).

Hence, reproduction is viewed not only as *shadow labor* that adds value to the final merchandise, but also as the focal point of the process itself: from training to commuting, from consumption to debt. To apply for a loan, to get a mortgage or an insurance policy for a son who wants to graduate, or to insure one's life or health, to retire: these are in a category that, once again, belongs neither to the formal nor to the informal, without which no good, no relationship, no link can materialize. The merchandise produced today through cognitive capitalism is consumption; it is words, information, knowledge, mobility, desire, narcissism, cooperation, image and investment. And the value attached to this linguistic/symbolic/relational merchandise produced by contemporary biocapitalism is *time* or, more precisely, *life;* reproduction, therefore, also in the sense of the extension of production spanning an entire existence and all its spaces, from the first cry to the tomb; reproduction as a minor becoming of production that no longer has (only) codified, institutionalized (visible and tangible) merchandise but which is continuous and invisible action, changeable and *common* according to reality. On the other hand (Vignola 2011: 136),

> It is necessary to realize the conceptual opposition between majority and minority, whose confrontation surpasses the quantitative aspect. The former implies a constant as unit of measure with which it can be measured; whereas minority differs from the constant and can be considered a subsystem or something outside the system.

That which reproduction transforms, the merchandise that is dramatically transformed by the process, produced in social labor, in the networks of social labor, is the *human being*: it is our I in the social sphere, our being in relationships, giving rise to desire and need that, as always, encourage, from the origin, invariably, the instances of social reproduction. Reproduction is neither flat nor lineal;

it cannot be measured and cannot be imposed but imposes itself; it is distant from the logic of efficiency and profit and yet generates efficiency and profit.

What to reproduce? Incessantly producing images, relations, producing meanings, eroticization and de-eroticization, behavioral models, education, and the codification of knowledge. Reproducing is understood, first and foremost, as "producing an infinite number of times" so that the matter to be produced is not consumed, is not scarce, has no end and, inversely, develops and broadens with use, a "collective concatenation which embraces the forces which interact in the language and in society" and that also encompasses a "machinic of bodies," drawing on the "Deleuzian concept of body, according to which bodies may be social, moral and monetary rather than physical – even the representations are bodies." (Ibid. 133f.).

Reproduction no longer has the scope or the sense of recovering (or reviving) the strength with pauses, breaks, interruptions of effort once one reaches home, the private sphere; it has turned into a dramatic exposition of a public *continuum* (traceability, cell phones, messages, Internet, contacts) that confirms the fact that our life is constantly productive.

We are never paid for this productive continuum, it is not even considered, not even this time, as always happens to reproduction, the fascination of reproduction and its enigma, its ancestral secret. Why is it neither compensated nor sensibly considered, then as now, and in that sense remain unchanged? Because we assume that it exists, that is it there, as it quite simply cannot cease to exist. We cannot abandon reproduction without abandoning ourselves at the same time. There is no such thing as exodus from social reproduction. Abandoning it—and is it even imaginable, admissible, desirable, even before it is deemed feasible?—would mean abandoning what we are and what gives us substance through a network of relationships in which/for which we exist, condemning us to a life of infertility, loneliness, and the absence of stimuli and contacts, words, caresses, and relationships. It is part of what we are. Even the *hikikomori* (prisoners), who achieved notoriety a few years ago, young Japanese who never leave home and, as much as possible, do not even leave their own rooms, maintain links to the outside world through the Internet and the media.

In short, one can sabotage production and be absent from productive labor. Abstaining from reproduction, however, is impossible. This is the distinctive feature of reproduction, which means that social reproduction should not be interpreted as only a form of modern social production. That would render the notion obsolete. I believe that because of the immanent features of social reproduction or because neither "opting out" nor any form of subtraction or replacement is possible, resorting to the concept of social reproduction holds its own specific and inescapable peculiarity. This becomes evident in the very generalization of the production of surplus inside the regimen of gratuity taken up by contemporary precarious labor, that is, the chronicization of precarity that today seems to have been normalized by contemporary forms of political organizations. And that must be recognized and questioned through the *microphysics of resistance*, in all the bodily forms that this resistance may take, as argued by Judith Butler (2013).

Hence, reproduction, irrevocable and cumulative, not subject to scarcity or lost under ethical pressures. Let us examine the example of knowledge as raw material, the basis of current capitalism, drawing on Carlo Vercellone (2012):

> Compared with the classic goods, the particularity of the knowledge as a common good consists, in effect, in its character: unrivaled, hardly restricted and cumulative. Unlike material goods, knowledge is not destructed under consumption. In fact, every new piece of knowledge becomes enriched as it freely circulates among individuals. Every new piece of knowledge generates new knowledge, in a cumulative process. This is why private appropriation of knowledge is only feasible through the creation of artificial barriers to its access. This attempt encounters, however, significant obstacles. Those obstacles have to do both with the individuals' ethical demands and with the way in which the use of computer and communication technologies renders the enforcement of intellectual property rights increasingly difficult.

As such, ultimately, reproduction is a form of production directly grafted into our life, in our vital impulses, upon the ineludible human pressure to continue to exist, to do, to create, to act. What has remained unchanged in time and space is the *price* of reproduction: even though reproduction has a *cost* to each woman and man, it is not remunerated. In spite of the fact that reproduction constitutes the substance of current production, it continues to be considered non-labor and to be subjected to a non-salary. Hence, cognitive biocapitalism has deepened its own exploitation capacity extraordinarily by appropriating itself of all sectors and transforming them into merchandise. It has also replaced the direct exploitation implicit in the conditions of the dependence of salaried labor, compensated by the guaranty of subsistence, with independent labor, formally exempt from all forms of (voluntary) subordination but which is, nonetheless, subordinate (Fumagalli 2007: 145). This non-permanent (precarious) labor has been degraded to the level of *gift* for which it is recognized, through the very process of explaining and developing itself within the mechanisms of reproduction.

And one may ask is there no more measure? Which measure can we adopt? Granted, there is no lack of attempts to introduce algorithmic estimates and new metrics (e.g., expert opinions, number of quotes, number of clicks on an article's link, life-hours spent in the subway, time spent on Facebook), all conforming to the uncertain nature of the investment on human capital by those who retain power, but it is also, inversely, the space where we can play. For the time being, the answer to the question is political and concerns first and foremost all of us: the measure is carried out the other way around, from the negative, and it is found in the progressive reduction of our energies-freedoms vis-à-vis the reproductive-productive labor that we carry out. It is to be found in the time we lack, constantly subtracted from us, and the time that is no longer enough.

New instances of reproduction

The productive subject of reproduction has an evident ancestress: the proletarian housewife. Today, as we attempt to draw a profile, we could venture to say that this subject tends to be feminine, lives in urban areas, and is of undetermined age. She walks, breathes, and exists but, at the same time, has to come to the world, surpassing its own self-representation, aiming at the collectivization of an awareness whose dimension involves and touches all and already stimulates all the recesses of the real.

The ideas expressed by Dalla Costa echo in our ears (Dalla Costa 2002):

> Due to the very fact that with her labor she used to produce the merchandise essential to capitalism, the very labor force, the woman held in her hands a fundamental lever of the social power: *she could refuse to produce.* For this very reason, she was a central player in the "social subversion" as expressed then, that consisted in the struggle that could lead to a radical transformation of society.

And thus, today, we are all called upon to produce collectively, generally, and outside the walls of our own homes the raw material of capital, that is, ourselves. *All of us, the housewives of today's capital, who consume our time cleaning up a room, perhaps without even realizing the effort, and as always without payment* (continuous education, continuous production of curricula, continuous search for work, continuous relationship activity, continuous care of the body). We must identify a way of carrying out the struggle that leads us to a radical transformation of society. And because we have claimed that it is not possible to exit relational-cognitive reproduction—unlike what could be done at the time of the Fordist factory—we have to find a way to transplant ourselves from the capitalistic market and from its logic to *somewhere else,* to understand what to produce-reproduce and for whom to produce-reproduce, refusing to reproduce inside this scheme, holding on to the knowledge that the world around us has been entirely created, from the very beginning, by our social labor.

Industrial capitalism has provided us with walls and borders within which the balance of power was clear. It was so that one could stake one's own fight, lending meaning to one's identity, politically speaking. The woman, then, incarnated the current precarity ("the woman has a working relationship with the man, *which is only interpreted in personal terms*: it is a personal fact between the woman and the man who can appropriate himself of her labor"(Pompei 1971: 35)). This order has crumbled and the domestic factory where the social labor performed by the woman could be understood has become the current city-factory that leaves no one out, wants everything and all, indistinctively. And this is, obviously, because social reproduction can only stem from the blending of differences. What should our reaction be before such a vast process? For one thing, we can try to find out how it has come about (*investigate life*). None of us can own social reproduction, but neither can "they"; not even the mighty have this possibility. We each have generic information on social reproduction. But the same is true for "them". Social reproduction goes on—let us admit—on its own, but that also means that it can never be completely deterred, guided, or twisted. It absorbs value, leading it to *the where* in which it is carried out. But *the where* is, indeed, something we can finally decide for ourselves.

As stated, being outside is not an option—seen as "social reproduction is something from which there is no escape," lest everything should come to an end—and that which we have described may also be called biopolitics, with its framework of social rules and appropriation of the living. It is society vampirized and translated into a market, where the conditions are produced so that the intertwining of exchanges can never be directed to the collective good. The device of biopolitics subtly coordinates competition among individuals, interiorized and opposing interests, a device of unhappiness and presentism that triggers anxiety. The device of biopolitics triggers depression because it discourages the essence of cooperation (commonality), forcing its extinction. It does, on the other hand, produce surplus, a mechanism that has enormous importance for existence, the revenge of life over all forms of production aimed toward profit, the transformation of levels of production and of social production itself. Surplus that we understand as the critical capacity to produce independent thought, the production of unproductive materials vis-à-vis the productivity criterion associated with all forms of production geared toward profit - thus, also, as the capacity to take a responsible stance and the capacity to detract from all social and ideological programs in which surplus is embedded.

As such, could the marvelous inevitability of reproduction or, for that matter, of biopolitics find more fitting (self-determined) forms of expression in the common, in the inventions of commoning or of commun-ism?

Experimental forms of alternative life, experimental forms of subjectification and of submitting experience and knowledge to common use; of practicing, outside the factories but within the cities, forms of re-appropriation of ourselves; of practicing reproduction and social work outside production, re-appropriating social reproduction that is expropriated and turned into income: all brand-new challenges.

Could occupied theaters—understood as spaces of reproduction (a network of cultural and social factors), that is, as spaces that embody the multiform precipitate of a society completely imbued in knowledge—function as an example of creation of sociality and independence of reproduction? The roofs of the factories or of the universities we have climbed constitute the first step, showing our bodies as precarious, at risk, the self-representation of fragility but also of might within the biopolitical dispositive. This experiment has a limit, however, since it stops at the level of witnessing and resistance. But let us go a step further: occupying a factory is an old idea that serves very little purpose, while we have seen that, for the purpose of pointing out expropriated social reproduction, it is very useful to concoct an Occupy Wall Street. A further step could embody the form of occupied theaters: they are an opportunity for the imagination and, notably, more than suffering (precarity and debt, with their demoralizing aftermath of fragmentation, individualism, passivity, and sense of defeat)—it is the imagination of remaining united.

From that point of view, could theaters be thought of and lived as experiences of the revenge of life over the death of a market economy? As a form of biopolitical struggle, of the heightening of cognitive biocapitalism? And could this, or something close, be the *common*, something resembling the coagulation of a self-determined project, aware of its own might around a community (e.g., Val di Susa)? Could we say that attention should be directed to this new *instance of production-common*, understood as a self-governed formulation of our desire to act upon the things we care for and upon the world? Thus, inventing affirmative (bio)politics capable of generating a new outlook within autonomous circuits, through performative tactics and through fundamental practices is the idea. If subjectivity takes note of the reality of the bios put to work, what are, then, the possible leverage points? Could those attempts be useful to make us aware of the determinant role of reproduction? Could one envisage paths or processes that could help us leave behind the categories of social control and internalization? Do they represent a way to reclaim our lives? I undoubtedly think so.

References

Bataille, Georges. 2003. *La parte maledetta.* Turin:Bollati Boringhieri.

Butler, Judith. 2013. *A chi spetta una vita buona?* Florence: Nottetempo.

Caffentzis, George. 1996. "Sulla nozione di crisi della riproduzione sociale: un riesame teorico," *Donne, sviluppo e lavoro di riproduzione. Questioni delle lotte e dei movimenti*, edited by M. Dalla Costa and G. F. Dalla Costa. Milan: Franco Angeli.

Chisté, Lucia; Del Re, Alisa; and Forti, Edvige. 1979. *Oltre il lavoro domestico: il lavoro delle donne tra produzione e riproduzione*. Milan: Feltrinelli.

Dalla Costa, Maria Rosa. 1974. "Riproduzione e emigrazione," in A. Serafini (ed.), *L'operaio multinazionale in Europa*. Milan: Feltrinelli.

Dalla Costa, Maria Rosa. 2002. "La porta dell'orto e del giardino," *Congress-seminar at the Rialto,* Rome, June 1–2, 2002. Available at http://www.generation-online.org/p/fpdallacosta.htm.

Dalla Costa, Maria Rosa, and James, Selma. 1972. *Potere femminile e sovversione sociale*. Rome: Marsilio Editore.

Del Re, Alisa. 2012. *'Le Ambiguità Del Lavoro' Congress*, Turin, October 12, Women's archives in Piedmont.

Federici, Silvia. 1980. "Wages against housework," *The politics of housework*, edited by Malos, Ellen. London: Allison & Busby.

Federici, Silvia and Fortunati, Leopoldina. 1984. *Il grande Calibano*. Milan: Franco Angeli.

Forti, Chiara. 1999. *Le redazioni pericolose. Come fare la giornalista e vivere infelicemente*. Rome: DeriveApprodi.

Fortunati, Leopoldina. 1981. *L'arcano della riproduzione social. Casalinghe, prostitute, operai e capital*. Venice: Marsilio.

Foucault, Michel. 1991. *La volontà di sapere*. Milan: Feltrrinelli.

Fumagalli, Andrea. 2007. *Bioeconomia e capitalismo cognitive*. Rome: Carocci.

Haraway, Donna. 1995. *Manifesto cyborg. Donne, tecnologie, biopolitiche del corpo*. Milan: Feltrinelli.

Latouche, Serge. 1993. *In the wake of the affluent society: an exploration of post-development*. London: Zed Books.

Marx, Karl. 1964. *Il Capitale, Book I*. Rome: Editori Riuniti.

Marx, Karl. 1969. *Il Capitale, Book I, Chapter VI*. Translated by B. Maffi. Florence: La Nuova Italy.

Mazzone, A.: "Autogoverno e tirannide. L'idea di stato: preliminari per un'analisi del potere presente." *Contraddizione* 73, July–August, 1999.

O'Brien, Mary. 1981. *The politics of reproduction*. London: Routledge & Kegan Paul.

Pompei, Guilina. 1971. "Salario per il lavoro domestic." *L'Offensiva, Quaderni di Lotta Femminista* 1.

Rossi Landi, Ferruccio. 2002. "L'autore tra riproduzione sociale e discontinuità: dialogo con Ferruccio Rossi-Landi." *Segno, Autore e Riproduzione Sociale Seminar*, Bari University, April 19, Lectures 15, 149–172, 1985. Republished in *Corposcritto*, 2, 2, Edizioni dal Sud, Bari, 2002, with an introduction by Susan Perilli.

Rossi Landi, Ferruccio. 2003. *Il linguaggio come lavoro e come mercato*. Milan: Bompiani.

Smith, Adam. 2008. *La ricchezza delle nazioni*. Translated by. F. Bartoli, C. Camporesi, and S. Caruso. Rome: Editore Newton Compton.

Tronti, Mario. 1973. "Capitale sociale," in *Telos*, 17, pp. 25-62.

Vercellone, Carlo. 2012. "La legge del valore nel passaggio dal capitalismo industriale al nuovo capitalismo." *UniNomade*. Available at http://www.uninomade.org/vercellone-legge-valore.

Vignola, Paolo. 2011. *La lingua animale. Deleuze attraverso la letteratura*. Rome: Quodlibet.

5. Seizing Europe. Crisis Management, Constitutional Transformations, Constituent Movements

Sandro Mezzadra

It is safe to contend that the shattering of old spatial hierarchies and the emergence of new geographies of capitalist development and accumulation figure prominently among the tendencies underlying the global economic crisis (Mezzadra & Neilson 2013a). New regionalisms and new patterns of multilateralism are taking shape and, although no new world order is clearly discernible, the present disorder already bears the traces of a decline of Western hegemony. No "civilizational" emphasis, of course, behind this statement—but I am convinced that there is a need to take stock of the meaning and relevance of the new global geographies in the making to better understand the specific challenges, risks, and opportunities we are currently confronted with in Europe. A process of "provincialization" of Europe, to put it as in the title of an important book by Dipesh Chakrabarty (2000), is actually underway, but the direction of this process, its political interpretation, is still open. The crisis of sovereign debt, the specific and most visible way in which the global economic crisis hit Europe, has nevertheless created a profoundly new situation in the European Union (EU). A section of the European elite and capital is attempting—indeed quite successfully to date—to exploit the crisis as a chance to "reform" the institutional architecture of the EU, to foster a new compromise between financial capital and export-oriented industry, and to establish new center–periphery relations. The proposal by Hans-Peter Keitel, President of the Federation of German Industry, to turn Greece into a special economic zone is a good reminder of the importance of the last point (see German Industry Leader 2012), while the continuity of "austerity," with its disruptive social effects, is the general hallmark of the project and the best illustration of its ferocious class nature.

In this essay I highlight some aspects of this new situation in Europe, focusing on the resulting consequences for such important political and legal concepts as citizenship and constitution. It is important to keep in mind that these concepts have been part and parcel of European history and even "identity" for centuries. Their contemporary transformations therefore provide an effective angle on the stakes of the current crisis in Europe. Highlighting the shifting configurations of power within the material constitution of the EU compels us to go beyond any rhetoric of "democratic deficit" and to posit democracy and citizenship themselves as concepts and practices that need to be radically reinvented in Europe. In other words, it leads us to contend that there is a need to imagine a *constituent* movement and moment in Europe. It is only within such a movement and moment that we can think of a left capable of politically expressing the claims and needs of the composition of contemporary living labor—and at the same time realistically interpret the challenge of the provincialization of Europe as a chance for a new project of freedom and equality.

Citizenship, democracy, and constitution

Although French and Dutch voters rejected the Treaty establishing a Constitution for Europe in 2005, bringing to an end the process of its ratification, it is hard to deny that the EU has a constitutional structure and rank. This is not only due to the existence of a Charter of Fundamental Rights, adopted in December 2000 and given full legal effect by the Lisbon Treaty (2007); more generally, the development of an elaborate web of European legal norms and of a sophisticated jurisprudence, combined with the forging of governmental standards and "best practices," has steadily produced a series of transformations within the very structure of the Constitutions of the Member States. Both the sphere of action of public powers (sovereignty) and the status of citizens, the two main fields of constitutional regulation, have been altered by these developments, which started in the 1960s but acquired a fully new dimension with the signing of the Maastricht Treaty (1992). The Constitutions of the Member States, even the most powerful, have been displaced from the center of the legal and political stage and transformed into "partial orders" (Grimm 2012, 335). This means that they are no longer the supreme legal source for the organization of political power and the rights of citizens. A process of hybridization of law leads to a weakening of the constitutional system, challenging its unity as well as its effectiveness. At the same time, at the European level it is precisely the absence of a constitution in the traditional sense of the word that creates the space for a huge flexibility of "governance" and for the development of multi-level regulations (Chignola & Mezzadra 2008).

There is a need to historicize these complex transformations. The history of constitutionalism and constitutional law in the 20th century in Europe was dominated by a process of constitutionalization of labor. Since the Weimar Constitution, faced with the challenge of the Soviet Revolution, this has always meant at the same time an attempt to constitutionalize class struggle. This attempt marks the transition from the liberal constitution, centered on the individual and market exchanges mediated by the legal institution of contract, to the democratic constitution, which is compelled to acknowledge and articulate the centrality of labor and its subjects. In an essay written in 1964, Antonio Negri (2009) provides an impressive discussion of the specific dynamics, unbalances, and even contradictions that this acknowledgment inscribes onto the constitution. In the framework of the socialization of capital corresponding to mass industrial production, the democratic constitution, on the one hand, represents and "contains" the productive power of labor, while, on the other hand, it expresses and articulates the primacy of capital's command and planning. The entire dynamics of constitutional checks and balances as well as of political representation in the democratic constitution appears, in Negri's eyes, subordinated to the development of this contradiction. It was the time of the Welfare state, of "social rights of citizenship" (Marshall 1950), and of what Étienne Balibar (2003, 125–134) calls the "national (and) social state." Balibar mobilizes a reference to Machiavelli (to the "Machiavellian theorem") to carve out of his analysis of this particular moment in European constitutional history the existence of a "contentious democracy," which he posits as "the other side of the national-social state" (2003, 129). This was not, of course, an ideal model but, rather, a political form predicated upon the existence of specific organized subjects (parties as well as unions), institutional channels for industrial conflict and negotiation, political cultures of organization, mobilization, and struggle. It was, above all, inscribed within a specific "container" (the nation state) and rooted within the specific class composition of postwar capitalism in (Western) Europe, which means mass industrial production, or Fordism.

What is commonly described as the acceleration of the pace of European integration in the late 1980s, culminating in the Maastricht Treaty, must be understood against the background of the profound transformations of capitalism in the wake of the uprisings and struggles around 1968, the declaration of the inconvertibility of the US dollar in 1971, and the crisis of 1973. It is in the framework of these transformations—of the new dimension of the processes of financialization of capital and of the neo-liberal turn globally announced by Pinochet, Thatcher, and Reagan—that the constitution of labor and the national-social state entered a deep crisis. This is the moment when what I have described in terms of a hybridization of law reaches a new stage. From this point of view—that is, the point of view of a materialist interpretation of constitutional processes and changes that is a privileged point of entry into any discussion of the present political predicament in Europe—the acceleration of the integration process, and particularly the move toward the Economic and Monetary Union prompted by the establishment of the Delors Committee in 1988, can be interpreted as the opening of a peculiar type of *crisis management*. The crisis to be managed was (also) the crisis of a specific constitutional form and experience underlying the development of the welfare state rhetorically associated with the "European model". This crisis management, which stitches together economy and politics (and eventually an economic and political crisis), is the real unifying thread of the constitutional development of the EU in the last two decades. It is not necessary to dismiss as mere ideology the "neo-functionalist" rhetoric surrounding the Maastricht Treaty, according to which the sharing of a single currency would produce a virtuous "spillover", creating the conditions for further progress in the political unification and eventually for European social policies capable of replicating at the continental level what was no longer sustainable at the national level. Some people may have sincerely believed this. The fact remains that, as Fritz Scharpf (1999, Chapter 2) timely stressed, "negative integration" (to put it shortly, sharing the limits to national social policies and market regulations) was not significantly matched by "positive integration," in other words, by an effective attempt to build a European welfare system.

Nevertheless, considering the Maastricht Treaty as the opening of a constitutional crisis management event does not mean dismissing the potentialities associated with the new stage of the European integration process. While the institutional left has oscillated between skepticism and uncritical acceptance in front of this process, a series of social movements started, in the 1990s, to develop a quite different attitude. Especially movements connected with the struggles of migrants, the unemployed, and precarious workers, as well as with media activism and the claiming of civil rights, attempted to immediately "seize" the European space, combining a sharp criticism of specific EU policies (e.g., its border regime in the making and its neo-liberal economic constitution) with an option for action, campaigning and networking at the European level, occasionally including the use of European courts and jurisprudence. It was not the option of the majority of social movements and it did not produce spectacular successes, but it was widespread. It began forging a common European language among activists and became particularly visible during the first European social forums held in the early 2000s. In a way, one could say that the attempt was made to struggle *within and against* the European citizenship in the making. The establishment of a European citizenship appeared to many observers in the 1990s to pave the way for a process of delinking citizenship from the principle of nationality, a process that could potentially weaken the EU's exclusive nature and become the framework for the expression of new democratic movements in the welfare state crisis. Scholars working in the field of migration played an important role in this conversation (e.g., Hammar 1990; Soysal 1994), while a more general rethinking of the concept of citizenship was prompted by the work of Balibar (1994, 2003) and Engin Isin (2002). To put it shortly, the attempt was made to distinguish the institutional framework of citizenship from its movement, and to shed light on the transformations produced within that very framework through the practices and struggles of subjects often constructed as "excluded," or differentially included.

This is a concept of citizenship that has allowed the combination, as mentioned above, of even radical criticism of the European integration with an attempt to seize the European space (and at the same time keep the borders of this very space open). I participated in this attempt as both a scholar and an activist, particularly as far as migration is concerned (e.g., Mezzadra and Neilson 2003; Mezzadra 2004, 2008). While I am convinced that the work done around the concept of citizenship still constitutes an important source of inspiration for critical thinking and political action in Europe, I also think that there is a need to test that work against the background of the profound transformations of the very institutional framework of European citizenship in recent years. In a recent article on the European crisis, Balibar (2012a) restates a position he held with remarkable coherence since several years: a

> Political Europe, outside of which there is indeed only decline and inability for the people of the continent, will only be legitimate, and therefore possible, if it is more democratic than the nations that create it, if it allows them to step beyond their historical conquests in terms of democracy.

The problem that arises here is whether we can imagine this "surplus" of democracy along a line of *continuity* not only with the national history of democracy in Europe—particularly with the "contentious democracy" of the "national (and) social state"—but also with the evolution of the institutional architecture of the EU. It seems to me that the very constitution of European citizenship can no longer be taken for granted as a political space for the invention of the surplus of democracy mentioned by Balibar. I thus turn to an analysis of recent constitutional transformations and disruptions within the EU. Such an analysis provides a particularly effective angle on the transformations and disruptions of European citizenship itself.

Constitutional borderlands

The very concept of constitution has been tested and placed under duress by recent developments within the EU. Take, for instance, the influential discussion of the present state of constitutional law in Europe provided by Dieter Grimm (2012). According to his analysis, the "external success" of constitutionalism in the world after 1989 has been met by a process of "internal erosion" of the effectiveness of the constitution, which can be observed in its clearest form in the

European case. What the German jurist emphasizes is the relevance of economic, political, and even legal dynamics that increasingly compel states to "share" their power with "a series of non-state actors," leading to a situation in which the state has lost "its monopoly of public power." Grimm is quick to note that this is more than a mere widening of the gap between "norm and reality," which has always existed without threatening the "potential of constitutionalism." The new situation that he describes in terms of an "internal erosion of the constitution" challenges the very capacity of the latter to "comprehensively regulate public power in its sphere of validity" (Grimm 2012, 315–16). The concept of deconstitutionalization nicely captures this tendency toward the multiplication of levels and actors of power that escape constitutional regulation while at the same time intervening within fields that have been traditionally defined as being of "constitutional relevance."

What further interests me in Grimm's analysis is his discussion of this process of erosion of the constitution in terms of the two "borders" on which the development of modern constitutions and constitutional states has been historically predicated. On the one hand, he refers to political boundaries, which traditionally circumscribed the territory of the state and therefore the "validity of the constitution." On the other hand, he has in mind the "constitutive" relevance of the border between private and public for the very existence of a constitution (Grimm 2012, 328–331). Both these lines of demarcation appear to be blurred in the present and, once again, this is particularly apparent in the case of the EU. European governance structurally works the boundary between public and private, both as far as the variable geometry of its actors is concerned and as far as the shifting patterns of its governmental "styles" are considered. At the same time, European institutions and law are now internal moments to any "national" space, intensifying a process of multiplication of legal orders that is challenging the unity of the traditional concept of state territory independently of the developments within the EU. One should add that both the process of "enlargement" and the emerging European border regime make the borders of the EU themselves elusive and "open", that is, quite different from the cartographic representation of political borders as clear-cut lines of demarcation of the "inside" from the "outside" (e.g., Beck and Grande 2007; Mezzadra and Neilson 2013b, Chapter 6).

Grimm's diagnosis of an internal erosion of the constitution in Europe (and, indeed, beyond Europe) can be fruitfully paralleled with the theory of societal constitutionalism developed over the last two decades by another German jurist, Gunther Teubner. To be sure, Teubner's combination of the systemic sociology of Niklas Luhmann with insights from theories of legal pluralism is quite different from Grimm's more traditional view of law, constitution, and state. Teubner does not seem to be particularly concerned by the blurring of borders between public and private or the inside and outside of a state's territory. Instead, he is engaged in an attempt to further push the process of "de-centering" of the state that has been at the core of many theories of legal pluralism and, in particular, to build upon the criticism of the omnipotence of legislation provided in the early 20th century by Eugen Ehrlich (Teubner 1997). What Teubner has been describing in recent years is the emergence of a "global law" that, contrary to the most influential legal theories of the last century (that can be epitomized by the names of Carl Schmitt and Hans Kelsen), is predicated neither upon a political decision nor on a "basic norm" (*Grundnorm*). Writing of the emergence of a global economic law, Teubner (1997, 7) contends that it "is a law whose 'centre' is created by the 'peripheries' and remains dependent on them." "Fragmentation" is a defining feature of the emerging global legal "regimes," which are presented by Teubner as results of sector-based processes of legal self-organization that take place outside the traditional (constitutional) framework of the state. The transnational copyright regime, the so-called *lex constructionis* and its standard contracts on transnational construction projects, the new *lex mercatoria* and human rights regimes are among the instances discussed by Teubner. According to his analysis, this fragmentation can neither be curbed nor fought, because legal fragmentation is itself "merely an ephemeral reflection of a more fundamental, multi-dimensional fragmentation of global society itself" (Fischer-Lescano & Teubner 2004, 1004). At best, a "weak normative compatibility of the fragments might be achieved. However, this is dependent upon the ability of conflicts law to establish a specific network logic, which can effect a loose coupling of colliding units" (Fischer-Lescano & Teubner 2004, 1004).

Decoupling the concept of constitution from the state, Teubner charts multifarious, fragmentary, and heterogeneous processes of *constitutionalization* that develop from within regimes corresponding to "partial social systems" defined in "functional" terms. The irreducible and structurally proliferating multiplicity of regimes radically challenges the unitary dimension of the concept of constitution. "Collisions" and "conflicts" among regimes are to be considered the norm rather than the exception according to Teubner's theory of societal constitutionalism. "Hybrid" arrangements must be deployed to both facilitate the crystallization of constitutional norms and structures within the partial regimes and articulate their collisions. "Constitutional fragments" can only be tactically "coupled" within "networked structures" and often "*ad hoc* constitutional norms" emerge to supplement existing frameworks at the national, transnational, and global levels in an attempt to limit and regulate the "expansive tendencies" of social systems (Teubner 2012, Chapter 3). From Teubner's point of view, in any case, multiplicity comes first and his entire theory is built upon this kind of ontological statement, which explains the reasons why post-workerism in general, and Michael Hardt and Antonio Negri in particular, paid great attention to his work and engaged in lively discussion with him (Hardt and Negri 2009, 347–48; Chignola 2012). At the same time there is a need to stress that Teubner's theoretical framework (particularly his Luhmannian theory of the social) leads him to adopt a view of partial social systems that often overemphasizes the autonomy of "sectors," obscuring the structural pervasiveness of the logics of capital as a "cross-sector" binding (and indeed disrupting) element.

Whereas Grimm describes an "internal erosion of the constitution" due to powerful dynamics of deconstitutionalization, Teubner maps a proliferation of processes of "constitutionalization" that saturate legal and political spaces across the borders of nation states. Grimm is explicitly skeptical toward such an extensive use of the concept of constitutionalization, which leads, in his opinion, to diluting and eventually losing the historical and theoretical specificity of the constitution (Grimm 2012, 324). At the same time, one could note that the proliferation of partial legal regimes described by Teubner is part and parcel of the factors that converge to produce the erosion of the constitution discussed by Grimm. This means that, insofar as they limit the regulatory effectiveness of the constitution, partial legal regimes have, at least "negatively," constitutional relevance for Grimm as well.

If one considers the analyses of the two Germans jurists together, what emerges and needs to be emphasized from the point of view of the analysis in this essay is a crisis of the constitution as a *unitary* system. Be it displaced from the center of the legal and political space by processes of deconstitutionalization (Grimm) or be it included into elusive and fragmentary constitutional networks and assemblages (Teubner), the constitution is undergoing profound transformations that take a peculiar shape in the European case. While national constitutions have been placed under duress and formally and materially transformed by the process of European integration, the Charter of Fundamental Rights and the jurisprudence of European courts actually seem to represent constitutional fragments whose inscription within a unitary framework remains highly problematic. At the same time, the organization of powers within the EU continues to be characterized by structural tensions between the European Commission and the European Council, while the European Central Bank's autonomy in the management of the single currency establishes and crystallizes a huge power to intervene beyond any constitutional regulation into the very fabric of social relations.

Legal scholars who have worked on the process of European integration from an angle close to Teubner's theoretical framework have often emphasized the need to prompt a "proceduralization of the category of law" to come to grips with the challenges inherent to these developments. As Christian Joerges (2007, 15–16) writes, "the Europeanisation process should seek flexible, varied solutions to conflicts, rather than striving to perfect an ever more comprehensive body of law," which means, from a political point of view, instead of striving toward a traditionally federal solution. There is much to learn from such attempts to develop a "conflict-law constitutionalism" for the EU. What seems particularly interesting here, as in Teubner's case, is precisely the chance to work through the multiplicity of legal institutes and categories connected to the conflict of law viewpoint and to imagine the emergence of a multitude of claims from the composition of contemporary living labor as the material condition for constructing the constituent dimension of a new "law of the common" (Chignola 2012).

Without dismissing the potentialities of this theoretical perspective, there is, however, a need to acknowledge that its emphasis on flexibility and elusiveness make it particularly sensitive to the shift of relations of power, a point that remains under-theorized in the work of legal scholars such as Teubner and Joerges. In the wake of the global economic crisis, the moment of financial command, crystallized in the management of the euro, affirmed not merely its autonomy but also its direct constitutional relevance (Negri 2012). While the so-called Fiscal Compact and European Stability Mechanism (ESM) are the main formal expressions of this moment of command, the continuity and the violence of the austerity programs they dictate show the narrowness of the field that remains open for the kind of negotiations and flexible solutions to conflicts recommended by legal scholars such as Joerges. While in the South the European crisis has taken the shape of a violent disruption of what was left of the achievements of several decades of working class struggles and social movements, coupled with mass unemployment and poverty, what seems to emerge at the EU level is a peculiar form of "executive federalism" (Habermas 2011). A vast centralization and increase in the power of European "executive" institutions goes hand in hand with budget cuts, a re-nationalization of political rhetoric, and a further shift toward the bureaucratic at the expense of democratic criteria of legitimization.

More Europe?

As stated above, the development of the European integration process since the late 1980s can also be understood as an attempt (or a series of heterogeneous attempts) to manage the crisis of a specific constitutional form and experience, usually associated with the establishment of the democratic welfare state after World War II. Since the beginning, the "hegemonic project" for the management of this crisis was shaped by the influence of a peculiar historical form of neo-liberalism, that is, that of German *Ordoliberalismus* (Buckel et al. 2012). One could say that in the wake of the global economic crisis the model of the "social market economy" prompted by this school of economic and political thought has been stripped of any social elements. The stability of prices, the autonomy of the monetary union from any political intervention, rigid budgetary controls over Member States, further liberalization and flexibilization of the economy, and the labor market go hand in hand with the violent opening up of new fields for the accumulation of capital through the dismantling of welfare systems, the pervasiveness of debt, and the privatization of "public goods." Neoliberalism has thus taken on a pronouncedly authoritarian shape (Lazzarato 2012). The call for more Europe that circulates among relevant sections of the continental political and economic elite basically does not question the continuity of this crisis management (which also means the continuity of austerity programs) and is widely limited to an invocation of the kind of executive federalism mentioned above. To be sure, within social democratic (and even liberal) parties there is a growing awareness of the need to imagine and implement strategies of "re-regulation," especially of financial markets (Buckel et al. 2012, 32), but the general economic and policy framework of the European crisis management is only very rarely challenged.

Ernst-Wolfgang Böckenförde, a former German constitutional judge and well-known legal scholar, was among the first to bring into the discussion of the European crisis a reference to the concept of the "state of exception" (*Ausnahmezustand*). He was also quick to note that the state of exception and the powers to confront it are not regulated in the European treaties. The resulting risk was, in Böckenförde's (2010) opinion, a transformation of the treaties themselves—that is, the European constitutional foundations—into "soft law" and a huge increase of the arbitrariness and self-referential logics of the European institution in the management of what seemed to him an existential crisis, a crisis of the European project as a whole. The concept of state of exception definitely grasps some important features of the European crisis, particularly the exceptional amount of pain, exploitation, and dispossession it has occasioned among "the oppressed" (to recall Walter Benjamin). But it would be misleading to connect the current state of exception in Europe with a sovereign political decision capable of founding a new order and a new normative system along the lines of Carl Schmitt's (2006) *Political Theology*. What has emerged in Europe over the last years is, instead, a web of soft law and governmental standards, best practices, and administrative procedures that channel and articulate the violence of financial capital making its command immediately effective. The dilution and indefinite iteration of the state of exception, and not the decision to terminate it, seems to define the horizon of this form of crisis management.

There is a need to acknowledge that a fundamental transformation occurred within the very institutional framework of the EU in the wake of the global economic crisis. While some scholars speak of an impending transition from the "democratic deficit" to a "democratic default" (Majone 2012, 21) and others denounce a "preemption of democracy" (Scharpf 2011) or the sharpening of the "elitist" and "post-democratic" nature of the EU (Streeck 2012), even from a juridical point of view it is easy to see that the whole project of "integration through law," the trademark of European integration, has been confronted with its limits and contradictions in recent years (Joerges 2012). The balance between legal supra-nationalism and political bargaining processes classically envisaged, for instance, by Joseph H. H. Weiler (1981), has been destabilized and legal processes have steadily developed an autonomous dynamics, entering into new alliances with European bureaucratic machineries and interest groups. What has consequently emerged is the crystallization of a new assemblage of power capable of dictating standards and norms that increasingly restrict the field of action of any politics. This is true both at the national level and in the European arena, where politics is, paradoxically, increasingly identified with the representation of the very "national interests" that are placed under duress by the new assemblage of power mentioned above. At the same time, as Christian Joerges aptly notes, law itself has become fully political, challenging the very idea of a balance between law and politics that was at the core of the integration through law project. The normative integrity of the latter has thus been undermined. Even before the current crisis started, three judgments of the European Court of Justice in 2007–2008—the *Viking*, *Laval*, and *Rüffert* judgments—set new market-oriented standards and criteria for the regulation of industrial relations and established the clear primacy of market rights over labor rights. Without going into the technical details of these judgments, it is important to emphasize their political relevance. They were "no less and no more than the judicial toppling of the post-war *acquis* of the common European labor law constitution" (Joerges 2012, 46).

This is, of course, an important point for this essay, since what Joerges calls the post-war *acquis* of the common European labor law constitution was part and parcel of the constitutional form discussed earlier as characteristic of the national and social state (Balibar 2003) prevailing in Western Europe since the end of World War II. The primacy of market rights over labor rights (or, as some neo-liberal scholars would have it, the reframing of labor rights in terms of market rights) is a pervasive element that shapes not only European jurisprudence but also European institutions as a whole. It is indeed inscribed into the material constitution of the EU, at least since the founding of the European Monetary Union and the Stability Pact, which made a "return to Keynesian policies" very difficult (Joerges & Weimer 2012, 20). But the request for a balanced budget in the so-called Fiscal Compact of 2012—which led, for instance, to a kind of "automatic" change (and, indeed, profound alteration) of Article 81 of the Italian Constitution (Mattei 2013, 94)—goes a step further. With the Fiscal Compact and the ESM, the straitjacket of monetary stability, fiscal discipline, and austerity programs was further entrenched and consolidated. As a basic norm of European integration, "the independence of the European Central Bank and its commitment to price stability, which cannot be changed by anybody" (Joerges & Weimer 2012, 25), is the driving force of a process of reshaping and reassembly of the European institutions, governmental agencies, and normative structures. This process seems oriented toward the elimination of any political mediation, not to mention any form of contentious democracy (to quote again Balibar). The Commission indeed received new powers through the ESM, but they are eminently negative ones, to scrutinize national budgets and impose fines on deficit violators (Majone 2012, 20). While national governments represented in the Council continue to cut the European budget and to manage the continuity of austerity programs in both the "rescued" and the "rescuing" countries, we are confronted with a "fundamental transformation of the EU and its core legal principles into a managerial regime of the state of emergency" (Joerges & Weimer 2012, 28).

To define as "negative", in the sense suggested by Fritz Scharpf several years ago, the powers hold by the Commission does not imply, of course, that they are harmless or ineffective. While the violence of austerity programs is apparent especially in many Southern European countries, it should be clear that the profound transformation of the European institutional framework in the wake of the great economic crisis has both its disruptive and its "constituent" sides. Even beyond the institutional (and constitutional) dimension analyzed so far, what seems to be at stake is a reshuffling of the alchemic composition of European capital, that is, the relations between its constitutive "fractions" and at the same time of the variable geography of European integration. Service, industrial, and knowledge economy, as well as cognitive and financial capitalism, post-Fordism, and disorganized capitalism, to mention a couple of key labels circulating in critical debates over the last two decades to grasp the "novelty" of contemporary capitalism, are all at stake in these processes. In other words, in the framework of the current economic crisis, social disruption, and political turmoil, the very shape of European capitalism in the following decades, its spatial distribution within the continent as well as its position within global capitalism, will be decided. While the European space and its borders have been profoundly destabilized by the uprisings in North Africa and the Middle East since late 2010, a process of rescaling the European space is underway, finding, for instance, expression in the constitution of new regions as governmental units (Bialasiewicz et al. 2013; Smith 2013). Taking together these processes of spatial rescaling and the tensions crisscrossing the crisis and development of capitalism provides us with a particularly effective angle on the current European situation, its potentialities, and its inherent risks.

The transformation of the institutional framework of the EU sketched in this section does not aim at overcoming the crisis. Even independently of the intentions of the actors involved in this transformation and of the interests prompting it, its effects seem to be the opposite. No great solution is in sight to save the day. The indefinite prolongation of the crisis, as argued by Fumagalli and Mezzadra (2010), is not necessarily a catastrophe for capital today. In Europe it is clearly conceived of as a chance to foster the processes of economic, institutional, and spatial reshuffling discussed so far and, at the same time, to "discipline and punish" unruly populations not merely at the Southern edge of the continent. The battle over the future of the euro itself, part of a larger global "currency war", appears to be used as a kind of blackmail to nurture the continuity of the European crisis management. At the same time, I am convinced that there is a political need to realistically bet on the instability and non-sustainability of this project, or of the multiple, heterogeneous, and fragmentary projects underlying the current hegemonic project in the EU (Buckel et al. 2012). The attack on welfare (both in the narrow and wider senses of the word) is too radical and generalized, incurring too much hopelessness across diverse geographic scales in Europe to be sustainable in the long run. The drastic decline of consensus surrounding austerity policies and the EU itself, widely identified by the threatening diktats of the so-called troika in too many countries, should be a warning but does not seem to be taken seriously by the European elite. This is not to say that social struggles and unrest will spontaneously take political shape and speak the political language we would like them to take and to speak. Just think of the rise of nationalist and fascist forces from Hungary to Greece or of the recent success of the five-star movement at the Italian elections of February 2013. It is really not a time for easy political enthusiasm in Europe, but the fragility of the current EU project is laid bare by recent developments. A call to action becomes necessary.

Seize the time

Myriad social conflicts and struggle against austerity have shaped everyday life in the last years in several European countries, involving students, migrants, workers, and the unemployed, a heterogeneous multitude of people stripped of social rights in the fields of housing and pensions, healthcare and education. Spectacular uprisings, for instance, in the United Kingdom and in Italy against university reforms in late 2010 have occasionally lent great visibility to the intensity of rage and refusal, whereas more fragmented but widely spread practices of resistance have been the counterpoint to the development of the crisis and crisis management in Europe. Forms of social and even economic self-organization have sprung up, for instance, in Greece, to confront mass poverty and destitution. The same is true in the case of Spain, where the amazing continuity of the initiative of social movements since the first emergence of the *indignados* in May 2011 provided the basis for an extraordinary experimentation with new political forms, tools of organization, and patterns of social relations. The list goes on, including the recent mass mobilizations in Portugal and Slovenia. What is striking, however, is the radical gap between the articulation and intensity of struggle and the practice of resistance within and against the crisis and its management in Europe, on the one hand, and their lack of political effectiveness and success, on the other hand. It is precisely this radical gap that constitutes the most striking form of manifestation of the crisis of democracy in contemporary Europe, at both the level of the EU and that of the Member States.

The contentious democracy identified by Balibar as the other side of the national and social state seems to have been severed in Europe from the institutional framework of democracy itself; the dialectics between the "insurrectional" and the "constitutional" dimensions of politics, to put it in terms of another seminal essay by Balibar (1994, 51), appears interrupted. What results from this separation and this interruption is a *division* that runs through the concepts of democracy and politics, which means an opposition without any mediation between their contentious and insurrectional moments (that persist within social struggles and movements) and their governmental and constitutional moments (crystallized in the EU managerial regime of the state of emergency, to recall

Joerges and Weimer [2012], as well as in pro-austerity national governments). There are good reasons to connect this division of the concepts of politics and democracy and their absolutely concrete implications in Europe with the dramatic transformations of capitalism in recent years, particularly with processes of financialization.

In *Commonwealth*, Hardt and Negri (2009, 290–95) refer to one of Mao Zedong's most famous slogans—"The one divides into two"—to grasp the novelty of this situation and the intensity of the antagonism between capital's command and living labor's claims for autonomy. Far from uncritically celebrating this situation and its undeniable potentialities, I already noted the implicit risks, particularly in Europe. These risks are due not only to the violence and power of capital, but also (briefly put) to the huge heterogeneity of contemporary living labor. There is definitely a need to take stock of the ruptures that characterize the present political constitution in Europe, of the impossibility of imagining a movement of democratization and reappropriation of social wealth in a line of continuity with the contentious democracy of the postwar age or the development of a European citizenship stripped of any social and progressive meaning in the eyes of a wide majority of the European population. A "counter-rupture," from below and from the left, is urgently needed in Europe. At the same time, we also need to imagine a new and original system of mediations, both within the composition of living labor and at the institutional level, to establish a more favorable power relationship with financial capital and to create the conditions of a totally different crisis management.

One thing is clear: This is not possible at the national level in Europe. I totally agree with Balibar (2012a) on this point: outside of a political Europe "there is indeed only decline and inability for the people of the continent." Neo-nationalist and "populist" politics, even when vested with "leftist" tones and rhetoric, are often just the reverse side of the neo-liberal crisis management. They are unable to come to grips with the exhaustion of the nation as a spatial unit of reference for economic and social policies, at least in this part of the world, and, above all, they structurally deploy exclusive traits against migrants. Briefly put, they are part of the problem (even though they often contribute to shedding light on it) and not part of the solution. This means that there is an urgent need to reinvent the European space as a site of struggle and political experimentation. While I have already stressed that a counter-rupture is necessary for such a reinvention (and this is what qualifies as *constituent* in the task we are confronted with), this counter-rupture should not be sustained by such vague political discourses as the claim for a "social Europe" against the "Europe of capital" or by even more ambiguous slogans such as the "Europe of the peoples." We cannot ignore the huge and decades-long accumulation of power, knowledge, and wealth within the existing European institutional framework. A new political project for a new left in Europe, radical and realistic at the same time, should aim at a *reappropriation* of this power, knowledge, and wealth. A huge intellectual and political effort needs to be mobilized to concretize this goal and to build around it a left that does not exist in Europe today. Only bits and pieces of the forces of the European left can, indeed, be conceived of as part of this process. Nothing less than a multiplication, intensification, and increasing coordination of social struggles can open up the space within which a new political project can emerge and become the political constitution of a new left.

Speaking of a constituent moment does not necessarily imply the realism or even desirability of a constituent assembly and drafting of a new European constitution in the short run. Instead, it means, first, to emphasize the need of what I have been calling thus far a counter-rupture and to work toward the production of its conditions. A new political discourse must be collectively forged, capable of inscribing within the European space the multifarious claims expressed by contemporary struggles and movements. To do so, a selective reading of the origins of the European integration process and particularly of the federal imagination that emerged from World War II and anti-Fascist resistance, would definitely be a productive move, in the spirit of what Machiavelli calls a return to the principles (Negri 2003). Analogously, the Chart of Fundamental Rights of the EU should be selectively read to carve out those elements that represent in it, as in most charters of rights, the crystallization of the "power of the people," achievements of past struggles that can form the basis for present and future struggles for freedom and equality (Balibar 2012b, 32). Take, for instance, Article 34 of the European Charter of Rights, which recognizes the need "to ensure a decent existence for all those who lack sufficient resources" and could be claimed as the basis of a European campaign for basic income and against the social consequences of austerity programs (Rodotà 2012, Chapter 9). I am convinced that such a selective reading could nurture a constituent politics in contemporary Europe, made up of a variable geometry and geography of political campaigns animated by the claims of the protagonists of struggles and resistance within and against the current crisis.

Needless to say, this is, however, not enough. On the one hand, this is because contemporary experiences of exploitation and dispossession need to be articulated in a new program of radical transformation. The political campaigns to be constructed in Europe today (first against poverty and for a new welfare, including migrants as well as "autochthonous" populations) should therefore also be instrumental in the definition of key aspects of this program and in the emergence of the coalition of subjects and forces that will make it politically effective. On the other hand, there is a need to work toward the production of a *destituent* moment, of the counter-rupture, of the interruption of the continuity of the European crisis management without which any constituent politics are hard to imagine. There is no need to think of this destituent moment in terms of a great "event." It can come about through the accumulation and the spillover effect of several ruptures in a number of countries. Its temporality as well as its spatial coordinates will likely be as heterogeneous and spurious as its nature. What is certain is that social struggles and practices of resistance will play the main role in producing this counter-rupture, if it is to happen in the near future.

In this essay I have tried to shed light on some of the defining features of the present political constitution (and political predicament) in Europe. It seems that addressing the European question should become an urgent priority for intellectual, political, and social forces engaged in the resistance against austerity programs and neo-liberal crisis management. I attempt to schematically sketch three levels of political action and theoretical intervention: the invention of a new political discourse for a new left in Europe, the organization of political campaigns for the definition of a program and construction of a coalition of subjects and forces struggling for radical transformation, and the intensification, multiplication, and coordination of struggles and practices of resistance working toward the production of a counter-rupture. What counts is the overlapping and interlacing of these three levels. I am convinced that the fragility and instability of the hegemonic project provide plenty of opportunities for the construction of a new political project for a new left in Europe. Seize the time, to invoke Bobby Seale's (1970) history of the Black Panther Party. The time is now.

References

Balibar, Étienne. 1994. *Masses, Classes and Ideas. Studies on Politics and Philosophy before and after Marx*. London/New York: Routledge.

Balibar, Étienne. 2003. *We the People of Europe. Reflections on Transnational Citizenship*. Princeton: Princeton University Press.

Balibar, Étienne. 2012a. "What democratic Europe? A response to Jürgen Habermas." *Green European Journal*. Available at http://www.greeneuropeanjournal.eu/what-democratic-europe-response-to-jurgen-habermas.

Balibar, Étienne. 2012b. *Cittadinanza*. Turin: Bollati Boringhieri.

Beck, Ulrich, and Grande, Edgar. 2007. *Cosmopolitan Europe*. Translated by Ciaran Cronin. Cambridge: Polity Press.

Bialasiewicz, Luiza; Giaccaria, Paolo; Jones, Alun; and Minca, Claudio. 2013: "Re-scaling 'EU'rope: EU macro-regional fantasies in the Mediterranean." *European Urban and Regional Studies* 20: 59–76.

Böckenförde, Ernst-Wolfgang. 2010. "Kennt die europäische Not kein Gebot?" *Neue Zürcher Zeitung*, June 21.

Buckel, Sonja; Georgi, Fabian; Kannankulam, John; and Wissel, Jens. 2012. "Wenn das Alte nicht stirbt und das Neue nicht zur Welt kommen kann," Kräfteverhältnisse in der europäischen Krise. In *Die EU in der Krise. Zwischen autoritärem Etatismus und europäischem Frühling im Auftrag der Assoziation für kritische Gesellschaftsforschung,* Foschungsgruppe "Staatsprojekt Europa," 12–49. Münster: Westphälisches Dampfboot.

Chakrabarty, Dipesh. 2000. *Provincializing Europe: Postcolonial Thought and Historical Difference*. Princeton: Princeton University Press.

Chignola, Sandro (ed.). 2012. *Il Diritto del Comune. Crisi della Sovranità, Proprietà e Nuovi Poteri Costituenti.* Verona: Ombre Corte.

Chignola, Sandro, and Mezzadra, Sandro. 2008. "Gli spazi d'Europa. Aporie del processo di costituzionalizzazione e pratiche di libertà." *Rassegna di Diritto Pubblico Europeo*, 7(1): 129–148.

Fischer Lescano, Andreas, and Teubner, Gunther. 2004. "Regime-collisions: the vain search for legal unity in the fragmentation of global law." *Michigan Journal of International Law* 25(4): 999–1046.

Fumagalli, Andrea, and Mezzadra, Sandro (eds.). 2010. *Crisis in the Global Economy. Financial Markets, Social Struggles, and New Political Scenarios*. Cambridge: Semiotext(e).

German Industry Leader. 2012. "Greece Should Become a Special Economic Zone." *Spiegel online International.* Available at http://www.spiegel.de/international/europe/spiegel-online-interview-with-german-industry-leader-hans-peter-keitel-a-855040.html

Grimm, Dieter. 2012. *Die Zukunft der Verfassung II. Auswirkungen von Europäisierung und Globalisierung*. Berlin: Suhrkamp.

Habermas, Jürgen. 2011. *Zur Verfassung Europas. Ein Essay.* Berlin: Suhrkamp.

Hammar, Tomas. 1990. *Democracy and the Nation-State: Aliens, Denizens and Citizens in a World of International Migration*. Aldershot: Avebury.

Hardt, Michael, and Negri, Antonio. 2009. *Commonwealth*. Cambridge: Harvard University Press.

Isin, Engin F. 2002. *Being Political. Genealogies of Citizenship*. Minneapolis: University of Minnesota Press.

Joerges, Christian. 2007. "Democracy and European integration: a legacy of tensions, a re-conceptualization and recent true conflicts." *EUI Working Paper LAW No. 2007/25*.

Joerges, Christian. 2012. "What is left of the Integration through Law Project? A reconstruction in conflicts-law perspectives." In *The European Rescue of the European Union? The Existential Crisis of the European Political Project, ARENA Report No 3/12 RECON Report No. 19*, edited by Edoardo Chiti, Agustín José Menéndez, and Pedro Gustavo Teixeira, 37-67. Oslo: Arena.

Joerges, Christian, and Weimer, Maria. 2012. "A crisis of executive managerialism in the EU: no alternative?" *Maastricht Faculty of Law Working Paper 2012/7*.

Lazzarato, Maurizio. 2012. *The Making of the Indebted Man: An Essay on the Neoliberal Condition*. Los Angeles: Semiotext(e).

Majone, Giandomenico. 2012. "Rethinking European integration after the debt crisis," *Working Paper No. 3/2012*. University College of London: European Institute.

Marshall, Thomas Humphrey. 1950. *Citizenship and Social Class, and Other Essays*. Cambridge: Cambridge University Press.

Mattei, Ugo. 2013. *Contro Riforme*. Turin: Einaudi.

Mezzadra, Sandro. 2004. "The right to escape." *Ephemera*, 4(3): 267–275.

Mezzadra, Sandro. 2008. "Citizen and subject. A postcolonial constitution for the European Union?" In *Conflict, Power, and the Landscape of Constitutionalism,* edited by G. Tarabout and R. Samaddar. London/New Delhi: Routledge.

Mezzadra, Sandro, and Neilson, Brett. 2003. "*Né qui, né altrove – Migration, Detention, Desertion: A Dialogue. Borderlands*," e-journal 2(1). Available at http://www.borderlands.net.au/issues/vol2no1.html

Mezzadra, Sandro, and Neilson, Brett. 2013a. "Extraction, logistics, finance. Global crisis and the politics of operations." *Radical Philosophy* 178: 8–18.

Mezzadra, Sandro, and Neilson, Brett. 2013b. *Border as Method, or the Multiplication of Labor*. Durham, NC, and London: Duke University Press.

Negri, Antonio. 2003. *L'Europa e l'Impero. Riflessioni su un processo costituente*. Rome: Manifestolibri.

Negri, Antonio. 2009. *Il Lavoro nella Costituzione.* Verona: Ombre Corte.

Negri, Antonio. 2012. "*A proposito di costituzione e capitale finanziario.*" Available at http://www.uninomade.org/costituzione-e-capitale-finanziario/

Rodotà, Stefano. 2012. *Il Diritto di Avere Diritti.* Rome: Laterza.

Scharpf, Fritz. 1999. *Governing in Europe: Effective and Democratic?* Oxford: Oxford University Press.

Scharpf, Fritz. 2011. "Monetary union, fiscal crisis and the preemption of democracy," Discussion paper from Max-Planck-Institut für Gesellschaftsforschung, November 11, 2011.

Schmitt, Carl. 2006. *Political Theology. Four Chapters on the Concept of Sovereignty.* Chicago: Chicago University Press.

Seale, Bobby. 1970. *Size the Time. The Story of the Black Panther Party and Huey P. Newton.* New York: Random House.

Smith, Adrian. 2013. "Europe and an inter-dependent world: uneven geo-economic and geo-political developments." *European Urban and Regional Studies* 20: 3–13.

Soysal, Yasemine. 1994. *Migrants and Postnational Membership in Europe.* Chicago: Chicago University Press.

Streeck, Wolfgang. 2012. "Das Ende der Nachkriegsdemokratie." *Süddeutsche Zeitung,* July 27, 2012.

Teubner, Gunther. 1997. "Global Bukowina: legal pluralism in the world society." In *Global Law without a State,* edited by G. Teubner, 3-28. Aldershot: Dartmouth Gower.

Teubner, Gunther. 2012. *Verfassungsfragmente. Gesellschaftlicher Konstitutionalismus in der Globalisierung.* Berlin: Suhrkamp.

Weiler, Joseph H. H. 1981. "The community system: the dual character of supranationalism." *Yearbook of European Law* 1(1): 257–306.

6. KORPOBRAZ: The Power of the Poor

Giuseppe Cocco

> 'Beware, sir, of men who don't have no power, who don't have no money! [....] Suddenly, those men turn into many, a whole lot, thousands and hundreds of thousands (with the) power of their entire and detached poverty.'
>
> João Guimarães Rosa

Anthropoemy?

The theme of the IV Seminar for researchers in the University of Rio de Janeiro Humanities Graduate Program was "Anthropoemic Practices in Art and Culture."[1] The proposition of the event, introduced in the folder, hinged on two considerations. First, the organizers recall the 1998 24th International Arts Biennial Exhibition in São Paulo and recall the cultural and political "tradition" stemming from Oswald de Andrade's 1928 Cannibalist Manifesto. Second, it prompts the concept of anthropoemy, based on ideas formulated by Claude Lévi-Strauss in *Tristes Tropiques* (1955):

[Lévi-Strauss] envisaged two types of society, the anthropophagic societies [...] for which the absorption of certain individuals of fearful forms represents the only manner by which to neutralize or even exploit them [...] and those societies which adopt anthropoemy [from the Greek emein, to vomit] and which, [...] before the same dilemma, suggest the opposite solution, i.e., [the ousting of] those fearful individuals from the body of society, isolating them either temporarily or permanently ("Vomit and no" 2012).

The ingenuity of the seminar proposition, as the very title suggests, rests on this latter dimension, a choice backed primarily by two arguments. The first argument is the exploitation of an alternative path, contrary to a generalized and (allegedly) simplified use of anthropophagy in the wake of a so-called "multiculturalism": 'The discourse on 'social inclusion' or 'responsibility for the *other*' is a clear example of a civic dimension of the anthropophagic principles,' as stated in the seminar folder.[2] The second reason is the suggestion that the anthropophagic discourse (dating from the early 20th century), for its inclusive method, would in the 21st century face a "somewhat adverse" cultural and eco-

1 "Vomit and no," seminar held August 20–24, 2012.

2 See the seminar at http://ivseminarioppgartesuerj.blogspot.com.br.

nomic context. In Gilles Deleuze's societies of control, 'characterized by the dispersion and internalization of disciplinary norms – the power of anthropophagy could be scaled down.' The folder also quotes Sueley Rolnik, for whom 'capitalism is also Tupinambá.'[3] Thus, "capitalism becomes cannibalistic," devouring its own anthropophagy while toning down its radicalism and emancipatory character. Faced with a system that "devours all and adapts to all things," one would wonder whether "it would be opportune to revisit the concept of anthropoemy as a practice adopted to resist a cannibalistic capitalism," for, "in view of the generalized devouring which we must relentlessly endure—and of which the institutionalization of art is a symptom—what space is left for the *vomit*, for the excretion, for the *no*?"[4]

The justification behind our exhaustive reconstruction of the "Vomit and No" seminar's proposition is twofold: first and foremost, the organizers' well-defined, courageous, original, and provoking proposal is the reason behind the interest (and polemics) it incurs. Second, on the one hand, it helps us identify a series of important constraints to the manner one uses and construes the philosophical and anthropological concepts of difference and, on the other hand, it supports the introduction of our counterpoint approach to the issue.

From a conceptual point of view, it would seem that references to Deleuze (and Foucault) are biased and disarrayed, particularly when dealing with the transition from a discipline-based to a control-based society. This bias encompasses, therefore, a doubly inappropriate definition of capitalism, its transformations, and relations with the resistance: it does not take into account the relation between the development of capital and the struggle (resistance); neither does it take into account the political point of view behind the theoretical contributions by Foucault and Deleuze to the analysis of the relations of power and knowledge in today's capitalism. Notwithstanding, the seminar's theme is a valid opportunity to reopen the discussion on anthropophagy and contemporary capitalism. This debate hinges on two basic premises: (1) contemporary capitalism is not anthropophagic but, instead, parasitic; (2) the relation between anthropophagy and anthropoemy is not dialectical, for the former is the politics of life (biopolitics) and the latter the politics of death (biopower) (Pelbart 2003). In other words, learning how anthropomorphic and anthropoemic forms function today is tantamount to learning the functioning of contemporary capitalism.

3 In "O Brasil da Virada" (Brazil at a turning point), in "Panorama Histórico Brasileiro" (Itaú Cultural), http://www.youtube.com/watch?v=NDkGVPmYjh0&list=PL2CCF74F3B149F96D&index=14&feature=plpp_video, referred to me by Amanda Bonam.

4 Ibid., the author's italics.

Hence, we would venture to suggest that today relations between anthropophagy (forms of social relations that absorb the other, that are "inclusive") and anthropoemy (forms of social relations that banish the "other" from the body of society, that are selective) are modulated with exclusion and inclusion continuously intertwined.

A Tupinambá[5] capitalism?

We state that the relation between anthropophagy (inclusion) and anthropoemy (exclusion) is not dialectic, since it does not develop in duality; neither does it produce, necessarily, a synthesis. Rather, contemporary capitalism is characterized by the very fact that those two dimensions no longer function in isolation but, rather, in modulation, typical of Brazilian hybridism. It is *within* this modulation (and not in its extremes) that answers and clues to the criticism of relations of power are to be found. At the same time, this modulation of inclusion and exclusion functions as a trap, precisely as read in the seminar folder: contemporary capitalism is inclusive to the point of appearing to be anthropophagic; accordingly, the resistance seems to rest on the edges of the "no," of denial of the other, that is, anthropoemy.

Suely Rolnik, who worked with Oswald's political and poetic cannibalism in terms of "anthropophagic subjectivity" from the first half of the 1990s, anticipated this pitfall and addressed it by expanding the concept of anthropophagy that leads to two opposite dimensions: initially, she suggests a concept of "low" and "high" anthropophagy; later, she introduces the distinction between "active" and "reactive" anthropophagy. For the purpose of our approach and summarizing those distinctions to the utmost, we could say—emulating Rolnik—that there is high, or active, anthropophagy that enables "creation from chaos," as well as a low, or reactive, anthropophagy, which is the "denial of chaos and refusal to plunge into it," and, thus, a "mere consumption of worlds available in the market of ideas and images." (Rolnik 1998, 468) In our view, however, this does not seem to be an adequate "solution" to a critical stance. Far from escaping the pitfalls of flexible capitalism and the modulations of a society of control, breaking up the concept of anthropophagy into two opposite ideas (low and high and creative and reactive anthropophagy) only leads to a watering down and reduction of the concept to an element internal to the determinism of capital and its divisions, which, as we shall see, become "necessary." One of the reasons for that is continued dichotomy chaos/order, whereas, as Hélio Oiticica points out,

5 The Tupinambá are a South American Indian people who spoke Tupian languages (translator's note).

there is more in chaos than rhythm; chaos is a precondition to all rhythms, all order: it is by plunging into dance (samba), he explains, that we find the rhythm of an "individual and collective force" where those two concepts are intertwined. The search for "one total and irreversible act of life" is, according to Oiticica, the search for an "imbalance" as the basis of the "balance of being" (Oiticica 2011, 76). Althusser (1994, 554) echoes him in his "philosophy of the encounter" as he discusses the rain of atoms and aleatoric encounters (*clinamen*): order stems from the materiality of chaos and fortuity. Its origin is to be found in deviation rather than in reason and it must reach duration, in other words, order.

To define flexible capitalism as "anthropophagic *zumbi*" or *tupinambá* is tantamount to accepting its capacity of modulation as the annulment of conflict, precisely as Rolnik (2010, 15) does in the same article, considering the "negotiation between the interests of the capitalistic economy and the poetical demands for artistic creation" as necessary. On the contrary, it would seem that the interest of the Oswaldian political "anthropophagy" concept resides precisely and, on the one hand, in the affirmative dimension of a radical alterity in the face of capitalism and, on the other hand, in the connection it establishes between this non-modern (Southern) Brazilian radicality and European modernity alternatives. In other words—and contrarily to those applications—by means of anthropophagy Oswald takes the point of view of an Amerindian alterity that allows him to radically break off from the Western world (and, in particular, from the positivism and enlightenment of the Communist Party's orthodox Marxism), since it continues to exchange points of view with the European alter-modernity associated with the struggles and constituent power, the same alter-modernity found in the Stalingrad resistance against Nazi racism (Negri 2002). It is important, therefore, to insist on the dyad suggested by Lévi-Strauss between anthropophagy and anthropoemy; to that effect we need to revisit the concept of anthropoemy, not that of anthropophagy.

Brazilianization (anthropoemy) versus Mundobraz (anthropophagy)

One way of evading pitfalls is to reformulate this contraposition in terms of an alternative between two different dimensions of time. This is possible through the Deleuzian criticism of time, a concept also addressed and enriched by Peter Pál Pelbart: as "time that splits continuously towards uncountable futures" (Pelbart 2003, 90; Pelbart 2007). Thus, in a "crescent and vertiginous web of diverging, converging and parallel times" (Pelbart 1998, 91), one must choose between the linear time of Eurocentric and anthropocentric progress and the other dimension of time, which is anthropophagic: no longer *Chronos*, but becoming. "The tree is not green, it becomes green! (Gil 1998: 71); the meaning is not in the characteristic but, rather, in the verb, in the action. Likewise, João Guimarães Rosa (2009) writes, "Then, I turn into a real leopard, you see. ... Suddenly, see, I *became a leopard*" (De Campos 2009, ccxli).

Chronos is the time of "action" or, rather, of the denial of idleness (as Oswald put it) through the discipline or control of work, the curse of labor. It is the time when the Indian leaves the forest for the fields or the city to become a peasant or proletarian or to join the great masses of "the Brazilian poor" and its "relative population surpluses" (Guimarães 2007, 32). It is the time when the periphery shifts toward the center, from underdevelopment toward development, or toward the population surplus. It is the time for Brazil, the "country of the future": its path has been laid out and no options remain but "accelerating .... the growth" toward this preconceived and deterministic path. As we refer to the current context of capitalist globalization, we call it the time of the "Brazilianization" of the world and ... of Brazil. The future has become Brazil: by shifting toward the "center," modernizing itself, and becoming industrialized, Brazil moves speedily toward insecure labor conditions, social fragmentation, and civil violence, which increasingly characterize economies in the center based on the ways the accumulation regime of modern capitalism functions. It is at this point that one sees the inclusion of the excluded as such, following a seemingly anthropophagic modulation (low or reactive) but that is, in fact, anthropoemic, for this inclusion modulates exclusion, bringing it into the society of control: between subordination of labor and slavery, along the flexible lines of precariousness. Before and beyond this chronological linearity of "progress," time is perceived as intertwined, mixed, miscegenated, and anthropophagic: "more shore than river, more mass than flow, coexistence rather than succession ... endless variation rather than order" (Rosa 2009, 95). It is the time of becoming, of the multiplicity of relations involving man–instrument–animal, culture–nature. It is the time Oswald defines as that of idleness and which we call the time of denial, of refusal of work and the discipline it entails. Fabricio Toledo (2012) writes,

> To escape, to deviate, to lie, to deny, to silence, to paralyze, to yield, to hide, to avoid. A sequence of gestures that could be perceived as negative, which to us may seem more a retreat of movement than action proper.

This new dimension of time is what we call "Mundobraz," (see Cocco 2009) the becoming-Brazil of the world, in other words, a time of inclusion that is both departure (denial) and self-worth (transmutation of values), a dual process—in short, the generation of new values and thus of new rights within and against capitalism. Inclusion is considered a component capable of, through a shift in perspective, decentralizing Eurocentrism and its instrumental and totalitarian rationality (the rationality of capital).

In fact, the Brazilianization of the world and Mundobraz go hand in hand, within the same modulation. But where does the difference lie? Where do we find the *clinamen*, the ethical divide? Where does the truth lie? We know that Michel Foucault says that the answer is on the side of the "courage of truth," in the struggle. As such and referring to a general feature of Marxist analyses, he says, "What calls my attention is that one always refers to 'class struggle,' but pays little attention to one of the components of the phrase, namely 'struggle' (Foucault 2001, 268). In another interview he emphasizes, "It is only in the struggle that the favorable conditions will emerge" (Foucault 2001, 349). In a debate with Noam Chomsky, who defines struggle as the search for justice (or, rather, as the affirmation of the truth that is independent of the search process), Foucault suggests that we should rather think of justice as being the struggle itself (Foucault 2001, 471–512). In his latter lessons, he suggests that truth is associated with courage, in other words, with life (*bios*) as the "*mise à l'épreuve de soi-même*" and a combat in and against this world" (Foucault 2009, 310). In similar terms, Deleuze claims there is no creation without resistance and that, in the "flight," we need to "take up arms." It is in those very terms that de Andrade (2000, 110) refers to the universal miscegenation based on what he defines as the "Canudos,[6] the hired gunmen's Stalingrad." (see also Cocco 2009, chapter 4)

The art of the struggle

There is no art without resistance. "Only by the furious tearing down, will it be possible to erect something credible and legitimate: our reality," says Oiticica (2011, 85). Jean-Luc Nancy adopts the same line: "no being is devoid of a fold, there is nothing before the fold." Continued creation is one of struggle and resistance. The meaning is in the path and never deviates from it" (Nancy 1998, 121). For Oiticica the fold unfolds in a piece of creation that is action: the "dressing" opposes and is linked to the "seeing" (Oiticica 1964, 74).

But, are we aware of what struggle is and what struggling means today? What are the struggles that allow us to go beyond modulation and control? If struggle is what defines the divide between Brazilianization of the world (modulated inclusion of the poor as poor, through fragmentation of the whole world

6 "Stalingrado jagunça de canudos" refers to the group of quasi-insurrectionaries (made up of former black slaves, uprooted indigenous groups, and impoverished and landless mestizos) who settled in Canudos and put up fierce resistance against the established power during 1896–1897 (translator's note). Euclydes da Cunha wrote about Canudo's war in the masterpiece Os Sertões.

and of the entire time under the regime of capitalist accumulation, real subsumption) and the world's becoming-Brazil (restoration of fragments as peculiarities that make up "a new people and a new land," a crowd), this conflict could then be redefined as one that integrates the idea of the poor, defined by de Andrade as a struggle that opposes the "technicized barbarians" and the "new troglodytes."[7] To learn about the struggle, we present two radically opposed paths or perspectives.

The Indians versus the poor?

Let us examine the first clue, which has been formulated and circulated on the Web as follows: "The poor is the other whom we should assimilate (inclusion). The Indian is the other who wishes to continue being different ('living well'[8])." The statement implies that the Indians are outsiders and, are, unintentionally, considered from their anthropoemic stance, that is, a refusal to undergo any form of assimilation: the only way out of assimilation is the denial of the other. Living well would be defined as something tantamount to a chosen rather than imposed exclusion, to a policy of the no and to an unlikely and Heideggerian power of powerlessness. To eliminate any possible doubt, the statements above should be completed as follows: "The Indian who thinks of himself as poor is lost/He has become raw material waiting to be liberated by human kindness which, as we know, abounds around here." This obviously leads to the political conclusion according to which "there would be an old and hardly mendable fracture between two very different lefts: that which considers the Indian as poor and that which considers the poor as Indian." We are, as the phrases suggest, in the "conceptual" realm, whereas, we should be in the realm of the struggle—the only possibility to change viewpoints—and to observe where the struggles are leading.

Two issues therefore emerge: that of living well and that of the poor. In the statements above, the reference point of living well is not, as one might think, the cosmology of the Andean Indians recovered by the Bolivian constitutional process. Instead, the reference point is neo-Malthusian. Malthusianism, also when qualified as neo-, remains conservative moralism and, as in "any Moral fabrication ... it implies relinquishing the process of value building/generation" (Santiago 2012). This omission refers precisely to the economy of scarcity and limits. The neo-Malthusian discourse on degrowth introduces a fully paradoxical

7 For more on the "technicized barbarian" and on the dispute between the Indians and the poor, see "General Intellect," Global/Brasil, no. 16, http://www.revistaglobalbrasil.com.br/?p=1236.

8 This is a reference to the Bolivian constitutional process (see Schavelzon 2012).

element to this debate, since it links the values of the "limits" to the values of living well when, they are values that cannot be measured against each other. The Malthusian concept of social wealth is neoclassic, as defined by Léon Walras, linked precisely to the concept of scarcity: "I call social *wealth* the set of material or immaterial goods which are *rare*, that is, which are not, on the one hand, *useful* and, on the other hand, are only at our disposal in *limited amounts*" (Walras 1952, 21). This is, as we know, the utilitarianistic and neoliberal dogma. Deleuze and Guattari (1972, 36) suggest that

> It is the art of the ruling class, this practice of the void as market economy: organizing scarcity within the abundance of production, and plunging any desire into the deep fear of scarcity, of dependence on the object of real production which should be dissociated from the desire (the demands of rationality), while the production of desire becomes a ghost (nothing but the ghost).

Living well, on the other hand, rests on a different level, outside the system of set values in the process of the production of values and is, contrary to the limitations of political economy, unregulated.

Scarcity and the limits associated with it or that determine it are critical mechanisms for the organization of the moral and the command; furthermore, when they do not manifest themselves as the objective form of limits to growth or scarcity of resources, they do appear in the form of command and also in the *enclosures* of communal land (during the Industrial Revolution) and more recently in the *enclosures* of intellectual property and of networks. (see Belisário & Tarin 2012; see also Boutang, particularly number IV.2) It is the logic of the limits and of scarcity that produces and legitimizes the instrumental relations to nature and its destruction: first, because through these limits all inequalities and other forms of biopolitics (e.g., mandatory birth control) are justified and, second, because they imply that progress is equivalent to the constant search for new conditions to push those limits; however, those "natural" limits refer to, first and foremost, human labor. For Lévi-Strauss there is a direct relation between the exploitation of nature and the exploitation of man by man. It would be naïve, to say the least, to think that those reactionary issues could be propelled in a different direction—for example, the Amerindian direction—based on its extenuation by the issues of catastrophe and the "degrowth to come." It is no coincidence that Félix Guattari and Gilles Deleuze (2010, 318), when discussing "a possible revolutionary path—withdrawal from the world market ... in a peculiar renewal of the fascist 'economic solution' ... or, in the opposite direction, i.e., going further in the movement of the market, decodification and reterritorialization?"—choose "going further, instead of withdrawing from the process, 'accelerating the process,' as Nietzsche put it: in fact, in this respect, we still have not seen anything." In an interview with Deleuze and touching upon the concepts of purity and consumption, Félix Guattari insists even more forcefully on those issues. With regard to purity, he claims, "A constantly threat to the revolutionary apparatus is drawing a puritan conception of the interests, which will be realized only by a specific fraction of the oppressed class." To remove any doubt, Guattari adds,

> There has never been a struggle against the consumption society, the notion is stupid. We claim, on the contrary, that there is not enough consumption: the interests will never shift to the side of the revolution unless the lines of desire reach a point where the desire and the apparatus mix, desire and artifice, to the point of turning against the so-called natural data of the capitalist society, for instance. (Deleuze & Guattari 1972, 32).

This is precisely how the Xingú Indians, who take a firm position against the Belo Monte Dam, see things. Their fierce struggle against the dam's installation, which included occupation of the construction site and the sabotage of trucks, is linked to the claims of consumption that the media have defined as extravagant but which lead the struggle to its limits and transfer it to the terrain of the production of other values and, as such, to a state of living well.[9] "Before Belo Monte," writes Barbaro Technizado,

> We do not hesitate ... we choose exodus. We want a hill of 'Amaroks, Hiluxes, L 200's, F 4000's, trucks, passenger cars, busses, motorcycles, boats, fat bank accounts plus 1,3 thousand heads of cattle – 500 of which Nelore, preferably.' And we want all the iPhones, iPads along with all the other "I"'s, from A to Z. The way out is not an exit, because the empire has no outside. The way out is the exodus. Exodus with our hands full of the best consumption goods available! (General Intellect 2012).

This is how in 1969 and 1970 Taylorist workers at Fiat refused work (Balestrini 1969). It is precisely the Oswaldian theme: "I want everything that does not belong to me," "I want to eat the finest biscuit." Riobaldo (2009, 329) echoes the sentiment: "I wanted everything, without anything!"

By crossing all limits, it is possible to transmute all values, precisely like the struggles of the Indians—in line with those carried out by the workers—who destroy limits and break away from any chains that bind them to the logic of proportions and capitalist accounting, inverting the discourse of the landowners and of the media against reservations— "too much land for too few Indians"— into "too few farmers for too much land." By overcoming the limits that bind us (and force us to destroy nature), we can carry out democratization, tapping into

---

9 To read the letter by the Indians who occupied the Belo Monte construction site, see http://www.valor.com.br/empresas/2729734/o-que-pedem-os-indios-de-belo-monte.

the mixture of culture and nature, just as the living well of the Andean Indians does.

The poor and the Indian

We turn now to the second aspect of our analysis: the issue of the poor. To better explore this second path, we adopt the line of the French anthropologist who, in 1955, classified societies into two types according to the way they dealt with the issue of alterity. In 1986, in a lecture in Tokyo, Lévi-Strauss summed up the civilization mutation that he was observing in the capitalist restructuring at the outset of the neo-liberal reaction as follows: while in the industrial world the trend has been the transformation of men into machines, in post-Fordism the orientation was toward transforming machines into men:

> The advances in electronics ... allow us to envisage the day when it will be possible to shift from a civilization that inaugurated the historic becoming, though forcing men into machines, to a wiser civilization which would be able to – as in the case of the robots – transform machines into men. (Lévi-Strauss 2011, 92f)[10]

Conceivably, Lévi-Strauss was influenced by the sociological literature that explained industrial performance in Japan with the country's high level of robotization. He insisted, however, on the wide range of opportunities available under this civilization shift. Robotization would allow "culture [to receive] entirely the task to generate progress [and thus] society would be liberated from the Millennial curse which turns men into slaves so that progress can be achieved" (Lévi-Strauss 2011, 92). Indeed, on the one hand, the French anthropologist does not have a negative view of the crisis of industrial modernity but, rather, sees it as expanding the realm of possibilities and as a liberating change; to the Japanese, on the other hand, he speaks of a technically possible liberation from the curse of labor. To him, the release of nature (the change to civilization) and the liberation of labor are one and the same, which is very similar to what de Andrade (1990, 218) claimed in his later period when, in the 1950s, he formulated innovative theories on matriarchy:

> Aristotle claimed man leaves his condition as slave when the spindles work by themselves. And what has mankind been doing for centuries, in all its efforts and endeavors, in all its pioneering and conquests, but to seek that the spindles start working by themselves? Nothing crowns the industrial revolution as majestically as the productive and intimative domain of technique. The Robot is an ideal ... because

10 Obviously, Lévi-Strauss referred to the role of automation and of the Robots, which, at the time, were thought to be elements that characterized the emerging Toyotistic model (Coriat 1983). However, his reflection is far more subtle and enduring, because, it involves the criticism of the relationship between culture and nature.

> it is around the Robot that today's civilization is being built. The slave will only disappear when he can be replaced by mechanics, i.e., when the spindles start to work by themselves.

Rosa (2009, 329) had a similar view: "The day will come, said Riobaldo, when we can lay in the hammock or in bed, and the shovels will march by themselves to do the work in the fields." Oswald added something to this when he claimed that robotization and freedom will lead to the "conquest of idleness" (Andrade 1990, 329). For Oswald, technology is social rather than technical, an idea also found in Deleuze, who, in his work on Foucault, referred to Mario Tronti, founder of Italian workerism. By the mid-1960's, Tronti wrote, "Science and technique will not be the trophy of class struggle, but its battlefield, instead." (Tronti 1976b, 32) In his comments on *Anti-Oedipus*, Guattari draws on the following idea: "What we denounce are all issues based on the opposition man-machine, men alienated by machinery" (Deleuze & Guattari 1972, 32). Technique is neither a given objective of a path to progress that would be sufficient to reach and follow nor is it something that one would have to relinquish to protect untouched nature with its savages. Technique is the battlefield. Years later, in the midst of the democratic turmoil following 1968, a leaflet produced by the Porto Marghera Workers' Committee read,

> The workers do not oppose ... the machines, but rather those who use machines to make them work. To those who claim that work is a necessity, our answer is that the mass of accumulated science ... is such as to immediately reduce labor to a purely secondary fact of human life. (Santiago 2012, 261)

So, where do the poor fit in all this? Once more, Deleuze and Guattari (1972-73, 34) provide a clue:

> The poor and the destitute ... are aware that they are close to the grass, and that "desire" involves very few things, not necessarily those that are left to them, but rather those same things that they are constantly deprived of.

Destitution is a mechanism fundamental to the transformation—through limits and scarcity—of desire into need, of the transformation of desire into repulsive fear of scarcity (Deleuze & Guattari 1972-73, 34). The poor are not the image of absence but, rather, the image of desire and the

> Desire lacks nothing. It does not lack its object. It is rather the desire that lacks its subject, or rather the desire that lacks a permanent subject; and a permanent subject can only exist through repression. The desire and its object are one and only thing, it is the machine, while machine of a machine.

In other words, "the machine is everything" and the poor is this image of the "men who dive deeper into life ... who are life itself": men who do not "eat enough, sleep enough, and who have but a few possessions, if that" (Deleuze &

Guattari 1972-73, 35). For the poor, social production and desire production coincide, just as in the savage logic the desiring machine is a "production of producing." Among the poor "there is no longer man or nature, but only processes which produce the one within the other and pairs of machines" (Deleuze & Guattari 1972, 8).

Immaterial labor and the body

We should now pose the question: what has happened to the relationship between capital, technique, and labor during the past few decades? We have said that today's capitalism is determined by its (global) networks, its intangible (cognitive) value, and its (financial) governance. If, on the one hand, value has become intangible, on the other hand, labor has become immaterial and its immateriality is not tantamount to "intellectuality" but, rather, to the recomposition of the intellectual and manual functions of the worker's body. Indeed, in the shift from industrial to cognitive capitalism, the conversion expected and also desired by Lévi-Strauss, of the transformation of men into machines to that of machines into men, did not take place. Robots do not release men from labor, nor nature from instrumental reason. On the contrary: factory automation has led to new forms of slavery, since the robotized line works according to the recomposition of labor (immaterial: intellectual, and manual), which depends on the level of subjectivity: it is the very soul that is explored. The production of subjectivity becomes the terrain of exploitation.

But the production of subjectivity has also become the terrain of liberation, that is, the installation of idleness. In this context, we can recall another of Oswald's intuitions. In his text "Utopia Antropofágica" the "crisis of the messianic philosophy," he settles his accounts with Stalinism, the USSR, and, more broadly, with orthodoxy, indicating that the word *idleness* comes from the Greek *sxolé*, school, "so one can clearly identify within the ancient society the idle as men who escaped manual labor to dedicate themselves to speculation and the achievements of the spirit." (Andrade 1990, 106) The horizon of the struggle envisaged by Oswald was that of the subjection of time: not the deterministic chronology of Western capitalist progress but, rather, the becoming, an "age of idleness and a different form of matriarchy." One cannot avoid venturing into Marxist allusions to the era of Marxist claims as an era of *General Intellect*, i.e., an era in which the Intellect becomes inseparable from the commonness of the social networks: mass intellectuality, collective and social intelligence fostered by knowledge, technique and *know-how* accumulated in and by networks of brains!

In his "Letter to Raul on the body," Antonio Negri (2009, 107) suggests a definition of post-modern metamorphosis similar, yet different, to that advanced by Lévi-Strauss: "Yesterday, the abstract assimilated life. Today, it is life that assimilates the abstract." In other words, capitalism had robbed us from the concreteness of life. Today, the unique once again recovers the abstraction, the merchandise, the value. "The abstract has become live matter [content and driver] in all forms of expression" (Negri 2009, 107). This exercise implies a different form of knowledge, recalling the "Parangolé experience": not the knowledge of an object, since the

> Work is no longer object insofar as the knowledge it contains, but rather a relation which transforms that which is known into new knowledge and into what still remains to be learned, an unknown side, so to say, what is left to the imagination which is recreated from this work. (Oiticica 1964, 67)

In his last publication on the metamorphosis of capitalism, André Groz argues, "Labor for material production, measurable into units of product by time units is replaced by the so-called immaterial labor, to which classical measuring standards no longer apply" (Oiticica 1964, 11). The centrality of immaterial labor is a fact that implies double movement: it has to do with a process of appreciation that tends to leave the shop floor and spread throughout the social networks of circulation and reproduction, beyond the salary relation; simultaneously, immaterial labor is the result of the recomposition of material (manual) production labor with (intellectual) conception labor. Immaterial labor is not synonymous with either abstract labor or intellectual labor: it is, on the contrary, live labor, labor of association—in the *bodies*—of mind and hand, labor that again becomes concrete production of the senses and which qualifies the process and appreciates assets (whether intangible services or tangible goods). Labor becomes immaterial as it becomes the direct producer of value through its biopolitical dimensions. Its "immaterial sense is the result of bodily things, of its mixture, of its actions and passions" (Gil 1998, 74). It is labor whose power is close to that of the schizophrenic referred to by Deleuze and Guattari. The "schizo" manages to destroy the frontiers between the series, transforming words into bodies and sense into action and passion. For the schizo, every word is physical and has a direct effect on the body. "Word is action" (Gil 1998, 74) and the "logical operations are also physical operations" (Gil 1998, 84). Thus, we could venture that the words are Parangolés, referring to a specific experimental position and the production of another form of work, *action–work*, participatory work.

Recapping some of the claims: *in today's capitalism, labor is immaterial, a concrete generator of value in a biopolitical context. Immaterial* labor means that the activities generating value are cognitive, communicative, linguistic, and affective, comprising this soul that capital must deliver to the shop floor. This does not mean that material labor has disappeared (although it has brutally shrunk in some regions of the world) but, rather, that the value it generates has become dependent on its immaterial dimensions, those of the soul of the labor incarnated in the *body* of the worker.[11] We therefore touch the biopolitical dimension of immaterial labor: the recomposition of the mind and hand in the *body of the worker,* who, in cooperation with other bodies within a "population," produces life from life. As such, *production* becomes *generation*: a crowd of singularities cooperating among themselves while preserving their character.

In this context, that is, under the regimen of accumulation of today's capitalism (organized in networks and whose intangible, cognitive value is governed by finances), the radical change resides in the relationship between "inclusion and exclusion." From the perspective of this transformation, the relationship between anthropophagy and anthropoemy could reveal a new type of conflict: in this modulation of relations between inclusion and exclusion, this conflict consists in what we could call the *paradoxical centrality of the poor*. It is precisely the conflict we defined as the alternative that sets the Brazilianization of the world against Mundobraz, the becoming-Brazil of the world. On the one side, Brazilianization and anthropoemy: social fragmentation, endless exclusion (of the poor as poor), the Indian dead as Indian, the deported Haitian immigrant, and the illegal Bolivian made slave in the factories supplying the multinational Zara in São Paulo. Here the Neo-Malthusian stigma applies, precisely because global capitalism appears as a double catastrophe: both social and environmental! The image of the poor is an exact match for the stigma that the "super Anthropologist from Pindorama" prepares for him[12] in the form of a straightjacket: raw material, the "Indian–loser." On the other side, Mundobraz and anthropophagy: a renewal de Andrade referred to when he spoke of the capital São Paulo: "São Paulo owes its power to the immigration of live forces from the four corners of the globe,"[13] in other words, to universal miscegenation. The image of the poor is then the authentic difference, miscegenation and multiplicity. The power of the poor is profiled as the becoming-Brazil of the world and the becoming-world of Brazil. The power of the difference of the poor found its expression in the protest organized on the June 20, 2012, at the People's Summit in Rio de Janei-

11 This metaphor was coined by Yves Clot, Jean-Yves Rochex, and Yves Schwartz, *Les Caprices des flux. Les Mutations technologiques du point de vue de ceux qui les vivent*, Matrice, 1990.

12 Barbaro Tecnizado, "General Intellect," cit.

13 "Ainda o matriarcado," Utopia Antropofágica, cit., 215.

ro: slum dwellers, landless workers, young intellectual workers holding precarious jobs, women, and Indians gathered at the Vila Autódromo slum to challenge the official Rio+20 Summit. The poor became a multitude and together they voiced their grievances: against removal from the slums during mega-events, in favor of land reform, and against agribusiness and the mega-dams that displace the Indians and destroy forests.

At Vila Autódromo, standing before the police force appointed to protect the official delegations at Rio Centro, the poor made a statement of their power: a multitude of Indians, slum dwellers, the landless, women, and young people holding precarious jobs gathered around the similarities of their differences, stating the uncommon in their struggles, the field of a policy of the immanence *terraTerra*: "Giving the earth back to the earth," as in Oiticica's (1980, 183) words and Décio Pignatari's ideogram.

In this paradoxical centrality of the poor as multitude, we (again) find the labor of the poor and the body of the worker and part of the world's becoming-Brazil and Brazil's becoming-world, that is, with a possible transmutation of all values: the construction and exodus of a new people and of a new land. The centrality of the poor is a becoming-South of politics, a becoming-Brazil of the South. Oiticica's extremely anthropophagical poem illustrates that: "SOU EU[14] – É VOCÊ – É AMÉRICA LATINA – *Subterrania do mundo para o Brasil ... subterrania é a glorificação do sub – atividade – homem – mundo – manifestação.*[15]"

Pier Paolo Pasolini (1976, 54) claimed that "every thousand years ... the world comes to an end" and that is because the nature of things has "radically [and] totally changed." Until the 1950s, according to the director, things had a "mysterious quality," the quality of the handcrafted. It was so in the 1950s and until the first part of the 1960s. Objects were still created by human hands: the old and patient hands of woodworkers, tailors, upholsterers, and others. Those objects were meant for humans, persons. The objects were in the image of the individuals, almost as in the photographs comprising the "typological catalogue" with which August Sander depicted the "types and hierarchic structures of the German people" in the 20th century (Peres-Oramas et al. 2012, 108). Later, regrets Pasolini, the "craftsman or his spirit suddenly died" (Peres-Oramas et al.

14 IT IS ME – IT IS YOU – IT IS LATIN AMERICA – South – underground of the world for Brazil... undergroundness is the glorification of the under – activity – man – world – manifestation: not at the price of glori-condition → yes: as conscience to overcome the super – paranoia - repression – impotence – negligence of living – critical – creative – active (translator's note).

15 Oiticica, "Subterrânia," cit., 145. The poem is obviously anthropophagic precisely for the transformation of Underground into Subterrânia.

2012, 55f). Indeed, in poor labor Pasolini fails to see the "other" craftsman, for he thought that only the poor could produce and nurture meaning.[16] It is Merleau-Ponty (1962, 82) who describes this craftsman when he refers to the "admirable language of the craftsman of being," the activity of *seeing* as the "window of the soul," a cycle of vision and encounter "devoid of rupture," where "it is impossible to claim that nature ends here, and here begins the man" (Merleau-Ponty 1962, 82). In essence, it is a question of viewpoint and relation, a "double encounter of the world and the body which is in the source of all knowledge" (Lefort 1962, III). While Pasolini argues that "reality only has the language of things and can only be lived,"[17] Merleau-Ponty admits a language of the body, somewhat along the lines of the results of the photographic work by Hans Eijelboom, who identifies "amidst the chaos of the streets" the anthropological presence of patterns, systems, and criteria (Peres-Oramas et al. 2012, 166). Oiticica (2011, 73), in turn, echoes Merleau-Ponty and places the body in the center of his new concept of artwork as a unit of structure and action:

> It is *there* the work of art requires the direct participation of the body, beyond the dressing of the body, it asks it to move, to dance.... The very act of "dressing" the piece of work demands from the spectator an expressive-bodily transmutation, a fundamental trait of dance, its paramount condition.

How can we avoid to establish the relation, on the one side, of this "vision as a thought that deciphers the signs given by the body," in the words of Merleau-Ponty, and, on the other side, the new corporeality or "dance" of immaterial labor, with the political aesthetics of Glauber Rocha and its extremely powerful statements and inflections?

KORPOBRAZ: The power of the poor

"And suddenly, all by itself, when we least expect it, the wilderness looms." This is how Riobaldo (2009, 249f) stumbles upon a multitude of ragged and ill-armed poor and asks himself,

> How could they fight? How could they live?... Beware, sir, of men who don't have no power, who don't have no money!... Suddenly, those men turn into many, a whole lot, thousands and hundreds of thousands (with the) power of their entire and detached poverty.

---

16 As a young man, Pasolini (1976, 57) said, "I walked around the outskirts of a city (Bologna, Rome, Naples...), and what those outskirts told me in the 'Latin' was: her live the poor, and life here is poor. But the poor are laborers. And laborers are different from you, the bourgeois. The future they want is therefore different."

17 Lettere Luterane, cit., 53.

Rocha echoes the same concerns. First and foremost, he suggests an extremely fruitful inversion of the approach to the issues of underdevelopment and poverty. Furthermore, while eschewing the naïf that springs from colonial thinking, Glauber takes the path of a naïve poetry stemming from a wholly different viewpoint. Based on the poetic experience of seeing "for the first time," the "aesthetics of the poor" opens to a totally materialistic view of the world and of the existence: an experience of detachment the poor are able to achieve to the fullest. To explore that path, we could attempt to rank Glauber's aesthetics into three political phases: the first phase is the aesthetics of hunger, followed by the aesthetics of the dream, and, finally, Korpobraz political aesthetics.[18]

In "*Eztetyka da fome* [The Aesthetics of Hunger]," a manifesto produced by Glauber in January 1965,[19] he argues that

> While Latin America bemoans its general wretchedness, the foreign interlocutor cultivates a taste for this wretchedness not as a tragic symptom, but rather as simple formal information for his field of interest.... Latin hunger ... is not, then, just an alarming symptom: it is the very nerve of its own society.... Our originality is our hunger, and our greatest woe is that, because it is felt, *it is never understood.* (Rocha 2004, 64f)

The majority of Europeans and Brazilians do not understand hunger: "for Europeans it is a strange surrealism. For Brazilians, it is a national disgrace" (Glauber 2004, 66). It is precisely from that shame that stem both the motto of Dilma's government (*Brasil, País Rico é País sem Pobreza* [Brazil, a Rich Country is a Country without Poverty]) and the speculating stance of anthropologists who claim that the "poor are raw material."

Making poverty disappear, in the words of Rociclei da Silva (2011), the young director gears his criticism toward illusions of intending to "cure" hunger by "cabinet formulations", arguing that "only a culture of hunger, drenched in its own structures, can take a qualitative leap. And the noblest cultural manifestation of hunger is violence." The aesthetics of hunger that Glauber (2004, 66) conceives and produces (in *Cinema Novo*) is politics:

> [The] aesthetics of violence is revolutionary rather than primitive ... only by becoming conscious of the colonized's one possibility, violence, can the colonizer under-

18 It is not our intention to write about Rocha except to draw, by means of a transversal reading, on some of his concepts introduced in his essays, articles, interviews, and correspondence.

19 Thesis introduced during the exhibit in connection with the V Rassegna del Cinema Latino-Americano, January 1965, Genoa (Rocha 2004: 63ff). João Guimarães Rosa also took part in the event. Glauber was proud to be greeted by the Brazilian writer and writes about it in "Glauber Fellini" (Rocha 2006, 255).

> stand, to his horror, the power of the culture that he exploits. As long as he does not rise up, the colonized is a slave.

This is very similar to Franz Fanon's ideas. Glauber continues: "There had to be a first dead policeman for the French to see an Algerian" (Glauber 2004, 66).

A few years later, in 1971, still abroad, Glauber issued a new manifesto: *Eztetyka do Sonho* [The Aesthetics of Dream].[20] In it, revolution takes on a central role, since Western thought is seen as the fundamental mechanism of domination: "*The great majority of the prophets of (this) social revolution are artists.*" This is because they have a "more sensitive and less intellectual" relationship with the poor masses" (Rocha 2004, 249). The struggle of the poor and the struggle in the Third World becomes a struggle against colonizers and their rationalism. Suddenly, criticism is also directed toward leftist progressive positivism:

> The cultural systems in place, both on the right and on the left, are bound to a conservative rationale. The failure of the left in Brazil arises from this vice of the colonizer. The *right* thinks according to the reason of order and development. Technology is a mediocre ideal of power that has no other ideology except the submission of man through consumption. The answers from the *left* ... have been paternalistic with regard to the central issue of the political conflicts among the poor masses. (Rocha 2004, 249)

In other words, the "reasoning of the poor is transformed into the reason of the bourgeoisie over the people" (Rocha 2004, 250) and the reason of the left appears to be the same reasoning of the bourgeoisie (positivist and enlightened): "Struggling against the colonizing rationalisms is the only way out." (Rocha 2004, 250) Struggle is no longer opposed to the other two reasons, for it is anti-reason, anti-modernity: "Revolution is the anti-reason which conveys tensions and rebellions from within the most *irrational* of all phenomena: poverty" (Rocha 2004, 250).

Through his political innovation, Glauber therefore manages to seize the paradox that affects the very image of the poor as a two-headed "animal": one "fatalistic" and the other "mystical." The fatalistic head is the result of submission to the reason that exploits it. The mystical head is the realm of resistance, a resistance based on the fact that "the poor cannot explain the absurdity of their own poverty." Revolutions are plotted by non-reason, whereas reason—even when presented as stemming from power—is always repressive. It is the dream, the mysticism that one needs to touch: "To the revolutionary, his most powerful weapon is the liberating irrationalism." Love is no longer second place but, ra-

20 "Eztetyka do Sonho," presented in January 1971, at Columbia University (Rocha 2004, 248).

ther, fundamental. Violence becomes absolute second place: "Liberation, even when encountering violence provoked by the system, will always mean *eschewing violence* on behalf of a *community* founded on the meaning of unlimited *love* among men" (Glauber 2004, 251), of poor men while poor men, it is wise to underline. "When in flight," says Deleuze, "grab a gun."

Finally, in his "Foreword to a revolution" from December 1980, Glauber expresses his concern before a

> *Cinema novo* (that) is waging a war within and without, a war that threatens to destroy the *cinema novo* from its origins up to our days. Internally, the twenty most prominent members of the movement are split into revolutionary and conservative. Externally, imperialism seeks to sabotage the industrial development generated by Embrafilme. (Rocha 2004, 35)

The proposal, however, remains powerful and Glauber (2004, 36) suggests radicalization of the criticism of rationalism formulated in "*Eztétyka do Sonho.*" The idea is to break away from the structures of the prevailing aesthetics, whether they belong to "commercial populism" that "wishes to recover Hollywood through the re-introduction of the *chanchadas pornoxykz* (refined porn-comedy)" or to the "revisionist avant-garde that seeks to create obstacles to the challenge of the popular art forms." Glauber formulates a "*terceyro modelo*" (third model), that is, an anti-model, intended to function as a "*síntese neobarroka*" (neo-baroque synthesis) of the "'*internacionalismo épico & didático & transconstrutivista*' [internationalism that is epic, didactic, and transconstructivist] ... *Ynvenção Polytyka da socyedade brazyleyra* [Political invention of the Brazilian society]" (Rocha 2004, 36).

Also in 1980, the director wrote a new foreword, which was never published. In it, he reveals the same concerns before the lack of cohesion amid the "*Irmãos do Cinema Novo*"; only a few did not succumb to a war of egos but instead autophagically reconstructed the "Kynematrographic space in a *Brazyl* pre-colonized by the *Cinema Novo.*"[21] Glauber's intention is to counter the attacks from "the Communist Party, from the different organizations on the left (as well as) from the porn-comedy advocates on the right," and he pushes the idea that the Cinema Novo was and should remain the "*third force: images and sounds of the people*" (Rocha 2004, 516). A third force that, as we know, is not an intermediary force but, rather, a line of escape, the third bank of the river. Here controversy becomes violent:

> [The] Marxist pseudo-aesthetes who, irresponsibly classified the *cinema novo as a petty-bourgeois subjectivist movement* are defined as "ignorant public sub-

21 "Préfacio 80" (Rocha 2004, 515). Note the author's peculiar spelling (the use of z, k, and y).

> philosophers", importers of the European thought, as they, genetically, are Italian, Spaniards, Portuguese, but never *brazileiros*, not because of their race or color, but because they lack the *tropycal* spirit. (Rocha 2004, 517)

Curiously, this "tropical spirit" is a concept that Glauber borrows from Liberation theology: In *Brazyl*, Marxism does not convert the Catholic Church; instead, it is the Church that absorbs it, as it did with the Afro-*Brazylycal* religions. The tropical spirit is the very cauldron of a generalized anthropophagic miscegenation. "I tap from all [religions]" and "drink water from every river ... To me, one [religion] is too little, perhaps not even enough" (Rosa 2009, 12).

"The future is a *feijoada* stew that can cause indigestion, vomit or diarrhea, but ends up hardening" yet another model: the "baroque-satirical-mythical-lyrical" (Rocha 2004, 518). Despite the anthropoemic crisis and pitfalls, the battlefield is anthropophagic. The baroque suggested by Glauber is perhaps closer to the neo-baroque of de Campos' "programmatic prediction" formulated in a 1955 article: "this neo-baroque, which might intrinsically meet the cultural-morphological needs of today's artistic expression, may instill fear for the simplicity of its calling and the lazy spirits that long for the steadfastness of concerted solutions."[22] (Rocha 2004, 518)

In a 1969 interview Glauber discusses "*Transe da América Latina*" and says, "We are underdeveloped countries and this is a problem which no political regime or ideology can solve. That can only be achieved through work, construction and organization" (Rocha 2004, 184). In other words, "we can only struggle through production" (Glauber 2004, 236). In 1970, the Porto Marghera Workers' Committee repeated this same idea in an impressive exchange of points of view: "Progress is not a neutral event, because it is decided exclusively according to the particular point of view and according to the political control over the forces that can sever the power of capitalism." (Santiago 2012) *Struggle is the production of other values and meanings*, such as a result of technological innovation: in idleness meaning school, as Oswald put it. Thus, the workers' struggle must be global, taking into account the situation of the periphery. The Workers' Committee writes,

---

22 "A Obra de Arte Aberta," originally published in the daily newspaper Diário de São Paulo, on July 3, 1955,
was republished in Augusto de Campos, Décio Pignatari, and Haroldo de Campos' Teoria da Poesia Concreta (Textos Críticos e manifestos 1950–1960), Ateliê Editorial, Cotia, São Paolo, 53, 2006. In an article dedicated to Deleuze in 1988, de Campos reclaims the concept of neo-baroque and defines it as a "contemporary semiotic practice which quotes the past translating it again and trans-modelling it into the present context ... Barroco-Ludisme deleuzien" (Alliez 1998, 545).

> Through the development of machines it will be possible to work a lot less, as long as the machines conceived by modern science do not become the monopoly of the USA or the Soviet Union, as is the case today, but are made available all over the world. (Santiago 2011, 262-63)

Produce, yes, but how? Based on which values? Glauber answered that by insisting on the ontological dimension of poverty and pain: pain and poverty as viewpoints for the production of new values: "We have to face our reality with deep pain. There is nothing positive in Latin America except pain and destitution .... This is the starting point in the construction of a civilization that has a long road ahead" (Glauber 2004: 172). Therefore, one should not fear the "primitive" or "savage"; one "must be anthropophagic," rather than a false patriot or the naïve mimic of the prevailing culture (2004, 236).

The subjects of the becoming-Brazil of the world are the poor, for they are the ones who produce wealth while transmuting all the values. In this regard, de Campos notes that the "idea of progress" does not entail a "sense of hierarchy of value, but ... rather of a sense of vectored metamorphosis, of qualitative transformation, of culture-morphology: *make it new*" (de Campos 2006, 43): invention, resistance, and creation. The neo-baroque of the concrete poet is in dialog with Deleuze's "polyphony of polyphonies" (de Campos 1998, 548), with the becoming-work[23]: pieces of work without authors and pieces of work without production, we could venture to say. The Deleuzian definition of baroque hinges on the concept of folds: "the baroque does not cease to fold.... The baroque line is the fold that reaches the infinite" (De Campos 1998, 549f). As Nancy (1998, 118) puts it, there is no being devoid of folds and there is nothing before the fold; he adds that there are different ways to handle the fold, to fold it, unfold it, and fold it again."

It is in those transmutations and metamorphoses that the political force and the force of bodies coincide, because the body of immaterial labor, the biopolitical production, finds in the body of the poor the image "of productive discourse of the *beautiful bodies* against the power over the beautiful." (Negri 2009, 115) A feeling-thinking that, according to João Rosa, is the best definition of *brasilidade*, because "one cannot explain *brasilidade*" but live it, for "understanding *brasilidade* requires, above all, learning to recognize that wisdom and logic are two different things.... Logic ... is the power through which man, one day, will kill himself (Lorenz 2009: IX–X). This "life that takes the form of language,"

23 Curiously and significantly, de Campos anticipated Humberto Eco on the open-becoming of the work of art, despite the fact that the Italian never managed to learn about his work (see Eco's note on the anticipation of the concept by de Campos, "Barroco-Ludisme deleuzien [Allienz 1998, 548]).

concludes Rosa, is what one calls "baroque" (Lorenz 2009, LXIII). The origins of Mundobraz are to be found in Glauber, who argues that "Utopya becomes a metaphor in the symbolic baroque language of our *tropicalism*, expressed as it structures the collective unconscious and the high poetics of Aleijadinho & Vila-Lobos, visual arts and sounds of Korpo Brazyl, *KORPOBRAZ.*" (Rocha 2004, 518)

References

Alliez, Eric, and Deleuze, Gilles. 1998. *Une Vie philosophique.* Paris: Les Empêcheurs de tourner en rond.

Althusser, Louis. 1994. "Le Courant souterrain de matérialisme de la rencontre." In *Écrits philosophiques et politiques, Tome II (Textes réunis et presentés par François Matheron),* edited by Louis Althusser. Paris: Stock/Imec.

Balestrini, Nanni. 1969. *Vogliamo Tutto*. Milan.

Belisário, Adriano & Bruno Tarin (eds.). 2012. *Copyfight: Piratairia e Cultura Libre*. Rio de Janeiro: Azougue.

Boutang Yann Moulier. 2007. *Le Capitalisme cognitif, La Nouvelle grande transformation*. Paris: Amsterdam.

Cocco, Giuseppe. 2009. *Mundobraz: o devir-Brasil do mundo e o devir-mundo do Brasil*. Rio de Janeiro: Record.

Coriat, Benjamin. 1983. *La Robotique*. Paris: La Découverte/Maspero.

De Andrade, Oswald. 1990. "Ainda sobre o matriarcado." In *A utopia Antropofágica*. São Paulo: Globo.

De Andrade, Oswald. 2000. "Atualidade dos Sertões." In *Feira das Sextas*. São Paulo: Globo.

De Campos, Haroldo. 2009. "A linguagem do Iauaretê." In *Ficção Completa, Vol. 2* edited by João Guimarães Rosa. Rio de Janeiro: Nova Aguilar.

De Campos, Haroldo. 1998. "Barroco-Ludisme deleuzien." In *Une Vie philosophique,* edited by Eric Alliez and Gilles Deleuze. Paris: Les Empêcheurs de tourner en rond.

De Campos, Haroldo. 2006. "Poesia e paraíso perdido" (originally published in *Diário de S. Paulo,* June 5, 1955). In *Teoria da poesia concreta. Textos críticos e manifestos 1950–1960,* edited by Augusto de Campos, Décio Pignatari, and Haroldo de Campos. São Paolo: Ateliê Editorial, Cotia.

Deleuze, Gilles, and Félix, Guattari. 2010. *Capitalisme et schizophrénie 1, L'Anti-OEdipe*, 1972. São Paulo: Editora 34.

Deleuze, Gilles, and Félix, Guattari. 2003. "Entretien sur l'Anti-Oedipe." in L'Arc, no. 49, 1972, reprinted in *Pourparlers (1972–1990)*, edited by Gilles Deleuze. Minuit, Paris, 1990–2003.

Foucault, Michel. 2001. *Dits et Écrits, 1976–1988* (II). Paris: Gallimard.

Foucault, Michel. 2009. *Le Courage de la vérité, le gouvernement de soi et des autres II*, Cours au Collège de France, 1983–1984. Paris: Gallimard, Seuil, EHESS.

General Intellect. 2012. "Bárbaros tecnizados" in *Revista Global Brasil*. Available at http://www.revistaglobalbrasil.com.br/?p=1236

Gil, José. 1998. "Un Tournant dans la pensée de Deleuze." In *Une vie philosophique,* edited by Eric Alliez and Gilles Deleuze. Paris: Les Empêcheurs de tourner en rond.

Guimarães, Alberto Passos. 2007. *As Classes Perigosas. Banditismo urbano e rural (1982).* Rio de Janeiro: Editora UFRJ.

Lefort, Claude. 1962. "Introduction." In *L'Oeil et l'Esprit,* edited by Maurice Merleau-Ponty. Paris: Gallimard-Folio.

Lévi-Strauss, Claude. 2011. "L'Anthropologie face aux problèmes du monde moderne." Conferências pronunciadas na Fundação Ishizaka de Tókio, 1986. Paris: Seuil.

Lorenz, Günter. 2009. "Dialogo com Guimarães Rosa." In *Ficção Completa, Vol. I,* edited by João Guimarães Rosa. Rio de Janeiro: Editora Nuova Aguilar.

Merleau-Ponty, Maurice. 1962. *L'Oeil et l'Esprit.* Paris: Gallimard-Folio.

Nancy, Jean-Luc. 1998. "Pli deleuzien de la pensée." In *Une Vie philosophique,* edited by Eric Alliez and Gilles Deleuze. Paris: Les Empêcheurs de tourner en rond.

Negri, Antonio. 2002. *Poder Constituinte. As alternativas da modernidade.* Translated by Adriano Pilatti. Rio de Janeiro: DP&A.

Negri, Antonio. 2009. "Lettre à Raúl." In *Art et multitude* 1999. Paris: Stock.

Oiticica, Hélio. 1964. "Bases fundamentais para uma definição do Parangolé." In *Museu é o Mundo* 1965. Org. César Oiticica Filho. Rio de Janeiro: Azougue.

Oiticica, Hélio. 1980. "Devolver a terra a terra." In *Museu é o Mundo* 1965. Org. César Oiticica Filho. Rio de Janeiro: Azougue.

Oiticica, Hélio. 2011. "A Dança na minha experiencia." In *Museu é o Mundo* 1965. Org. César Oiticica Filho. Rio de Janeiro: Azougue.

Pasolini, Pier Paolo. 1976. *Lettere Luterane*. Milan: Garzanti.

Pelbart, Peter Pál. 1998. "Le Temps non-réconcilié." In *Une Vie philosophique* edited by Eric Alliez and Gilles Deleuze. Paris: Les Empêcheurs de tourner en rond.

Pelbart, Peter Pál. 2003. *Vida Capital, Ensaios de Biopolítica*. São Paulo: Iluminuras.

Pelbart, Peter Pál. 2007. *O Tempo Não-Reconciliado. Imagens do tempo em Deleuze*. São Paulo: Perspectiva.

Peres-Oramas, Luis, Severo, André, Maier, Tobi, and Villanueva, Isabella (eds.). 2012. *Catálogo doa Trigésima Bienal de São Paulo*, A Iminência da Poética, September 7 to December 9, São Paulo.

Rocha, Glauber. 2004. *Revolução do Cinema Novo*. São Paulo: Cosac & Naify.

Rocha, Glauber. 2006. *O Século do Cinema*. São Paulo: Cosac & Naify.

Rolnik, Suely. 1998. "Schizoanalyse et anthropophagie." In *Une Vie philosophique,* edited by Eric Alliez and Gilles Deleuze, 463-476. Paris: Les Empêcheurs de tourner en rond.

Rolnik, Suely. 2010. "Políticas da Criação na Deriva Transnacional." *Cadernos de Subjetividade*, 14–21. São Paulo.

Rosa, João Guimarães. 2009. "Grande Sertão, Veredas." In *Ficção Completa, 1956, Vol. 2*. Rio de Janeiro: Nova Aguilar.

Santiago, Homero Silveira. 2011. "A recusa do trabalho." *Cuadernos de Etica e Filosofia Politica* 19: 249-257.

Santiago, Homero Silveira. 2012. *Entre Liberdade e Servidão*, Tese de Livre Docência apresentada na FFLCH da USP, June 2012.

Schavelzon, Salvador. 2012. *El Nacimiento del Estado Plurinacional en Bolívia. Etnografia de una Asamblea Constituyente*. La Paz: Clacso

Silva, Rociclei da. 2011. *Informação, cultura e cidadania no coração da periferia pelas batidas do hip hop*. Dissertation, Universidade Federal do Rio de Janeiro/Instituto Brasileiro de Informação em Ciência e Tecnologia, Rio de Janeiro.

Toledo, Fabricio. 2012. "Recusar" in *Global/Brasil*, no. 16. Available at http://www.revistaglobalbrasil.com.br/?p=1263

Tronti, Mario. 1976a *Operários e Capital*. Porto: Afrontamento.

Tronti, Mario. 1976b. *La Linea di condotta*.

Walras, Léon. 1952. *Éléments d'économie politique pure ou théorie de la richesse sociale*. Paris: Librairie Générale de droit et de jurisprudence.

7. Pathogenesis, Financialization and the Politics of Time

Timothy S. Murphy

At the very beginning of the book that arguably first introduced the full range of autonomist theory and practice to English-speaking audiences, the *Semiotext(e)* volume *Autonomia: Post-Political Politics* (1980), edited by Sylvère Lotringer and Christian Marazzi, Marazzi insists that

> It is in fact crucial to understand that what is called [the] 'autonomous movement' (*movimento autonomo*) is anything but homogeneous. It is composed of many different and sometimes opposing experiences. It includes organizational and theoretical paths which may be traced back to a single 'origin' (the so-called Italian 'workerism'), but this doesn't mean that they can be grouped today under the same definition…it is exactly these political differences, the internal variety of the autonomous movement, that allowed it to grow. (Lotringer & Marazzi 1980, 10)

Indeed, in the course of the '60s and '70s the Italian autonomous movement grew primarily as a result of internal fractures that multiplied both theoretical positions and forms of militant practice. This started with the 1963 schism that broke up the editorial board of *Quaderni Rossi* and ended (more or less) with the unbridgeable chasm that separated the creative movements of 1977 from the regicidal elitism of the Red Brigades. The importance of this proliferating heterogeneity or intensive difference that lies at the core of the autonomist impulse has long been acknowledged by historians and scholars of the movement—the works of Sergio Bianchi and Steve Wright have been and continue to be crucial in this regard—but the dissemination of autonomist ideas and practices throughout the global network of militants has sometimes obscured it. This is particularly true for the Anglophone context, in which the reception of autonomist texts has taken place more slowly than in other European languages and over which the collaboration of Michael Hardt and Antonio Negri has cast a very long shadow.

I do not mean to suggest that Hardt and Negri's influence on the reception of autonomist ideas in the English-speaking world has been pernicious, quite the contrary. I believe that the success of their work, more than any other single factor, paved the way for the adoption of autonomist frameworks and references by both militant and academic discourses on globalization, as well as for the current availability of other autonomist theorists' work in English translation. Anyone who recalls how difficult it once was—say, back in the '90s—to persuade publishers to publish translations of recent Italian philosophy and social theory must admit that circumstances are quite different now, though no one is sure how long this situation will last. If we look more closely at these effects, however, we can see that Hardt and Negri's influence on the reception of autonomist thought in English goes even deeper; for example, their enthusiastic borrowing and revision of critical concepts invented by Gilles Deleuze and Michel Foucault have tended to focus interpretive attention on that admittedly extremely important line of contemporary thought, often to the exclusion of other important lines. Likewise, their philosophical and juridical approach to the structures of transnational capitalism and the powers of the global multitude has tended to inspire similarly qualitative analyses of those matters, as opposed to other kinds of analysis.

All of this is perhaps nothing more than a circuitous way to paraphrase what Hardt and Negri themselves repeat many times: that their work is nothing other than a partial synthesis—a Sartrean totalization, if you will—of many divergent analyses, conceptualizations, and struggles that should not be mistaken for a grand unified theory. Their collaboration exemplifies and enacts the heterogeneity of autonomist thought and is a new starting point rather than a conclusion. Indeed, with the translation into English of a widening array of autonomist theorists, English-speaking readers can finally appreciate both the importance of Marazzi's claim regarding autonomy's originary heterogeneity and the enabling limits of Hardt and Negri's powerful but partial synthesis. In the remainder of this essay I focus on two major autonomist thinkers of the "second generation," who are becoming increasingly relevant for the adaptation of autonomist theories and practices to the contemporary context: the media theorist Franco "Bifo" Berardi and Marazzi himself. I argue that Bifo's focus on the psychopathologies of what he calls 'semiocapitalism' constitutes a productive counter-reading of the affirmative Deleuze–Guattari–Foucault model of biopolitics that Hardt and Negri popularized, while Marazzi's econometric studies of the "language economy" and financial capitalism offer an important quantitative supplement to the qualitative approach that Hardt and Negri have offered for the analysis of the breakdown of common measure characteristic of capitalist globalization. To conclude, I examine how all four authors' works converge in a shared commitment to a new politics of time, conceptualized in Negri's distinction between a future of capitalist repetition and the time to come of the multitude's creation of new being.

The psychopathologies of semiocapitalism

If the autonomist catechism has a first article of faith, it is undoubtedly the claim that gives the movement its name: the "autonomist hypothesis" most famously articulated by Mario Tronti in his essay "Lenin in England" (1964, 1):

> We too have worked with a concept that puts capitalist development first, and workers second. This is a mistake. And now we have to turn the problem on its head, reverse the polarity, and start again from the beginning: and the beginning is the class struggle of the working class. At the level of socially developed capital, capitalist development becomes subordinated to working class struggles; it follows behind them, and they set the pace to which the political mechanisms of capital's own reproduction must be tuned.

This hypothesis held for all the heterogeneous components of Italian *autonomia* in the '70s and still holds for autonomist thinkers in the present; Bifo and Marazzi share it and Hardt and Negri refer to it explicitly in both Empire and Multitude. Indeed, for Hardt and Negri it constitutes the ontological horizon of their critique as well as the methodological inflection point that enables a passage between Italian communism and French post-structuralism. The convergence between those two terrains, which constitutes one of the most influential aspects of the authors' collaboration, authorizes them to escape the sclerotic tradition of Hegelian Marxism into a universe where dialectical negation is an antagonist rather than an ally, a universe of irreducible singularities whose differences are relentlessly affirmative. Benjamin Noys has recently labeled this joyful a-Hegelianism "affirmationism" and traced its genealogy primarily (though not exclusively) to Deleuze's legacy.[1] The problem with it, according to Noys and other critics such as the Adornian John Holloway[2] and the feminist Ida

1 "If we consider contemporary theory as polarized between the antithetical figures of Alain Badiou and Antonio Negri – an austere Platonism versus a joyous Spinozism – this apparent antagonism conceals their shared commitment to affirmation. In very different forms they both affirm the creation of unashamedly metaphysical ontologies, the inventive potential of the subject, the necessity for the production of novelty, and a concomitant suspicion of the negative and negativity. Beyond these two figures, and unnoticed in all the disputes, debates and metaphorical wars that have wracked contemporary theory, this 'affirmationism' constitutes a dominant and largely unremarked doxa" (Noys 2010, ix). See also pages 1–2 and 9–18 and Chapters 2 and 4 of Noys (2010), which offer full-scale critiques of Deleuze and Negri.

2 "The working class becomes the positive subject: that is why the positive concepts of class composition and class re-composition are on the side of the working class, while the negative concept of de-composition is placed on the side of capital. In the reversal of the polarity, identity is moved from the side of capital to the side of labour, but it is not exploded or even challenged. This is wrong. Subjectivity in capitalism is in the first place

Dominijanni,[3] is that not only does it subordinate critical negation to metaphysical affirmation, but the thoroughness with which it does makes it extremely difficult (if not impossible) to distinguish practices of critical negation—on the part of Empire or the multitude—from those of metaphysical affirmation. Put crudely, if the multitude produced Empire by its innovative struggles against Fordist capitalism, as Hardt and Negri insist, then how and why should we imagine that the multitude's current struggles will overcome Empire and not simply reinvigorate a post-Fordist capitalism? In other words, if the multitude's struggles are purely affirmative, how do they differ from the destructive positivity (positivism?) of capital? And how can the affirmative power of those struggles account for the enormous scale of suffering we see global capitalism producing on all sides, now as much as in earlier stages of its development?

This is where Bifo's work can usefully critique and supplement Hardt and Negri's formulation. Bifo shares with them many fundamental assumptions about contemporary capitalism, though he uses different terms. He views contemporary capitalism as the continuous effort to capture the creativity of the affectively—and intellectually—developed, self-organizing working class that emerged during the '60s and '70s to undermine the industrial order of Fordism. Contemporary capital's reliance on the independent, non-synchronous communications and semiotic productivity of its workers marks the consolidation of a new mode of production that Bifo calls semiocapitalism instead of Empire (or Marazzi's biocapitalism/cognitive capitalism). However, in opposition to Hardt and Negri's metaphysical affirmations of the power of the multitude, Bifo views the defining characteristics of the new cognitive proletariat, or "cognitariat," as fundamentally negative and often pathological. Cognitive labor works with and through information to produce surplus value and it delivers the material and/or immaterial results of its informatic labor processes in a time that is unbounded by the old eight-hour working day and at the same time reduced to zero through instantaneous networking. This scenario means that cognitarians live and work under conditions of permanent information overload on the intra- and internets,

---

negative, the movement against the denial of subjectivity. A truly radical reversal of the polarity involves not just transferring subjectivity from capital to the working class but also understanding that subjectivity as negative instead of positive, as the negative subjectivity of the anti-working anti-class" (Holloway 2005, 164).

3 "The multitude moves, like capital, in a linear and progressive temporality, ignoring the obstacles of regression.... In short, it is neither traversed by the negative nor by negative feelings such as fear, anxiety and dependence. Thus, in one gesture it eliminates all the work done by feminist practices to reintroduce into the constitution of subjectivity the mass of material that has been disavowed by political rationality" (Dominijanni 2005, 32).

continuous subjection to control via cell phones and GPS tracking, and the inescapable precariousness of employment due to the erosion of the welfare state's safety nets.[4] These intensely negative working conditions necessarily give rise to the explosion of psychopathological reactions that have marked the past decade of infoculture: panic disorders, ADD/ADHD, digital addictions, dysfunctions, and depression. Such illnesses are not aberrations or anomalies but, rather, the global productive norms of a "Prozac economy."

Bifo diagnoses these disorders through an intriguing combination of Deleuze and Guattari's late works (especially *What Is Philosophy?* and *Chaosmosis*) and Jean Baudrillard's theories of simulation. From Deleuze and Guattari's works on old age, he derives tools for theorizing information overload as "chaos," as well as models of how to accommodate that chaos through the "refrains" or temporary stabilizations offered by philosophical concepts and artistic affects and percepts. This emphasis on chaos as a form of suffering is usually overlooked in most interpretations of Deleuze and Guattari, but for Bifo it provides the means for linking their work to Baudrillard's, which is usually assumed (for good reason; see his *Forget Foucault* [Baudrillard 1987]) to be antagonistic to theirs. Baudrillard's concept of simulation, which Bifo elaborates as "the projection of signs that neither reproduce nor record any facts [or] the effect of the projection of ghosts never preceded by a body" (Bifo 2009b, 157), corresponds to the experience of chaos in Deleuze and Guattari's last work: it constitutes

> The infinite replication of a virus that absorbs desiring energy to the point of exhaustion. A sort of semiotic inflation explodes in the circuits of our collective sensibility, producing effects of mutation that run a pathological course: too many signs, too fast, and too chaotic. (Bifo 2009b, 159)

This is the cause of the psychopathologies of semiocapitalism, which include not only the depression, dysfunction, and ADD striking even well-compensated Western cognitarians, but also the aggressive forms of suicide that link September 11 hijackers, self-immolating Iraqi insurgents, hyper-regimented Asian factory and office workers, and the various campus shooters in the United States. Borrowing from Baudrillard's analysis of 9/11, Bifo argues that "these are two convergent pathologies, two different manifestations of the unbearable pain affecting both the hyper-stimulated and competitive psychologies of those who see themselves as winners, and the rancorous ones of the humiliated" (Bifo 2009b, 168). Using Baudrillard's ecstatically negative yet disturbingly accurate anal-

---

4 Hardt and Negri have recently drawn further attention to this mode of exploitation through their identification of the "mediatized" as one of the figures of the contemporary multitude (Hardt & Negri 2012, 14–19).

yses to displace the too-easy Deleuze–Guattarian optimism or affirmationism that he finds in Hardt and Negri,[5] Bifo articulates a highly original pessimistic or negative reading of schizoanalysis as a protocol of treatment for the structural disorders of semiocapitalism (Bifo 2009b, 214–17). Its application, however, remains uncertain as well as apparently interminable; "degrowth" is the closest thing to a program that has emerged so far (Bifo 2009b, 219–21) and in other texts Bifo seems to suggest that the "end of growth" is structurally unavoidable (2012, 75–77).

Quantifying the immeasurable

If Bifo's work helps us to acknowledge and resituate the negative in contemporary autonomist theory, thereby putting the depression and panic that many have experienced, in both the psychological and economic senses, on the agenda, then Christian Marazzi's work helps us to materialize and grasp the crisis of measure that Negri and other autonomists have been theorizing since the '70s. The crisis first appears in the context of the workers' rejection of both exchange value and its corollary use value during the struggle over the wage; at that time Negri (2005, 272) proposes to use the workers' "invention-power" as the measure of their autonomous "self-valorization":

> In the first place, then, the progress of the process of self-valorization is measured, negatively, by the progressive reduction of individual and overall labor-time, that is, the quantity of proletarian life that is sold to capital. In the second place, the progress of the process of self-valorization is measured positively by the multiplication of socially useful labor dedicated to the free reproduction of proletarian society.

This is still relatively easy to grasp as an early model of what autonomists now call exodus, but the transformations in labor that have taken place since the '70s have rendered the disjunction more profound. In *The Labor of Job,* Negri reads the biblical text as a parable of the absolute breakdown of measure: Job's experience of suffering at God's whim teaches us that "value, labor, and justice cannot be apportioned according to a common measure" (Negri 2009b, 36). In the collaborations with Hardt, this generalized immeasurability arises from the

5 Occasionally Bifo goes a bit overboard in his critique of Negri's approach, as when, for example, he bemoans Guattari's collaboration with Negri in the eighties: "The relationship between Negri and Guattari is the encounter of two old militants who had seen so much, and who at that moment, that is, in the 1980s, were living through a moment of defeat, of difficulty, but as 'real men.' And there one finds a 'macho' element … if Guattari had not met Negri, he would have been able to take stock of his aging, he would have faced his feminine side and his depression" (Bifo 2008, 159).

breakdown of the division between labor time and reproduction time, which spreads labor time to the whole time of life, and from the putting to work of not just generic (and hence interchangeable) labor power but the common (but singular and hence not interchangeable) faculties of human sociality in general—thought, language, affect—for the purposes of capitalist exploitation. This process is clearly revealed in the increasingly massive and abstract financial markets, whose disarray following the subprime mortgage market collapse triggered the current global economic downturn. As Hardt and Negri (2009, 157) insist, although it cannot actually *measure* the productivity of the common,

> Finance capital is in essence an elaborate machine for *representing* the common, that is, the common relationships and networks that are necessary for the production of a specific commodity, a field of commodities, or some other type of asset or phenomenon.

The implications of this breakdown of measure are profound but hard to identify concretely. Perhaps Marazzi's work can help here, for he (and the younger economists he inspired, best represented in the collection *Crisis in the Global Economy* [Fumagalli and Mezzadra 2010]) provides the tools to establish a broadly accessible quantitative Marxism. As Paul Dunne (1991, 2–3) notes, in the introduction to an anthology that attempted to popularize just such a form of Marxism 20 years ago, Marxists have generally dismissed the techniques of quantitative analysis used by orthodox mainstream economists:

> The tools and data of orthodox analysis were not considered of any value or interest, since many Marxists would argue that the very attempt to capture the dynamics of capital accumulation with statistical analysis and the available data was useless. The available techniques and the data focus on appearances, with the data being merely phenomenological forms which give little insight into what is happening.

In other words, econometrics was viewed as ideology, pure and simple. However accurate this view may be, the dismissal that ensued has been a tactical error, in that it has deepened the gulf of incomprehension between Marxist critique and popular economic discourses and reduced the ability of radical critics to engage in productive debates with conventional economic ideology. As Dunne tried to do, Marazzi demonstrates that

> The increasing supply of empirical research techniques should be seen as an opportunity, rather than as something to ignore. They can be used to attack the orthodoxy in a positive manner in presenting alternatives and in influencing students and academics who only know the orthodoxy but are unhappy with its failure to explain most economic phenomena. (Dunne 1991, 3)

This is particularly true at present, I think, when a quantitative understanding of the causes and effects of the financialization of the global economy and the return of rent can benefit every thoughtful leftist, especially in the English-speaking world.[6]

Marazzi is remarkably clear regarding the underlying causes of the past several financial crises, in which he follows other analysts in tracing back to the use of public pension funds to bail out the New York budget back in the '70s. This marked the advent of pension fund capitalism, the massive and systemic injection of retirement funds (and other social investments) into the speculative investment markets to maintain the level of Fordist welfare assistance during the welfare state's dismantling. The social safety net's dependence upon the state's redistributive tax policies declines and dwindling social benefits are ever more fully underwritten or replaced by investment returns (not only stocks and bonds but also real estate). The acceleration of this injection over the intervening decades has fundamentally altered the landscape of capital and therefore the logic of anti-capitalist struggle. As Marazzi summarizes it, "in the name of his interests as a *shareholder*, the *waged* employee (in the public or private sector) is prepared to fire himself if Wall Street should demand it" to increase the return on investment (Marazzi 2008, 22).[7] Like it or not, we are all on the financial market now, as subjects as well as objects and whether we speculate individually or collectively, because the market is the single greatest force that will determine our living conditions while we work and after we retire. Consequently, I am convinced that we must acquire the critical tools necessary to grasp the market's quantitative logic of finance. Especially in the United States, we live in the shadow of an "*empire without credit*", the formula describing the paradox of the largest world power that is also the largest global debtor" (Marazzi 2011, 84).

How did we get sucked into and subjected to this empire without credit? The process was complex and I do not attempt to outline it all here. Let me simply focus attention on the expansion of debt that was a cornerstone of the financialization. Marazzi analyses the transition from Fordism to post-Fordism in terms of capital's need to find alternative sources of profit once worker struggle had forced the rate of profit to show signs of impending collapse in the '70s. It found those sources not in further fixed and variable capital investments (new plant

---

6 I hasten to add that I do not claim to grasp the quantitative aspects of the current global crisis in their entirety. I have simply found the work of Marazzi and his comrades to be the clearest source of insight into the quantitative side of the situation and I believe it deserves to be more widely read and used, especially by autonomist theorists and militants.

7 Maurizio Lazzarato (2012, 110) confirms this in his analysis of "indebted man": "Whereas the 'real' economy impoverishes the governed as 'wage-earners' (through wage freezes, precarization, etc.) and possessors of social rights (through narrower income redistribution, decreases in social services, unemployment insurance, and student grants, etc.), finance claims to enrich them through credit and stock."

construction and new hiring) but, rather, in the much more rapid turnover of the financial circulation cycle. To realize this, however, capital had to find sources of liquid capital to circulate and it found them in both state and private (consumer and mortgage) debt, which could be packaged into securities and exchanged on an increasing scale following the deregulation of financial markets in the Reagan era. The debt market required continuous new infusions of such securities to stabilize its own expansion and thus promoted global expansion of debt. As Marazzi (2011, 39) notes,

> The expansion of subprime loans shows that, in order to raise and make profits, finance also needs to involve the poor, in addition to the middle class. In order to function, this capitalism must invest in the bare life of people who cannot provide any guarantee, who offer nothing apart from themselves. It is a capitalism that turns bare life into a direct source of profit.

That profit—which is really a return to the logic of rent that capital was supposed to eliminate as it developed (Hardt & Negri 2009, 137–41, 258; Carlo Vercellone in Fumagalli & Mezzadra 2010)—constitutes a stand-in for the impossible measure of that "bare life" that we are (at least from the viewpoint of debt financing itself).

This process of financialization was tremendously successful up to the point of its crisis, and the efforts currently underway nationally and globally aim to restore it to its previous mode of functioning. As Marazzi (2011, 52–53) shows,

> The quantity of surplus-value created by new apparatuses of extraction is *enormous*. It is based on the compression of direct and indirect wages (retirement, social security cushions, earnings from individual and collective savings), on the reduction of socially necessary labor with flexible network company systems (precarization, intermittent employment), and on the creation of a vaster pool of free labor (the "free labor" in the sphere of consumption, circulation and reproduction, with a more intensified cognitive labor). The quantity of surplus-value, i.e., of unpaid labor, is at the root of the increase in the profits not reinvested in the production sphere, profits whose increase does not, as a consequence, generate the growth of stable employment, let alone wage increases.

The crisis of measure results, as we already know, from the displacement of production from its formerly quantifiable, measurable place in the factory during working hours and into the measureless space of general human sociality everywhere and all the time. Its ubiquity is the source of its immeasurability, but also the key to its logic of exploitation.

The crisis of measure affects not only individual and collective productive agents bought and sold by capital, but also the gatekeepers of the financial system, who find their existing measures—the indicators that central bankers use to set interbank interest rates that are supposed to control the economy by controlling access to credit—failing to function accurately. Marazzi (2011, 80–81) follows the crisis of measure all the way to the top, demonstrating how the evaluation errors of ratings agencies and other measuring instruments must be understood

> Not so much, or not only, as mistakes attributable to the conflict of interests scandalously typical of rating agencies, but as the expression of an (ontological) impossibility of making rules or meta-rules able to discipline markets in accordance with so-called rational principles.

Rationality, of course, is at root a ratio: a determinate or quantitative proportion between two variable values, for example, between the industrial/material and financial economies. According to Marazzi and others, a new epoch of economic accumulation has emerged, in which financialization is no longer a parasite weakening a supposedly more basic material or industrial economy but is, instead, the driving force of the global economy as a whole and it throws all the existing management mechanisms, which are essentially tools for measuring determinate ratios of value, into crisis. In sum, "financialization allowed *global* capital to grow thanks to the production of financial rents and consumer debts that endowed international exchanges with *systemic coherence*" up to the point of its internal crisis, the moment when the debt circulating within the system went bad and no further debt could be found to use as input (Marazzi 2011, 69). This crisis may even portend a period of radical "deglobalization" as nations and regions erect protectionist barriers to the abstracted flows of finance (Marazzi 2011, 112).

Time, debt, and struggle

The value of both Bifo's and Marazzi's work as supplements or corrections to Hardt and Negri's, which by no means exhausts their individual significance,[8] can perhaps most clearly be revealed through an examination of the radical politics of time that ultimately emerges from the analyses of all four thinkers. Negri first broached this issue in his earliest prison writings, especially "The Constitution of Time" (1981), where he argues that

> The transition to real subsumption, in so far as it affirms the collective as sole temporal and real substrate of action, not only does not reduce it to the formal indifference of equilibrium, but reproduces, reproposes, refounds the antagonism of subjects. So collective time and the temporal *Umwelt* [surrounding world] tend to pre-

8 In particular, I think it would be valuable to pursue the convergence between Bifo's emphasis on a looming era of degrowth with Marazzi's warning against the pursuit of national or regional policies of deglobalization, which I cannot do here.

> sent themselves to us immediately within *two horizons*: that of the closed time of legitimation and of equilibrium, the zero tendency of the absolute circularity of the social; and that of multiple, antagonistic, productive, constitutive, open time. (Negri 2003a, 40, trans. modified)

The former is the time of capital, the latter the time of living labor; the former produces the future as a predictable continuation of the present's logic of accumulation, while the latter constitutes an unpredictable "time-to-come [*tempo a-venire*]" that Negri's later prison text, *Kairos Alma Venus Multitudo*, further refines:

> The materialist theory of knowledge is … an irreducible construction of being that is both hazardous and absolute. A radical epistemological *displacement*, since the common name, so as to guarantee the conditions of the event, is implanted within the horizon of a fundamental ontology of time, marked by the arrow of time, in the struggle that separates the opening of *being-to-come* from the senseless repetition in the void of the 'future.' (Negri 2003a, 134)

This is suggestive but extremely abstract, so perhaps an examination of Bifo's and Marazzi's articulations of the struggle over time can help to clarify Negri's meaning.

Like Hardt and Negri, Bifo (2009a, 69–70) focuses on the qualitative consequences of the capitalist attempt to command and control time:

> The colonization of time has been a fundamental objective of the development of capitalism during the modern era: the anthropological mutation which capitalism produced in the human mind and in daily life has been above all a transformation in the perception of time. Yet with the spread of digital technologies, which allow absolute acceleration, something new occurs. Time becomes the primary battlefield, as it is the space of the mind: mind-time, cybertime. Thus we must introduce a distinction between the concept of *cyberspace* and the concept of *cybertime* …. [Cyberspace] can grow indefinitely, because it is the point of intersection between the organic body and the inorganic body of the electronic machine … [but cybertime] is not a purely extendable dimension, because it is connected with the intensity of experience that the conscious organism dedicates to the elaboration of information coming from cyberspace.

Not only has capital imposed circularity and equilibrium on the temporal cycle of production and valorization, as Negri argues, but it has in the process accelerated, condensed, and ultimately fractalized labor time, as Bifo (2009a, 81) goes on to explain:

> In the net economy flexibility has evolved into a form of the fractalization of labor. Fractalization means the fragmentation of time-activity…. The worker (a mere machine possessing a brain that can be used for a fragment of time) is paid for his punctual performance. The working time is made fractal and cellular. Cells of time are on sale on the net, and the corporation can buy as many as it needs.

This fractalization is a key contributing factor to the chaotic pathogenesis that Bifo locates in the pervasive simulated negativity of semiocapitalism and it also blocks the formation of collective forms of resistance: "Because solidarity is based on the territorial proximity of social bodies, you cannot build solidarity between fragments of time" (Bifo 2012, 55). Bifo sums up his analysis in a slogan borrowed from the Sex Pistols' punk anti-anthem "God Save the Queen": "No future, no future for you!" In response to this foreclosure of the future, which amounts to the perpetuation and intensification of present modes of temporal exploitation, Bifo advocates forms of withdrawal from the capitalist tyranny over time as a means to reestablish the control over singular or subjective time that is necessary for the creation of new being that Negri encourages.

Marazzi, on the other hand, emphasizes the reciprocal negativity of the role played by time for both living labor and capital and does so precisely by examining the quantitative aspects of the attention economy (a concept originally proposed by Thomas Davenport and John Beck in their book of that name, on which Bifo also explicitly draws (Davenport & Beck 2002)). Marazzi (2008, 140) explicates the negative feedback loop that underlay the 2001 crisis of the so-called New Economy of digital information and immaterial labor:

> On the supply side, the New Economy is characterized by *increasing returns* by virtue of the intangibility and reproducibility of its capital goods (the infinite possibilities for cloning software, for example). On the side of demand for goods and services, however, attention (its allocation) has *decreasing returns*, because attention is a highly perishable and scarce commodity.

This might be paraphrased roughly as a situation in which production costs go down as consumption costs go up. Why do consumption costs rise? Because when the common faculties of human sociality are put to work at all times but compensated according to the microtemporal units of the fractal model that Bifo describes, a radical devaluation of labor takes place that undermines and reverses the expansiveness of the digital economy:

> If in order to command attention it is necessary to invest increasingly more money (in addition to holding the intellectual property rights), in order to sell/realize the supply after eliminating the competition, it is necessary that, on the demand side, the side of the consumption of attention, there is sufficient disposable income to purchase the informational goods supplied by the market. But in the *attention economy*, income, instead of increasing, *diminishes* in direct proportion to the increase in the amount of time dedicated to work. (Marazzi 2008, 141)

Not only is the acceleration and fractalization of time intensely pathogenic for cognitarians, it is also directly contradictory to capitalist valorization, which throws the entire production cycle into disarray. Informational capital is valorized by attention, which takes subjective time that is comparatively scarce and inelastic, but that time is increasingly monopolized by the demands of cognitive production and cannot accommodate the overproduction of digital goods (see also Bifo 2012, 98), hence the 2001 crisis of the New Economy.

The current crisis of sovereign debt, from Marazzi's point of view, illuminates the other end of capital's spectrum of temporal domination: the economics of expanding and accelerating debt circulation. The construction of ever-more abstractly derivative investment vehicles out of repackaged corporate, government, and consumer debt, which allows it to be multiplied through exchange until its magnitude dwarfs the output of the material and digital economies combined (another important aspect of the crisis of measure), is the source of the finance regime's ability to recover from the attention deficit crisis that devastated the New Economy a few years earlier. The circulation of debt permits the generation of profit in the form of rent even when the underlying economic factors that produced profit in Fordism—productivity, wages, consumption, and so forth—precipitously decline:

> The indebtedness of domestic economies, to which a more or less pronounced reduction of savings according to whether one is in the US or Europe corresponds, is what allowed financial capitalism to reproduce itself on an enlarged and global scale. It is possible to affirm that, parallel to the reduction of the redistributive function of the social state, it is now assisted by a kind of privatization of deficit spending à la Keynes, i.e., the creation of an additional demand by means of private debt.... Consumption was fueled by so-called remortgaging, the possibility of renegotiating mortgage loans in order to get new credit, thanks to the inflationary increase in house prices. This mechanism, called home equity extraction, played a fundamental role in the American economic growth. (Marazzi 2011, 33–34)

The effect of this is the continuing growth of debt as a means to continue "servicing" it, a circular process that threatens to reach Nietzschean proportions (by which I mean the infinitization of debt that he uncovered lurking behind Christian morality and bad conscience[9]). As discussed earlier, this procedure functions only so long as new debt and new debt servicers can be added at the bot-

9 See Section 21 of Essay 2 in Genealogy of Morals (Nietzsche 1968, 527–528): "The aim now is to preclude pessimistically, once and for all, the prospect of a final discharge ... the aim now is to turn back the concepts 'guilt' and 'duty'—back against whom? There can be no doubt: against the 'debtor' first of all, in whom from now on the bad conscience is firmly rooted, eating into him and spreading within him like a polyp, until at last the irredeemable debt gives rise to the conception of irredeemable penance, the idea that it cannot be discharged ... God himself makes payment to himself, God as the only being who can redeem man from what has become unredeemable for man himself—the creditor sacrifices himself for his debtor, out of love (can one credit that?), out of love for his debtor!" Lazzarato (2012, 77–81) discusses this infinitization in some detail in the context of a more general Nietzschean analysis of neoliberalism.

tom of the Ponzi scheme; when that possibility is foreclosed, as it was after the subprime mortgage meltdown, only state entities can provide the means for continued deficit spending, but they too are hemmed in by existing debt. Both our private loan payments and the taxes we pay end up in the same place: the debt cycle of the financial markets. We are mortgaged, as individuals, institutions, and collectives, for an almost infinite amount and, consequently, for the foreseeable future. This is the other pole of Bifo's complaint about cellular time and it reminds me of Thoreau's complaint about people becoming the property of their property through debt at the start of *Walden*. As Maurizio Lazzarato notes, "Economists tell us that every French child is born 22,000 euros in debt. We are no longer the inheritors of original sin but rather of the debt of preceding generations" (Lazzarato 2012, 32). This is the qualitative meaning of residential properties that are quantitatively "underwater" and retirement accounts that register a negative rate of return—our time, individually and collectively, is not our own and may never be again. We are in debt from here to eternity and if we have a future—Bifo thinks not—we owe it all to capital.

How can we struggle against this infinitization or eternalization of debt, this mortgaging of our future? At one time Marazzi (2011, 95) saw a reformist possibility in the Obama administration's attempt to coordinate two levels of relief:

> This New Deal action of the new American democratic administration seems to be able to conjoin two levels, two plans that usually conflict with each other. On one hand, there is *local* intervention, with help oriented to a determined level of demand aggregated by intervening precisely where the crisis destroys incomes, job positions, and existences. On the other hand, this action has a *global* dimension to the extent that it aims at restoring economic value to financial instruments that, by definition, are created to be immersed in the global financial circulation, i.e., in portfolios of institutions and investment funds of every kind.

The bank bailout and state attempts to impose higher reserve ratios on lenders are the most visible aspects of the global level, while the administration's attempt to negotiate (or litigate) the revaluation of outstanding mortgages to reduce or eliminate the underwater effect, along with conventional measures such as the extension of unemployment compensation, represents the local level.[10] We all know the result of the bank bailout: a brief interval of circumspection followed by a return to "normal" operations and remunerations, along with a renewed resistance to heightened "regulation" of financial markets. I suspect that the agreement for limited mortgage revaluation, approved by litigators in

10 Obama's challenge to higher education, to reduce its cost increases if it wants to continue receiving federal funding, is also part of the local response and is similarly troubling in its implications. But that is a whole other essay.

many of the US states in 2012, is also a not entirely unexpected disappointment to Marazzi (and, of course, to many struggling homeowners). Nevertheless, the efforts themselves are significant in that they practically acknowledge

> The absolutely crucial dimension of *time*, the fact being that the help to families in the form of the guarantee to a social rent is a veritable investment in the future. As we said, the interventions from the base not only allow one to avoid instantaneous and massive increases in the public debt, but these interventions are carried out on a *long* temporal horizon, a horizon within which the qualitative development of the new generation can be better ensured with investments in early childhood, in school and in entering the job market. (Marazzi 2011, 95–96)

This is, then, a reformist policy of time, an attempt to resolve the crisis economically, but, more than this, we need a radical or revolutionary *politics* of time to forestall the recurrence of the debt-trap economy. As Marazzi (2011, 92) says, "what is at stake are the possibilities or impossibilities of overcoming the ongoing crisis *politically*, rather than economically," as virtually all national and global institutions are now trying to do.

What might such a revolutionary politics of time look like? How might we not only escape from the pathogenetic dialectic of accelerating cellular work time (in Kantian terms, a sublime rhapsody of the infinitely small) and the looming eternity of debt servitude (the sublime rhapsody of the infinitely large) but also, as Negri demands, create new being in a time to come? That remains to be debated and tested; Bifo (2012, 57–58), for example, recently insisted upon a "right to insolvency" that aims to go beyond the practical demands of movements such as Occupy Student Debt: "The concept of insolvency implies not only a refusal to pay the financial debt, but also, in a more subtle way, a refusal to submit the living potency of social forces to the formal domination of the economic code." Hardt and Negri (2012, 33–36) too advise us to "invert the debt" to reclaim our living time. Perhaps Marazzi can offer us some guiding principles for what he calls "taking time":

> Taking time means giving each other the means of inventing one's own future, freeing it from the anxiety of immediate profit. It means caring for oneself and the environment in which one lives, it means growing up in a socially responsible way. To overcome this crisis without questioning the meaning of consumption, production, and investment is to reproduce the preconditions of financial capitalism, the violence of its ups and downs, the philosophy according to which "time is everything, humanity is nothing." For humanity to be everything, we need to reclaim the time of its existence. (Marazzi 2011, 96, trans. modified)

This is surely one concrete sense of the concept of exodus in contemporary autonomist thought. Only after taking back time from capital—in other words, negating the entire spectrum of repetitive times that indebt and oppress us—can we create new being.

References

Baudrillard, Jean. 1987. *Forget Foucault*. Translated by Nicole Dufresne. New York: Semiotext(e).

Berardi, Franco and Guattari, Félix. 2008. *Thought, Friendship, and Visionary Cartography*. Translated by Giuseppina Mecchia and Charles J. Stivale. New York: Palgrave/Macmillan.

Berardi, Franco. 2009a. *Precarious Rhapsody: Semiocapitalism and the Pathologies of the Post-Alpha Generation*. Translated by Arianna Bove et al. London: Minor Compositions.

Berardi, Franco. 2009b. *The Soul at Work: From Alienation to Autonomy*. Translated by Francesca Cadel and Giuseppina Mecchia. Los Angeles: Semiotext(e).

Berardi, Franco. 2012. *The Uprising: On Poetry and Finance*. Los Angeles: Semiotext(e).

Davenport, Thomas H., and Beck, John C. 2002. *The Attention Economy: Understanding the New Currency of Business*. Cambridge: Harvard Business Review Press.

Dominijanni, Ida. 2005. "Rethinking Change: Italian Feminism between Crisis and Critique of Politics." *Cultural Studies Review* 11, 1: 25–35.

Dunne, Paul (ed.). 1991. *Quantitative Marxism*. Cambridge: Polity.

Fumagalli, Andrea, and Mezzadra, Sandro (eds.). 2010. *Crisis in the Global Economy: Financial Markets, Social Struggles, and New Political Scenarios*. Translated by Jason Francis McGimsey. Los Angeles: Semiotext(e).

Hardt, Michael, and Negri, Antonio. 2009. *Commonwealth*. Cambridge: Harvard University Press.

Hardt, Michael, and Negri, Antonio. 2012. *Declaration*. Argo Navis Author Services.

Holloway, John. 2005. *Change the World without Taking Power: The Meaning of Revolution Today*. London: Pluto Press.

Lazzarato, Maurizio. 2012. *The Making of the Indebted Man: An Essay on the Neoliberal Condition*. Translated by Joshua David Jordan. Los Angeles: Semiotext(e).

Lotringer, Sylvère, and Marazzi, Christian (eds.). 2010 (1980). *Autonomia: Post-Political Politics*. Los Angeles: Semiotext(e).

Marazzi, Christian. 2008. *Capital and Language: From the New Economy to the War Economy*. Translated by Gregory Conti. Los Angeles: Semiotext(e).

Marazzi, Christian. 2011. *The Violence of Financial Capitalism*. Translated by Kristina Lebedeva and Jason Francis McGimsey. Los Angeles: Semiotext(e).

Negri, Antonio. 2003. *Time for Revolution*. Translated by Matteo Mandarini. New York: Continuum.

Negri, Antonio. 2005. *Books for Burning: Between Civil War and Democracy in 1970s Italy*. Translated by Timothy S. Murphy et al. New York: Verso.

Negri, Antonio. 2009. *The Labor of Job: The Biblical Text as a Parable of Human Labor*. Translated by M. Mandarini. Durham, NC: Duke University Press.

Nietzsche, Friedrich. 1968. *On the Genealogy of Morals in Basic Writings*. Translated by Walter Kaufmann. New York: Random House.

Noys, Benjamin. 2010. *The Persistence of the Negative: A Critique of Contemporary Continental Theory*. Edinburgh: Edinburgh University Press.

Tronti, M. 1979. "Lenin in England." In *Working-Class Autonomy and the Crisis*, 1964, Translated by Ed Emery. London: Red Notes.

Part II. Post-Crisis Readings of Hardt and Negri

8. The Many Faces of Power – Subjectivity, the Common, and Fundamental Crisis

Lars Poulsen

Introduction

The work of Michel Foucault is an important inspiration for Michael Hardt and Antonio Negri, especially his analytics of power. In Foucault's conception, power is multifarious, decentralized, and complex. Hardt and Negri continue this line of thought but combine it with a more Marxist approach, focusing on basic developments in production. Their use of central Foucauldian tenets is distinct and original and has therefore also been controversial.

In this article, I argue that Hardt and Negri's Foucault-inspired approach to power allows them to make important and quite sophisticated analyses of the production of subjectivity at different nodal points in the present network of power. I first describe the basic elements in Hardt and Negri's use of the Foucauldian conception of power. Second, I show how the work of Hardt and Negri presents three distinct concepts of crisis at different levels of abstraction and historical perspective and scope. All are closely related to the central concept in their work: the concept of *the common*. These types of crisis actualize different forms of struggle over subjectivity and the common, involving different forms of power. Third, I describe how, according to Hardt and Negri, our present situation is characterized by multiple new kinds of struggle over the common and how, closely related to these, various forms of power and counter-power are producing specific forms of subjectivity. Lastly, I discuss classical Marxist and humanist ideas about alienation and authenticity. I argue that such ideas—understood in a way appropriate to present societal conditions—may still play an important role in a critical analysis of society, and in attempts at resisting and creating alternatives to the global power network of capitalist Empire, a role perhaps not fully recognized by Hardt and Negri.

My main purpose in this article is therefore to describe how, according to Hardt and Negri, the subjectivity of human beings in multiple and complex ways is influenced by diverse forms of power, some specific to the present age. My secondary purpose is to discuss the idea of some form of non-alienated, subjective and social being, which may be considered an alternative to the influence of this power.

The many faces of power

The concept of power is notoriously ambiguous. In his outline of different theoretical approaches to the concept, Steven Lukes (2005, 61ff) observes that power in some contexts and perspectives can be seen as a single, unitary concept with many expressions. From another angle it can be considered an impossible task to formulate such a unitary concept, and from a third perspective the problem is not the unitary character of the concept but, rather, its application. Such basic considerations are important and outlining a comprehensive typology of power may be a central future project for social philosophy.

Given this complex situation, my point of departure in this article is the fact that power has not just many definitions, but also many forms in social reality. Foucault (1982, 219) offers us a very broad and basic definition of power as "a way in which certain actions modify others"[1] and supplements this by stressing that power exists fundamentally as "fluid," as put into action, and as relations. Static or institutionalized relations of power are somehow derivative or secondary. Along this line of thought, it should come as no surprise that Foucault's multifaceted concept of power is simultaneously intuitively recognizable and yet heavily disputed. In his wide-ranging oeuvre Foucault describes various types of power: sovereign power, disciplinary power, biopower, governmentality, pastoral power, panoptic power, domination, technologies of the self, and so forth. It is fair to say that the relations between the different types of power, as well as Foucault's own periodization of the dominant forms of power in different ages, are not always entirely clear. For that reason, also interpretations of these aspects of Foucault's work are disputed among scholars.[2]

Hardt and Negri's common work is heavily influenced by Foucault's conception of power, but the authors simultaneously use his central ideas in an eclectic and somewhat controversial way. The general power structure in present society—what is called Empire—is best considered a global network[3] of power that is steadily expanding to all surrounding areas of the globe and society. In that sense, the authors claim, today there is nothing outside of Empire. These imperial structures are basically brought to life by the biopolitical flows of the multitude that constitute the crux of economic and social life. The passage from

---

1 Sometimes articulated as "conduct of conduct" (Foucault 1994, 237).

2 Compare, for instance, the different approaches of Nealon (2008, 45) and Dean (1999, Chapters 4 and 5; 2003, 113).

3 Foucault talks about specific dispositifs or apparatuses of power (e.g., a disciplinary apparatus). These are local and in a sense delimited networks or grids of power. For that reason, he would probably hesitate to adopt Hardt and Negri's concept of an all-embracing network, Empire.

Fordist to biopolitical production[4] and cycles of resistance from the multitude have forced capital to respond in a flexible way, thereby fortifying its control over production and society. Hardt and Negri describe the exercise of power "from above" aimed at stabilizing capitalist control and imperial rule as biopower,[5] while the counter-power or biopolitics of the multitude "from below" is actually primary: it is the power of life itself.

This network of power is multifaceted and incorporates what classical Marxism considers both base and superstructure. But Hardt and Negri's analyses show that while a basic "glue" keeping the network together is capital's wish to maintain and expand its control, in every nodal point of the network resistance—or at least its possibility—also resides.

The overall picture we get from Hardt and Negri's analyses can be described as follows: Today's complex network of power is marked by different figures of subjectivity at different points in the web, with specific social relations and struggles taking place. Throughout history this network constantly but slowly changes form (more along a Foucauldian line of thought than a classical Marxist understanding); that is, the relations of power have their specific forms in Empire, as well as in our age of crisis, although struggles over the common seem ever present. For a countermovement against imperial and capitalist power, it seems necessary, in this general network, to adopt a clear position for autonomy and authentic anti-capitalist practices based on the common.

The special focus on subjective nodal points in the power network is similar to the forms of power described as self-creation or "technologies of the self," a main interest of Foucault, especially in his later works (see also Foucault 1984). This concept may approach what Hardt and Negri call subjectivity production, although this term seems to allude more to a shaping of the subject from outside—that is, through external powers—than to an active self-fashioning initiated by the subject. As should become evident, this is not necessarily a contradiction but, rather, a matter of complementarity. In any case, this duality corresponds in a certain sense to Hardt and Negri's distinction between biopower from above and the biopolitical power of the multitude.

Hardt and Negri's conception of power can be considered more Marxist than Foucault's, in the sense that the multiple forms of power in the global structure of Empire are tightly connected to the societal development of production. Roughly put, changes in labor—from the Fordist regime to biopolitical or immaterial labor—are the cause of changes in the dispositifs of power. This new form

---

4 In biopolitical production what is produced are not just commodities, but affects, relations, subjectivities, and forms of life—indeed, life in general.

5 A concept taken from Foucault, designating power over a population's life processes.

of social production is the bios that "drives the system." Consequently, they can say that "what Foucault fails to grasp finally are the real dynamics of production in biopolitical society" (Hardt & Negri 2000, 28). These changes in the regime of production are, for instance, the explanation for the general passage from disciplinary society to a "society of control."[6] Some commentators, for instance, Mitchell Dean (2003, 111–14, 116–18), criticize Hardt and Negri for misinterpreting Foucault and reducing the multifarious character of power when describing historical development as such clean cuts between different formations of power (discipline and control, respectively), especially when these are explained by changes in production. Furthermore, Dean claims the authors turn the complexity of power and the relation between Empire and the multitude into too simple and binary an opposition between repressing biopower from above and counter-power from below, that is, bad and good power.

Although there may be some truth to these criticisms, I describe below how Hardt and Negri's analyses of subjectivity production also have an eye open for other kinds of power that are not tightly connected to the realm of production or other parts of what is traditionally considered the economic base of society. For this purpose, in this context it may be useful to employ categorizations of power inspired by Foucault, but broader than the specific Foucauldian ones, especially the categories of structural, discursive, and practical power.[7] As should become clear, the most important inspiration from Foucault is the general focus on the ways in which multiple forms of power shape subjectivity in present society and the way Hardt and Negri use this to emphasize how practices of resistance specific to our time of crisis can attempt to create alternative subjectivities based on commonality and autonomy.

Different types of crisis

When politicians and media talk about crisis, they usually mean the present crisis in economic growth. But for Hardt and Negri, as for many critical theorists, crisis is something much more fundamental. In their works, Hardt and Negri analyze at least three different kinds of crises. The historical period called modernity is characterized by a deep contradiction between the original, revolutionary cultural and societal forces discovering immanence and fighting transcendence and the reactionary countermovement trying to reinstall transcendent thought and political sovereignty (Hardt & Negri 2000, 74ff). Throughout history this divide has constituted a permanent crisis, constantly threatening stability but al-

6 A term taken from Gilles Deleuze (1992).

7 For a more detailed unfolding of these categories of power, see also Poulsen (2006).

so driving historical development. Today, according to Hardt and Negri, modernity and its institutions are no longer capable of holding back the revolutionary forces of the multitude.

Analyzing the present economic and financial crisis, we see at a deeper level what Hardt and Negri describe as a *biopolitical* crisis, that is, a much more fundamental crisis than can be seen from superficial economic and financial fluctuations. The authors' basic claim (Hardt & Negri 2009, 143ff) is that the capitalist form of management impedes productive potential in the present biopolitical production (see also Christensen et al. 2012, 113–114). The common foundation for innovation, creativity, and cooperation is undermined by the widespread attempts at privatization and monopolization, for example through patents. The increasing tendency toward precarization of work further supports this development, simply because tired, hungry, or unsecure workers have less creative energies and ideas to display the kind of autonomy and flexibility required by biopolitical production. A third element mentioned by Hardt and Negri (2009, 147–148) is the attempt to control or erect barriers for the global flows of the workforce, for instance expressed in national or regional policies directed at the exclusion or marginalization of migrants and non-citizens.

The basic analysis of Hardt and Negri is that capitalist production, as a response to the anti-capitalist struggles of the working class, has since the 1970s undergone a transformation from a Fordist, or disciplinary, regime to one of control and biopolitical production. For a certain period of time this paved the way for more innovation and flexibility in capitalist production, resulting in increased economic growth and social stability, but today this temporary solution to the fundamental crisis of postmodern capitalism is no longer attainable. In the present situation, only a supersession of capitalism can unleash the general intellect and productive powers of the multitude.

From a certain perspective, the above description is, nevertheless, still too narrow. The deeper crisis outlined above is caused not only by the change in the regime of production (from Fordism to biopolitical production), but also by broader changes in the role of commonality in present social life. Today, the common wealth of society, the common pool of resources and possibilities, is increasingly connected with social and cultural value and to a lesser degree with material necessities or economic growth. Capitalist control of economic and social life can hardly create more material growth, Hardt and Negri claim, but it can definitely not fulfill the social wishes and desires of the multitude, more generally. This requires the coordinated abilities and autonomous cooperation of all parts of society.

The present economic crisis has *intensified* struggles over the common. We have seen this in the social struggles around the globe in the last decades over basic common resources such as water and land, as well as in the neoliberal strategies for the extensive privatization of public goods and abolition of social rights, and, possibly more important, in the intensive and occasionally successful struggles to fight these policies and defend the common. In a way, it is the same fundamental struggle that has taken place throughout history, a struggle between the multitudinous forces of the common and the reactionary forces of sovereignty and private property. It is a contradiction that has constituted a permanent crisis internal to capitalist modernity.

Struggles over the common

One might consider the concept of the common as the most important in Hardt and Negri's work, even more important than those of Empire or multitude. A range of specific struggles over the common and the common origins of societal life are taking place in our age. The *dynamic* character of these struggles is possibly better understood through this concept than, for instance, through the overarching and more structural concept of Empire.

Hardt and Negri's description of the fundamental role of the common turns the traditional perspective on its head: capital profits from society and the productive activities of its members, not the other way around, and most people contribute in creating value—material, social, cultural, or, in some other way, human value—whether they work in a factory or similar institution or not. This common pool of value and resources is utilized or even drained by capital. As a matter of fact, the quest for profit and growth is dependent on the common, a fact that mainstream economic science and even the media and politicians, for that matter, do not seem aware of. Hardt and Negri call capital a parasite or, inspired by Gilles Deleuze and Félix Guattari (1987, 442ff), an apparatus of capture feeding on the common.[8] In that sense, today exploitation is a violating phenomenon to which most members of society may consider themselves subjected to.

In the traditional Marxist understanding, exploitation means the theft of the value of surplus labor, which, in principle, can be calculated from the extra work hours the worker labors for the capitalist without being paid. Those who are exploited are the workers, who can count the amount of hours they work in the factory—not the women working at home, the students, or the unemployed or other groups outside the traditional industrial working class. But Hardt and Negri

8 This perspective has a basic affinity with the old anarchist statement that property is theft: community and common property are somehow primary and the privatization of common values must be considered a derogation.

break with this logic. In the age of biopolitical production, the whole of society is a social factory.

Given their concept of the common, Hardt and Negri present not only an alternative description of the foundation of economic and social life, but also a new theory of value, that is, of who *creates* value and of what *is* of value. People working at home, students, volunteer workers, and the poor all contribute to the common production of value. This further paves the way for a new strategy of thinking political organization and alliances, at least in the sense that it becomes easier for traditionally divergent groups to see themselves as part of a common struggle—a struggle *for* the common, *through* the common.

Hardt and Negri call this multifaceted assemblage of social actors the multitude, but the concept has been notoriously criticized as being too diffuse and too speculative in various ways. Their confidence in the spontaneity, creativity, and solidarity of the multitude seems too often unfounded (Dyer-Witheford 2001, 70–80). On the contrary, their emphasis in their later work, especially *Commonwealth* (2009), on the common as something more fundamental and *integral* to the dynamics and reproduction of society—a dimension of society under continued construction and development—seems to constitute a stronger analysis, for several reasons:

- The concept of the common provides us with an understanding of the fundamental role of the common resources for capitalist valorization (what is conceptualized as externalities by mainstream economic science).
- We obtain a new understanding of exploitation as capital's "expropriation of the common" (Hardt & Negri 2004, 150) compared to certain traditional Marxist analyses (see also Christensen et al. 2012, 99).
- We can analyze how the present crisis is connected to various forms of corruption of the common, including different expressions of social pathologies.
- We obtain a tool to understand how different subjectivity figures are involved in, or are expressions of, struggles over the common, related to specific forms of power.
- As argued below, this concept facilitates a more individual psychological perspective in relation to which Hardt and Negri otherwise seem hesitating.

Following these reflections, it is clear that the concept of the common should be understood as both an economic, social, *and* psychological category.

Figures of subjectivity in the age of crisis

In their later text, *Declaration*, Hardt and Negri (2012) describe, how "the triumph of neoliberalism and its crisis" have fabricated "new figures of subjectivity," whom they call the indebted, the mediatized, the securitized, and the represented. One can identify many forms of subjectivity in present society, so what is the purpose of specifically distinguishing these four figures of subjectivity? At least one interesting perspective on these figures, unfolded below, is that it enables us to identify how different forms of power influence the subject in ways specific to our time. Furthermore, it is exactly in relation to these fields of subjectivity that change and resistance become not only necessary but also possible.

The represented

As a general claim, Hardt and Negri (2009, 346) tell us that parliamentary and other types of political representation take the form of a "disjunctive synthesis." This concept, which they borrow from Deleuze and Guattari, highlights the double character of representation: it simultaneously draws the multitude closer to the rulers and distances it from them (Hardt & Negri 2012). In this way representation is an integral part of modern sovereignty, since it gives people the impression of having a say in decision making and at the same time limits this to the minimum necessary (in parliamentary democracy a vote every four or five years).

This basic characterization is even more accurate today, with globalization and the diminished role of nation states. The possibility of simply feeling represented has vanished for large parts of the population and the politicians who should be representing us seem even more distant than before. According to Hardt and Negri, this development has played a crucial role for the many protests and rebellions in the last years, even in countries such as the United States or in the southern part of Europe, where the financial crisis has made evident the flaws of the institutions of parliamentary democracy.

The indebted

In the same way, Hardt and Negri explain how the phenomenon of debt has attained a central role in the present financialized economy and society, epitomized in the figure of the indebted. Everybody is indebted nowadays, to get a place to live, an education, or other basic means of subsistence, especially in a situation that cuts back on social welfare: "Today's new poor are ... the property of masters ... who rule through finance" (Hardt & Negri 2012). To be integrated in society, one must have debt.

But this indebtedness should be understood not only in the basic economic sense, but also in a much broader, psychological sense. We carry the burden of a permanent debt, a constant tendency to feel guilty and responsible toward current and future creditors or toward society or life as a whole.[9] It is almost, as Friedrich Nietzsche would say, a way of being human that is weighed down and inhibited by an eternal sense of guilt.

The securitized

The present societal situation is characterized by a permanent state of emergency (Hardt & Negri 2004, 7). The global institutions of Empire and the nation states have continuously developed new political and technological means to make life secure for their fearful citizens. This increasing securitization of society can be seen from the most general global level to everyday life, in the war on terror, the war on drugs, the war against rogues states and rebellions, and preemptive measures against crime, rebellions, and social unrest, all mixed together (Hardt & Negri 2012). The figure of the securitized is a form of subjectivity nurtured by lawmakers and security institutions, as well as the media.

The mediatized

Technological development in general and the development of the media and mediatization in particular have possibly been the most important factors in questions of identity and related social pathologies. This is probably the field where Foucauldian power and sneaking technologies of the self are mostly proliferating. Whether one wants to blame technology and social media and so forth in themselves as intrinsically bad or dangerous or, rather, as specific cultural forms that lead to isolation, superficiality, narcissism, and other pathologies, the basic fact of intensified social acceleration and informational overload can hardly be denied (Rosa 2010). We are all in the whirlwind of bigger and smaller self-technologies, whether or not we consciously wish for them, whether in social media or in the quest for a career, whether apparently self-determined or imposed upon us through social demands and expectations.

Once again, Hardt and Negri (2012) mainly focus on changes in present working life and biopolitical production: "Mediatization is a major factor in the increasingly blurred divisions between work and life." With our smartphones and wireless connections, we are always at work and thus always controlled—if

---

9 A condition exacerbated by the fact that in the present culture we always lack time (Rosa 2010).

nothing else, then at least through our conscience and self-monitoring.[10] But, furthermore, the media do not really make us passive, claim Hardt and Negri. On the contrary, we are supposed to participate, checking, liking, and commenting all the time, but this participation is not really being active in an ordinary sense. We are kept in some kind of intermediary position: "The mediatized is … a subjectivity that is paradoxically neither active nor passive but rather constantly absorbed in attention" (ibid.).[11] Hardt and Negri's analysis can extend to many other aspects of postmodern mediatization: one further phenomenon would, for instance, be how fear and media spectacle are today woven together in everyday culture and so-called democratic debate. The big news channels and debate programs seem to take pride in reducing the spread of information to fearmongering, toward your fellow citizens or the terrorists across the border (Hardt & Negri 2012).

These are just delimited examples of the ways in which subjectivities are formed and produced today, and the general power network is full of diverse connections and contradictory tendencies. However, for this context, the important theoretical point to stress is how the general Foucauldian perspective facilitates analyses of relations between specific forms of power and figures of subjectivity. The general picture may be persuasive: a (through media) *disquieted* population permanently oppressed by *guilt*, seeking *security* and wanting to transfer responsibility to the *representative*. For such a population a chaotic multitude constitutes no alternative but the experience and vision of commonality, the common, might. For that reason, my argument goes, the concept of the common seems more elucidating and promising.

Power and the figures of subjectivity

A very important point from the perspective of resistance is that we should not think of these forms of precarious subjectivities identified by Hardt and Negri as simply instances of straightforward repression. They are also points of struggle, in the sense that these societal problematics may also be places for people to meet and create commonality. In all these areas, we also find *potentials* for opposition and alternative organization. For instance, the new information technologies, social media, and so forth obviously offer improved possibilities for

10 Such panoptic power expressed as bad conscience and self-surveillance seems, interestingly, to apply to the figures of the mediatized, the indebted, and the securitized (for his original analysis of panopticism, see Foucault 1977, 195ff).

11 Current theorists go even further in their analysis of how our bodies and desires are affected by constant exposure to media (e.g. Berardi 2005, "Inconclusive excitation takes the place of orgasmic release)."

communication and cooperation—and therefore for resistance and the creation of commons. Similarly, as Hardt and Negri stress, protests against false representation and hollow political institutions and procedures give people the opportunity to experiment with other ways of being together, alternative ways of living and producing, and new forms of organization in general. In that sense these figures of subjectivities can act as both distorted, or corrupt, forms *and* as community-based forms of subjectivity, that is, forms based on the common.

The four points of struggle and their respective figures of subjectivity have become increasingly important nodal points in the power network of the society of crisis. This power can be understood as structural, practical, as well as discursive (or "ideological"). When all these dimensions of power are combined, the effect of this specific exercise of power is evidently stronger, which means they constitute an important foundation for the stabilization of the imperial network of power.

Throughout history, institutions such as the family, the corporation, and the nation state have been important forms of corruption of the common (Hardt & Negri 2009, 297ff), mainly because they are exclusive, narrowing their benefits to a delimited group, keeping others out. Nevertheless, they also constitute primary institutions, in which people in our society experience the common and express commonality and productive cooperation. Similarly, the new figures of subjectivity exhibit this same ambiguity and duality. One might consider whether the fundamental crisis throughout modernity has found a new and possibly radicalized form in (some of) these figures, in these important points of conflict for social being today.

It is important to note that, from a political perspective, the question of representation has a primary role in Hardt and Negri's (2012) analysis: "The figure of the represented gathers together the figures of the indebted, the mediatized, and the securitized." The struggle for a real democracy, an absolute democracy, can potentially counter all the other forms of subordination. Experimentation with democratic organization and new forms of being together can potentially break the "spell" of the other forms of impoverished subjectivity:

> Forces of rebellion and revolt allow us to throw off the impoverished subjectivities produced and continually reproduced by capitalist society in the contemporary crisis. A movement of organized refusal allows us to recognize who we have become and to set out on becoming different. (Hardt & Negri 2012).

We are all influenced by the norms and discourses tying us to the negative consequences of mediatization and securitization of (post)modern life, and possibly by the fading hope in the representative political system as well. We are also coerced by the practical necessities and structural constraints of our working life and specific societal position and possibly debt as well. The important point, however, Hardt and Negri make is that the production of subjectivity through the different forms of power described above can be counteracted by forms of subjective and social being, which are oriented toward experimentation and commonality. One objective for such practices of resistance may be seen as counteracting the widespread alienation in present culture.

Alienation today

With the visions of alternative, self-controlled forms of organization and being found in Hardt and Negri, one basic question is what hinders such potential from materializing itself? One straightforward although traditional answer may be the all-pervasive alienation in our culture. How does this answer fit into the theoretical framework of Hardt and Negri?

The concept of alienation is understood in many ways, in Marxism as well as other strands of thought, but one basic sense of the word might be the experience of being alien or distanced vis-à-vis the world or parts of it (possibly including oneself), which means a somehow "impoverished" being. In this sense, certain features of the world or society create this alienated condition and further make it impossible to avoid. Traditionally, implicit in the concept is the notion of either a more original situation or a still unattained future condition without this experience of alienation.

Hardt and Negri apparently do not spend much time on the classical Marxist concept of alienation. They do, however, point out that alienation is more pervasive today, compared to earlier regimes of production (Hardt & Negri 2009, 140). One definition of alienation in Karl Marx (specifically the younger Marx) is that the worker in capitalist industrial production loses the possibility of experiencing and unfolding his or her skills as a creative being, the power to creatively transform reality. Marx contrasts this monotonous, divided, and externally determined working process in the capitalist factory or agricultural production with previous forms of craft production, in which the individual worker had control of the entire production of a commodity, and not just part of the process.

However, even though such alienation can be profound, it was, in Fordist production, still confined to the walls of the factory or workplace. In the rest of one's life, one could still be something other than a wage earner, as it were, and not all aspects of workers' subjectivity were related to their job. Given the expansive character of work time in biopolitical production—specifically with the increasing importance of affective labor and the production of knowledge, subjectivity, and social relations—Hardt and Negri (2004, 111) conclude that a broadening of alienation has taken place; it now permeates even people's experiences with themselves as affective, social, and intellectually creative beings:

> When affective production becomes part of waged labor it can be experienced as extremely alienating: I am selling my ability to make human relationships, something extremely intimate, at the command of the client and the boss. Alienation was always a poor concept for understanding the exploitation of factory workers, but here in a realm that many do not want to consider labor – affective labor, as well as knowledge production as well as symbolic production – alienation does provide a useful conceptual key for understanding exploitation.

An important point is that the most intimate—and most human—of our personal traits and abilities are appropriated and (partly) controlled by the capitalist, or at least utilized for purposes that are not our own.

But this idea that alienation has become more widespread or more profound seems only to make sense if we have an implicit notion of a real existential (if not ethical) difference between various ways of using one's creative and social skills. We seem to approach a classical concept of *authenticity* (and of alienation). If there is a "false" manner of being on the job that can haunt us even when we are no longer at work, then there also has to be a state of being without such alienation. Imagine, for instance, the stereotypical salesperson with a big smile and servility.[12] A spontaneous critical reaction might in certain cases be to feel this fellow human being is acting superficially, exaggeratedly, or falsely to make us buy a product. The very interesting point is that in most cases such situations do not involve conscious behavior, nor is it a question of either/or, of simply being false or not. On the contrary, most people experience this form of being stretched between social expectations, our roles,[13] and staying true to oneself. In other words, the described form of alienation in present work life is alienation in its standard form; it occurs in subtle and complex ways that none of us fully understand or know how to avoid.

This is the basic idea of alienation (in the workplace) of Hardt and Negri, but the concept of alienation seems to apply more extensively, to broader phenomena in present culture. Still, the relation between such alienation and the figures of subjectivity, which Hardt and Negri analyze, remains to be determined.

---

12 One might also recall Jean-Paul Sartre's (1994, 59–60) famous depiction of the waiter in Being and Nothingness.

13 Usually supported by various forms of discursive power promoting specific norms or ideals for how to be successful, and so forth, in your job, your social (and virtual) relations, and life in general.

Alienation and the common

The kind of alienation described above (epitomized in the salesperson) seems affiliated with the kind of superficiality and attention captivity potentially resulting from the mediatization described by Hardt and Negri. That such psychological pressure in the work sphere or, more broadly, in our culture, can lead to pathological forms such as exaggerated other-directedness and narcissism is, of course, not a new phenomenon.[14] The new element might, instead, be the intensity and extension of these phenomena.

While Hardt and Negri claim that alienation has deepened for the worker and spread to all parts of the worker's life, it seems the authors do not want to extend the concept to other obvious parts of our culture: "Whereas the consciousness of the alienated worker is separated or divided, the consciousness of the mediatized is subsumed or absorbed in the web. The consciousness of the mediatized is not really split but fragmented and dispersed" (Hardt & Negri 2012).

Whether split or fragmented, we are in many such situations confronted with comprehensive, discursive and practical types of psychological pressure (or power), creating broader forms of social pathology, all of which are in a certain humanist tradition labeled alienation.[15] Do the authors, in this context, fail to see a certain type of power connected to alienation, alienation understood in a more traditional sense? One can point to recent, extremely interesting analyses of social and technological acceleration and its tendency to cause various forms of alienation, most notably in the work of Hartmut Rosa (2010). The entire network of what Franco Berardi (2005) calls the infosphere is part of a hypermodern power dispositif of mediatization, which stresses and tendentially splinters human beings and impedes the possibility of self-determined self-creation.

From such considerations, it seems obvious that we need some notion of a way of being, which is the positive alterity of alienation. One candidate would be the concept of authenticity, that is, the idea of a subjective and social mode of being that (to some degree) succeeds in resisting the dominant forms of capitalist ideology and power. Such a notion of authenticity does not, however, really seem to fit into Hardt and Negri's (2012) theoretical framework:

> The old cultural projects against alienation wanted you to return to yourself. They battled the ways in which capitalist society and ideology have separated us from

---

14 See, for instance, the classical social psychological works by Thomas Ziehe (1975) and Christopher Lasch (1979).

15 They want, of course, to avoid some kind of old-fashioned essentialism associated with "humanism" with a very simple scheme of some real, inner self as opposed to the false being or consciousness of capitalist society (see also Hardt & Negri 2012).

> ourselves, broken us in two, and thus sought a form of wholeness and authenticity, most often in individual terms. When you become a singularity, instead, you will never be a whole self. Singularities are defined by being multiple internally and finding themselves externally only in relation to others.

One could ask whether Hardt and Negri's presentation here of traditional humanist conceptions of alienation and authenticity allows us to fully appreciate the depth of these concepts. It is a basic feature of the authors' philosophy, however, to avoid focusing on individuals. Human beings are political forces, social groups, singularities, or, at best, subjects, but they rarely stand forth in Hardt and Negri's texts as individuals, specific personalities, or psychological enigmas. The authors' focus is sociological or political, never psychological or what they might call humanistic. Nevertheless, they declare sympathy to the "humanism of Foucault's final works."[16] Concluding a discussion of the apparently contradictory notions of humanism in Foucault (and in their own work), Hardt and Negri (2000, 92) state, "This is humanism after the death of Man ... the continuous constituent project to create and re-create ourselves and our world."

In their analysis of the different social uprisings and movements in recent years, Hardt and Negri point in a similar direction. When people act and live together in an intense manner with very concrete practices, profound meetings between people unfold in spontaneous although unexpected ways. The important element in people creating common understandings is often simply their being together, as they have been for weeks or months in city squares or the streets during the multiple protests around the globe in the last years. Hardt and Negri (2012) stress the importance of the protestors' experiences when organizing infrastructure for occupations and protest activities, providing solidarity measures and daily comfort among the participants, and simply being intensely and physically together.

This is, in a way, a very Foucauldian (or Althusserian[17]) conception of power—and counter-power. Power is, first, something practical. Continued, maybe even ritualized activities form our subjectivity. This phenomenon is similar to the disciplinary practices that Foucault (1977) analyzes in great detail: Simply

---

16 One might be tempted to say that Hardt and Negri keep struggling through their works with this ongoing ménage à trois between humanism, Marxism, and post-structuralism (see their discussion of the concept—and tradition—of humanism in Hardt & Negri 2000, 91–92; 2009, 136, 139–140).

17 See Louis Althusser's (1970, 127) interpretation of Blaise Pascal's injunction: "Kneel down, move your lips in prayer, and you will believe." The practice itself will change your subjectivity.

participating in certain practices, in principle regardless of theoretical reflection, will form your body and subjectivity: a very practical form of power.[18]

Hardt and Negri further note that these protest movements have somehow created an autonomous time. The slow pace of decision making in direct democracy and the practice of waiting at occupied squares and simply being there together constitute an alternative to the pressure of capitalist time schedules and neoliberal efficiency mania. The opposition between the alienating powers of capitalist Empire and social and humane ways of being is evident.[19] A very important point drawn from the analyses of Hardt and Negri is that subjectivities based on the common unfold or develop forms of *unmediated*—or non-alienated, if one prefers—social connectedness. As a very broad statement, individualization and isolation, that is, distancing oneself from the common foundations of social life, is a form of alienation.[20] Such forms of alternative being could be seen as a point connecting authenticity understood individually, or "existentially," with authenticity understood as a collective and political concept.

One might therefore say that this critique of Hardt and Negri concerns more certain topics their work does not address—work that my reflections may then supplement—rather than proper flaws in their analyses. In any case, my claim would be that neither Hardt and Negri nor any of their congenial theorists have yet offered an alternative language regarding the problematic of subjectivity and authenticity. We are, for better and for worse, stuck in the language and thought of humanism; social pathologies brought about by the dominant structures of power are a corruption of humanity, of a better way of being together, of the common.

18 In contrast to a more rationalistic conception of (discursive) power as ideology, understood as false thinking.

19 In a similar vein, we can see refreshing glimpses of moral indignation pointing toward a notion of authenticity in Hardt and Negri (2012), for instance, when they talk about "the deafening imbecility of the media circus." In their discussion of mediatization today, they even point to Deleuze's statement that the problem is "providing little gaps of solitude and silence in which [people] might eventually find something to say" (2012).

20 This very general social philosophical statement does not, of course, imply that specific ways of being per se—for instance, concentrating on individual or solitary life projects—constitute alienation (see also the analysis above of social norms and pressure as a main cause for certain forms of alienation). The point is, rather, a certain attitude of commonality in contrast toegoism or forced isolation.

Being outside, being against

Our time of crisis, with people struggling for survival and trying to defend their basic social rights, has brought about many new forms of social organization for coping with harsh living conditions. Even in formerly wealthy parts of the world, such as Southern Europe, large parts of the population have been pushed toward precarization and marginalization. Larger groups than ever, for instance, have lost their homes or their jobs or, if they still have a job, they must work for a minimal salary that cannot support them. In this situation, we find people gathering to squat houses to live in or to organize concrete resistance, often physical blockades, to avoid that people get thrown out of their homes when they cannot pay the debt. In some countries workers have occupied factories or other workplaces to start self-governed production. Other groups have started agricultural production to provide for their own means of subsistence, while still others have established self-governed local exchange trading systems (LETS), transcending the logic of the capitalist market. Certain neighborhoods and cities have even introduced their own alternative currency.

The long-time tradition and practice of house squatting and social centers have also proliferated, although in many countries the state has responded with severe repression. Generally, experiments with alternative forms of life have become accessible to larger parts of the population. In a sense, old left radical practices and the idea of creating "free spaces" that are to some extent real alternatives to capitalist structures have been revitalized because of the present crisis. For many people today, they represent the best or only solution to the immediate threat to their ways of life. In academic and political fora, such alternative organizations of ways of life based on the common and on self-government have been increasingly discussed in recent years under the term *commons* (see e.g. Caffentzis 2004). Just as commons are in permanent development as a social phenomenon, so is the *concept* among participants, reflecting their own practices in various contexts.

Since natural commons have been increasingly appropriated and enclosed by capital through the last centuries, many leftist groups focus on cultural or social forms of commons, that is, the places or institutions in which people cooperate on a collective basis and/or with a sense of commonality. With their concept of the common, Hardt and Negri similarly emphasize the *cultural* dimension of our economic and social life.[21] For many anti-capitalists today, the basic

---

21 In their main writings, Hardt and Negri do not address the question of commons or social projects outside of market logics directly, but in Empire (2000, 44–45) they offer a critique of projects on the Left defending the 'local' or trying to create local 'spaces' outside of the capitalist global market (which they consider an impossible project). It is not

task is partly to defend and partly to develop such commons in their various forms. But since commons can very well be capitalist in nature, or at least under its control and utilized by capital, it seems essential for an anti-capitalist countermovement to have some criteria for what constitutes a real alternative to capitalist logics. In addition to the presence of a common pool of resources, a well-defined community with certain shared values and caring among the participants seems essential. Furthermore, collectively developed and accepted rules and obligations for the organization of the common, that is, some form of participatory democracy, seem crucial.[22]

We can see two important dimensions in these reflections on anti-capitalist commons: the common *practices*, through which people live and develop, and certain shared *values* and discourses on their common project. From a Foucauldian perspective, one might say that these commons, as a cultural movement, combine elements of practical and discursive counter-power and, as such, forms of power that oppose the *structural* power of capitalist Empire. This discursive counter-power could then, as explained above, be understood very broadly as a discourse and self-understanding aware of shared non-capitalist values and a consequent attempt at subjective and collective authenticity and autonomy.[23] The important point is, of course, that we are all heavily influenced by the society in which we live. In that sense no social projects or ways of being can be fully outside the social logics of capitalism. The general outcome of such experimentation in alternatives is thus, of course, always uncertain, but for Hardt and Negri (2012) stating a clear oppositional position is certainly necessary: "An alternative is … a new dispositif that is based in a radically asymmetrical standpoint.… Its autonomy makes coherent the rhythms of its temporality, as well as its production of subjectivities, struggles, and constituent principles."

---

entirely clear how these arguments relate to considerations like the ones I undertake here. But at least their central claim that there is no more any 'outside' to the imperial network of power (2000, 186ff) might seem difficult to reconcile with the idea of (relatively) autonomous commons. See also Negri et al. (2008) for Negri's skepticism regarding such attempts of "soft" forms of societal change.

22 These points are inspired by Silvia Federici and George Caffentzis (public talk, Copenhagen, 26-01-13).

23 Such an awareness could hopefully make it possible to avoid the new production of subjectivity and commonality turning into traditional structures of identity and domination, or a defense of particularistic interests, as it has been seen in many leftist experiments and organizations throughout history (e.g., Hardt & Negri 2004, 354ff). See also Hardt and Holloway (2010) for a discussion of the creation of "new, democratic institutional forms".

Whether we talk about smaller, local projects or larger-scale organizations of commons, a basic awareness of the values involved in different forms of social organization seems crucial. For countermovements today and critical thinking about society, clearly articulating the *difference* between the subjective and social logics[24] that characterize the capitalist network of power and alternative, anti-capitalist commons seems a basic task.

Conclusion

To conclude, Hardt and Negri offer a genuine analysis of the global network of power, Empire, heavily inspired by Michel Foucault. Their analysis emphasizes the pluralistic character of power together with the relation of the general power structure to capital and the development of capitalism (thereby linking Foucauldian post-structuralism with a Marxist perspective).

The authors present a profound historical understanding of the present crisis and the common. The present crisis is a fundamental cultural and political crisis, with certain figures of subjectivity—analyzed by Hardt and Negri—being more central to social struggles than before. Hardt and Negri's analyses offer fruitful insights into the ways in which individuals and social groups in present society stand vis-à-vis diverse forms of power. Today, in times of economic crisis, new forms of subjectivity are produced by various forms of power, leading either to subjectivities weakened by apathy and isolation or to new forms of commonality and resistance.

Especially in the authors' later works, the concept of the common plays a central role; it might be considered the *normative* pivotal point in their thought: the dimension of society around which social struggles take place. Their unfolding of this concept is important as an alternative to neoliberal politics, economics, and subjectivities. I have discussed the phenomenon of alienation in the context of present society and hint at the idea that we need a notion of some form of counter-identity oriented toward the common to clarify basic contradictions in our way of being social creatures. My discussion offers critical questions to Hardt and Negri's understanding of classical 'humanist' concepts such as alienation and authenticity. Finally, I have argued that such concepts, in an up-to-date political form, are still useful for a critical understanding of the various forms of capitalist power in present society and for attempts at resisting and creating social alternatives.

In conclusion, Hardt and Negri's analyses provide important conceptual tools for understanding the present struggles over the common as part of a fun-

---

24 See also Poulsen (2009).

damental cultural crisis, with multiple forms of imperial power and counter-powers confronting each other in the struggle over what kinds of subjectivities we should become.

References

Althusser, Louis. 1994. "Ideology and ideological state apparatuses" (1970). In *Mapping Ideology,* edited by Slavoj Žižek. London: Verso.

Berardi, Franco. 2005. "Biopolitics and connective mutation." *Culture Machine* 7.

Caffentzis, George. 2004. "A Tale of Two Conferences: Globalization, the Crisis of Neoliberalism and Question of the Commons." Available at http://sduk.us/silvia_george_david/caffentzis_a_tale_of_two_conferences.pdf

Christensen, Pil; Nielsen, Peter; and Poulsen, Lars. 2012. *Magt og modstand. En introduktion til Michael Hardt og Antonio Negris tænkning.* Frederiksberg: Frydenlund.

Dean, Mitchell. 1999. *Governmentality. Power and Rule in Modern Society.* London: Sage Publications.

Dean, Mitchell. 2003. "Empire and governmentality." *Distinktion: Scandinavian Journal of Social Theory* 3.

Deleuze, Gilles. 1992. "Postscript on the societies of control." *OCTOBER_* 59, winter. Cambridge: MIT Press.

Deleuze, Gilles and Guattari, Félix. 1987. *A Thousand Plateaus. Capitalism and Schizophrenia.* University of Minnesota Press.

Dyer-Witheford, Nick. 2001. "Empire, immaterial labor, the new combinations, and the global worker." *Rethinking Marxism* 13(3/4): 70-80.

Foucault, Michel. 1977. *Discipline and Punish. The Birth of the Prison.* London: Penguin Books.

Foucault, Michel. 1982: "The subject and power." In *Michel Foucault. Beyond Structuralism and Hermeneutics,* edited by Hubert L. Dreyfus and Paul Rabinow. Chicago: University of Chicago Press.

Foucault, Michel. 1994. *Dits et écrits IV.* Paris: Gallimard.

Foucault, Michel. 1997. "The Ethics of the Concern for the Self as a Practice of Freedom." In *Foucault 1997: Ethics: Subjectivity and Truth, Essential Works 1*: 281-301.

Hardt, Michael, and Holloway, John. 2010. "Creating common wealth and cracking capitalism: a cross-reading." *Shift Magazine* 14 & 15.

Hardt, Michael, and Negri, Antonio. 2000. *Empire*. London: Harvard University Press.

Hardt, Michael, and Negri, Antonio. 2004. *Multitude – War and Democracy in the Age of Empire*. New York: Penguin Press.

Hardt, Michael, and Negri, Antonio. 2009. *Commonwealth*. Cambridge: Belknap Press.

Hardt, Michael, and Negri, Antonio. 2012. *Declaration*, pamphlet distributed by Argo Navis Author Services. Available at http://antonionegriinenglish.files.wordpress.com/2012/05/93152857-hardt-negri-declaration-2012.pdf

Lasch, Christopher. 1979. *The Culture of Narcissism: American Life in an Age of Diminishing Expectations*. New York: Warner Books.

Lukes, Steven. 2005. *Power. A Radical View*. New York: Palgrave Macmillan.

Nealon, Jeffrey T. 2008. *Foucault beyond Foucault: Power and Its Intensifications since 1984*. California: Stanford University Press.

Negri, Antonio; Petcou, Constantin; Petrescu, Doina; and Querrien, Anne. 2008. "What makes a biopolitical space? A discussion with Toni Negri." *Eurozine* January 21.

Poulsen, Lars. 2006. "Kapitalismens subtile magtformer." In *Økonomi og samfund 2007,* edited by Peter Nielsen. Copenhagen: Frydenlund.

Poulsen, Lars. 2009. "Fællesskabets forsvinden." In *Værdikampe,* edited by Peter Nielsen and Lars Poulsen. Copenhagen: Frydenlund.

Rosa, Hartmut. 2010. *Alienation & Acceleration. Towards a Critical Theory of Late-Modern* Temporality. Malmö: NSU Press.

Sartre, Jean-Paul. 1994. *Being and Nothingness*. New York: Gramercy Books.

Ziehe, Thomas. 1975. *Pubertät und Narzissmus Sind Jugendliche entpolitisiert?* Frankfurt-am-Main, Cologne: Europäische Verlagsanstalt.

9. The Creative Democratic Potential of the Multitude: Solidarity and Love as Transcendence in Immanence

Christian Ydesen

> 'Every act of love, one might say, is an ontological event in that it marks a rupture with existing beings and creates new being, from poverty through love to being.' (Hardt & Negri 2009, 181)

Introduction

In Michael Hardt and Antonio Negri's works, love as a political philosophical concept plays a privileged role in understanding the creative political potential of the Common in general and the Multitude in particular. On the other hand, the historically powerful concept of solidarity is left to only play a role as a survival mechanism of the poor (Hardt & Negri 2009, 180). But while the ontological status, content definitions, and interconceptual relations of the two concepts remain somewhat blurred in Hardt and Negri's writings, such an undertaking might be remedied through construction of the concepts as transcendence in immanence.

This article analyzes the social ontology of the common—the very foundation of the multitude's democratic potential—using the interconnected philosophical frameworks of Martin Buber and Michael Theunissen with a specific focus on the two concepts of love and solidarity. Buber's and Theunissen's frameworks provide the opportunity to analyze precisely the ontological status, content definitions, and interconceptual relations of the two concepts as transcendence in immanence, using dialogical thinking and thematizing the *Other* in relation to universality.

The purpose of the article is then to uncover what is specifically constitutive of love and solidarity used as political philosophical concepts in relation to the common in general and the multitude's creative democratic potential in particular. On this basis, the article sets out to address and validate the universal outlines of love and solidarity as inevitable human phenomena, thus claiming validity in a post-crisis scenario.

Rehabilitating the concept of solidarity vis-à-vis Hardt and Negri's thinking, this article argues that love and solidarity both represent indispensable dimensions in human existence that hold considerable creative and democratic potential, compatible with Hardt and Negri's general notions about the Multitude and the Common. A modified understanding of the Common's social ontology holds the potential to reconstitute and reconfigure democracy in a post-crisis scenario.

The creative democratic potential of the multitude

A core feature of Hardt and Negri's philosophical writings is the democracy of the multitude based on its immanent potential for self-governance, that is, "the rule of everyone by everyone" (Hardt & Negri 2004, 100). According to the authors, this democracy is a genuine and absolute democracy, as opposed to the present states of democracy under the reign of empire (Hardt & Negri 2004, 351).

Hardt and Negri present a meticulous analysis of the failures, paradoxes, and inadequacies of contemporary democracy which have resulted in the distortion of power, failures of representation, and ultimately oppression (Hardt & Negri 2004, 231ff). These systemic failures, characteristic and closely tied to the functionality of empire, optimistically provide hope that the omnipresent crisis of empire will create a space for the emergence of a new absolute democracy from the creative and innovative ranks of the Multitude. The ontological foundation of this hope is the transition of sovereignty to the plane of immanence, meaning that empire and multitude operate on the same level. There is no longer a transcendent realm able to suppress the creative forces of the multitude.

This transition to the plane of immanence with no transcendent power hubs and the ubiquitous inadequacies of contemporary democracy require questioning the nature of democracy in a post-crisis scenario because the current economic crisis can be viewed as a process reshuffling and creating new openings and possible solutions and developments that were formerly barred and beyond reach. In this respect the many recent uprisings—such as the Arab Spring, the Occupy movement, and *Los Indignados* in Spain—can be seen as evidence of this reshuffling (Hardt & Negri 2012). In fact, the common currency of so many struggles and movements for liberation across the world today—at local, regional, and global levels—is the desire for democracy (Hardt & Negri 2004).

Investigating the nature of the multitude's democracy, Hardt and Negri (2009, viii) explain that

> A democracy of the multitude is imaginable and possible only because we all share and participate in the common. By "the common" we mean, first of all, the common wealth of the material world – the air, the water, the fruits of the soil, and all nature's bounty.... We consider the common also and more significantly those results of social production that are necessary for social interaction and further production, such as knowledges, languages, codes, information, affects and so forth.

As clearly indicated by the quote, the central component in the creative potential and ontological nature of the multitude's democracy is the common. The potential is augmented by the transition to the hegemony of immaterial labor under the age of empire, which dramatically increases the significance of the common. As demonstrated, the production of knowledges, languages, codes, information, affects, and so forth, taking place in the common negates the Hobbesian dictum of "*bellum omnium contra omnes*" that has permeated Western political thinking for centuries, installing a regime of scarcity rooted in material industrial production and an accompanying mindset puzzled by how to distribute material goods (Hardt & Negri 2004, 310f).

But what is the social ontology of the common? This is an important question to approach an understanding of the creative potential of the multitude's democracy and thus grasp and subsequently reconstitute and reconfigure democracy in a post-crisis scenario.

The social ontology of the common

As a way of describing the social ontology of the common, Hardt and Negri seek to revive the medieval English figure of the "commoner," This figure was associated with being productive and Hardt and Negri make it clear that the commoner in fact "commons," that is, makes the common (Hardt & Negri 2012). More concretely, the commoner is

> Opening private property to the access and enjoyment of all; transforming public property' controlled by state authority into the common; and in each case discovering mechanisms to manage, develop, and sustain common wealth through democratic participation. The task of the commoner, then, is not only to provide access to the fields and rivers so that the poor can feed themselves, but also to create a means for the free exchange of ideas, images, codes, music, and information. We have already seen some of the prerequisites for accomplishing these tasks: the ability to create social bonds with each other, the power of singularities to communicate through differences, the real security of the fearless, and the capacity for democratic political action. The commoner is a constituent participant, the subjectivity that is foundational and necessary for constituting a democratic society based on open sharing of the common. (Hardt & Negri 2012)

However, it is important to understand that

> Commoning does not involve ... imagining that identities can be negated such that all will discover they are, at base, the same. No, the common has nothing to do with sameness. Instead, in struggle, different social groups interact as singularities and are enlightened, inspired, and transformed by their exchange with each other. They speak to each other on the lower frequencies, which people outside of the struggle often cannot hear or understand. (Hardt & Negri 2012)

Thus, the multitude inhabiting the common remains a swarm of singularities. In this context, the singular refers to the uniqueness of each individual as it pertains to different practices and ways of life. This fundamental uniqueness prevents singularities from melting together but ensures that their idiosyncrasies are preserved, even though they share a number of common characteristics, values, and methods of organization. To Hardt and Negri, singularity is the one crucial binary of the multitude, the common being the other. Thus, the multitude can at the same time be one and internally diversified.

To understand the innovative and creative production of the common, Hardt and Negri (2009, 57) find inspiration in Foucault and introduce the concept of the biopolitical, meaning "the power of life to resist and determine an alternative production of subjectivity." The biopolitical must also be understood as an opposition to *biopower*, that is, the power over life exercised by empire.

However, Hardt and Negri's outline of the social ontology of the common has not been received without criticism. The following presents some main points of criticism and uses them as a starting point for an expanded and corrective analysis of the common's social ontology with a focus on the key concepts of love and solidarity.

Criticism and potential for further analysis

The recent book by Danish researchers Pil Christensen, Peter Nielsen, and Lars Poulsen (2012, 135) about Hardt and Negri makes the point that "the all-encompassing and – in part – speculative character of the multitude is a drawback; e.g. in relation to the optimistic belief in the almost spontaneous unification and ability to resistance [my translation]." These points of criticism suggest that the actual conceptual construction of the Multitude in general and its potential in particular remain somewhat blurred and unclear, with detrimental effects on the potential to understand the nature of the multitude's democracy constituted by the biopolitical production and interaction between singularities and between singularities and the common.

Although Hardt and Negri reject this criticism of the multitude's creative potential, it resonates with Slovenian philosopher Slavoj Zizek (2005), who starts his criticism with Karl Marx and subsequently aims it against Hardt and Negri:

> If we abolish the obstacle, the inherent contradiction of capitalism, we do not get the fully unleashed drive to productivity finally delivered of its impediment, but we lose precisely this productivity that seemed to be generated and simultaneously thwarted by capitalism – if we take away the obstacle, the very potential thwarted by this ob-

> stacle dissipates ... or, in the case of Hardt and Negri, the illusory vision of multitude ruling itself, no longer constrained by any totalizing One.

This critique attacks the very construction of the plane of immanence, suggesting that the loss of transcendence—and thereby the workings of dialectics—will result in the loss of productivity and thus the very ability of the multitude to rule itself.

However, I argue that Hardt and Negri's ontological framework holds the potential for overcoming this critique, but in the authors' eagerness to praise the importance of the plane of immanence and distance themselves from any type of transcendence and dialectics, they are unable—or mistakenly unwilling—to realize this potential. It only lives a life in the shadow of their writings.

A shadow figure in Hardt and Negri's writings is Franz Rosenzweig (1886–1929), who was a key figure in the movement of dialogical philosophy and a central inspiration for Martin Buber (1878–1965) and his dialogical thinking (e.g., Hardt & Negri 2009: 182). Buber's main work, *I and Thou*, was published in 1923 and German professor of philosophy Theunissen (1932–) later took up his thinking in his own works on social ontology. What the movement of dialogical philosophy has to offer the philosophical framework of Hardt and Negri and their description of the common's social ontology and thereby the creative potential of the multitude's democracy is transcendence constructed as immanence, making it compatible with Hardt and Negri's concept of the plane of immanence.

To understand the full implications of transcendence in immanence and its compatibility with Hardt and Negri's framework, it is necessary to take a closer look at the social ontology presented in Buber's writings, as well as in the corrective expansions made by Theunissen. This will be the focus of the next section, with the addition of a careful discussion of transcendence in immanence in relation to Hardt and Negri's notion of the social ontology of the common.

The social ontology of Buber and Theunissen: introducing transcendence in immanence

"The question what man is cannot be answered by a consideration of existence or of self-being as such, but only by a consideration of the essential connexion of the human person and his relations with all being" (Buber 2002, 214). Thus writes Buber in his famous work *What Is Man* from 1938. His point may sound ordinary and harmless, but it reflects a radical redefinition of what it means to be a human being, as opposed to the majority of Western thinking. The discovery of the *thou* has even been labeled the Copernican turn of modern thinking (e.g.,

Heim 1930, 333). Neither collectivism nor individualism is able to describe the human being in its totality, because each subscribes to a fixed starting point: individualism sees only the human being in relation to itself, while collectivism does not see the human being but only society: "With the former man's face is distorted, with the latter it is masked" (Buber 2002, 237). Not until the singular human being knows the other in all his or her otherness, as himself or herself, as a human being, and breaks through to the other, the singular human being will have broken his/her solitude in a transforming encounter. That is the central point of dialogism.

Buber argues that the inter-human sphere is a special category that escapes the normal human approach to handling objects. The inter-human sphere potentially contains an unfinishedness constitutive of being human. Prominent Buber interpreter Maurice Friedman (2002, xvii) writes, "Man becomes man with the other self. He would not be man at all without the I–Thou relationship." It is from that realization that Buber introduces the distinction between *I–Thou* and *I–It* in his description of human existence.

The I–It relation is characterized by speaking about something *qua* the intentionality of consciousness. This means that all entities are oriented toward the I as the world center. In other words, the I–It relation is a subject–object relation. The It exists in time and space and is subject to causality. Furthermore, the essence of the relation is prior to the relation itself, since the It is given beforehand. The same is true of the subject, which, to function as a pole of intentionality, must be present prior to the relation. I–It is therefore only in the past, because objects gain their existence from having been. They must necessarily have been objects in my consciousness before I can speak about them. Any assertion is thus a prejudice based on the past, because the presence of the It is rooted in the past (Theunissen 1984, 306f).

The central issue for Buber (2004, 13) is that I–It is not participating because the two entities exist independently of each other:

> The man who experiences has not part in the world. For it is 'in him' and not between him and the world that the experience arises. The world has no part in the experience. It permits itself to be experienced, but has no concern in the matter. For it does nothing to the experience, and the experience does nothing to it.

The division between I–It and I–Thou is clearly reflected in Buber's (2004, 12) quote:

> The life of human beings is not passed in the sphere of transitive verbs alone. It does not exist in virtue of activities alone which have some *thing* for their object. I perceive something. I am sensible of something. I imagine something. I will something. I feel something. I think something. The life of human beings does not consist of all

> this and the like alone. This and the like together establish the realm of *It*. But the realm of *Thou* has a different basis.

The crucial difference between I–It and I–Thou is that the Thou is not an intentional object. The Thou contains possibilities and potentialities reaching beyond the assignment of predicates. Being has more qualities than there are predicates and is not determined by the totality of qualities (the I–It relation). Countless predicates do not lead one closer to being and the Thou is thus experienced as nothingness. In other words the Thou is something elusive that remains undetermined to the I, but at the same time the Thou exists on the same plane as the I (i.e., transcendence in immanence). I–Thou is characterized by "talking to" instead of "talking about."

The Thou cannot be characterized by traits and there is no prescribed set of rules:

> Life is not lived by my playing the enigmatic game on a board by myself, but by my being placed in the presence of a being with whom I have agreed on no rules for the game and with whom no rules can be agreed on. (Buber 2002, 197)

On the contrary, I am present for him/her I am speaking to and the other is present for me. Thus, a room for future—the undecided and surprising—is created; the I lays its future in the hands of the other, so to speak. Talking-to requires correspondence. The expectation of correspondence constitutes the talking-to. Between the intention of correspondence and the actual correspondence opens an abyss that the intending subject cannot overcome (i.e., transcendence in immanence). Talking-to requires an answer, or pain arises. The act is delivered to the other in hopes of fulfillment.

The I–Thou relation is exclusive and not subject to time and space. Any It borders another It, but the Thou is infinite. Although the Thou appears in space, its duration as a purely intensive phenomenon can only be decided on the basis of the Thou itself, and not with the ruler of the "It-world" (Theunissen 1984, 325f). The "Thou-world" is thus not coherent in time and space and hence escapes causality. Buber (2004, 15) writes, "So long as the heaven of *Thou* is spread out over me the winds of causality cower at my heels, and the whirlpool of fate stays its course." Everything is background for the I–Thou relation and thus the meeting is the true now. The communication reaches out toward the other, seizes the other, and transforms the other from a listener to a speaker. Between I and Thou, there is no purpose. It is a reciprocal relationship.

Contemplating the social ontology of human interaction, Buber (2002, 22) mentions three types of dialog: the true dialog (I–Thou relation), the technical dialog (objective understanding), and finally the monolog disguised as dialog (I–It relation). Assessing these types of dialog, Buber (1965, 84) recognizes significant inspiration from Immanuel Kant (1724–1804) and his categorical imperative. Buber (1965, 84), however, modifies Kant significantly because the human being is not treated in isolation, as in Kant's case: "Man exists anthropologically not in his isolation, but in the completeness of the relation between man and man; what humanity is can be properly grasped only in vital reciprocity."

Central to true dialog are spontaneity and self-exposure. The reason is that self-development is dependent on the presence of these two key elements, because the dialog will otherwise degrade into the I–It relation, not allowing room for the realization of the universal structures of the I–Thou relation:

> If genuine dialogue is to arise, everyone who takes part in it must bring himself into it. And that also means that he must be willing on each occasion to say what is really in his mind about the subject of the conversation. And that means further that on each occasion he makes the contribution of his spirit without reduction and without shifting his ground. (Buber 1965, 85)

With this claim, Buber (1965, 86) runs into antagonism between *Sein* (life as being) and *Schein* (life as semblance): "Because genuine dialogue is an ontological sphere which is constituted by the authenticity of being, every invasion of semblance must damage it." Buber, however, segregates the genuine Sein as expressing human beings communicating with each other as what they are. But Buber (1965, 77) also points out that it is necessary to liberate the concept of uprightness from the "thin moralistic tones which cling to it" to defeat the semblance of lies, deceptions and constraints and "let it take its tone from the concept of bodily uprightness."

Theunissen worked extensively on this issue and one of his main works even bears the title "*Sein und Schein* [Being and Semblance]." This work addresses on what grounds human self-development can take place in light of Sein and Schein. Theunissen emphasizes that this antagonism expresses a limitation in Buber's dialogical thinking, since he does not find Buber's use of the dialogical potential adequate. The problem is that Buber, working with the dichotomy of Sein and Schein, is forced to overcome the abyss *qua* the single human being's sincerity and Buber's dialogical thinking is thereby still connected to a transcendental approach (Grøn 1983, 253f). This, however, does not drive Theunissen to write off dialogical thinking; instead, he finds a solution to the problem in Hegel's dialectical logic where he uses dialogism and dialectics to correct each other (Theunissen 1982, 17).

Hegel thus takes on an anchoring role in understanding the connections between *Allgemeinheit* (universality) and the individual. According to Hegelian logic, the antagonism between Sein and Schein is negated because they are each contained in the other (Theunissen et al. 1980, 136). The central point is that Hegel's logic is seen as an attempt to develop a concept of mutual recognition and, as such, a foundation for developing a communicative ethics rooted in freedom. To Theunissen, communicative freedom means that a human being does not experience the other as merely a limit but, rather, as a genuine condition for emancipation (Theunissen et al. 1980, 46). Communicative freedom is, however, only possible against the background of *Allgemeinheit* and that is the logic of concepts or, in Hegel's words, "the concept as absolute in itself" (Hegel 1977). To draw closer to these deductions, one might say—along with Hegel—that the singularity through which the individual human being differs from objects is in itself, first and foremost, a result of the realization of *Allgemeinheit*. Qualified self-development is only possible through the realization of *Allgemeinheit*. The reason can be found in the dialectics of I-saying.

When I say, "I," I mean myself and simultaneously what everyone means when they say "I" (Theunissen 1982, 19). Hence, *Allgemeinheit* consists in the infinity of the self-relation, which again consists of the recurring movement of the self-relation. In other words, *Allgemeinheit* is not concrete until the subject relates to its content in such as way that it simultaneously relates to itself (Theunissen 1982, 21). Consequently, the individual can only be a true self by giving up its particularity in favor of recognizing *Allgemeinheit*. Hence, in I-saying lies a totality of subjects that all have that in common that they are subjects; self-consciousness is therefore rooted in recognition from others (Theunissen et al. 1982, 22). The mutual relation of recognition is an expression of freedom: since I recognize the other as free, I can see myself as free. Theunissen (1984, 369) writes,

> The dialectic is most deeply rooted in the conversion of the making own of the Other into the alter-ation of the own. On the basis of alter-ation, however, the human being who, as transcendental midpoint of the world, at first maintains his I against the Other does not turn back into his self through integration of the Other, but through the grounding of his self upon the Other. He discovers the Other as the basis of his capacity for self-being.

This dialogical facticity demonstrates the movement of human self-development realizing itself through love. Thus, Theunissen has significantly modified Buber's dialogical thinking and this is the right track to understand how transcendence in immanence can be a beneficial addition to Hardt and Negri's social ontology. A crucial step along the way, however, is to understand the concept of "between", which is central to dialogism and constitutes the very core of transcendence in immanence. The term *between* must be understood as having an ontological character and at the same time it reflects a fundamental category in human existence:

> "Between" is not an auxiliary construction, but the real place and bearer of what happens between men; it has received no specific attention because, in distinction

> from the individual soul and its context, it does not exhibit a smooth continuity, but is ever and again re-constituted in accordance with men's meetings with one another; hence what is experience has been annexed naturally to the continuous elements, the soul and its world. (Buber 2002, 241)

Between cannot be found with the I (neither in the subjective pole of intentionality nor in a perceived world oriented toward the I and dependent on it). Nor can between be found with the other and not in an objective world of ideas. Between *is* the encounter.[1]

Between is the ontological premise for the I–Thou relation and transcends all that is present. Hence, it is transcendence in immanence. The beginnings of the transcendence are known, but not its goal or end. It is a movement from the determined to the undetermined and thus Buber claims that all real life is encounter.

Furthermore, Theunissen emphasizes the destruction of the concept of intentionality rooted in transcendental phenomenology. The Thou exists in the language as a basic word. The language (*Allgemeinheit*) puts the human being into the world and moves beneath the sphere of subjectivity, which is crucial to the idea of intentionality (Theunissen 1984, 291ff). Therein lies the existence of the ontological *between* and thus transcendence in immanence.

Following this brief presentation of the concept of between construed as transcendence in immanence, it is clear that dialogism entails high demands for the ethical (reciprocity), the political (the urge to jointly realize the universal good), and the religious (the infinite obligation toward the Other). Without these dimensions, the philosopher cannot even begin to understand what it is to be a human being and Theunissen has, fittingly, worked on these questions.

Theunissen's work should be seen in light of the inherent danger of Hegelian dialectics that the other merely is transformed into a controlled element in my self-realization, making the other "my other" through an integration of the other in myself (Lübcke 1999, 193). In this perspective, self-realization is undermined because its conditions disintegrate and Theunissen seeks to apply dialogism as a corrective because it offers a demand for reciprocity through spontaneity (Grøn 1983, 258f). The political and religious demand that springs from this line of reasoning is, however, constantly threatened by the lurking shadow of the Hegelian power perspective. The situation gets even worse when Hegel points out that, through the integration, the universal (*Allgemeinheit*) becomes superior to

---

1 To illustrate this point, Buber (2004, 19) draws on love as an example: "Feelings dwell in man; but man dwells in his love. That is no metaphor, but the actual truth. Love does not cling to the I in such a way as to have the Thou only for its 'content,' its object; but love is between I and Thou."

otherness (in a dialectical process). In this manner, Hegel ends up with a conflict between the unknown, which the human being constantly seeks, and the life offered and allowed (by *Allgemeinheit*). Within this perspective, the human being must submit to the dialectical development of *Allgemeinheit*. This point is precisely the main criticism Hardt and Negri (2000, 97ff) have against Hegel in ranking him among the thinkers of the counter-revolution. Theunissen, however, corrects Hegel at this point, introducing a division between the sought after and the unknown. The sought after is *Allgemeinheit* (the driving force, that which leads to all ethical striving) and this search reveals itself as an objection against the life at hand. The unknown is the determination for the human being that is missing from consciousness (Theunissen 1982, 29, 38). This means that the universal good is not something given beforehand but, rather, something absent. This distinction is thus crucial to the construction of transcendence in immanence instead of transcendence in transcendence.

The human being cannot know what it means to be a self and Theunissen thereby presents a critical perspective rooted in this negative fundamental experience of absence.[2] Consequently, self-realization can only take place in a community characterized by communicative freedom and only a normative concept of the "universal" derived from that makes it possible to reveal twisted forms of communication. In practice, such examples can be found in institutions pursuing private rather than common interests, which evidently connects with the concept of Hardt and Negri's Empire.

The major breakthrough from introducing Buber and Theunissen's dialogical thinking to Hardt and Negri's analytical framework is a well-established social ontology centered on transcendence in immanence, compatible with Hardt and Negri's concept of the common centered on the plane of immanence. Transcendence in immanence reinstalls transcendence, thus negating Zizek's critique mentioned above, but, more importantly, it does so with reference to *Algemeinheit*, which is the common and thus it stays at the plane of immanence simply because the other is present there.

Transcendence in immanence does not entail negation of the subject or the other—they are not antagonists—which makes it possible to incorporate the Spinoza- and Deleuze-inspired vitalism (i.e., inherent human creativity, wonder, growth, and discovery) so central to Hardt and Negri and their notion of the multitude's inevitable political potential. Following Deleuze, Hardt insists on

2 It is in this connection that Theunissen's big interest in Søren Kierkegaard should be seen (Theunissen 1991), because he intricately treated the situation of the human being in despair (e.g., see Kierkegaard's Sickness unto Death).

understanding social encounters and interhuman relations as productive and constitutive (Hardt 1993, xvii).

To put this compatibility into perspective, Theunissen's critique of Heidegger is very telling. Adjacent to Hardt and Negri's (2009, 30) critique where "the critique and affirmation of bodies that characterizes phenomenology's revolution in philosophy ... gets completely lost in Heidegger," Theunissen criticizes Heidegger for his concept of *mit-sein* not being able to incorporate the between (proximity); it is merely a projection of the self onto the other (Theunissen 1984, Chapter 5). The concept of mit-sein entails that "the Other, like the remaining inner-worldly entities, is caught up in my world project, Heidegger, just as much as Husserl, robs it of its alienness and its contrariness" (Theunissen 1984, 179).

To further elaborate on the compatibility of transcendence in immanence with Hardt and Negri's thinking, I call upon my reader to reflect on the following quotes from Hardt and Negri's writings at face value in light of the dialogical thinking of Buber and Theunissen presented above. First, Hardt and Negri (2009, 181) speak of being as "a living relation." Second, they write that "it requires a leap from the individual to the collective in order to become an autonomous and participating political subject" (Hardt & Negri 2012). Third, they talk about the "the reciprocal recognition of the social debts we owe to one another and to society" (Ibid.). Fourth, they emphasize that "in being together a collective intelligence and a new kind of communication are constructed" (Ibid.). Fifth, they make it clear that "we are able to create new truths only when we cease to be individual and constitute ourselves in our relationships to others, opening ourselves to a common language" (Ibid.).

The central concept where ends meet is the concept of becoming. Drawing on Deleuze, Hardt and Negri (2009, x) point out that "the ethical horizon has to be reoriented from identity to becoming." In the same way, dialogical thinking and transcendence in immanence focuses on the becoming-other—the creative and constitutive processes of the between functioning on the background of the human search for meaning and the human being's missing determination.

The other is surrounded by *Allgemeinheit*, an indispensable entity in human existence compatible with the common. It places the other in a whole other league from "*Homo homini lupus est* – to other men, man is a dangerous wolf," which Hardt and Negri (2012) similarly try to move beyond. The encounter with the other constructed as transcendence in immanence is the very essence of what happens within the multitude and the common's social ontology, that is, the very presupposition for producing "cooperation, communication, forms of life, and social relationships" (Hardt & Negri 2004).

Having presented the social ontology of transcendence in immanence using the dialogical thinking of Buber and Theunissen and argued for its compatibility with Hardt and Negri's notions of the multitude and the common, it is time to analyze how this corrective (in relation to Hardt and Negri's presentation of the social ontology of the common) social ontology functions on the common in general and in relation to the multitude's creative democratic potential in particular. To accomplish this, I scrutinize the concepts of love and solidarity in constant dialog with the way Hardt and Negri present them. I argue that Hardt and Negri employ too narrow a conceptual understanding of love and solidarity and that these concepts are central pillars in understanding the social ontology of the common and the very roots of the multitude's creative democratic potential.

Political concepts of solidarity and love

Solidarity, according to Hardt, requires mutual interests and is therefore founded on a calculation of interests (Hardt 2007). As demonstrated in the introduction, Hardt and Negri perceive the concept of solidarity as a survival mechanism for the poor. But while solidarity is thus a concept most commonly regarded as linked with sameness and calculation of interest, it is also a dynamic concept applicable to multiple levels, for example, local and global levels, subject to differing diachronic mental constructions and political discourses. Using Buber and Theunissen's dialogical thinking with its strong focus on the other—those who are different—casts a completely new light on the concept of solidarity. Perhaps this is best illustrated in a quote from the German theologian Martin Niemöller (1892–1984) about the Nazi regime in Germany:

> First they came for the Socialists, and I did not speak out – Because I was not a Socialist.
>
> Then they came for the Trade Unionists, and I did not speak out – Because I was not a Trade Unionist.
>
> Then they came for the Jews, and I did not speak out – Because I was not a Jew.
>
> Then they came for me – And there was no one left to speak for me.

The quote gives us an inkling that solidarity reaches out toward those who are different; it points to the necessity of engaging and expressing solidarity with other people, people with whom you may not feel you have anything in common or, even less, feel that you can identify with. This is especially true in times of oppression, just as under the reign of Empire. The multitude must express solidarity across its internal diversifications. Solidarity begins with the other and not the self, as Hardt and Negri seem to imply with their conceptual understanding.

Using the social ontology of dialogism, this argument about the origins of solidarity is supported by the notion that human self-realization is dependent on the existence of otherness. This dialogical self-realization implies a demand for solidarity in human existence through the recognition and respect for otherness in its totality (empathy). Solidarity springs from what we share (*Allgemeinheit*). The German sociologist and philosopher Axel Honneth's explicit thoughts on solidarity are compatible with the social ontology of dialogism. According to Honneth (1995: 128), solidarity must be understood as a reciprocal relation where human beings take part in each other's different ways of life. This takes place against a background of a shared experience (*Allgemeinheit*), generating a value constellation where subjects can recognize and appreciate each other's accomplishments and abilities because they can see in them a realization of the interests of the totality and the community. Honneth (1995, 129) refers to this as solidarity emanating from symmetric appreciation:

> To esteem one another symmetrically means to view one another in light of values that allow the abilities and traits of the other to appear significant for shared praxis. Relationships of this sort can be said to be cases of 'solidarity', because they inspire not just passive tolerance but felt concern for what is individual and particular about the other person.

The realization is that only through caring for the unfolding of the other's individuality in its totality can the human being realize common goals. This point is in perfect harmony with Buber and Theunissen's thoughts on the human being discovering the other as the very basis for his or her own existence. Human self-realization is, thus, rooted on otherness as transcendence in immanence and the recognition of this interdependence calls for a solidarity that surpasses imagined communities, since even the existence of communities and differences depend on otherness—they are simply invisible without otherness. This situation does not entail a static anything-goes attitude; on the contrary, the dialogical interdependence implies a dynamic dialectic, because "the entity" roots its being in "the otherness." Honneth (1995, 129) thus speaks about "societal value-horizon(s)." But how can such a dialogical solidarity be identified?

Human search for *Allgemeinheit,* the root of self-realization, calls for consciousness about the social ontology of self-realization. In other words, if the human being is to recognize the other through solidarity participation in his or her way of life, an experience pointing toward connectedness via universality must have taken place beforehand (Honneth 1995, 91). Dialogical solidarity cannot be identified if the other is seen as a competitor, because that would leave only very limited space for the ontological manifestation of the between. By looking at the other as a competitor, an I–It approach is activated through the allocation of predicates via categorizations, stigmatizations, and classifications.

The growth conditions for dialogical solidarity are instead diversity, pluralism, tolerance, and empathy. The key to these growth conditions and experiences pointing toward connectedness is love as a political concept.

Using love as a concept of political philosophy is an outsider's endeavor in Western political thought, because the discourse surrounding the concept of love ties it to the private sphere or at least to notions of identity, that is, love of family, race, and nation. But Hardt and Negri (2009, 179) insist that "love is an essential concept for philosophy and politics, and the failure to interrogate and develop it is one central cause of the weakness of contemporary thought." To that end, they emphasize that "love is really the living heart of the project we have been developing, without which the rest would remain a lifeless heap" (Hardt & Negri 2009, 180). The centrality of the concept of love in Hardt and Negri's thinking is thus beyond doubt.

The main feature of Hardt and Negri's conception of love is its ability to generate the transformation and production of subjectivity; love is the very process behind the production of the common (Hardt & Negri 2009, 180). Drawing on Spinoza, Hardt and Negri (2009, 181) claim that love is closely interwoven with joy and production, including the production of subjectivity. Much as in Buber and Theunissen's dialogical thinking, Hardt and Negri (2009, 182) point out that "what distinguishes the beneficial forms of love ... is the constant interplay between the common and singularities." They even speak about loving alterity and that love means precisely that our expansive encounters and continuous collaborations bring us joy (Hardt & Negri 2004, 351).

To Hardt and Negri, love facilitates creations out of joy and not out of duty as a consequence of paid labor or force, as can be found in hierarchical organizations. At the same time, love is intrinsically linked with democracy, understood as the space of free interaction of differences because love facilitates joyful encounters (Hardt 2007). In other words, these joyful encounters are inevitably linked with experiences of connectedness, tolerance, and empathy, which are the roots of dialogical solidarity, as mentioned above.

However, one might object that these musings about the social ontology of solidarity and love are out of touch with empirical facts, since the world displays numerous examples, such as wars, conflicts, and uprisings, where solidarity and love are absent. But, according to dialogism and the social ontology presented here, solidarity and love are connected to *Allgemeinheit* and thus are always present, because they are woven into the very existence of human beings. To demonstrate the omnipresent forces of love and solidarity, I call upon the reader to think about a person you dislike. Then think about this person as someone who is or has been loved by someone, for example, his or her mother and father and children. Consider the change this perspective adds to your sense of dislike toward that other person. My point is that seeing the other as incarnated love commands respect and awe. This is not to differentiate between those who are loved and those who are not, but in reverence to the immense and unfathomable potential and integrity facing you.

That is, however, but one objection one might raise against the conception of solidarity and love presented here. Another objection is that the concept of solidarity loses its political substance when defined as a general communal feeling (Stjernø 2005: 304). In this construction of solidarity, the concept presupposes an us–them dichotomy, for example, cultural communities or communities of interest. It is clear that this perception draws upon an understanding of the other as a competitor or opponent. The objection apparently offers a lot because it builds on the notion than an entity is the negation of something else. Hence, a given community can form a self-understanding and an identity by defining itself in opposition to otherness.

However, starting from the social ontology of dialogical solidarity, two objections against the criticism arise. Beginning with the very foundation of the critique, the notion that an entity is the negation of something else holds the seed to override the criticism. This notion implies that the entity cannot exist without otherness. Entities do not emerge *ex nihilo*. A given community will disintegrate without otherness. Therein lies the demand of solidarity to respect and recognize otherness in its own totality; by doing so, one is actually respecting and recognizing oneself (see the Niemöller quotation). Thus, it is pointless for a given community to expand its own logic (ethnocentrism) or seek to absorb otherness; according to Hegel this will only result in otherness being the stronger part, because the entity depends on the recognition of the other and this constitutive recognition disintegrates with the absorption. Human beings and communities must therefore form their identities from their respect and recognition of otherness, realizing their inherent interdependence (*Allgemeinheit*).

A third critique pertains to the emotional and cognitive aspects of solidarity and love. A certain cognitive element is clearly necessary to realize dialogical solidarity and love. Emotions and empathy seem to be central to the realization of solidarity and love. Solidarity and love are, in other words, not rooted in universality but in emotions such as infatuation and compassion.

This critique draws on a discussion of whether solidarity and love require consciousness or whether they might be realized unconsciously. This is an interesting area of tension and the ontology of dialogical solidarity and love is ambiguous at this point, but this ambiguity negates the dichotomy. Overall, it is clear that the idea of solidarity and love as inevitable phenomena in human existence implies that an external reality exists, one that is something else and more than something tied to the individual. On the other hand, the realization of solidarity and love requires consciousness about the interdependence of oneness and otherness. Therefore much depends on the individual human being's perception of reality, but that is not the same as reality being entirely constructed by this perception of reality. Reality is something qualitatively different and contains more than all the dimensions the singular human being chooses, consciously or unconsciously, to include in his or her frame of reference when acting. One might say that reality is transcendence in immanence. This means that twisted and stunted perceptions of reality can emerge, a point that gains momentum upon contemplation of just how complex reality is; it is plausible to claim that all human beings, to a certain extent, subscribe to illusions, because it is impossible to see through all the connections of which one is part. One might therefore say that the social ontology of dialogical solidarity and love implies a certain ontological realism combined with an epistemological relativism.

This statement has wide repercussions for the critique, because the dichotomy, as mentioned, is negated. If a human being defines reality based on illusions, she will encounter opposition in meeting reality. If the definition is not revised and corrected, the human being will ultimately undermine herself as an actor by excluding her own possible actions. Regarding the conscious or unconscious roots of solidarity, one might say that a human being may turn a deaf ear to the universal demand for solidarity because he does not ascribe the demand significance in his horizon of actions. The social ontology of dialogical solidarity and love—as a fundamental element in human self-realization—implies, however, that such an approach to life will be twisted vis-à-vis reality because it is unable to incorporate the human condition. This misperception might find its expression in various ways (e.g., loneliness, sadness, violence, or even death). The world—reality, otherness—will necessarily assume a position with respect to this human being that will result in different scenarios. In the long run, the skepticism and distrust in the world perceived by the unloving human being with no sense of solidarity will be confirmed (self-fulfilling prophecy), limiting her horizon of actions. The concepts of solidarity and love are both consciously and unconsciously rooted, thus negating the criticism.

In Hardt and Negri's thinking universal concepts of solidarity and love do not lose their political substance. According to Hardt and Negri, one might say that the political sphere itself has become universal under the reign of empire. At the same time, the social ontology of dialogical solidarity and love do not imply that it is no longer possible to form communities (including political ones) and identities; on the contrary, the analysis indicates the very conditions for doing so. At the same time, recognition and respect for otherness is not a static condition where anything goes. A dialectical relation between oneness and otherness exists due to the inevitable room for interpretation in light of Theunissen's statement (mentioned above), that the human being cannot know beforehand what it is to be a self. Under these dynamics, a political field rules where human beings, groups, and communities strive for the democratic realization of a good society.

References

Buber, Martin. 1965. "Elements of the interhuman." In *The Knowledge of Man – Selected Essays*, edited by Martin Buber and Maurice Friedman. New York: Harper and Row.

Buber, Martin. 2002. *Between Man and Man.* London and New York: Routledge.

Buber, Martin. 2004. *I and Thou.* London: Continuum International Publishing Group.

Christensen, Pil; Nielsen, Peter; and Poulsen, Lars. *Magt og modstand – en introduktion til Michael Hardt, and Antonio Negris tænkning*. Copenhagen: Frydenlund.

Friedman, Maurice S. 2002. "Introduction". In *Between Man and Man*, edited by Buber, Martin. London and New York: Routledge.

Grøn, Arne. 1983. "Dialektik og dialogic." *Fønix* 7(4).

Hardt, Michael. 1993. *Gilles Deleuze. An Apprenticeship in Philosophy*. London: UCL Press.

Hardt, Michael, and Negri, Antonio. 2000. *Empire*. Cambridge: Harvard University Press.

Hardt, Michael, and Negri, Antonio. 2004. *Multitude – War and Democracy in the Age of Empire.* New York: Penguin Group.

Hardt, Michael. 2007. *About Love*. Presentation at the European Graduate School, available at Youtube http://www.youtube.com/watch?v=ioopkoppabI

Hardt, Michael, and Negri, Antonio. 2009. *Commonwealth*. Cambridge: Harvard University Press.

Hardt, Michael, and Negri, Antonio. 2012. *Declaration*. E-book, Argo Navis Author Services.

Hegel, G.W.F. 1977. *The Phenomenology of Spirit*. London: Oxford University Press.

Heim, Karl. 1930. "Ontologie und Theologie." *Zeitschrift für Theologie und Kirche*, Neue Folge XI.

Honneth, A. 1995. *The Struggle for Recognition – The Moral Grammar of Social Conflicts*. Cambridge: Polity Press.

Lübcke, Poul. 1999. *Vor tids filosofi: engagement og forståelse*. Copenhagen: Politikens Forlag.

Stjernø, S. 2005. *Solidarity in Europe – The History of an Idea*. Cambridge: Cambridge University Press.

Theunissen, Michael. 1984. *The Other – Studies in the Social Ontology of Husserl, Heidegger, Sartre and Buber*. Original German publication 1977. Cambridge: MIT Press.

Theunissen, Michael; Fulda, Hans Friedrich; and Horstmann, Rolf-Peter. 1980. *Kristische Darstellung der Metaphysik – eine Diskussion über Hegels Logik*. Frankfurt-am-Main.

Theunissen, Michael. 1982. *Selbstverwicklung und Allgemeinheit – zur Kritik des gegenwärtigen Bewusstseins*. Berlin.

Theunissen, Michael. 1991. *Das Selbst auf dem Grund der Verzweiflung*. Berlin.

Zizek, Slavoj. 2005. "Objet a as inherent limit to Capitalism: on Michael Hardt and Antonio Negri." Last accessed January 31, 2013 available at www.lacan.com/zizmultitude.htm

10. The Art of Non-Playing Chess: The Institutionalization of the Common

Óscar García Agustín

In 2001 the Zapatista National Liberation Army set out on the so-called March for Indigenous Dignity from Chiapas, in southern Mexico, to the capital, Mexico City. After 60 years in power, the Institutional Revolutionary Party had lost the election and a new government had come to power, led by the conservative Vicente Fox. The Zapatistas saw this change as the last possibility to retrieve the dialog with the government and achieve an agreement, among other issues, on indigenous rights and cultures that should be recognized in the Mexican Constitution. The march around Mexico was a success and the population showed their sympathy and support to the Zapatista cause. The arrival in Mexico City was spectacular, with the Zócalo, the main square of the capital, completely filled up.

Among the various encounters held by the Zapatistas with representatives from civil society in Mexico City, the movement's famous speaker, subcomandante Marcos, met with a group of prestigious international intellectuals, such as José Saramago, Alain Touraine, and Bernard Cassen, in the intercultural meeting The Paths for Dignity: Indigenous Rights, Memory and Cultural Heritage. In his speech, subcomandante Marcos told the story "The Other Player," preceded by a poem by the Argentinian author Jorge Luis Borges of the same title. It is a story about chess.

An indigenous person watches a group of chess players engrossed in a high-level chess game. The indigenous person observes the game, trying to understand it, and asks repeatedly what they are playing. The only answer he gets is that he would never be able to understand it. It is a game for specialists, for wise and important people. In the meanwhile the indigenous man dares to question the meaning of the game: "And why do you play if you already know who is going to win?" The indigenous man leaves and when he returns,

> Without so much as a word he approaches the table and places, right in the middle of the chessboard, an old boot covered in mud. The players are perplexed and look at him angrily. The indigenous man smiles maliciously while asking: "Check?" (Marcos 2001)

A few days later the Zapatista delegation left Mexico City. The Mexican congress approved a new law regarding the indigenous people, that was far from satisfactory to the Zapatistas, entailing huge disappointment. Since the Zapatistas understood that the institutional way, led by the political parties as the main actors of the representative system, was closed, they decided to set up an alternative process by creating their own institutions to develop indigenous autonomy. Instead of playing chess, as all the other players, they placed the old boot covered in mud on the political arena.

In his analysis of the economic crisis and the very relevant question about whether there is a way out for humanity, Franco "Bifo" Berardi also deploys the chess metaphor. Berardi points out that chess is a finite game in the sense that we must follow certain rules if we want to play. On the other hand, "love, life and history are not finite games in the sense that there are no rules which impede to break the rules" (Berardi 2012a). Thinking of the current situation, Berardi claims that the modern game of politics is over. If we play following the rules of politics, we can be sure of defeat. This means that breaking the rules is the only way of creating possible alternatives to avoid checkmate, that is, the defeat of humanity. The results are not going to be instantaneous and how to do so is still unclear. However, every form of resistance and collective organization can be the beginning of that alternative:

> To fight, to act collectively, will not be able to stop this process, but it is not useless, because it makes it possible to accumulate somewhere (in places which are not necessarily geographic) the schismogenetic energy that will produce, if the world will go on being habitable, the conditions for post-apocalyptic communism. (Berardi 2012a)

It is not casually, either, that John R. Searle, in his account of social reality, speaks of "constitutive rules" to cite those rules that create the possibility of certain activities and do not only regulate them. And it is no coincidence that Searle (1995, 28) uses the metaphor of chess to explain such rules:

> The rules of chess create the very possibility of playing chess. The rules are *constitutive* of chess in the sense that playing chess is constituted in part by acting in accord with the rules. If you don't follow at least a large subset of the rules, you are not playing chess.

Institutions (what Searle calls institutional facts) exist only within systems of constitutive rules. Checkmate is only checkmate if we accept the (constitutive) rules of chess.

The institutional problem is that the constitutive rules they are based on can remain unquestioned: everybody is playing chess because if they try to do something different, they are simply not playing chess. To play chess becomes a matter of political closure: what must be thought, done, or said or not is delimited by the chess board as a space in which all actions follow the rules of the game. The question raised by the indigenous man is not about the constitutive rules but about the players who accept those rules and, even more important, the possibility of playing differently. The Zapatistas suggest that alternative institutions can be built right now, while Bifo recognizes that the alternative is not yet possible but the struggles are necessary to be ready when the alternative comes.

In this contribution, I explore the options of non-playing chess, namely, the possibility of creating institutions (or developing processes of institutionalization) that challenge, change, or replace the existing ones. I begin with the considerations of Michael Hardt and Antonio Negri on institutions, particularly in their latest work. Subsequently I present the notion of institutionalization as a productive way of understanding how alternatives are emerging and how they are developing. I exemplify this with different cases—the Zapatistas in Mexico, the idea of "living well" in Ecuador, and the Plataforma de Afectados por la Hipoteca (PAH), or Platform for those Affected by Mortgage, in Spain—that reflect the variety and complexity of these processes. The economic crisis has not caused a crisis for the institutions that support capitalism. However, various social struggles have already started processes of institutionalization of the common, which, independently of whether they are destituent rather than constituent, aim to constitute and configure alternatives in a post-crisis scenario.

Against spontaneity: institutions by Hardt and Negri

Hardt and Negri's rejection of negativity and dialectics presented in Empire and their defense of the power of multitude as being immanent has led several authors to the conclusion that Hardt and Negri understand social struggles as spontaneous without the need for any articulation (e.g., Laclau 1991). There are two consequences: social struggles do not need to do anything and must wait until a hypothetical change comes. Consequently forms of articulation or organization are not an issue. It is true that, after a reading of Empire and Multitude, it is quite unclear how the multitude could fight against the Empire and how alternatives could be constituted. However, Hardt refutes that when he claims, "These experiences, in general, with new ways of organization, autonomous forms, face a huge challenge, that of 'becoming institutionalized', albeit this is not the right word. I mean to create instruments to give political continuity to these struggles" (Hardt, in Gainza 2006).

Indeed, Negri bring forward, in *Fabrique de porcelaine*, some of the aspects that would be developed more extensively in Commonwealth. Organization becomes a relevant topic. All doubts about spontaneity should be cleared up when Negri maintains immanence in the affirmation of constituent power as a continuous and determined ontological construction of the common. The concern about organization as a way of continuity contradicts the supposed spontaneity but, even more importantly, introduces institutions ("becoming institutionalized," as Hardt puts it) as a central aspect to account for the possibility of alternatives to the dominance of Empire. One initial inconvenience is that institutions, as Negri (2008) points out, usually have been detached from forms of life, or, in other terms, from the *potentia*, the constituent power. Institutions (in a sense similar to constitutions) must acquire a new social meaning that enables organization and the constant construction of the common. The question is how to do so.

In a very convincing way, Raúl Sánchez Cedillo (2008) contributes to the reconceptualization of institution as a tool for the struggles of social movements and not as a dispositive of repression and control against them. Sánchez Cedillo refers to *institutio* as a foundation, a plan, a project, a well-founded design, and *instituere* as in its meaning to prepare, get ready, establish but also to organize something already existing and to train and educate. This etymological reflection allows us to move toward the *instituere*, the instituent, meaning the positive creation of institutions to organize the innovative power of liberty and equality. Institutions are needed if the insurrection as a deconstituent movement against the instituted power must be transformed into a constituent power to organize the expressions emerged from insurrections (Negri 2001). By unfolding institutions, as Sánchez Cedillo does, in *institutio* and *instituere*, a similar dichotomy is created that is comparable to that between *potestas* and *potentia*. This makes it possible to consider institutions as a determinant aspect of social struggles, as it is presented in depth in Commonwealth, where Hardt and Negri explicitly state that insurrection needs institutions of a different sort. Three characteristics of institutions can be identified:

- Institutions are defined by (internal and external) conflict,
- Institutions invent and institutionalize a new form of life,
- Institutions are open to transformation by singularities.

First, Hardt and Negri's institutional approach is based on conflict. The main risk of institutional continuity is to neutralize the social rupture caused by insurrection and assume the dominant form based on identity. Social rupture must be extended and developed instead of being negated. Thus, the conflict is double: externally, against the ruling powers through the rupture created by the revolt, and internally, by constantly maintaining openness to discord.

Second, institutions consolidate "collective habits, practices, and capacities that designate a form of life" (Hardt & Negri 2009, 357). This consolidates revolts in alternative institutional forms and makes them powerful and long-lasting. Through institutions, disruptive social struggles find a way of continuing and developing common practices and behaviors.

Finally, institutions are continuously transformed by the singularities that compose them. Far for anchoring a closure, institutions are consequently open-ended. This is related to the idea of "training in love" because "it does not reduce the multiplicity of singularities but creates a context for them to manage their encounters: to avoid the negative encounters, which diminish their strength, and prolong and repeat the joyful ones, which increase it" (Hardt & Negri 2009, 357). The reference to training in love is distanced from spontaneity, since love is not something spontaneous but acquired by training. Institutions entail an organization in which social struggle is a learning and planning process and not just the result of a spontaneous manifestation of singularities.

The conception of institutions developed by Hardt and Negri is specified further through their response to two hypothetical objections: the sociological, summed up as institutions compel individuals to follow established patterns of behavior (assuming predetermined identities), and the political, as far as institutions exist on the basis of sovereignty. Regarding the sociological objection, the locus of agency is different: instead of showing how institutions adapt individuals to identities (conditioning their behavior), the interest lies in showing how singularities form institutions, which are in constant change. While the sociological conception assumes what we have called *institutio*, Hardt and Negri opt for *instituere*, the institutional process of creating a form of life in conflict with the ruling power. On the political objection, the argument is based on the idea that the mutual encounters (training in love) of the singularities of multitude hinder the formation of sovereign power.

With these clarifications it is clear that the concept of institution is moving between two terrains: stability (as a form of life constituted by collective habits, practices, and capacities) and process (as openness). This becomes evident when Hardt and Negri state, "Institutional norms and obligations are established in regular interactions but are continually open to a process of evolution" (Hardt & Negri 2009, 359). To avoid possible closure, Hardt and Negri consider institutions as a process rather than a set of norms. This is one of the reasons I prefer to talk about institutionalization since the focus is on openness and process, or institutions embedded in processes of institutionalization. But first I turn to the way in which Hardt and Negri deal with the tendency toward closure, inherent to institutions, and the need for openness, which characterizes the institutional process.

In an exchange with John Holloway, Hardt makes an effort to reformulate the combination of closure and openness. Hardt initiates the discussion by underlying the entwining between destruction and construction: the destruction of a world implies the creation of a new one. Therefore the creation of a new society must be developed right now in its cracks, following Holloway's (2010) idea developed in *Crack Capitalism*. Since cooperation and coordination are not spontaneous, institutions are required. Hardt defines institutions in a rather loose sense: "by institution here I do not mean a bureaucratic structure but rather, as anthropologists use the term, a repeated social practice, a habit, that structures social relations" (Hardt & Holloway 2011). The opposition between *institutio* (bureaucracy) and *instituere* (practices) is recognizable here. However, the stability of institutions is predominant, since practices and habits that structure social relations are stressed. Even the creative dimension and the capacity of producing new forms of life are blurred by the emphasis on practices and habits.

Holloway, who is opposed to the use of institutions in any sense and proposes using two different words instead, points out the contradiction in Hardt's definition, since repeated social practices slip easily into a bureaucratic structure. Trying to find a shared ground, Hardt accepts Holloway's critique and his proposal of institutionalization-subvert. According to Holloway, "Institutionalisation may be inevitable at times, but in the tension between institutionalisation and subversion we have already taken sides. Thought is subversion" (Hardt & Holloway 2011). Despite this common reconceptualization, Holloway still mistrusts institutions and focuses on rupture. Hardt, on the other hand, is positive about the idea of organization as an alternative to spontaneity and he redefines institutionalization-subvert as "repetition with difference," which includes the idea of openness missed in his previous definition.

This debate between Holloway and Hardt is very relevant. First, Holloway is probably right about the need to use two words to make a clear distinction. Second, the formulation institutionalize-subvert reflects the tension, pointed out above, between the tendency toward closure and the need for openness. Third, both authors agree that they are talking about institutions but, in reality, and this is observable in the terms they use, they are talking about institutionalization. It means a process. To Holloway a process of becoming fixed and a bureaucracy and to Hardt a way of organizing cooperation and social struggles.

My proposal in the following is to move from institutions to institutionalization to better grasp the dynamic of processes and the relation with institutions. As far as institutionalization is a process and not a fixation, it cannot be assimilated with bureaucracy but contains both tendencies: stabilization (inherent to the attempt of organizing) and openness (as a process that challenges existing institutions).

Institutionalization: social meaning and materialization

A very productive way of deepening the institutional dimension suggested by Hardt and Negri is to take institutionalization as the central aspect. The creation of institutions as demanded by Hardt and Negri has more to do with institutionalization as a process than with institution as relatively stable social practices.

Institutions assume a more dynamic perspective and, above all, they acquire sense in a process of institutionalization that relates to the construction not only of institutions but also of social meaning. The symbolic dimension, not successfully integrated in Hardt and Negri's account, gains a central role.

Especially in the literature on social movements, institutionalization is considered to have an internal and an external dimension. Within the organization, institutionalization is a matter of differentiation whereby participants are assigned different roles (Seippel 2001), creating a division between active and more passive members, leadership and regular activists, and so forth. Externally, it is associated with the process of being institutionalized, understood as part of the official terrain of formal politics (Suh 2011). Institutionalization is considered mainly political, as part of political system, while mobilization is primarily social. To participate in policymaking and influence policies, a certain degree of institutionalization of social movements is expected.

My starting point is quite different: I consider institutionalization a movement away from institutions (an openness), at least the existing ones, rather than a way of becoming institution. It is clear that the moment of being institutionalized is a plausible option, but it designates the result of institutionalization and not the self-process. Actually becoming a part of existing institutions or a more hierarchic or bureaucratic organization comprises only two of the imaginable possibilities. The political power of social movements is diminished if institutionalization is reduced to becoming part of the political system, as if this were their only aim, not reaching for societal change, and if the political and the social were strictly distinguished. The characteristics of institutionalization, which assume, reformulate, and expand Hardt and Negri's notion of institution, can be listed as follows:

- Creation of values (not preexisting values),
- Composed by a symbolic dimension (discourse) and a material one (institutions),
- Development of conflict by the interruption of consensus,
- Promotion of new interpretations and social meanings (rupture),
- Intersubjectivity as political (constitutive) activity.

Institutionalization is a creative process and, as such, a process of generating meaning and social imaginaries. In this sense I refer to Castoriadis' (2002) theory of the institution of society according to which institutionalization entails the creation of new values and not the realization of preexisting ones (Joas 1989). Similar to the Negrian *potestas* and *potentia*, the instituent creates new meanings that transcend the instituted (Castoriadis 2002). Since institutionalization is the process set up by such creation so that the point of departure is the questioning of the instituted (the existing institutions), it cannot be seen as the process of becoming instituted (or institutionalized) but of producing new institutions or altering existing ones.

The movement initiated by institutionalization is consequently double: questioning and creating. Castoriadis (1998) argues that social movements consider the central imaginary meanings of the instituted society and at the same time create something: different conceptions of sustainability, family, private property, democracy, and so forth. Thus the instituent contains the imaginary dimension as well as an ensidic one (Castoriadis 1998), meaning the creation of a certain unity and identity. That is true in what Castoriadis calls the institution of society and likewise in the process of institutionalization. It is similar to the idea of institutionalization and subversion developed by Hardt and Holloway. There is a tendency to organize and establish certain norms, values, tools (repetition), and the creation of new social forms (difference). In sum, the initial process of questioning and creating is developed by reiteration and difference, reflecting the need for stability (as a result of organization) and transformation (as a process that creates institutions without becoming institutionalized).

It must be noted that institutionalization is broader than institution because it is principally based on social meanings. Even when institutions are just altered or remain unchanged because they ignore or repress the demands of social movements, new meanings are put into play to modify the understanding of society and the role played by institutions, in that order. Institutionalization entails meaning, but when it materializes, it does so through institutions. I understand social imaginary and meaning in a way similar to what Hajer (1993) calls discourse institutionalization to indicate that discourses, when successful (meaning that people use them to conceptualize the social world), will solidify into an institution. Discourse institutionalization facilitates the reproduction of a given discourse and materialization into institutions facilitates its continuity.

The questioning and creative moment corresponds with the insurrection as social rupture in the case of Hardt and Negri. It is possible to claim that institutionalization emerges from the interruption of consensus, in parallel with Jacques Rancière's (2011) political moment. When consensus is interrupted, the agreement on a certain image of community (who belongs and who does not) is suspended through questioning. In other words, institutionalization, as a movement away from existing institutions, constructs a new scenario in which another configuration of society is opposed to the former one. The importance of maintaining the conflict is essential in both the discourse (social meaning) and the institutions (materialization). Consequently, a central question raised by the interruption of consensus and the persistence of conflict is how to constitute such institutions based on conflict, reflecting the new ways of interpretation.

Chantal Mouffe (1993) shares the idea of institutions based on conflict. She talks about the need for transforming social antagonism into what she calls agonism. She considers that the different ways of interpretation coexist in a common terrain, which enhances dialog. This does not mean that the conflict expressed by the different interpretations disappears. She considers pluralism to be a form of conflictual consensus that implies an agreement on shared common principles (such as liberty and equality) and disagreement regarding their interpretation when they are applied. How is the shift from antagonism to agonism possible? By means of institutions. Nonetheless, this conception of institutions based on conflict differs from Hardt and Negri's as well as my own account of institutionalization.

The challenge in Hardt and Negri's approach and my own is how to preserve social rupture and challenge existing institutions before the conflict becomes institutionalized. The challenge is then to construct an alternative scenario, both in discourse and in institutions, which allows for a new configuration of society or of the singularities emerged in the political moment of rupture. Contrary to this, Mouffe's theory suggests that a common scenario must be constituted to reach a new sort of consensus and make social spaces for the coexistence of different interpretations. The starting point is also different: I assume that social rupture entails an interruption of consensus, while Mouffe considers consensus an aim to avoid the social excesses of antagonism.

Emphasizing that the objective of institutionalization is to maintain social rupture and configure and develop other ways of interpretation, which are in conflict with the existing ones, it must be acknowledged that quite often institutions acquire an agonistic sense. When social movements alter institutions or influence policymaking, a common terrain is imagined in which the political system is opened to the demands of civil society. However, seen from the institutionalization angle, the fact that some demands are assumed by institutions does not imply that the conflict dimension, based on an opposite interpretation as well as alternative social meanings, becomes dissipated because it has been fulfilled.

A last word must be said about the political subjectivities, social movements, or communities, which embody institutionalization. As mentioned before, institutionalization is movement away from current institutions. In this sense, I share the critique of the sociological objection formulated by Hardt and Negri. The beginning of institutionalization can be placed "when a number of people begin the same habitualized pattern of activity, to possess some sense that they are doing it, *and* to communicate to each other in the same terms about what they are doing" (Jenkins 2004, 158). Two aspects must be underlined here. First, the intersubjective relation, that fixes certain stability through practices, meaning, and communication, relies on the singularities, that, as Searle (2005) reminds us, can stand for the reproduction of the dominant institutions or the beginning of a revolution. Indeed, it is the potential of creating and questioning to alter existing institutions or creating new ones by social movements that is interesting from an institutionalization approach. Second, political activity is the main form of activity. Intersubjectivity is a constitutive and transformative practice. Singularities engaged in processes of institutionalization do not reproduce given identities. Instead, they participate in creative and generative processes by negotiation and renegotiation of their political identifications. Institutionalization constitutes identities and relations between singularities. The perspective offered by institutionalization differs partially from the idea of Hardt and Negri about how identities form institutions, since both identities and institutions are embedded in a constitutive process of institutionalization.

Applying this approach to institutionalization, it is relevant to empirically explore how social struggles and movements set up processes of institutionalization of the common and how their impact on both discourses and institutions can be understood. The Zapatistas in Mexico started their struggle a long time before the economic crisis and can be considered a precedent of the 2011 struggles that are still under development. Living well in Ecuador responds to the collaboration between social movements and the progressive government as a response to the neoliberal policies applied in Latin America in the 1990s. Finally, the cause of the PAH in Spain is clearly intensified by the economic crisis and the increasing precarity in Spain. All of these struggles, despite the differences in terms of countries and times, point to some of the failures and abuses of capitalism in crisis and share the need for creating an alternative based on the principles of the common.

Struggles for the common

In *Declaration*, Hardt and Negri (2012) raise the following question: "How can the multitude become prince of the institutions of the common in a way that reinvents and realizes democracy?" Their answer is that it is the task of a constituent process. The problem is that the creation of a democratic society, based on institutions of the common, depends on the event of the commoner, an event that makes that change possible. It is unpredictable to know when the event will occur. However, Hardt and Negri suggest that "we must prepare for the event even though its date of arrival remains unknown" instead of just waiting for its arrival. To be prepared implies organization and to hold "passionately" on to the principles of freedom, equality, and the common.

It seems quite difficult to imagine how a constituent process can develop successfully under the constraints of global capitalism, especially if it is necessary that the event occur. Thus, I prefer to talk about the institutionalization of the common to refer to these open processes, which are being organized and foster alternative discourses or social meanings (those based on freedom, equality, and the common). As Christian Marazzi (2011, 122) points out,

> The forms and objectives of the struggle 'inside and against' crisis capitalism are at the same time local and global.... However, the first step in constructing new alternative paradigms, new forms of common government, is totally subjective. There are no predefined recipes, there is only the challenging awareness that any future depends on us.

Looking at the different social struggles for democracy and equality, including the 2011 cycle of struggles that mostly motivates *Declaration*, it is effectively evident that there is no single way or model to create alternatives inside and against capitalism. Social struggles entail a diversity of forms of institutionalization, which produces different kinds of discourses and institutions, although all of them conform to the "alliance of the common" (Hardt & Negri 2012), a constitutive action to transform society. In the following, I present some of these struggles, which assume different forms of institutionalization: the Zapatista movement in Mexico develops probably the most complex institutional framework as a project of autonomy, the principle of living well (*buen vivir*) in Ecuador is an alternative way of understanding development, and the struggles for housing in Spain, centered around the eviction of citizens who cannot pay their mortgages, create new social bonds and reject the oppressive effects of the debt, both individually and socially. Besides struggling for different aims and representing different dynamics between social movements and the state, all share the intention to institutionalize the common as an alternative against capitalism.

Autonomy and non-hegemonic alternatives

The Zapatista movement in Chiapas, Mexico, is the most developed example of autonomy as an alternative to representative democracy. As mentioned in the introduction, the Zapatistas stopped short of achieving an institutional agreement with the state and initiated (more precisely, deepened) a process of self-government. In 2003 the Zapatistas created the Councils of Good Government and the Caracoles, not as a result of negotiation or consensus with other political or social forces but as a decision taken independently (Rodríguez Lascano 2007). The institutions are grounded on previous institutions but the process of institutionalization is expanded since they aim to create non-state institutions and articulate government networks between Zapatista and other likeminded communities (González Casanova 2003).

Hardt refers to the Zapatistas as a clear example of institutionalization and subversion and Hardt and Negri (2012) acknowledge these successful experiences and synthesize their virtues by underlining that they "give substance and meaning to their projects to lead by following and to walk forward questioning." This echoes the Zapatista idea "to walk while questioning," deployed repeatedly to define their political project as an openness, avoiding any closure, and a continuous process. This notion of process, as institutionalization, does not mean that their project is not being materialized. The Zapatistas have been capable of changing discourse along their long-term struggle, starting from classical revolutionary Marxism to the defense of indigenous rights, fostering alter-globalization connectivity and prefiguring the struggles of 2011. At the same time, they have set up institutions, momentary or perdurable, to settle a new social imaginary opposed to capitalism. These institutions have been local, developing autonomy to different degrees, national, trying to articulate dissent against the political system, and international, recognizing that local struggles must be fought at all levels, including globally.

The Councils of Good Government materialize an alternative to capitalism through the concretion of new social meaning such as democracy, understood as the power of the community to decide and participate in decision making (under the premise to "lead by obeying"); development based on sustainability and respect for nature; *real* rights of singularities (indigenous people whose rights have been rejected), maintaining their difference (through institutions such as education and health care); and constant communication and cooperation with other members of civil society (through the institution of Caracoles).

The interruption of consensus initiated in 1994 has preserved and been redefined over the years and the conflict has indeed intensified. While the movement before 2001 tried to negotiate with political parties, any conversation with political parties was rejected afterward. Using Mouffe's terms, the Zapatistas do not consider agonism to be a possibility and have decided instead to create a logic opposed to the state. Autonomy shows the difficulties of construction against and within, with constant interference aimed to destabilize the area and a strategy of low-intensity war adopted by the government. It makes internal conflict and coexistence between Zapatistas and non-Zapatistas communities more complicated.

Since these institutions make sense in a process of institutionalization different from that of the state, the Zapatistas want to embed their project in a broader process, in dialog and collaboration with other social struggles that share their values. Besides organizing the local struggle, the challenge is to organize a national (or international) alternative to the political system. With this aim the so-called Other Campaign was launched in 2006 to explore such possibilities and break the representative logic (supported by the electoral system). The combination of respect for singularities and the constitution of a shared common ground is formulated in the Sixth Declaration of the Selva Lacandona:

> Perhaps united with other social sectors who suffer from the same wants as we do, it will be possible to achieve what we need and what we deserve. A new step forward in the indigenous struggle is only possible if the indigenous join together with workers, peasants, students, teachers, employees. (Ejército Zapatista de Liberación Nacional 2005)

A common condition (those who suffer from the same wants) with a common desire (what we deserve) must be developed by respecting singularities and, even more importantly, struggling together creates the possibility of each and every struggle.

In their search for connecting with other forms of social production contrary to the capitalist one, the Zapatistas prioritize being together with the Others by listening to them and their experiences. There is no intention of imposing a Zapatista point of view but, rather, to constitute a political identity that shares different ways of organizing against capitalism. In other words, the Zapatistas do not want to be hegemonic or to foster a homogenous organization. Far from spontaneity, organization is a central issue in the Other Campaign. Although it sounds a little paradoxical, the rejection of centralized structures implies a stronger effort of organization. I would add that it has entailed major complications, which show the difficulties of organizing social struggles without a hegemonic position. The assemblies, for example, are an example of how complex it was to reach consensus when the claims were so heterogeneous (Barrera & Rey 2007) and even contrary to some of the Zapatistas' principles.

From the perspective of institutionalization, as conceptualized above, the Zapatistas' successful experience relies on a process of institutionalization in constant redefinition in which conflict with political institutions has intensified. The project of autonomy has been translated into innovative stateless institutions, which makes sense in an alternative social imaginary. However, the expansion of their experience in dialog with other struggles still faces difficulties in producing new institutions but a new discourse is collectively being boldly developed.

Living well: an alternative development paradigm

Hardt and Negri talk about a quasi-institutional relationship between social movements and progressive governments whereby both actors maintain an antagonist and cooperative dynamic. It creates a special situation in which political parties take the power supported by social movements and later the permanence of the former in the government depends on the latter. Some parties, such as the Movement Toward Socialism in Bolivia, even have a loose organizational structure and are composed of social movements and local communities. This relationship contributes to an institutionalization in which social practices can become institutions within the state apparatus. It strengthens the possibilities of the continuity of social struggles but the risk consists in becoming "institutionalized" and missing the role of social movements as a constituent force. I find it quite interesting how the philosophy of *buen vivir* (living well) is the basis of an alternative development paradigm as institutionalization of the common. Although the model is applied in different countries, I have chosen to focus on the case of Ecuador.

After a national assembly in which multiple members of civil society participated, a new Ecuadorian Constitution was approved in 2008. The principle of living well was adopted as a transversal value and attached tightly to development, especially through the National Plan of Development of 2009 (Walsh 2010). The idea originates in indigenous cosmovisions, translated from Quechua (*sumak kawsay*) and Aymara (*suma qamaña*), and it marked a change of priorities in economic growth. The questioning of growth, as it is known in modernity, is accompanied by the questioning of production, which separates the object (nature) from the subject (humans). Living well entails a shift from an anthropocentric vision to a biocentric one or, in Cocco's (2012) words, the indigenous cosmology, and introduces an immanent and materialist basis without dualism between subject and object, since human and nature are intertwined. In the Ecuadorian Constitution nature holds its own rights as subject. According to Gudynas (Hernández 2009), this makes nature independent of its use or of whether it is economically usable.

The rights of nature and the balance between nature and human life makes the idea of living well different from welfare, although social and health policies have a similar goal. Furthermore, the fact that nature becomes independent of its use allows us to perceive its logic against capitalism. Ecuadorian President Rafael Correa stresses

> The primacy of use value over exchange value, and this has helped to shape our policies. While we insist that we need real development, we do not identify this narrowly with GDP [gross domestic product] defined in monetary terms, but instead take

> full account of its costs and consequences at every level, imposing the most stringent controls. (Correa 2012, 99–100)

Considering that financialization is the "form of capital accumulation symmetrical with new processes of value production" (Marazzi 2011, 48) extended into the sphere of goods and services, it is understandable why David Harvey (in Arellano 2012) considers capitalism to be overcome by the prevalence of use value over exchange value. That is why Correa emphasizes the need to ground a new concept of development against one of the capitalist pillars.

Living well synthesizes the encounter of the common as "common wealth of the material world" and as "the results of social production," combining humanity and nature. It highlights what Hardt and Negri (2009, viii) consider central, namely, "issues of maintenance, production, and distribution of the common in both senses and in both ecological and socioeconomic frameworks." The social practices and production based on living well precede the constitution, but with the constituent process it became an alternative paradigm of development against capitalism and recognition of the value of indigenous knowledge to the national common value. To avoid the fixation of living well and to diminish its social value, the constitution presents it as "an investment for change that is constructed continually from these claims (stemming from social actors) in order to reinforce the need of a wider vision, which overcomes the tight margins of economicism" (Article 275). It responds to the intention of opening up politics to the participation of civil society as occurred with the Constitution and the National Plan of Development.

The space opened by living well toward an alternative against capitalism coexists with the contradiction of having emerged within capitalism. The attempt to create a new form of development collides with economic interests and a model still dependent on mineral and oil extraction, from which one can derive a neo-developmental model similar to that of Brazil (Torres-Tovar & De Vos 2013). It has provoked increasing protests and a radicalization within social movements that aim toward a more ecological model. Correa laments the change in support of indigenous communities depending on the issue, but he trusts the possibility of reconciling differences.

Although it is true that the state assumes a great part of the responsibility for the policies that apply the principle of living well, the actions taken by social movements work as a corrective agent of the government's control of interpretation. Social movements try to hold the government accountable if they consider that their claims are not being heard. As far as participation in policymaking is ensured or social movements can influence (and even reorient) measures taken by the government, institutionalization, in this case, contains the potential to produce new social meanings (an alternative discourse of development) as well as the institutions that materialize them.

Social bond: spaces of mediation and interpretation

The *indignados* movement in Spain was embedded in the global cycles of protest initiated with the Arab Spring. Due to the movement's rejection of participating in the local elections in 2011 and its critical revision of the institutions created to foster the Spanish transition from dictatorship to democracy in the 1970s and 1980s, Hardt and Negri (2012) see the movement as a "*destituent* rather than a *constituent* process, a kind of exodus from the existing political structures," adding that "it is necessary to prepare the basis for a new constituent power." From the broader perspective of institutionalization and without being restricted, like Hardt and Negri, to the encampments set up by the movement, I consider the destituent and constituent moments to be part of the same process. New meanings of democracy, participation, and the active role of citizens constituted a strong civil discourse that interrupted political consensus and made the emergence of new issues and social actors possible. The expectations of discourse were too high compared with its materialization into institutions (albeit there are remarkable institutions, such as local assemblies and independent media). It must nonetheless be noted that the process of institutionalization opened up by this political moment allows for other social movements to formulate their claims and develop their struggles within the same framework. That is the case of the PAH.

The PAH refers to one of the subjective figures of the crisis, the indebted man, whose subjectivity is configured on the foundation of debt (Hardt & Negri 2012). The main objective is to condemn and struggle against the asymmetric relation between creditor and debtor. The economic crisis increased the impoverishment of citizens and made it impossible for many families to pay their mortgages. As a consequence, they were evicted because of Spanish eviction law. The PAH initiated protests in the houses to stop evictions and its success created a sense of collective power for justice by emphasizing new forms of solidarity. Their claims gained great support in the public opinion and they combined protests in the streets and civil disobedience with a popular legislative initiative.

The spaces of mediation and interpretation are placed between the sphere of fundamental rights and concrete spaces (Marazzi 2003). People affected by mortgage open up such a space as a reaction against the "ferocious domination of mathematical exactitude" (Berardi 2012b), which conceives of the problem as only technical and not social, political, or even human. Thus, the PAH has institutionalized a space of trust to build new bonds and debts not grounded on the power of money (Hardt & Negri 2012). According to the PAH, it is

> A space of regular meeting where the affected people experience 1) that their problem was not individual but collective, and caused by structural reasons; 2) as a consequence, there was no reason to feel guilt or shame; 3) reality can be transformed by collective action and what seemed to be impossible can become possible. (Colau 2011)

The intersubjective relations constitute a political identity within the space that allows the participants to abandon the subjective figure as debtor and its individualizing effects, characterized by guilt, bad conscience, and responsibility (Lazzarato 2011).

The interpretations and social meanings generated by the space of mediation (and trust) compete with the dominant ones. Although the PAH questions the core logic of debtfare, it must deal with the contradictions of being within capitalism. Spanish laws, a conservative government, and the privileged position of the banks make it difficult to create autonomous institutions or establish quasi-institutional relations. However, the attempt to alter existing institutions and institutionalize social practices is accompanied by the power of a discourse that has dismantled the capitalist discourse and its coherence. When evicted writer Cristina Fallarás claims (in França 2013), "I am not a criminal, what I am is fucking poor," she rejects the logic of capitalism and renames it: the debtor has not done anything wrong but is exposed to the precarity of a system based on debt. But the exploitation of their lives and their future does not annul the production of political subjectivity. Negri (2008) defines poverty as having to develop relationships and cooperate to fulfill lack and privation. Singularities find possibilities of acting and fostering the production of the common.

The rejection of culpability and the affirmation of the creativity of the poor reveal capitalism's lack of legitimacy. Although the PAH cannot offer an alternative to the debt system, the defenders of capitalism find serious difficulties justifying the eviction of families because of their condition as poor people in a situation of impoverishment and indebtment that is shared by the majority of the population. The discourse of the dominant economic rationality does not contain satisfactory arguments that can be accepted by the citizens. The incapacity of power to refute the truth produced by social movements is reflected in the insistence on delegitimizing them due to their ways of protest and not so much because of the content of their demands.

Despite the instituted power's resistance to change, the PAH has been capable of setting the political agenda (Bouza 2013). The Spanish conservative party felt forced to accept a popular legislative initiative, backed by 1.4 million signatures, although later the proposals of the PAH were not reflected in the resulting law. Although major legislative reforms are missed, social and economic practices are being changed, including banks that have adopted "dacion en pago" (i.e., once the home has been handed back to the banks, the debt should be cancelled) or show more flexibility in its application. The Andalusian government has approved a law for the temporary expropriation of houses from the banks. This legislative action, unimaginable in Spain a few years ago, is grounded in the social function attributed to the house, which has been considered an attack against capitalism, representing the inclusion of social needs as formulated by social movements.

Because of political closure, the process of institutionalization developed by the PAH, continuing the political moment, which had emerged after the 15M, shows the problems of materializing their discourse in new institutions or even altering existing ones. However, the constitution of spaces of mediation and interpretation fosters the production of new social bonds and a discourse that directly challenges the capitalist logic, regardless of whether or not it assumes more reformist measures or is based on civil disobedience. The case of PAH thus represents a way of institutionalization, in which new values, social bonds, and political identities are constituted and the maintenance of conflict, grounded in a powerful discourse, is essential in trying to achieve material and concrete improvements.

Checkmate?

Returning to the original question posed above, regarding the possibilities of non-playing chess, it is necessary to look at the current processes of institutionalization of the common. Hardt and Negri have paid attention to the creation of institutions as a way of giving continuity to social struggles. Nonetheless, since the event has not occurred (and we do not know when it will), all institutions of the common are, in reality, institutions to come that are not possible within the immanence of capitalism. For this reason, my proposal is based on institutionalization of the common as an openness and a process of the continuous questioning of capitalism. Albeit social ruptures happen within and against capitalism, new processes of fostering alternative social meanings and materializing struggles into new institutions are constantly emerging.

The cases I have presented as processes of institutionalization of the common share their rejection of following the rules. They do so by altering the rules of creating a whole new game. But the variety of responses differs. The Zapatistas break any link to the state and political parties and initiate their own project of autonomy. The resulting new institutions develop the indigenous communities' interpretation of democracy, despite their difficulties and conflicts at the regional and state levels. The Zapatista discourse overcomes local struggles and tries to create a non-hegemonic alternative in cooperation with other social struggles. The idea of living well reflects the promotion of values that are not based on capitalist tradition but, rather, on the indigenous cosmovision. It grounds an alternative understanding of development, recovering the symbiosis between nature and human beings. This is possible because of the relationship between the government and social movements, which allow for the production of policies and institutions to contribute to a common goal. Constant effort is required to maintain the participation of social movements in decision making. Finally, the PAH gains strength from the institutionalization of democracy as undertaken by the *indignados* movement. The initiatives of the PAH address the constitution of social bonds and the production of an effective discourse that make it impossible for capitalism to legitimize its inhumanity through the imposition of exchange value in the name of accumulation. The main challenge still consists in how to alter the legal and political systems, although some changes are taking place.

It is true that there is no such thing as an alternative chessboard ruled by the social production of the common. However, the failed attempts to renew capitalism after the financial crisis in 2008 show us that the number of players who do not want to follow the prefixed rules is increasing and they are questioning not only the movements of the pieces, but the whole game. Multiple processes of institutionalization are developing the art of non-playing chess. Regardless of the existence of another chessboard, the efforts of social struggles in terms of organizing and consolidating the interruption of consensus raise the even more important question of who the other players are. Although chess is still played according to well-known rules, other unexpected players are appearing on the board and they want to be part of the game—their game and not the one from which they have been (or still are) excluded.

What is this art of non-playing chess about, then? “A light of possible intelligence and openness,” says Berardi (2012b, 43), admitting that “I am not actually sure of what I am talking about when I say the word art. You aren’t either – nobody is exactly.” The uncertainty of the art (and of all the processes of institutionalization) reveals one fact. Checkmate is an act of speech to enunciate the end of the game. But its performative effect is still pending on the willingness of the speakers to accept the utterance performed by the act. In other words, performative utterances can be socially contested. Checkmate is not an exception. Indeed, questioning it is a way of rejecting the power exercised by the rules of the game. Checkmate? is the starting point of the art of non-playing chess. It is the confirmation that the game is not totally under control and, indeed, far from being over.

References

Arellano Ortiz, Fernando. 2012. "*David Harvey: 'Para superar el capitalismo, el valor de uso debe prevalecer sobre el valor de cambio.'*" Aporrea October 22. Available at http://www.aporrea.org/ideologia/n216743.html

Barrera, Marcelo, and Rey, Juan. 2007. "El andar zapatista y la otra campaña." *Revista Sociológica de Pensamiento Crítico* 1(2): 1271–1237.

Berardi, Franco. 2012a. "Jaque (¿mate?)." *Rebelión* April 20. Available at http://www.rebelion.org/noticia.php?id=148272

Berardi, Franco. 2012b. *The Uprising. On Poetry and Finance*. Los Angeles: Semiotext(e).

Bouza, Luis. 2013. "*La PAH y la agenda política.*" Publico April 17. Available at http://www.eldiario.es/agendapublica/PAH-agenda-politica_6_122197789.html

Castoriadis, Cornelius. 1998. *El Ascenso de la Insignificancia*. Madrid: Cátedra.

Castoriadis, Cornelius. 2002. *La Insignificancia y la Imaginación*. Madrid: Trotta.

Cocco, Giuseppe. 2012. *MundoBraz. El Devenir-Mundo de Brasil y el Devenir-Brasil del Mundo*. Madrid: Traficantes de Sueños.

Colau, Ada. 2011. *Cómo se para un desahucio. La experiencia de la Plataforma de afectados por la hipoteca.* Plataforma de Afectados por la Hipoteca. Available at http://afectadosporlahipoteca.files.wordpress.com/2011/07/como-parar-desahucio_a-colau1.pdf

Correa, Rafael. 2012. "Ecuador's path. Interview." *New Left Review* 77: 88–111.

Ejército Zapatista de Liberación Nacional. 2005. "Sixth Declaration of the Lacandon Jungle." In *In Motion Magazine*. Available at http://www.inmotionmagazine.com/auto/selva6.html

França, João. 2013. "*Pobres armados de razones.*" Eldiario.es April 17. Available at http://www.eldiario.es/catalunya/diferencia-hijo-pobre_0_122837717.html

Gainza, Patricia. 2006. "*Entrevista a Michael Hardt. La lucha no es espontánea, necesitamos organizarnos.*" Revista del Sur 163: 42–45.

González Casanova, Pablo. 2003. "Los caracoles Zapatistas. Redes de resistencia y autonomía. Ensayo de interpretación." *Revista Memoria* 177.

Hajer, Maarten. 1993. "Discourse coalitions and the institutionalization of practice: the case of acid rain in Britain." In *The Argumentative Turn in Policy Analysis and Planning* edited by Frank Fisher and John Forester, 43–76. Durham: Duke University Press.

Hardt, Michael, and Holloway, John. 2011. "Creating Common Wealth and Cracking Capitalism. A Cross-Reading." *Revista Herramienta* 49. Available at http://www.herramienta.com.ar/revista-herramienta-n-49/creating-common-wealth-and-cracking-capitalism-cross-reading

Hardt, Michael, and Negri, Antonio. 2009. *Commonwealth*. Cambridge: Harvard University Press.

Hardt, Michael, and Negri, Antonio. 2012. *Declaration*. E-book. Argo Navis Author Services.

Hernández, Maribel. 2009. "Sumak Kawsay y Suma Qamaña, el reto de aprender del Sur. Reflexiones en torno al buen vivir." *Revista Obets* 4: 55–65.

Holloway, John. 2010. *Crack Capitalism*. London: Pluto Press.

Jenkins, Richard. 2004. *Social Identity*. London: Routledge.

Joas, Hans. 1989. "Institutionalization as creative process: the sociological importance of Cornelius Castoriadis's political philosophy." *American Journal of Sociology* 94(5): 1184–99.

Laclau, Ernesto. 1991. "Can immanence explain social struggles?" *Diacritics* 31(4): 3–10.

Lazzarato, Maurizio. 2011. *The Making of the Indebted Man*. Amsterdam: Semiotext(e).

Marazzi, Christian. 2003. *El Sitio de los Calcetines. El Giro Lingüístico de la Economía y Sus Efectos sobre la Política*. Madrid: Akal.

Marazzi, Christian. 2011. *The Violence of Financial Capitalism*. Los Angeles: Semiotext(e).

Marcos, Subcomandante. 2011. "'Roads of dignity' speech," 2001. Synthesis/Regeneration 25 (Summer). Available at http://www.greens.org/s-r/25/25-11.html

Mouffe, Chantal. 1993. *The Return of the Political*. London: Verso.

Negri, Antonio. 2001. "Contrapoder." *Contrapoder. Una Introducción*: 83-92. Buenos Aires: Ediciones de Mano en Mano.

Negri, Antonio. 2008. *La Fábrica de Porcelana. Una Nueva Gramática de la Política*. Barcelona: Paidós.

Rancière, Jacques. 2011. *Momentos Políticos*. Buenos Aires: Clave Intelectual.

Rodríguez Lascano, Sergio. 2007. "Caracoles Zapatistas: Creación heroica." *El Programa de las Américas del IRC*. March 2.

Sánchez Cedillo, Raúl. 2008. "Hacia nuevas creaciones políticas. Movimientos, instituciones, nueva militancia." *Producción cultural y prácticas instituyentes. Líneas de ruptura en la crítica institucional,* 217–241. Madrid: Traficantes de Sueños.

Searle, John. 1995. *The Construction of Social Reality*. London: Penguin.

Searle, John. 2005. *Libertad y Neurobiología. Reflexiones Sobre el Libre Albedrío, el Lenguaje y el Poder Político*. Barcelona: Paidós.

Seippel, Ornulf. 2001. "From Mobilization to Institutionalization? The Case of Norwegian Environmentalism." *Acta Sociologica* 44 (2): 123-137.

Suh, Doowon. 2011. "Institutionalizing social movements: the dual strategy of the Korean women's movement." *Sociological Quarterly* 52: 442–471.

Torres-Tovar, Mauricio, and De Vos, Paul. 2013. "The Correa 'phenomenon' in Ecuador: between 'buen vivir' and neo-developmentalism." *International Health Policies* March 21. Available at http://e.itg.be/ihp/archives/correa-phenomenon-ecuador-buen-vivir-neo-developmentalism/

Walsh, Catherine. 2010. "Development as Buen Vivir: institutional arrangements and (de)colonial entanglements." *Society for International Development* 53(1): 15–21.

11. Mendicancy on the Edge of Crisis: The Gift of Rights in a Time of Global Strife

Ben Dorfman

Michael Hardt and Antonio Negri's trilogy of Empire (2000), Multitude (2004), and Commonwealth (2009)—and, more recently, Declaration (2012)—paints a picture of an interesting world. Theirs—the contemporary, post-1989 world—is a world full of massive asymmetries. Asymmetry includes shifting identity groups, attempts to think beyond class, coalitions of movements challenging global systems, multiple concepts of power, and multiple sites of sovereignty and varieties of social organization in a range of activist movements. Nonetheless, in their central texts, Hardt and Negri present massive *symmetries* in the midst of global diversity. Symmetry largely involves the opposition of Empire and multitude, or "the multitude." What to make of this opposition, the opposition between system and the productive subjects who make it? Empire is a "logic and structure of rule," as Giovanni Arrighi (2003, 29) points out; Hardt and Negri (2000, xiii) call it a new global form of sovereignty. Empire attaches itself to no state, no corporation, no multinational entity, and no concrete form of armed or military enforcement. Empire transcends the bond between capitalism and the state argued for so forcefully by Marx (1994, 258) in *Capital.* Empire relies on deterritorialization to in fact territorialize identities it sought to free. An "uncontainable desire for freedom," write Hardt and Negri (2000, 52), is in fact the birth of Empire. This is as modern revolution undid the strictures of state control (absolutism); democratic revolution was the first mode of state decentralization. The denigration of absolutist centralization would only expand, however, determining the vast expanse of Empire's playing field: the globe itself. Multitude produces Empire. The multitude is, simply, all of us. Capital—power—no longer accumulates to institutions or individuals. No one is "behind" Empire. Power accumulates to the system. It is in the heart of this dark terrain, that of the system, that the forces of multitude attempt to find light. "Communality and singularity" define the multitude's "flesh" (Hardt and Negri 2004, 212). Humanity labors, or "works," but in different ways, even, ironically, the capitalists among us.

Capitalism's crisis is, of course, an important theme for Hardt and Negri. This is clearly the case in *Declaration,* written in response to events after the global financial crisis of 2008, but the issue is present in Commonwealth (though the book was under construction during the emergence of the crisis).

"The productivity of biopolitical labor," write Hardt and Negri (2009, 145), "is reduced every time the common is destroyed." Biopolitical labor becomes the production of social life; social life is the world by which we are surrounded (Hardt & Negri 2000, xiii). However, social life and biopolitical labor are complex; as we identify ourselves in part, if not fully, via our social world, biopolitical labor becomes the construction of subjectivity itself. The common is the shared space of the multitude; the common is where the multitude, as constituted subjects, "communicate and act together" (Hardt & Negri 2004, xv). The dramatic, fast-moving nature of economic crisis after 2008 raised the contradiction between Empire and multitude to a "higher power" (Hardt & Negri 2009, 149). True: post-2008, crisis has been fast moving and widespread, quickly going "viral." The destruction of the common, however, or the multitude's impoverishment by Empire, is nothing new. The destruction of the common is inherent to capitalist systems. Here, long-term economic cycles of capitalist expansion are involved, with contractions and the cyclical dispersion and retreat of capitalist systems (e.g., Hopkins and Wallerstein 1996). These are essential as "passages" into Empire, as Hardt and Negri (2000, 67) call them.

Can we expand our view of crisis? I would say yes. Undoubtedly, crisis is the 10 percent unemployment rates in the United States, as they reached their height in 2009 (US Department of Labor 2013). Crisis is roughly percent unemployment in Greece and Spain. Crisis is multiplicious, sometimes networked, sometimes independent social movements bridging, for example, Zapatistas, Occupy, and the manifold interests of the World Social Forum. Crisis is assertions of geopolitical power (e.g., American-driven wars in the Middle and Near East), wars potentially predicated on grabs for economic power and natural resources (e.g., Harvey 2003). However, crisis is also *all* of these things in conjunction. Crisis—one might prefer "strife"—is conflict itself. Crisis is all struggles for democracy and representation. Crisis encompasses all geopolitical conflicts, symmetrical or not, since the "desymmetricization" of world politics with the start of the post-Cold War era. Crisis is all deterritorializations of identity due to the globalization of the world economy, contemporary labor mobility, the "pastiche" of aesthetic forms (Lyotard 1992), and conflicts between local and global forces over the right to reterritorialize identity (if one can). Crisis, or strife, is more than an attack on the common. Times of global strife and conflict represent attacks on subjectivity itself: the self's sovereignty, self-governing power, and right to determine the contours of the social world around it as much as the social world determines the contours of the self.

I would like to do a number of things in this essay. First, I would like to pose human rights, or the regime of theoretically international rights as prosecuted since 1948, as the point of conflict resolution or the resolution of strife, that is, human rights *qua* concept or the realization of human rights. This concept is expressed most forcefully in the Universal Declaration of Human Rights, hereafter UDHR (United Nations, or UN, 1948), as the ultimate reason for attempting to emerge from a crisis, or a world of strife. In other words, we repair economies to engage rights. As Hardt and Negri state, the theorization, if not institutionalization of, global democratic systems are based on the attempt to achieve rights. Rights are the reason for the reduction of global social inequality and attempts to gain temperance in armed conflict. Rights are the reason for the realization and analysis of crisis itself; that fundamental, international human rights have been violated *is*, or *defines*, crisis, as such. As Hardt and Negri (2012, 52–53) assert, the declaration of "inalienable rights" reveals "the course of a historical movement … reaching its maturity." Rights, or their realization, are the teleological ends of historical social struggle. However, the power of human rights in the global environment emerges from their "mendicant" position within the system (Hardt & Negri 2000, 36). In other words, the power of human rights emerges from rights' (*human* rights') position as an *impoverished* discourse and practice in global society, a site where ultimate ideological power emerges from the exhaustion of an idea or an idea's irrelevance. I would like to explain what human rights are, how they fit into the spaces Hardt and Negri define via Empire and multitude, and how rights might be "beggars." Why are rights mendicant? And how "mendicant" rights connect to a world we might read through the lenses of Empire and its multitudinous opposition?

Second, however, I would like to note that the concept of human rights' mendicancy ties rights to notions of gift, or the idea that maximum power emerges from those who give gifts they cannot afford to give. This thesis, with formative theorizations of the gift coming from Marcel Mauss and Georges Bataille, suggest that human rights are a demonstration of power from a place that has none. Mauss and Bataille suggest that rights enthrall us with a majesty and munificence even though rights should not possess such qualities because they are forced to beg (i.e., accept the idea of their mendicancy). By impressing us this way—as a gift (or *gifts* [plural])—rights dominate us. Rights become "highest moral precepts and political ideals" of contemporary society (Moyn 2010: 1). This is despite the fact—or, perhaps because of it—that rights are hardly always treated in such ways (goals to be *fêted*, as such). This dual dynamic around rights—their mendicancy yet simultaneous governing power—is not unique to the notation of crises or the identification of times of crisis such as ours. It is, however, that which makes them relevant to crisis wherever it is found.[1]

---

1 The thesis formulation of this essay opens the question of whether it is about Hardt and Negri or something else (e.g., human rights in themselves, or the contemporary world). My answer is all of the above. Hardt and Negri, as do all significant theoreticians, pro-

What are human rights and why are they beggars?

It is in Empire that Hardt and Negri (2000, 36) note human rights' mendicancy: "Global, regional and local organizations that are dedicated to relief work and the protection of human rights," they argue—with Amnesty International, Oxfam, and Doctors without Borders as examples—are among Empire's "mendicant orders." Mendicancy is no easy concept. Human rights are an example of "just wars without arms"; "through their language and … action," assert Hardt and Negri, human rights define the enemy as "privation" and then "recognize the enemy as sin." By engaging humility, *à la* medieval mendicant orders (e.g., the Franciscans), human rights shine a light on, if not precisely the arrogance of the surrounding world, then at least the surrounding world's oblivion to the higher moral principles and notions of self-realization many of us would like to see as the surrounding, or social, world's end.

This is an interesting vision of human rights as it takes on human rights as practice and idea, or rights *qua* concept as well as rights "organization" (Amnesty, Oxfam, Doctors without Borders, etc.). The concepts are, of course, related: rights come alive in organizations. The rights non-governmental organization (NGO) is imagined by Hardt and Negri (2004, 294) as part of a (potential) global representative system; they wish to transcend the statist systems that dominate the contemporary world and have perhaps dominated the *modern* world since the 1648 institution of the Westphalian system. The question is how to realize the realities of citizenship—national self-determination and popular representation should not be forgotten—but bring rights outside the pure purview of the state. For rights to be enacted at the global level, "they will have to be grounded in powerful and autonomous institutions" (Hardt & Negri 2004, 297). Of course, powerful and autonomous global institutions shadow the central mechanisms of Empire, the surrounding world of the contemporary, including the International Monetary Fund (IMF), the World Trade Organization (WTO), the World Bank and, indeed, any political or monetary organization structuring the international order. This shadowing of existing organizations, however, refers to rights as an idea, the guiding principle behind organizations. Organization itself, or order, is justified via appeal to the right and the just, for betterment, process and development (the World Bank's slogan is "Working for a world free of poverty"). The organization, representative or not (and Hardt and Negri argue that the IMF, WTO, and World Bank are not, though arguments can be made to the contrary),

vide tools to analyze our times and our world. They ask us to refer to these tools, but also to explicate our ultimate referent as the world they help explain. Therein, we balance between thinking our world, as such, and provocative touchstones provided for that endeavor by theorists such as Hardt and Negri.

gains its life from rights, that is, the appeal to a concept of naturality and modes of justification that it (the organization) "should" be there.[2] Rights—and we return to this theme—work both in the service of the contemporary global system (Empire) and against it (multitude).

Human rights can, in fact, be understood as the "highest moral precepts and political ideals" (Moyn 2010, 1) of contemporary society, occupying a unique position in our life-world. This may be comprehensible in two ways: historically and theoretically. A historical account runs as follows. Though human rights potentially have archaic origins—for example, the very notion of law (Ishay [2004] dates this back to Mesopotamian law codes), notions of the "law of peoples" (the Roman *ius gentium*, or early imperial concepts of international norms), the notion of *droit divin* (the right of kings), and abstract notions of sovereignty itself (i.e., the thought that anything at all might be sovereign)—its most concrete origins lie in the revolutionary democratic movements of the late 18th century, specifically the French and American Revolutions. Hardt and Negri refer to these movements repeatedly; though they were led by bourgeoisies—and therein reproduced structures of inequality—they nonetheless provided the "pure" (Hardt & Negri 2000, 117) rhetoric of rights: liberty, equality, and brotherhood. "All men are created equal and endowed … with certain inalienable rights," claims the American Declaration of Independence, the late 18th-century attempt to break away the American colonies from the British Empire. Man, or humanity, claims the French Declaration of the Rights of Man and Citizen, maintains "natural, inalienable and sacred rights." These rights were to be invested in the social polity. Rights, as rights theorist Johannes Morsink (2009, 21) notes, precede "social custom, judicial announcement, or some act of parliament." Rights were had simply by virtue of being human. They were not achieved via elevated social position, as for the French Bourbon monarchs or the Hanoverians, who ruled Britain in the 18th century, checked by parliament though they were.

Such notions of rights, however—those emergent in the late 18th century—were not necessarily *human* rights. This is a distinction that needs to be made to provide a firmer sense of *human* rights. Late 18th-century rights fall into the category of what rights scholars Moyn (2010) refers to as the "rights of man." An essential distinction between the rights of man and human rights concerns citi-

2 Notions that the IMF, WTO, and World Bank are representative institutions are addressed by Zweifel (2006) and, specifically focusing on the WTO, Joseph (2011). Both authors note that these international financial governance institutions maintain "democratic deficits." That does not mean, however, that the architecture of those organizations is not intended to provide some modicum of representational capacity.

zenship. Revolutionary democratic traditions in the late 18th century and 19th century were nationalistic. As Moyn (2010, 26) points out, the point was "a whole people incorporating itself in a state." In his account of nationalism, Eric Hobsbawm (1992, 88) notes that, for citizens, rights made the state "to some extent our own'" (that of the social body)—an idea Hardt and Negri (2000, 104) note the French Revolution consecrated via the idea of the "general interest" (Rousseau, of course, referred to it as the "general will"). The institution of rights concerned proprietorship over the nation. *Human* rights circumvent the nationality, or perhaps national*ism*, of rights by crossing international borders. Human rights allow one state to criticize another for its "wrongdoings" (Moyn 2010, 26). Theoretically, human rights trump national law because the appeal to a higher authority—the universality of rights themselves or the idea of intrinsic humanity—means that all national law should be based on human rights. Human rights do not explicitly rely on citizenry or citizenship (i.e., an institutionalized association with a social polity). Hannah Arendt (1958, 297) famously posed this as the basis for human rights: a "deprivation of a place in the world," she wrote in *The Origins of Totalitarianism*, generates "the right to have rights." Human rights are the rights of the stateless as much as they are of those grounded in state identity.

Historically, such distinctions place human rights firmly within the post-Second World War regime of the United Nations (UN), an international body, though state based, claiming to look after the supranational interests of humanity itself—the body via which we would "practice tolerance and live together in peace and with one another as good neighbors" (UN 1945). There are two points here. First, over time, ranges of human rights have been declared outside of the UN: the European Convention on Human Rights (1950), the African Charter on Human and Peoples' Rights (1979), the American Declaration of Human Rights (1969), and the Cairo Declaration of Human Rights in Islam (1990), among others (representing, e.g., the European Union, the African Union, the Organization of American States, and the Islamic Council of Foreign Ministers, respectively). All of these declarations are, nonetheless, predicated upon the UN's engagement with human rights, whose primary document is the Universal Declaration of Human Rights (UDHR, 1948), which rights scholar Michael Freeman (2011, 4) calls the fountainhead of international human rights law. Two categories of rights emerge here: civil and political rights and economic, social, and cultural rights. Civil and political rights are largely the rights of the individual and the individual's right to be defended against the state. As Jiwei Ci (2005) notes, this largely corresponds to Isaiah Berlin's (2002, 169) concept of negative liberty: what one is able to do without "interference from other persons." Hardt and Negri (2004, 268) refer to it as the space of the *Cahiers de Doléances,* that is, the right of complaint (referring to pre-revolutionary complaints brought to the French Estates General). No institution or collectivity should intervene to curtail individual expressive freedom. These are liberal rights: the right to intellectual self-realization and the conception of the self as intellectual as much as material. Economic, social, and cultural rights address the material individual, which involves national self-determination (collective self-realization), the provision of basic welfare and material subsistence, and economic non-exploitation within the international system (the right to development). Within the UN regime, civil and political rights, on one hand, and economic, social, and cultural rights, on the other, are most extensively worked out in the International Covenant on Civil and Political Rights (1967) and the International Covenant on Economic, Social and Cultural Rights (1967). The division of human rights into these two covenants was a Cold War agreement: the Americans sought to emphasize the former (civil and political rights) and the Soviets the latter (economic, social, and cultural rights). Both covenants, however, conjoin with the UDHR to form the International Bill of Human Rights, the full UN vision of rights. Both covenants, however, are predicated on the UDHR itself. The UDHR encompasses the right to "freedom of thought, conscience, and religion" (Article 18), as well as the right to "equal protection of the law" (Article 7). The UDHR also encompasses rights concerning minimal living standards, however—for example, the right to work (Article 23) and the right to an adequate "standard of living," including adequate "food, clothing, housing and medical care" (Article 25).

This gives us two phenomena (the second point about human rights falling within the UN regime). First, the international human rights regime continued to grow along these two lines after 1948, expanding and specifying problem areas within both civil and political rights and economic, social, and cultural rights. This led to "topically" based rights treaties. The Convention on the Elimination of All Forms of Racial Discrimination (1965), the Convention on the Elimination of All Forms of Discrimination against Women (1979), and the Declaration on the Right to Development (1986) are all examples of such treaties. These emphasize legal equality and social development. Second, however, especially come the end of the Cold War, human rights came to occupy a special ideological pride of place on a global basis. Moyn (2010) notes this as a matter of "last utopias." Under Soviet and American competition, the end of history —social "completion"— theoretically lay with one of the two ideologies (capitalism and communism) those states represented. The defeat of Cold War ideological competition, however, defeated ideology itself; political economics were no longer necessarily the key to global happiness. This cleared a space for human rights as a non-ideological ideology of universal appeal. Hardt and Negri (2004, 60) note this in Multitude: "the logic of human rights is not in the specific interest of any nation or people but rather by definition universal to humanity." The logic of human rights is the property of a deterritorialized, fully globalized world.

This gives us a sense of human rights in our atmosphere; that human rights are "there," that they have arrived in the cultural–political discourses of the late 20th and early 21st centuries, whether we describe that world as Empire or not. Rights—that is, human rights—have evolved. However, rights theory (as opposed to history) nuances this picture. A *theory* of human rights tells us that rights are intended to liberate; the *raison d'être* of rights is to liberate peoples in both individual and collective forms. "All human beings are born free and equal in dignity and rights," asserts the UDHR; however, all human beings are also "endowed with reason and conscience." Rights grant conscious, reasonable, reflective subjects freedom; human rights grant these subjects the power of self-realization and action in relation to one's perceptions. Rights grant the ability to sustain perception by protecting the subject's material life. Economic sustenance is also within the purview of rights. This fact is important to Hardt and Negri's (2009) sense of justice; if we are to realize commonwealth, the authors maintain we must recognize the common *wealth,* a shared proprietorship of global wealth. The point is everything from the "right to nationality" claimed in the UDHR (Article 15) to the right to rights in a state of full internationality or globality. Cultural identification and self-determination are to be embraced in all their dimensions, intellectually and economically.

Important here for Empire—the political form accorded the contemporary by Hardt and Negri—is that human rights become a paradigmatic modern political form. Human rights engage a "centered" subject and provide for its liberation. Human rights engage a concept of mind and body. Reason and conscience are essential to the human being (UDHR, Article 1). Reason and conscience—the operations of mind—cannot be sustained however, without the body; the human being's material life is a necessity. Human rights preserve the motive subject, the individual who drives his or her physical person via thought. The will to associate with others both intellectually and physically—to form political associations—is also protected. The question, then, for both Empire and for "us" (the referent of Empire) is what makes rights beggars—mendicant? How are rights, in the conditions of the late 20th and early 21st centuries, especially in the face of a relative ideological cache, *impoverished*? How is a concept with a relatively high level, or seemingly high level, of historical presence, "mere," to the side, present but poor? How is an idea, one that in fact wields high levels of power, power*less*? How are rights a beggar in the contemporary landscape of the real?

One answer to this question is obvious: rights organizations need to beg. In other words, rights need to beg for raw finances and political capital. Amnesty

International, one of Hardt and Negri's examples (and an obvious one as perhaps the premier international rights organization), is a member-driven organization. Amnesty relies on "donations" (related to, incidentally, the French word for gift, *don*). Amnesty is a charity. It relies on states to *accept* its petitions; Amnesty can enforce nothing. Individuals, corporations, and federal tax breaks provide it funds. Amnesty relies on charity as an act. Human Rights Watch, the other preeminent rights organization, also maintains this status. Amnesty, Human Rights Watch, Oxfam, Doctors without Borders, Reporters without Borders—virtually all humanitarian organizations—are non-profit. They are prohibited from wealth. Wealth may be expended upon high levels of aesthetic presentations; it often is. Amnesty's barbed wire candle and yellow and black graphic are instantly recognizable and widely quoted in a visual sense. So is Human Rights Watch's blue background and white-lettered logo. The blue helmets of UN soldiers—those who fight "just wars" *with* arms—are also iconic (we gain here a prelude of human rights in the service of Empire). Despite aesthetic value, however, the economic status of rights is subsistence. The economic status of human rights is equal expenditure with consumption, at the least. The economic status of rights is the sustenance of the life of the rights organization, but not more. *Qua* their institutionalization, human rights may appear corporate (e.g., the title of Joseph Slaughter's 2007 book uses the designation *Human Rights Inc.* to indicate the possibility of corporatism in human rights). Political-economically, however, human rights are far from corporate. Rights are idealisms, based on the institution of radical social equality rather than any level of equality's destabilization, or the accumulation of power unto one's self as opposed to the other.

This is not the limit of human rights' begging, however. In terms of their association with international institutions—specifically, the UN (over and above the human rights NGO)—rights take their practical footing in weak institutions. Internationally, one cannot deny the effects of human rights. As Freeman (2011, 160) notes, there are pragmatic reasons for states' adoption of human rights standards. These include securing trade advantages or avoiding trade sanctions. States adopt human rights standards to avoid being "shamed" by the international community (or at least shamed by specific powers within it). Human rights can also enter multiple-step processes in terms of rights' adoption by states that traditionally violate them. These processes include attempts to prevent news of rights violations from leaking out, denial upon the leak, reaction of the international community with sanctions and shaming, tacit lip service to the necessity of rights, and, then, the actual adoption of rights standards. Human rights bring with them the issue of legitimacy; rights bring up the problem of adherence to standards of principle that few fully achieve but represent the ideal end political systems attempt to achieve. Even the most insidious revolutions have been conducted in the name of right, the liberation of peoples from oppressed states into a more "utopic," natural existence. Liberation and self-realization discourses lie deep within modern politics, even in their illiberal modes. Their notions govern the political discourse of the contemporary international stage.

Still, though human rights can be and have been adopted into national law, the 1998 British Human Rights Act being a prime example, the ultimate impetus to rights comes from abstract and universal institutions.[3] Again, the UN is a primary example. The ultimate force of human rights is an idea, a standard that represents a concept as much as a reality. Human rights are enforced by "hard" power only in the most extreme cases; even then, as in cases such as Bosnia and Rwanda in the 1990s, enforcement is extremely difficult (the essential issue being potential violations of national sovereignty). Such a situation often means that human rights gain their fullest meaning as a disembodied dream. Human rights gain their promise as a "come," as Jacques Derrida (1997, 306) termed it, a promise, a "might be" of potential, but potential oft unrealized.

What is unique is that the dream of rights, the claim of liberation as the basis for their organization, is the claim of both Empire *and* multitude—those entities seeking to resolve crisis (and whose conflicts *give* us strife). Multitude, at least as formulated by Hardt and Negri, seeks rights through resistance, "protest." Multitude is singular in its production of Empire; it always works in cooperation with itself to build the social world. Being multitudinous is an identity. In its modes of activity, however, multitude is not "one" (Hardt & Negri 2004, xiv). Multitude entails different "cultures, races, ethnicities, genders, and sexual orientations; different forms of labor; different ways of living; different views of the world." Identity multiplicity and sociopolitical as well as economic diversity constitute multitude's multiple lines of protest. Pro-democracy demonstrators in the Middle East, Occupy protestors on Wall Street, and Zapatistas in Mexico, claim Hardt and Negri (2012), share common identities in the act of struggle. This is whether the focus of struggle is neo-liberal economics, political oppression, or the paradoxical goal of ethnic liberation while simultaneously restructuring oppressive social power within so-called traditional societies—an important point for Hardt and Negri's (2009, 106) understanding of the Zapatistas, since they seek to both challenge and free indigenous identities. Multitudinal protest, if it might be called that—"altermodernity," a term that Hardt and Negri (2009) also use—concerns greater realization, locally or globally, of democratic practice. The multitude is interested in "reappropriation" (Hardt & Negri 2000,

3 This phraseology is borrowed from Lynn Hunt (2007, 153), who argues for the nature of human rights as lying in "abstract universality."

407); the multitude seeks to reassert a right to "self-control and autonomous self-production." This is as in producing Empire ("society"), the multitude has relinquished control to Empire. The multitude has used both its material and immaterial (intellectual) resources to constitute exploitative systems in which member of the multitude become posed against one another (this is why multitude is not a class: identities within it are managed *against* one another). Multitude has sought the liberation of its "selves" and its identities. However, in doing so, multitude has allowed for difference and power inequality. This scenario nonetheless represents the terms of its liberation—that it provides many levels of liberation. This becomes nature without nature in a postmodern sense. Difference in all its manifestations, claim Hardt and Negri, allows us to do things *together*.

Nonetheless, if multitudinal protest is righteous, if it represents freedom, anti-oppression and the realization of rights, why has the Empire not been dismantled? Why, even in the midst of a historical movement reaching its "maturity," have some supplicated to Empire? Why have not all acted to establish or restore what Hardt and Negri (2004) term the common, the site of multitudinal cooperation, and the embrace of brotherhood in difference? How is it that Empire represents, or utilizes, the dream of rights—such that Empire might claim defectors or prevent members of the multitude from realizing its power for strategic and fundamental opposition?

For one, this is connected to Empire's existence as a new historical form. Empire indeed represents the deregulation of capital markets (a move intrinsic to capitalism) and the dissolution of state-based authority that global capitalism can incur. Empire, however, also represents governance via tensions within such figurations: battles over which markets should be deregulated, precisely how much and where, precisely when the flow of economic resources should end, and the interplay of these forces to serve its (Empire's) productive ends— that is, the ongoing productivity of the global system itself. Empire, moreover, represents the flow between national and international justice; this is as state authority underpins global authority yet the authority of international rights, at least in theory, is or at least represents the ultimate site of legitimacy for national rights. Empire is not a site or "node" of control. Empire is not *some*where. Empire is control itself. Empire is the subject's integration in the "rhythm of productive practices and productive socialization" (Hardt & Negri 2000, 24). In a global economy, in congruence with the juridical-political forms that sustain it, this means less the production of selves with limitless geographical and identity horizons than it does the asymmetricization and possible displacement of traditional identities, yet their recovery when necessary. Within Empire, the subject's new territory is not localization in national or cultural pasts with concordant geographical spaces. The new territory of the subject is in the release of the subject into geographical, cultural, and political horizons that might challenge its history. The reinvocation of indigenous identities, or the "indigenization" of world politics, as Samuel Huntington (1996, 91) refers to it, is a war in this battle. Indigenization, or the recovery of traditional identity, is a strategic strike against imperial rule. In part, resistance is against modernization and universalization. Still, this provides a systemic element where production might be localized—this since the localization of one identity allows for the globalization of another. Just as tourists need locals for their travel, so, too, does Empire need indigenous identities and the crises created by them (their conflict with "modernity") to stand as repositories of a world we have lost—repositories of territorialized identities Empire claims to have overcome and at least partially cleansed.

Nonetheless, this does not prevent the full structure of Empire from hinging upon rights with rights as Empire's teleological end of crisis. As Hardt and Negri (2000, 14) formulate it, Empire is "governance without government." Empire is a set of oppositions brought into concert in the name of progressive freedoms, that global modernity will improve human life. Hardt and Negri (2000, 14) argue that within Empire,

> Systematic totality has a dominant position.... All conflicts, all crises, and all dissensions effectively push forward the process of integration.... Peace, equilibrium, and the cessation of conflict are the values towards which everything is directed. The development of the global system (and of imperial right in the first place) seems to be the development of a machine that imposes procedures of continual contractualization that [should] lead to systemic equilibria.

I have taken the liberty of adding the parenthetical *should* to the notion of systemic equilibria because Hardt and Negri's point is that, within Empire, freedom must be monitored. This may be "our" point as well. We can recognize what Hardt and Negri (2000, 17) call the "right of the police." In other words, we live in a world that recognizes the "exceptionality of intervention." As in the case of indigenous conflict—conflict over difference and the introduction of potential inequality (via both concepts and practices of us versus them and problems of "minorities")—Empire relies on a state of emergency. Such conflicts rely on dissension and torsion that point to the need to recover normality. Freedom of trade, for example, must be defended, as it has been in the face of capitalist-skeptical protests in Genoa (2001), Gothenburg (2001), and Seattle (1999), among others—Seattle being a favorite of Hardt and Negri (2004, 285). Market freedom is "normal." Democratic freedom must sometimes be imposed (e.g., in Afghanistan and Iraq). This involves preserving the rights of minorities and the repressed (those not allowed to speak by "regimes"). A world described by Empire involves prosecuting war criminals and the check and reform of national and international systems so that the international order defends what it says it does—economic and personal freedom writ large (few regimes present themselves as *not* doing so, even if the terms of freedom are socialistic or based on cultural particularities). Hardt and Negri describe this situation as entrapping. It may be. Even in the name of liberation, they argue, "every movement is fixed and can seek its own designated place only within the system itself, in the hierarchical relationship accorded it" (Hardt & Negri 2000, 14). Francis Fukuyama (1992, 338) rather defended this order: "Rather than a thousand shoots blossoming into as many different flowering plants," he wrote, "mankind will come to seem like a long wagon train strung out along the road." There are many alternative roads to rights and liberation. The route, however, is unified: history's "rationality" or the possibility of constructing human systems based on reasonable and conscientious subjects. "Imperial" rights—the rights of Empire—may be "tamer" than multitudinal rights, or rights sought by resistance. They may come via the opposition of logic to illogic, or order against spontaneity. Both sides, however, involve the invocation of the subject's reflective powers for peace and the realization of justice in concrete juridical and representational forms. Of course, for Hardt and Negri, "reflective powers"—those maintained by subjects—are relative. The subjects' biopolitical production does not necessarily mean a "false consciousness" or that the wool is pulled over the multitude's eyes—at least in relation to its own power to resist. It does mean, however, that rights are precisely the battle terrain between Empire and multitude; rights are the subject of "war and democracy in the age of Empire" (Hardt and Negri 2004). They are what we look for as we attempt to solve crisis or recognize it as a problem. The struggle of the multitude concerns a transcendent equality within itself: to regain what it has lost, to find a "place in the world," as Arendt phrases it. The struggle of the multitude is to realize what Empire supposedly provides it: the intrinsic equality of every human being. Empire will alternatively allow for and quash the multitude's struggles in the name of self-adjustment. This concerns the right to bring peace so that, within social orders, human subjects may realize themselves in relation to the rights that contemporary historical conditions grant us: orders of the natural, the "inherent" capacities of every human being, and the possibility of accumulating capital, or at least benefit, to a system we, in fact, built.

The gift of rights or the power to govern via an idea

That we appeal to human rights ideas—that they maintain a particular dominance in the world—does not answer questions about the mechanisms of that dominance. It does not answer questions about how mendicancy works. How can the mendicant idea of human rights—indeed, "only" an idea, untouchable, nowhere to be found, and only manifest in weak institutions and profitless organizations—govern such a system (Empire, our world), as well as its resistance (multitude)? How can human rights wield power over a system that both creates and resolves its own crises, as well as stand as a discursive and conceptual referent, perhaps the absolute referent, for those who would remake and transform the same system? What is it about an impoverished idea and practice that would make the granting of rights, or the idea of their granting, so powerful within crisis? And what is it that would make an impoverished idea so powerful that it would seem to be and becomes presented as the destiny of a potentially oppressive system, as well as the meaning of confrontation with that system, or at least calls for greater participation within it—claims that historically give us crisis and will probably continue to?

Such questions bring us the nature of the gift, the giving or receiving of a thing or concept. Such questions lead us to the nature of giving things—the gift as an article of that which is given—and the statuses from which gifts are given most powerfully. How do we deal with and what is the significance of a thing offered, held out as available or there to be had? How do we deal with the positions from which things and concepts are proffered?

In *The Gift: The Form and Reason for Exchange in Archaic Societies*, sociologist Marcel Mauss (2000, 13) presents us with perhaps the formative theory of the gift: the notion of giving as a form of rivalry. Gifts and giving, he asserts, are a means of establishing social hierarchy. Weight is placed on the idea of obligation; one is obligated to both give and receive gifts in social situations, lest one wants to marginalize oneself from the social body. "To refuse to give, or fail to invite," writes Mauss, "is like refusing to accept—the equivalent of a declaration of war; it is a refusal of friendship or intercourse." To not participate in the reciprocity of a given gift—*given* here meaning one in existence or one proffered—is to position oneself outside the social order. Non-reciprocity is to negate reliance on, contribution to, or recognition of the other; non-reciprocity is to say that one does not need, since one will not be given again. Non-reciprocity denies the existence of the other by asking for his or her non-engagement. Non-reciprocity is a mode of denying sociality itself. Non -recognition begs the non-recognition of oneself. Refusal to give or accept breaks the "spiritual bond" of society, as Mauss (2000, 13) puts it. One cannot dismiss a concept or object in social interchange; ideas, objects, and all other offerings present or in discourse or offered for exchange need to be entertained; otherwise one negates the bearer of the gift in question. This runs the risk of the future negation of oneself.

In *The Accursed Share*, philosopher Georges Bataille (1988, 69) radicalizes Mauss' notion of the gift: "Gift-giving has the virtue of … surpassing of the subject who gives." Gift giving is more than just recognition or one thing for another. Contrary to apparent economic logic, gift giving increases wealth or that which is proprietary to the subject. Gift giving is not just about participation in the social order or contractual obligation. Gift giving is about dominance in social situations. Obviously, in a rote sense, this is counterintuitive; gift giving would seem to be about economic loss. When one gives a gift, one departs with a resource. One loses potential capital: one loses money, time, energy, control over an object, and from the total resources one has to either exchange or expend on oneself, or for one's own benefit, in the future. Loss involves transformation, however. In gift giving, one puts oneself in a miraculous, "extra-economic" position. In gift giving, one suggests either (*a*) the irrelevance of one's life in the face of an idea (that one might just give) or (*b*) the ability to sustain oneself in the absence of material resources or, at the very least, in their paucity. In gift giving, one posits oneself in a position of mastery; one posits oneself anyway as able to transcend the material world, beyond fear and eschatology. One says implicitly, "I do not need the material world." In remaining in it (the material world), however, in giving—something one can only do in the material world—one returns to that world, though in a position of indifference. One might accept a gift. However, from such a position, the giver knows the gift is given in futility. *Qua* receiver who has already given, the reciprocal act becomes irrelevant. One says, in essence, the return gift is *not* needed to replace the resources lost in the initial giving. That was indicated in one's giving, an act of giving as "pure"—loss without qualification (non-profit). This situation puts the receiver, or "return gift giver," in a subordinate position. The return gift giver will never be able to return adequately, since it is understood that the return gift is not needed, regardless of the magnitude of the return gift.

What we are driving at here is that gift giving is a form of self-immolation; gift giving is a form of self-denial—one gives, at least most powerfully, *but* (*only*) detracting from the self. Self-immolation grants agency; the gift represents one's ability to move despite the other. The gift represents and grants the ability to take action regardless of the stature, status, or position of the other. In political-economic terms, the gift and the self become synonymous; the loss of the gift, an occurrence that takes place in the act of giving, is a loss of the self. One gives that which defines and allows the self, and hence one's selfhood itself. Self-immolation and gift immolation become synonymous. The thing represents ruin; the gift is ruin of the self and, in the acknowledgement of the irrelevance of the self, one acknowledges the irrelevance of that which one gives, of the thing given. Gift giving is an explosion of potential, an expenditure if not asking for then at least involving the degradation and devaluation of that which one gives. Gift giving is a form of destroying one's own riches. In relation to another, such destruction is a demonstration of social power. As Bataille (1988, 69) puts it, destroying the object of the gift is the ultimate gift. It is public self-immolation. The act must be public to have this effect, however. Destroyed "in solitude, in silence, no … power would result from the act" of self- or gift destruction. In the presence of another, giving, or destroying, the gift becomes a mode of enriching oneself via "contempt for riches." One accomplishes agency by demonstrating full autonomy. This autonomy stems from the demand for recognition and dissociation from boundedness to the material world and from social order itself. One holds others—the social—in thrall as one demonstrates oneself to be beyond them. One shows the ability to live without the means to do so.

In the context of human rights, the theory of the gift becomes relevant by realizing that rights give or offer themselves. Rights are given by no one. Historically, one once gave rights. Under divine right—the direct granting of power from the divine to the king to the public (if the king so chose)—rights were not conceived of as part of the social body. Rights might be given or taken away from the social body by the monarch *ad hoc,* the king as state ("*l'etat c'est moi*"). Revolutionary democracy transformed this notion by claiming rights as proprietary unto themselves. Rights were simply there to be had. Rights were inherent, inalienable, preceding political form (before social custom or act of parliament, as Morsink notes). Rights granted themselves. In their early form, that of popular, national sovereignty, rights claimed to be there for the national body. They were the gift of "natural man" for the nation. Human rights do not reject the nation; peoples retain the right to national self-determination. However, rights extend their gift to humanity itself, again, regardless of national citizenship. Rights are posited as present—available to all and at will. Rights were what we should all have and be, by virtue of their simple existence as something that can be taken—a universal sovereignty which might be possessed by all.

It is here that mendicancy enters the picture. What Bataille and Mauss suggest is that the most powerful positions from which to give gifts are either positions of ultimate wealth from which one runs one's wealth into exhaustion (expends it all) or positions of poverty, where one gives what one does not have (i.e., in poverty, any act of giving is necessarily more than one has because one does not have enough). As Mauss specifically indicates, this concerns the bonds of social recognition. To accept gifts or return them in kind is to disengage the intercourse via which one posits oneself in the social order or recognizes the boundedness and reliance of one on (or to) another. To deny gifts or not reciprocate them is to step outside the boundaries of obligation and hence the recognition of all others in all senses. *À la* Bataille, however, more may be at stake. Gift giving involves social mastery. Giving is by nature excessive; giving represents the erosion of one's agency by way of the expenditure of one's resources. Giving is economic self-undercutting, a self-destructive act in which one finds transcendence. As one gives in to ruination, as one explodes oneself or, via the equation of the self and the gift, destroys one's riches in front of another, one becomes ungovernable. One cannot be given a response. In a state of unrespondibility, however, one becomes ungovernable. One gains irrevocable power over others. One gains nonnegotiable agency. One accomplishes the status of a power, perhaps *the* power, to which others have to react. One is irrevocably part of the social order; one has given a gift whose reality is irrefutable. One might try to repay it. Such reciprocity, however, is impossible due to the magnitude of the gift in relation to he, she, or "it" who has given. The gift has left the giver in ruin. The giver is the ungovernable sovereign out of its, his, or her position of mendicancy, as the beggar.

Within the range of political ideas, many concepts cannot give themselves as gifts in this way. Capitalist accumulation cannot. Capitalist accumulation can never outspend itself, since it is always in the process of accumulation; the *raison d'être* of capitalist investment is the recuperation of further wealth: surplus value. Capitalism always holds something in reserve. Expenditure can never be fully self-immolatory. In Adam Smith's (1998, 168) words, capitalism's teleology is to "improve its productive powers." Capitalism will never attempt to destroy its own bases.

Socialism—control over the "means and modes of production" by those who produce—is also prohibited from giving excessive gifts. Socialism must recuperate the profits of capitalism for those who produced them. Socialism seeks to restore equilibrium in economic systems. Socialism concerns the reduction, if not elimination, of the alienation of the self. Excessive self-destruction is not known inside socialism. Socialism should reduce the physical, psychological, and material exploitation that erodes the life of the self. Socialism is not an engagement of or relinquishment to the idea of supplication, nor destruction of the self. Socialism's maxim, as Marx (1938, 27) writes in *Critique of the Gotha Program*, is "from each according to their abilities, to each according to his needs." Giving beyond ability or accepting beyond need is not within socialism's purview.

Democracy may give itself as an excessive gift or as a gift from a "mendicant" position, a beggar's gift. Democracy can and perhaps should encompass social diversity. As John Rawls (2005, 3–4) writes, the "political culture of a democratic society is always marked by a diversity of opposing and irreconcilable religious, philosophical and moral doctrines." The equality of religious, philosophical, and moral, or identity-based, doctrines need not be realized; people and concepts may maintain "dominant" positions, room for others though they must allow. In *The Social Contract*, Rousseau (1968, 72) challenges this with the concept of the general will. The general will, writes Rousseau, "studies only the common interest." Private interest and the potential for power differentiation are not in the general will's horizon. The general will recuperates sovereignty for the public since it concerns the common public control of sovereign power; the general will substitutes "moral and lawful equality for whatever … inequality that nature may have imposed on mankind" (Rousseau 1968, 66). The general will accepts no "right of first occupant"—the right of he or she who might have traditionally maintained higher social rank (*à la* the right of kings)—nor does the general will accept the right of the strongest. The general will invests or seeks to recuperate power fully in the name of "all," a kind of common. Such investments in the public, which imply and demand an overturning of monarchical power—or precisely the right of first occupant as well (as right of the strongest)—nonetheless demands the invocation of individual will. "If the general will is to be clearly expressed," writes Rousseau (1968, 73), "every citizen should make up his own mind for himself." Unity in social action is not ensured. If unity is to be achieved, it will do so naturally and spontaneously. Spontaneity involves allowing for radical decision making processes, ones that can lead to social inequality, and hence the exchange from unequal and potentially power-differentiated positions.

Rights can be invoked by capitalistic, socialistic, and democratic systems. The realization of rights (or right, as in justice) may be their goal. Capitalism, socialism, and democracy may claim rights' ability to free and liberate, but rights are supplicants within such systems. Rights—and specifically human rights—are present before management and conscious decision making. Capitalism, socialism, and democracy do not constitute right; they receive it. Capitalist, socialist, and democratic systems *take* right. They incorporate rights as an idea within their systems. Political systems may display rights; political systems may attempt to show they manifest rights. Political systems may *use* rights. In appropriating rights, however—in taking them—they receive them. Rights have to be recognized—seen—and accepted. Rights must be engaged as something that can be received, that is, a gift. No one offers rights; rights offer themselves. Returning to Arendt, it is in this way that everyone has the "right to have rights." Were rights to be offered by another, a system or person, there might be biopolitical power over rights; the ability to determine who might be a rights subject and who might not. Given of and by themselves, however, rights can be received by any person or any system. Rights are the ultimate gift as an impoverished idea that might be received and need not (and indeed never may) be repaid.

This notion is that of rights in their "mereness." Human rights are manifest nowhere except as a concept. Human rights offer themselves for sustenance in political systems; they can be donated to and taken by global systems as the framework for their governance as well as resistance. Non-profit rights must be donated to in the interest of their sustenance; rights have little practical life—a life that enters systems—without the institutional and financial support offered by specific actors (institutions, governments, or individuals themselves). When received, however, rights give from the most powerful position: that of the impoverished who has little or nothing *to* give. Rights give from outside systems. Of course, that becomes the trick—this is how rights exert the most power. With little or nothing to give, rights give everything. Rights exceed the need to accumulate. Human rights destroy their wealth before us all by giving more than they can. Intended or not, rights can but demand obedience—that we look in awe at their magnificence. Try though we might, we cannot master rights, because rights have already demonstrated that they cannot be mastered. This is as they will always, at least proportionally, give more to us than we give to them.

Conclusion: modesty in the face of rights poverty

In *Declaration*, Hardt and Negri (2012, 51), assert that "all people are equal" and maintain "certain inalienable rights." Using the wordplay of the American Declaration of Independence, Hardt and Negri argue that rights include the right to "life, liberty and the pursuit of happiness"—the right to free thought and action. Social rights are also important, however: "free access to the common, equality in the distribution of wealth, and the sustainability of the common" are non-negotiable absolutes. Again, the common is where production happens; the common is where labor takes place, if but only in communicative form (immaterial labor). Crisis is the destruction of the common, another round of which has taken place with the radical capital markets fluctuations since 2008. The realization of rights is the basis for the resolution of crisis.

Empire—the world Hardt and Negri ascribe as ours—does not avoid this logic. Crisis is useful for Empire—our world—because it allows for the right of the police. Crisis creates exceptional circumstances because it can—and often does—bring protest. The world has undergone waves of protest over the past several years. As Hardt and Negri (2012) point out, protest takes multiple forms: anti-capitalist protest, protests against austerity measures in high unemployment countries, and political protest against regimes preventing free expression and legal equality. Crackdowns against such protests are rights violations; at the very least, crackdowns question or impinge upon the full range of possible expressions within civic and communal spaces, potentially violating civil and political rights. Crackdowns, however, are invoked under the name of the preservation of civic space itself, a regular civic space where the quiet expression of dissenting opinion is governed by rules and where dissent is considered part of the purview of expression. This concept is important because it becomes a principle by which to intervene in other rights violations. Every instance of ethnic violence, tension over national self-expression, and denial of peoples' civil and political or social or cultural rights by the states in which they live is cause to proclaim order against the forces of chaos and against "exception" and the invocation of absolutism and the *ad hoc*. These strategic crises are useful for Empire. Such crises demonstrate that Empire also speaks to rights or finds its own end in their realization. That Empire realizes rights in terms of at least supposed freedom in labor markets, the realization of increasingly democratic political systems, the possibility of social mobility, and liberal flows of information demonstrates Empire's organization in its acceptance of rights' conceptual demands. Equilibrium in our world should result in a productive human state—that necessary for our continued existence.

It appears that massive parts of the global system are organized—governed even—by an idea owned by no one. Rights are self-proprietary in the sense that no one possesses them and no one governs their existence. Human rights maintain a special status: the idea we know we do not live up to but that represents the full majesty of sovereign possibility. We thus often protect human rights like beggars; rights become like the homeless receiving welfare. Like the homeless in welfare societies, rights are accepted as part of the landscape and even hoped for; rights are repositories for our social conscience. Rights "remind" us. However, when we take from rights—when we receive the gift of rights, a gift they are giving themselves—we are indebted in ways that cannot be repaid. In giving from a position of poverty, rights show themselves to be greater and more extravagant than those of us who give from any position of wealth. In this way human rights gain their dominant ideological position—that which we are supposed to repay—and the teleology of any kind of conflict resolution, or resolution of strife, whether strife is conceived of in civil and political terms (e.g., free speech) or social cultural and economic terms (e.g., economic crisis, social oppression and conflict, or debates over welfare). Of course, international relations are always within the purview of rights, or at least rights concerns.

Mendicancy on the edge of crisis, as in the title of this article, means that rights sit right where they should: not in the middle of crisis (otherwise crisis, or strife, would be resolved and we would be realizing rights), but as the reason why both parties in crisis, multitude and Empire, *would* resolve the crisis. As Hardt and Negri put it, it may be that the most recent crisis, the crisis in the world economy since 2008, has elevated the attack on the common to a "higher power." Beyond problems of connectivity between financial markets and the degree of mobility in contemporary labor markets, a key to the crisis may also be the informationalism that Hardt and Negri (2000, 115) consider central to contemporary global culture: We are in a state of "progressively intense communication among the spaces and people of the earth;" we are *aware* of crisis, or claims to its existence, due to the "postmodernization" of production. However, this situation increases the impetus to resolve crisis and facilitate human nature. It is via this ameliatory impulse that human rights govern us from their mendicant position. That is to say that, at the end of the day, in the context of crisis, rights are greater than we will ever be; they are the standard we can only hope to achieve. Before rights' mendicancy, we grovel, asking for their forgiveness, faced with the modesty of human rights' poverty.

References

Arendt, Hannah. 1958. *The Origins of Totalitarianism*. New York: Meridian.

Arrighi, Giovani. 2003. "Lineages of Empire." In *Debating Empire*, edited by Gopal Balakrishnan, 29-42. London: Verso.

Bataille, Georges. 2008. *The Accursed Share, Volume I: Consumption*. Translated by Robert Hurley. New York: Zone.

Berlin, Isaiah. 2002. *Liberty*. Oxford: Oxford University Press.

Ci, Jiwei. 2005. "Taking the reasons for human rights seriously." *Political Theory* 33(2): 243–265.

Derrida, Jacques. 1997. *The Politics of Friendship*. Translated by George Collins. London: Verso.

Freeman, Michael. 2011. *Human Rights: An Interdisciplinary Approach*. 2nd ed. London: Polity.

Fukuyama, Francis. 1992. *The End of History and the Last Man*. New York: Penguin.

Hardt, Michael, and Negri, Antonio. 2000. *Empire*. Cambridge: Harvard University Press.

Hardt, Michael, and Negri, Antonio. 2004. *Multitude: War and Democracy in the Age of Empire*. London: Hamish Hamilton.

Hardt, Michael and Negri, Antonio. 2009. *Commonwealth*. Cambridge: Belknap.

Harvey, David. 2003. *The New Imperialism*. Oxford: Oxford University Press.

Hobsbawm, Eric. 1992. *Nations and Nationalism since 1780*. Cambridge: Cambridge University Press.

Hopkins, Terrence, and Wallerstein, Immanuel. 1996. *The Age of Transition: Trajectory of the World-System, 1945–2025*. London: Zed.

Hunt, Lynn. 2007. *Inventing Human Rights: A History*. New York: W.W. Norton.

Huntingon, Samuel. 1996. *The Clash of Civilizations and the Remaking of the World Order*. New York: Free Press.

Ishay, Micheline R. 2004. *The History of Human Rights: From Ancient Times to the Globalization Era*. Berkeley: University of California Press.

Joseph, Sarah. 2011. *Blame it on the WTO? A Human Rights Critique*. Oxford: Oxford University Press.

Lyotard, Jean-François. 1992. "An answer to the question: What is the postmodern?" In The Postmodern Explained: Correspondence 1982–1985, edited by Julian Pefanis and Morgan Thomas: 1-16. Minneapolis: University of Minnesota Press.

Marx, Karl. 1994. *Capital, Vol. 1: A Critical Analysis of Capitalist Production*. Translated by Samuel Moore and Edward Aveling. New York: International.

Marx, Karl. 1938. *Critique of the Goth Programme*. New York: International Publishers.

Morsink, Johannes. 2009. *Inherent Human Rights: Philosophical Roots of the UDHR*. Philadelphia: University of Pennsylvania Press.

Mauss, Marcel. 2000. *The Gift: The Form and Reason for Exchange in Archaic Societies*. Translated by W.D. Halls. New York: W.W. Norton.

Moyn, Samuel. 2010. *The Last Utopia: Human Rights in History*. Cambridge: Belknap.

Rawls, John. 2005. *Political Liberalism*. New York: Columbia University Press.

Rousseau, Jean-Jacques. 1968. *The Social Contract*. Translated by Maurice Cranston. London: Penguin.

Slaughter, Joseph. 2007. *Human Rights, Inc.: The World Novel, Narrative Form, and International Law*. New York: Fordham University Press.

Smith, Adam. 1998. "The wealth of nations." In *The Human Record: Sources of Global History, Volume II: Since 1500,* edited by Alfred J. Andrea and James H. Overfield, 166-170. Boston: Houghton Mifflin.

United Nations. 1945. "Charter of the United Nations." Available at http://www.un.org/en/documents/charter/preamble.shtml

United Nations. 1948. "The UDHR of Human Rights." Available at http://www.un.org/en/documents/udhr/index.shtml

US Department of Labor. 2013. "Labor force statistics from the current population survey." Available at http://data.bls.gov/timeseries/LNS14000000

Zweifel, Thomas D. 2006. *International Organizations & Democracy: Accountability, Politics, and Power*. Boulder, CO: Lynne Reinner.

12. Private Debt in the Age of Crisis — Strategies of Resistance

Pil Christensen

Introduction

The bankruptcy of the American investment company Lehman Brothers in the summer of 2008 sent shock waves through the global financial markets (Christensen et al. 2012, 112). The share price in general was in free fall and shortly after it was clear that a global financial crisis had broken out (Marazzi 2011, 97). This crisis had debt at its epicenter. The extent of debt had reached an insupportably high level and the crisis began where the debt took its most extreme form: the American housing market (Larsen & Mjølhus 2009, 5).

In Denmark, the global economic crisis is also connected to an alarmingly high private debt. The media have repeatedly highlighted that the Danes are among the most indebted population in Europe[1] and that private debt since 2008 has become a much bigger burden to the average person. Many more people are now seeking debt counseling[2] than before the outbreak of the crisis and counselors report that the crisis resulted in a sense of panic (Torp Carlsen 2009). The total amount of debt in RKI (Denmark's biggest register of defaulters) has increased with 39 percent from January 2010 to July 2011. In general the economic crisis, including rising unemployment rates and falling housing prices, has created a tougher debt-situation for many more people (Bræmer & Overgaard 2011).

But debt is more than a phenomenon that just occurred with the crisis: private debt had been steadily rising since the mid-1990s. In Denmark private debt rose by 230 percent from 1994 to 2010 (Danmarks Statistik, private archive).[3] Denmark's total amount of private debt comprises 158 percent of its gross domestic product, making it one of the most indebted countries in the European Union. Furthermore, private debt comprises more than 350 percent of yearly income. In comparison, Spanish private debt is around 145 percent of yearly income while Italian private debt makes up only around 75 percent of income

---

1 For example, Rossau 2010, Bernsen 2010, Due 2011, Skovgaard 2010, and Kris 2010.

2 Over the last couple of years the Danish government has supported different social organizations and has thus been able to offer free debt advice, mostly aimed at economically disadvantaged people.

3 It was not possible to access data prior to 1994 (Christensen 2013, Appendixes 1 and 2).

(Organisation for Economic Co-operation and Development, national account database; Ritzau 2011).

Where debt used to be relatively unproblematic for most people, the 2008 crisis changed this radically: debt went from being a means to fulfill our dreams to a chain that ties us down. This article explores the role of private debt in the neoliberal paradigm and, among other things, the massive rise in private debt. I identify the important point of origin in relation to private debt in connection with the economic crisis beginning in the 1970s and a transition to neoliberalism. The crisis triggered transformations that have become decisive in the role of private debt. I pinpoint four pivotal elements: First, Hardt and Negri's understanding of the shift from Fordism to a post-Fordist biopolitical production seems vital and, in the light of this shift, a decrease in the relative purchasing power of Western consumers. Second, a general trend toward financialization[4] that 'unleashes' the creation of debt and makes debt central to the economy. Third, the important role of increasing and persistent private consumption, which—due to the relative weakening of purchasing power - to a greater extent is being financed by private debt. And, lastly, changed bank loan policies enabled by the growing deregulation, a main element of neoliberalism.

On the basis of this account I empirically explore the exercise of power with regard to how the production of subjectivity plays out in the debt relation within the context of the economic crisis in Denmark. My inquiry is based upon eight qualitative interviews with indebted individuals, two women and six men, all under the age of 40,[5] with different types of debt—for example, several of them technically insolvent. All the participants are from the Copenhagen area, four had jobs, three were unemployed, and one was a student. Furthermore, I analyzed the popular Danish reality show *The Luxury Trap*.[6]" Both analyses are based upon Maurizio Lazzarato's theories of the indebted man, as well as Hardt and Negri's ideas on the matter. I especially use Lazzarato's idea about how the individual must become both a guilty and a responsible subject. A certain morality is attached to the debt relation, a morality that makes the individual guilty in relation to debt and therefore feels a certain responsibility to repay what is owed. This responsibility shapes the way the indebted are able to live their lives and thus reimbursement is not only a question of money but also about living one's life in a way so one can honor one's debt obligations. Subsequently, I also draw upon Foucault's ideas of neoliberalism and power and the further development

4 Financialization is described in depth in Section 4.

5 For a thorough discussion of this subject, see Christensen (2013, Chapters 2 and 6).

6 My methodology involved watching all 12 episodes of one season of the program, Season 7, running from August 30, 2011, to November 22, 2011, and taking thorough notes.

of his thoughts, mainly by Lazzarato. Inspired by Foucault, I do not see subjectivation as a one-way process; by contrast, Foucault (1982, 794) says, "There is no relationship of power without the means of escape or possible flight. Every power relationship implies, at least in potentia ... struggle". Furthermore, my interviews show that the process of subjectivation is not all encompassing. Resistance against the indebted condition occasionally emerges. Therefore I find it necessary to draw upon Hardt and Negri (2012) to look at strategies of resistance emanating from indebtedness during the economic crisis, particularly their concept in Declaration (2012) of a *kairos,* as a certain moment when resistance becomes possible because the crisis, among other things, creates a common condition.

As underlined by the use of Hardt and Negri's framework, debt is not a position of absolute disempowerment; instead, the indebted subject is always capable of exercising some form of resistance against the indebted condition. This paper thus underscores how the two theorists can provide an important supplement to more pessimistic views on the potential for resistance that is also immanent in the current economic crisis.

Debt in the neoliberal paradigm

In this article I use Hardt and Negri's concept of a paradigm, as well as their understanding of the concrete shift from the pre- to the post-1970s society. A *paradigm* shapes the framework for how a society is structured politically, economically, and socially, what constitutes true knowledge, and what is possible to imagine and think (Hardt & Negri 2004, 142). The research literature agrees that the crisis in the 1970s initiated an economic, political, and social paradigm shift (Harvey 2005, 2011; Foucault 2008; Lazzarato 2009, 2012; Crouch 2011; Nielsen 2011; Pedersen 2011); however, the causal explanations for these shifts vary greatly.

In many ways the economic crisis that began in the 1970s radically changed the specific form of capitalism that had underpinned the postwar growing welfare states. This paradigm shift is key to understanding what role private debt plays in the emerging neoliberal era. While the paradigm of the postwar welfare state was characterized by extensive state regulation of market forces, expanding welfare, rising real wages, and mass consumption (Harvey 2005, 10-11; Nielsen 2011, 100-101; Pedersen 2011, 15-16), strong marketization is a crucial trait of neoliberalism. Thus market mechanisms and the logic of pure competition are integrated and become hegemonic over the entire societal fabric[7] (Foucault 2008). Neoliberalism is marked by both an entire range of breaks with the previous welfare state paradigm and a certain type of continuation (Nielsen 2011, 135). Because even though the free market and market interests play an important role, the neoliberal paradigm is not equal to less state involvement, control, or regulations; instead, the state's role is different (Foucault 2008; Lazzarato 2012, 51). The market cannot be truly free without interventions from the state to secure this position and one of the most important objectives thus becomes the integration of a competition logic throughout society (Foucault 2008, 12, 121, 139, 131, 144–145). The first tendencies, which pointed toward a neoliberal transformation in Denmark, began with a conservative transfer of power in 1982, but the real change did not happen until the beginning of the 1990s, when the Social Democrats came into power. The subsequent period has been characterized by outsourcing, privatization, and general marketization, especially in the public sector, using the private sector as a role model (Nielsen 2011, 153–54).

In relation to neoliberal development, Lazzarato points to a number of paradigmatic shifts that are important when considering the role of private debt: increasing real wages are replaced by access to consumer loans and investments on the stock market, while the right to housing is replaced by access to mortgage loans, and instead of increased social security options, the market for private insurances grows. At the same time, the consumer is subject to even more compelling norms of consumption, creating a paradox: the consumer is both a worker whose wages are not increasing at the same speed as before and the consumer is a citizen who needs a home. The paradox of relatively lower wages and the need for accelerating growth in private consumption is thus solved by increased private debt. But this only works as long as housing prices are rising, the stock markets are profiting, and access to cheap credit is steady and secure, all of which changed with the crisis (Lazzarato 2012, 57).

---

7 The emergence of neoliberalism as an economic, political, and social paradigm did not take place as a straightforward, unhindered development but, rather, in different paces and to various extents around the Western world. A neoliberal consensus was not established before the beginning of the 1990s (Harvey 2005, 13, 22-25; Pedersen 2011, 22). On this basis, I do not consider it to be problematic that my numbers for Danish private debt go back only to 1994, since a neoliberal consensus and therefore concrete neoliberal policies were not established before then. It is important to note that neoliberalism is far from a social paradigm reserved for the Western world: neoliberal strategies have been globally implemented. However, I deliberately focus on the Western world and therefore explain how the neoliberal paradigm unfolds here.

As Lazzarato points out, there is an intimate relation between economic, political, and social structures and the changes they undergo in the neoliberal paradigm and the production of subjectivity. Economic production cannot be separated from and is also always the production of subjectivity. Hardt and Negri (2012, 14) assert the same in Declaration:

> The triumph of neoliberalism and its crisis have shifted the terms of economic and political life, but they have also operated a social, anthropological transformation, fabricating new figures of subjectivity. The hegemony of finance and the banks has produced *the indebted.*

This way Hardt and Negri underscore how the neoliberal development of capitalism and important structures within the capitalist system—concretely, the vital role of the financial system—are shaping particular subjects, subjects who are aware of their indebtedness, living a life where debt is an important factor in the structuring of their possibilities.

I now take a closer look on what Hardt and Negri call "terms of economic and political life" (2012, 14) by examining three developments that are all part of and connected to the neoliberal development and play an important role in relation to private debt. First, I summarize the shift from Fordism to post-Fordism; second, I look at the process of financialization, and, third, I examine private consumerism and bank lending policies. This inquiry should be seen as creating a foundation for the analysis of the anthropological transformation fabricating the indebted man. Even though the use of the term *neoliberalism* points to both a certain understanding of the economic order and the development of social structures, *as well* a particular shaping of the subject, I separate the two analyses to maintain analytical clarity.

From Fordism to post-Fordism

Hardt and Negri (2012, 16) describe the transition from Fordism to post-Fordism by stating that "the center of gravity of capitalist production no longer resides in the factory but has drifted outside its walls." The Fordist production that was concentrated around the assembly line loses its hegemonic status, while the immaterial parts of the production, on the other hand, gain a more important position in the economy with respect to both cognitive and service work (Hardt & Negri 2012, 16). This change in *production hegemony* should be considered central to the role played by private debt in neoliberalism.

The postwar Fordist production was marked by both mass production and a corresponding mass consumption; real wages rose during the period, which guaranteed increasing private consumption. But the crisis in the mid-1970s had great consequences for the Fordist production system. Globalization of Fordist industrial production meant increased competition and, furthermore, the borders opened up to foreign investments and greater amounts of cheap labor. These developments simultaneous put pressure on Western workers' wages and working conditions (Harvey 2005, 22–26; 2011, 14–15; Crouch 2011, 112–13). The rising unemployment rate and general recession that followed the crisis, along with previously mentioned factors, negatively affected the relative purchasing power of Western consumers.

The hegemonic change in production also led to a change in the development of real wages.[8] During the 1980s real wages either dropped or stagnated or growth decelerated, as in Denmark.[9] This too, had an influence on people's consumption. These factors must be put in perspective with the rising inequality that has characterized the post-1970s era and which further weakened the relative purchasing power of certain groups in society. Where equality was a goal in the postwar welfare states, inequality effectively came to mark neoliberalism, because it was a way to strengthen modes of competition, which is absolutely central to neoliberalism (Foucault 2008, 142–43; Lazzarato 2009, 117)[10]. The rise in

---

8 According to Harvey, the Anglo-Saxon world experienced a decrease in real wages, caused by a new power balance between unions and the companies, where the unions were losing power. This is the reason for the decrease in real wages, as well as a broad range of social welfare cutbacks and a general strengthening of the neoliberal paradigm (Harvey 2005, 22–26; 2011, 14–15). There was no decline in real wages in Denmark, but since the middle of the 1970s growth in real wages has decreased (Danmarks Statistik). There is no evidence that Danish unions have lost power or that this explains the relative decrease in real wages; thus it is not possible to apply Harvey's model directly to the development in Denmark. Danish unions began to lose members after the mid-1990s, which could be interpreted as a loss of power. This finding can also be tied to the neoliberal development, which became prominent in the mid-1990s.

9 Sources: Danmarks Statistik 2001, 22; a spreadsheet from Danmarks Statistik for 2000–2011 (private archive; Christensen 2013, Appendix 14); and correspondence from the DST that documents there are no known omissions in the data (private archive; Christensen 2013, Appendix 15). Increases and decreases in real wages are distributed very differently according to occupation and there has not been taking any reservations in these calculations for this fact. It would be too complicated to discuss the issue in depth, but I think the upcoming discussion on the increasing inequality can be a part of creating a more nuanced picture.

10 The 2011 yearly United Nations Development Program (UNPD) Human Development Report ("Sustainability and Equity: A Better Future for All") states that inequality has increased in most countries: "Detailed studies show a striking increase in the income part among the riches groups in much of Europe, North America, Australia and New Zealand.... The difference between the rich and the poor has increased in the last two decades

inequality in Denmark has been striking, it being the country in Western Europe with the greatest increase in inequality from 2001 to 2012 (AE Rådet 2012).[11]

According to David Harvey (2011, 16–17) and Colin Crouch (2011, 114), the problem of the lacking purchasing power was solved by making cheap credit accessible to many more people, for example by means of the credit card. Furthermore, the increased private debt during the last 20 to 30 years also reflects the rise in cheap credit accessibility.

Hardt and Negri's conceptualization of post-Fordist production is valuable in continuing this discussion. When the center of gravity of capitalist production moves away from the factory, wealth is produced more autonomously, human life itself becomes productive, labor time and non-labor time become blurred, and hence the possible ways to control the worker must change. Control needs to happen at a distance, since capitalists can no longer oversee factories as they used to (Hardt & Negri 2012). Instead, debt becomes a way to control and generate profit off the worker, since debt is not restricted to work time; on the contrary, debt is a form of exploitation directed at the whole of human life. The change of hegemony (from Fordism to post-Fordism) is therefore also a change from a hegemony of profit, as the main way value is generated, to a hegemony of rent (Hardt & Negri 2012).

Financialization and debt in the neoliberal paradigm

Since the late 1960s, a range of global tendencies have been constitutive in changing the economy in several areas important to the development of the role of private debt. These tendencies can be collected under a single common designation: *financialization* (Nielsen 2011, 136–39; Pedersen 2011; Lazzarato 2012 10). Toward the end of the 1960s, the crisis began to reveal itself all over the social terrain and regulations that had governed the economy in the postwar period were gradually withdrawn. Hardt and Negri (2000) describe how the earlier stabile financial regulation created by the Bretton Woods system began to collapse. The system came under pressure and in 1971 President Nixon detached the dollar from the gold rate and abolished fixed exchange rates. The collapse of

---

in more than three quarters of the OECD Countries" (UNPD 2011, 29). The average increase in the countries was 20 percent from 1990 to 2005 (ibid., 30).

11 According to an AE Rådet report, this finding should be partly due to the income distribution policy carried out during the period—when tax releases were given to the highest earners and welfare benefits for low-income groups were reduced—as well as strongly increasing real estate prices, caused, among other things, by a whole range of new loans (AE Rådet 2012, 3).

the Bretton Woods system paved the way for extensive deregulation of the financial markets (Hardt & Negri 2000, 265–66; Harvey 2005, 12; Harvey 2011, 16, 32–33). This had an important impact on how banks and financial institutions could act in regard to lending, since detachment of the gold standard meant that the amount of money and thus the potential amount of debt no longer had to match the American quantity of gold. Hence the creation of debt was set free.

These changes in the monetary system shaped the beginning of the financialization, a process characterized by the growing influence of financial motives, markets, actors, and institutions in the economy. Moreover, profit is created to a greater extent by the financial markets compared to trading with and the production of commodities (Epstein 2005, 3), but at the same time the entire economy is penetrated by financial elements (Marazzi 2011, 27).

At the heart of finance is the capital management and, with the process of financialization, lending and debt became crucial to economic growth after the 1970s crisis (Harvey 2005, 161; Harvey 2011, 21–26; Nielsen 2011, 136; Pedersen 2011, 19). An outcome of finance becoming key to the neoliberal economy was a greater protection of the financial institutions, something which in practice meant further deregulation - for example of lending policies (Harvey 2011, 10). Another result of the financialization process can be seen in the accumulated values on the financial markets spreading to rest of the economy, leading to heavily increased housing prices, which yet again incurred the need to take on more debt.

The role of private consumption and lending practices

The issue of consumption is closely connected to private debt. Private mass consumption stimulated by increasing real wages only acquired a bigger role in the economy during the postwar period (Crouch 2011, 116) and today private consumption makes up more or less 50 percent of the Danish gross domestic product (Danish National Bank). Consumption thus plays an important role in the economy. Furthermore increased private consumption is closely connected to access to cheap credit.

Private consumption must be seen in light of the consumer society that built up in the postwar years and only came to play an increasingly important role in later decades. Signs of a consumer society can be seen in for example rising marketing and advertising expenses, which in turn contribute to stronger and more compelling social norms surrounding private consumption (Nielsen 2011, 114, 124–25). The individual's identity becomes more that of the consumer than of the worker (Hardt & Negri 2012). The strong imperative to consume should be seen in connection with developing norms in relation to borrowing. These norms made it more difficult to not borrow money, even though a loan is not absolutely necessary (Lauridsen 2012). It is thus possible to talk about a form of 'consuming and borrowing norm' especially dominating the years just prior to the recent economic crisis.

These intensified consumer and borrowing norms can be connected to what Crouch (2011, 114) characterizes as a transition from a public to a private Keynesian model: "Instead of governments taking on debt to stimulate the economy, individuals and families did so." Lazzarato makes the same point when stating how demand is no longer primarily stimulated by public debt but, instead, by private debt and how this is part of transferring the risk connected to debt to individuals and families. Public deficit has not disappeared, but "global demand has been maintained through financial markets and banks, as in the case of subprime loans" (Lazzarato 2012, 58).

Private debt, including social norms connected to both consuming and borrowing, has a significant influence on global economic growth, along with profit from other financial products, especially in the years before the economic crisis in 2008. Something, which makes Christian Marazzi claim that private debt and the consumption it allows, can be characterized as the *modus operandi* of the present economic system (Marazzi 2011, 39, 67–69, 88–89). These developments must be regarded as closely connected to the deregulation of the financial sector, which made it possible for banks to raise the limit of how much they can lend (Harvey 2011, 26–31). The aforementioned factors made it cheaper to borrow but less attractive to save and also made it possible for people with low incomes to take on debt and therefore maintain a relatively high level of consumption (Crouch 2011, 109–110). Moreover, a whole range of new and riskier types of loans were introduced on the market—for example, "interest-only loans" in Denmark—and at the same time the market for credit sales grew enormously (Pedersen 2011, 19). In this regard, it is worth noting that Denmark has almost no regulations concerning interest levels (Bernsen 2010).

The growth in lending was seen as beneficial to the whole society, but the economic crisis can be viewed as a culmination of an economic and societal model where necessary and growing consumption was being increasingly financed by debt. To take on debt can open up many positive possibilities, for example, the ability to buy a house. As already touched upon in the introduction, the economic crisis plays a large part in aggravating the problematic aspects of being indebted. In Denmark the economic crisis has been particularly tied to a housing bubble and a subsequent crisis on the housing market, with stagnating and declining prices, which has resulted in a distinct increase in the number of insolvent homeowners (Larsen & Mjølhus 2009, 42, 47–48). But dropping prices in the housing market are not the only factors creating economic problems for the Danes. Generally, more people with an otherwise healthy economy have experienced hardship, due to unemployment, as well as because of difficulties in taking on more debt to solve new economic problems brought about by the crisis (Rossau 2010).

One can conclude that private debt plays an important role in the neoliberal economic order and that political and economic shifts tied to neoliberalism are key to the development of private debt. The integration of debt into the societal fabric seems to go deeper and wider than before. The increase in private debt additionally suggests that debt has become a condition of our present society to a greater extent, or, as Hardt and Negri (2012) write, the "general condition of social life": not everybody, but many more today are indebted and, at the same time, debt has become much more of a concern for many.

I have given an account of the shifting terms of economic and political life created by neoliberalism and its crisis. The latter half of the article investigates the indebted condition in the context of the economic crisis, taking a closer look at the "anthropological transformation, fabricating new figures of subjectivity" (Hardt & Negri 2012). In a Foucauldian sense, power is characterized by always being productive (Foucault 2006, 100, 108). It produces subjectivity (Foucault 1982, 781; Milchman & Rosenberg 2009, 63) and thus there is no natural subject; on the contrary, the subject is being constructed in the process of subjectivation (Foucault 1997, 290; Milchman & Rosenberg 2009, 63).

In the following, I analyze the production of the indebted subject in the context of the economic crisis, mainly through two sources: the popular Danish TV show *The Luxury Trap* and qualitative interviews with indebted Danes.

The *Luxury Trap* as a part of the public discourse around debt

According to Foucault (Foucault 2006, 104, 106–107) discourses and the truth produced in the discourses about the individual are central to the production of subjectivity. *The Luxury Trap* can been viewed as an example of the public discourse created around debt and indebted individuals in the context of the economic crisis, since the program was launched precisely because of the crisis.[12]

Hardt, Negri, and Lazzarato point out how the individual is shaped as both a responsible and a guilty subject through the debt relation (Hardt & Negri 2012; Lazzarato 2012). On the one hand, the individual must be able to take on a very specific responsibility, a responsibility to live in such a way as to honor one's debt obligations as well as to commit and make promises. On the other hand, the

12 See correspondence from the TV station (private archive, Christensen 2013, Appendix 3).

individual must become a subject with a conscience, one who feels guilty in relation to the debt owed. Both the responsibility and guilt tied to debt became very evident among the participants in *The Luxury Trap*.

The program can be characterized as "emotional television." Although human drama is the center of attention, instead of competition between several individuals, the pivotal point involves individual competitions against oneself. In such programs one does not win a monetary award; instead, one gains the ability to control oneself, a particular characteristic of *The Luxury Trap*. However, the program participants are not capable of undertaking the self-transformation of becoming moral and responsible subjects by themselves. The program is therefore about how the participants, with the guidance of the TV hosts and other temporary authority figures, transform themselves from irresponsible and immoral to responsible and moral subjects.

The process of becoming a responsible subject is repeated in different ways in almost every episode. The participants often start out appearing ignorant or uninformed about the severity of their debt situation and, with the help of the hosts, realize that they must become (more) responsible. One example is when the female host Louise wants the participant Christian to become just as responsible at home as he is at work and she makes him sign a responsibility agreement. It is morally but not legally binding, as she puts it. In this situation, taking responsibility for one's debt becomes a moral responsibility toward one's family and surrounding people; debt is not only an abstract responsibility to a bank or credit institution.

But responsibility also involves making certain choices. The indebted subject is, in principal, free but is at the same time compelled to make the "right" choices to honor the debt (Lazzarato 2012, 14–15). This situation is accentuated and exemplified again and again in the program. Furthermore, the concepts of *time* and especially the *future* of the indebted and how these temporalities are controlled and directed by the debt relation are often addressed. Participants are shown how there is only one responsible future path to take, that of a particularly individual moral responsibility toward the debt.

As mentioned, the hosts use personal relations to exemplify the guilt the participants are expected to feel in relation to their debt. Almost every episode starts out with the hosts making the participants realize that their debt harms their family or friends. One example is Benita, who gained access to her daughter's relatively small savings. To exemplify the mother's "moral outrage", the story of the near-theft of the daughter's savings is told throughout the entire show. By the end of the show Benita has to work three days at a packing facility, arranging flowers for Mother's Day, to earn the money to repay her daughter. There will be no Mother's Day gift for Benita, and she must instead learn how to work "as a mother should," as one of the hosts claims. Even though the debt Benita owes her daughter is only a small part of her total debt, it is the episode's pivotal point, an example of how personal relations are used to underscore the fundamental wrong in having debt at all. The guilt the participants are expected to feel is verbalized in various ways, depending on the situation, but personal relations are continuously used as a point of departure to discuss issues of debt as related to responsibility and guilt.

By virtue of its status as a popular[13] TV show, *The Luxury Trap* has been shaping the public discourse around debt, specifically by contributing to an understanding of the indebted individual as someone who needs to take a certain responsibility and feel a certain guilt in relation to debt owed. The program leaves little, if any, room for the individual to create an autonomous or different story about him- or herself and debt. At the same time, the program omits opposition to the indebted condition. Because the program is completely orchestrated and edited, it is hard to say whether subjective resistance to the indebted condition is part of the participant's relationship to debt. In relation to resistance, Hardt and Negri (2012) point to the importance of constructing truth through discourse when shaping the public debate, but at the same time the authors accentuate the necessary collective dimension of truth construction (Hardt & Negri 2012, 37). The dimension of collective truth construction is something the program does not touch upon, insofar as issues of debt and responsibility pertain only to the individual. A broader take on the Danish public debate paints a slightly different picture: here, resistance to the indebted condition is present as a small part of the discourse around debt; however, the discursive gravity regarding resistance centers around concerns about the economic crisis as such and not debt specifically.[14]

Shaping the indebted subject in light of the economic crisis

The following presentation is a compressed version of the main analysis of my thesis. It is primarily focused on resistance in the work of Hardt and Negri, especially as formulated in Declaration (2012). Additionally, due to the length of

13 On average, there were 179,000 viewers for the season analyzed (Season 7). The average number of viewers for all seasons was 234,100.

14 Recently, a campaign launched by the biggest bank in Denmark, Danske Bank, received much social media criticism and created great dissatisfaction. The bank was, for example, accused of not taking responsibility for its part in the economic crisis.

this paper, I summarize the rest, inevitably revealing the risk of oversimplification.[15]

It became clear through my interviews that my participants had the impression that a very strong societal narrative, which made their debt and the act of borrowing appear legitimate and reasonable, prevailed before the crisis. At the same time, they felt it was easy to obtain loans from banks; as one participant expresses it, "[The banks] threw gold after me almost ... money was fucking chucked at me back then" (Bo, 44–47).[16] Bo's conception is supported by the fact that the whole financial sector was deregulated, in relation to lending as well. The participants are similar in their stories of how the prevailing narrative changed with the outbreak of the economic crisis and how it hugely influenced their understanding of themselves and their debt situation. Hence the crisis and the indebted subject cannot be separated, because the crisis is a constitutive part of the subjectivation of the indebted subject.

The crisis was important in all of the themes around which the interviews revolved. A central topic noted by Hardt and Negri, as well as Lazzarato, and that appeared to also have great meaning for the participants was the question of how the relation of debt limits the space for action on several levels. As Jason Read points out, neoliberalism is a regime of governmentality, which is characterized by arranging and organizing the conditions for action; power thus intensifies in its present form since it limits the space for action and possible actions (Read 2009, 6). The space left for the indebted becomes a site of responsibility that implies living a certain way and, instead of merely paying back economically, the indebted individual also pays back through a particular lifestyle arrangement (Hardt & Negri 2012; Lazzarato 2012, 14–15, 76).

My analysis shows that the indebted subject is shaped through both a materially and mentally limited space of action, which is also pointed out by Hardt and Negri (2012) when they discuss how debt disciplines consumption. The reduced space of action is tied to a particular form of responsibility. The commitment the individual experiences in relation to the responsibility of debt is completely individualized. Concepts of time as well as the future appear to be closely connected to a reduced space for action. As Lazzarato points out, debt is basically a promise to repay in the future (2012, 2, 21–23). My participants all experienced the fact that their debt froze the future to a certain extent and that some

15 For a thorough analysis of the matter, see Christensen (2013). The thesis is available through the University of Copenhagen or by contacting the author.

16 These numbers refer to the lines quoted from the interview with Bo. Unfortunately the interviews are not translated into English; for the Danish version, see Christensen (2013, Appendixes 5–12).

of the uncertainty that characterizes the future was lost. Hardt and Negri, as well as Lazzarato, emphasize how debt limits the space of action when it comes to the question of work-related choices and attitudes. For my participants, work seemed more closely connected to necessity than before the crisis and several felt that their indebted situation had an influence on their choice of work. Others told how they tend to complain less about unsatisfying working conditions. Almost all participants mentioned that they felt a reduced space for action in their relationship with their bank, which had changed dramatically after the crisis: before the bank had represented a gateway to freedom but now it had become a concrete limitation. As already mentioned, the crisis constituted a pivotal point in relation to all aspects of the limited space of action felt by my participants.

In addition, a particular morality and feelings of guilt connected to indebtedness constitutes another vital theme that I addressed and consider central to the production of the indebted subject (Hardt & Negri 2012; Lazzarato 2012, 4, 14, 24–25, 68). Lazzarato accentuates the close relation between debt and morality when, by way of Nietzsche, he calls attention to the fact that the words for *owing* and *feeling guilty* are the same in German, as well as in Danish, where the verb *to owe* (*at skylde*) originates from the noun *guilt* (*skyld*). So, owing a debt is connected to feelings of guilt and therefore another important aspect of debt morality becomes the *commitment* to repay. Through debt, morality raises a sense of guilt, shame, a bad conscience, and embarrassment. The moral dimension of debt consists in shaping the indebted subject into one who knows his or her debt obligations and feels morally responsible and guilty for them (Lazzarato 2012, 4, 14, 24–25, 68). Feelings of moral responsibility and guilt apply to almost all of my participants, even though their individual scenarios played out quite differently.

In connection to the discussion of morality and guilt, a moralizing discourse around debt as experienced by the participants, including the discursive expression of debt in *The Luxury Trap* and generally in the public debate, are important. This discourse accentuates the problematic behavior as well as personal flaws of the individual as main explanations for the problematic situation many people find themselves in with regard to their debt. This influences the fact that, in addition to responsibility, guilt was being individualized quite strongly by the indebted.

As also noted by Lazzarato (2012, 25, 68), the economic crisis intensified the guilt my participants felt in relation to their debt. This feeling of guilt proved to be important in establishing a corresponding feeling of responsibility toward the debt obligations. The strong moral injunction to repay one's debt under all circumstances became important, among other things, because it made it difficult for my participants to claim a structural critique insofar as holding, for example, the banks co-responsible for their debt situation. They felt that such a critique might wrongly reflect their unwillingness to repay their debt, which was not the case. Furthermore, as in *The Luxury Trap*, the participants' guilt as well as moral responsibility was personalized and became guilt toward their family and friends and not just an abstract guilt toward the bank.

Resistance

Lazzarato's ideas of the indebted subject are central to the analysis of my interviews, but he does not leave much room for the resistance and refusal that can materialize in the debt relation. Thus the process of subjectivation in Lazzarato's perspective becomes all encompassing and absolute. The same can be said in relation to the Foucauldian interpretation by Read of the neoliberal condition, which becomes an all-embracing paradigm that structures the space for action in an absolute fashion.

Both Lazzarato's and Read's theoretical courses are problematic in relation to a fundamental understanding of power and subjectivation - an understanding introduced by Foucault and used in this article; namely power as relational and always and already containing resistance or the potential of counterpower. Simultaneously, the interviews revealed that the power involved in the processes shaping the subjects in the debt relation did not always have a disciplining effect or an all-encompassing character as suggested. Thus the power at play is not solidified and the relation of power is not an exclusive relation of domination but, instead, implies resistance. I therefore consider it both necessary and enriching to include Hardt and Negri's perspectives on the potential resistance and counterpower among the indebted.

According to Hardt and Negri (2012), four subjective figures dominate present society, the indebted being one of them. All four subjective figures have the capacity to exercise resistance and counterpower against their different conditions. According to the authors, resistance becomes possible through what they call *Kairos*, a Greek word designating the optimal moment, the right instant understood as a form of opening. It is important that *kairos* not be understood quantitatively as a certain space of time or a particular occasion or event; instead, it should be understood qualitatively as certain conditions or circumstances. According to Hardt and Negri, a *kairos of resistance* is possible under the neoliberal condition and during the present crisis. Not only is individualization created, but also the crisis brings out the potential of "being-together," a *kairos of community,* because the same conditions largely apply to a lot of people, such as indebted individuals. The crisis thus also gives rise to a sense of community around the indebted condition or at least the potential for it (Hardt & Negri 2012). A sense of community is central for an individual to be able to act independently on the circumstances as an acting subject and in turn leave behind a non-acting subject (Hardt & Negri 2012).

Hardt and Negri, as well as Lazzarato, find the neoliberal debt relation to be fundamentally illegitimate, as applied to both the basic money relationship and the forms of subjectivation embodied in the debt relation. Therefore Hardt and Negri (2012) speak of a necessary violation of the debt relation where the first step must be refusal: one must refuse to repay debt. Hardt and Negri do not necessarily think that debt as such must disappear; however, it must be based on social ties, in contrast to relations of money. We should not be indebted to one another through money but via social obligations (Hardt & Negri 2012). The content of the debt we must cultivate should not be founded on guilt and the construction of a particular moral responsibility, but on commonalities and a mutual recognition of the social debt we owe to one another and to society as a whole (Hardt & Negri 2012).

Potential acts of resistance among the indebted participants

My participants expressed acts of potential resistance in different ways but it was possible to detect similarities among their statements. What could be called a counter-individualization strategy became apparent in the rejection of guilt connected to debt, as well as in a rejection of responsibility toward the debt. These refusals were expressed through accusations and anger aimed at banks, the political system, and the financial world. The anger resulted in some of the participants feeling less obligated toward, for example, banks. As one participant, Emil, said,

> As a matter of fact I actually accuse society in a way, anyway, at least the way the former government chose to do its things because ... from the outside every country can make it look like that they have this amazing economic growth ... just as I think it is saying to people that they can easily borrow up to 80 percent of their equity, which to a certain extent represents false money, because it is money that is not there. They made rules without telling people that everything could be taken away from them in one day or a half day. (165–170[17])

Another participant, named Noah, thinks a certain borrowing mentality existed, as he, together with many others, gave in to and therefore it is not exclusively

17 These numbers refer to the lines quoted from the interview with Emil, see Christensen 2013 Appendixes 5–12. All passages referring to interviews can be found this way. Unfortunately the interviews are not translated into English.

his fault that he is in so much debt (419–426). This also applies to Sofie, who thinks she actually made the right and logical decisions when she borrowed money:

> Well, it is not a problem that I made that decision or, well, yes, it is for me at least, but the problem is that these kinds of decisions were possible to make and logical to make. The decisions I made when I chose to get a loan and buy an apartment that was fucking expensive back then were realistic, logical decisions and they should never have been. Maybe I should not have made them and maybe I should have been able to foresee a lot of things but actually I think the problem is that these kinds of decisions were reasonable to make within the ruling logic of the housing market. (901–908)

The immediate anger against the way politicians and financial institutions acted in the years before the economic crisis provoked some participants to partly deny their responsibility,[18] which can been seen as a tendency toward a counter-subjectivation strategy, since some of the responsibility is removed from the individual and placed on structural and political conditions.

A collective crisis

Most of the participants think the economic crisis has had a huge influence on their situation and blaming it becomes a way to escape the individualization of the responsibility. Some of the participants tended to oppose the increased individualization of the indebted condition by focusing on the common features that the crisis creates for many people, just as Hardt and Negri (2012) noted. Several of them shared with me how they openly tell others about their indebtedness because they consider societal problems partly responsible for their situation and not exclusively their own fault. They wish to alternate the common presumption of pure overspending as the primary reason for indebtedness.[19] Furthermore, they express how it is a great support for them to know that others are in the same situation as they are.[20] One participant, named Lasse, tells it as follows:

> I have felt lonely, as I said before, because nobody felt sorry for me and nobody seemed to be in the same situation as me, but as the years have passed I found out that this was actually not the case. (578–580).

---

18 Jonas, 617–622, 735–738; Kira, 491–495; Sofie, 549; Kristian, 468–469, 483–489; Emil, 325–332, 400–401; Noah, 419–426, 322–327; Bo, 354–358. (These numbers refer to the lines from the some of my interviews, see Christensen 2013, Appendixes 5–12).

19 Kira, 473–478, 479–489; Bo, 409–417; Sofie, 881–888.

20 Kristian, 580–586, 627–633; Lasse, 412–414, 418–419.

The crisis thus enables one to reposition responsibility by withdrawing it from the individual. Furthermore, the crisis appears as a collective condition, which makes a structural critique possible based on a common understanding of the indebted condition that could establish a common ground from which to act. It is important, however, that some of the indebted individuals are also using strategies that have no critical potential—and in several ways seem just as individualized as the debt situation itself—to retreat from feelings of guilt and responsibility.[21]

Denial and ambivalence

According to Hardt and Negri (2012), the potential common condition created during the crisis can make the individual capable of becoming an acting subject, which is crucial to resistance. As discussed earlier, a first step in relation to resistance can be the denial of repayment. I asked my participants if they would consider joining an initiative where people collectively denied repaying their debts and most of them said yes; some of them had even thought about it themselves. When my participant Kristian explained what it would mean for him to be part of such an initiative, it became clear that it would make up a strong form of protection against the individualization he was experiencing. However, at the same time, the following statement underscores how far Kristian actually is from resisting this same individualization:

> The feeling of not being alone would be a great relief. I think you would remove a great burden from people, because I think people generally – I know it from myself – experience debt as something very personal and very lonely. It is almost religious, like a cross I must carry because of my sins. (768-772).

Several of the participants also expressed a great deal of fear at the suggestion of a collective denial of repayment because they worried about the consequences.[22] In other words, the idea of engaging in such a collective act appeared attractive to my participants, but none of them planned to actively pursue the option, which is not unusual, considering the consequences.

Only one participant had a critical attitude toward the suggestion:

> No, we could never agree that it was just the fault of the market and that it is not my fault [sneers] you can put it up your arse! You are the ones who have established the

21 Emil, 501–504, 514–516; Lasse, 178–187; Noah, 351–354; Kristian, 646–647, 457–465; Jonas, 539–541; Lasse, 66–67, 71–72, 405; Emil, 309–316; Jonas, 569–570; Kira, 426–432; Bo, 267–274; Emil, 444–448.

22 Kira, 454–456, 459–460, 644; Lasse, 592–596; Noah, 511; Kristian, 542–551, 560–564; Sofie, 985–989.

> debt, then you must be man enough to pay. If you are able to have the fun, you should be able to take the rough times as well. So I would never be a part of such an initiative. On the contrary, I would establish a counter-movement. Anybody who says that we don't want to pay our debts, well, okay, then, I will MAKE them pay because I have no respect at all for people who deny repaying their debt (Bo, 575–580).

Two other participants thought it important to note that not all kinds of indebted people could be a part of such an initiative; it is important that the debt not be self-inflicted.[23] This attitude emphasizes a paradox, since most of the participants simultaneously blamed nobody but themselves for their indebted condition. These insights suggest that some forms of debt are more morally repugnant than others; for example, indebtedness due to "pure overspending" is the worst.

The question of denial thus shows an ambivalence that is present in all my interviews. The ambivalence furthermore stresses the paradox concerning the different forms of debt and their moral status. While resistance does not dominate the indebtedness story, it is present and sometimes resistance and subjectivation seem closely intertwined. The ambivalence is apparent when the participants describe how difficult it is to overcome the social norms attached to debt. As Noah expresses it,

> I think the banks and the financial world have a huge responsibility for the current 'debt-crisis', they have a responsibility for the fact that many people are being evicted and must leave their homes, so well I think that the responsibility should be put on them as well, but it is very difficult to take a stand that is so radically different from the mainstream discourse because quickly it becomes a question of me, that I don't want to pay my debt, that I want money for free. (515–520)

Authoritarian tendencies

My interviews show that the individual is shaped as an indebted subject through a limited space of action and a space that is formed in several ways. Furthermore, a particular morality and guilt are tied to debt, which plays an important role in relation to the processes of subjectivation. In almost all aspects, the crisis plays a central role and in many ways the crisis radically changed the indebted condition. But it is important that these processes that shape the individual into an indebted subject are also met with resistance. The subjectivation is not all encompassing. My participants do not present an actual competing logic and mostly they do not exercise any form of resistance – but still some form of opening towards resistance occur once in a while. Most of the participants denied

23 Emil, 533–540; Jonas, 719–722.

being completely subject to the condition of debt and, even though none of them actually acted differently, a variety of logics besides the neoliberal logic are at stake here. The crisis plays a pivotal role in incipient resistance, just as it does for the process of subjectivation.

According to Lazzarato, the crisis is characterized by an important tendency: governing happens more through authority and restrictions and less through freedom, which otherwise normally characterizes neoliberal governmentality (Gordon 1991, 5; Rose 2003, 183, 189). Lazzarato accentuates how a duality characterizes the governmentality marking the crisis and emphasizes how the indebted are still free and the crisis is therefore not an expression of a return to earlier forms of servitude, as Hardt and Negri (2012) state. My own interviews revealed these authoritarian tendencies, especially in relation to the limited space of action created by the debt relation. The participants also often expressed how they felt that debt limited their freedom. However, I suggest that Lazzarato suppresses or misses the duality immanent to the crisis as such, namely, the possibility of resistance that accompanies the crisis - together with the authoritarian tendencies, as shown in my analysis.

Conclusion

In this article I show how a range of developments connected to and part of the neoliberal paradigm are important to the role of private debt in Denmark. The shift from Fordism to post-Fordism enables a weakening of real-wage increases and, together with growing inequality, requires increasing debt to maintain the purchasing power of Danish and Western consumers. Changes in global monetary systems have led to the process of financialization that gives debt a pivotal role in the economic system, since private debt, among other things, has become an important way of gaining profit. Furthermore, the necessity of a growing and persistent private consumption in connection with the relative weakening of purchasing power makes debt an important way to finance this consumption. This should be seen in light of the massive deregulation of the financial sector and, more concretely, of the banks and their lending practices. The deregulation of lending policies further enabled people to take out more loans. Altogether, these occurrences made private debt a condition for many more people.

With an analysis of the reality show *The Luxury Trap,* I demonstrate how public discourse around private debt is one that contributes to understanding the indebted individual as one who needs to feel a certain form of guilt, as well as moral commitment to repaying debt. Moreover, such individuals need to take responsibility for their debt and honor its obligations. The program shows how the individual must become an indebted subject, and leaves no room for the individual to be anything else.

The main elements in *The Luxury Trap*'s discourse recur in the analysis of my qualitative interviews with indebted individuals. The analysis shows how the individual is shaped as an indebted subject in mainly three ways. The first way is through a limited space for action concerning both the material and psychological dimensions, as well as the participant's relationships with work, the future, and change in the bank's role in the debt relation, which all shape the subject in a certain way. The limited space for action involves taking a certain responsibility and thus the debt relation makes the indebted arrange their life in such a way to honor their debt. The second important element in shaping an indebted subject is the particular morality characterizing the debt relationship and the guilt the individual must feel because of her debt. Here a moralizing discourse plays an important role together with a strong moral injunction to always repay your debt, because this made it difficult for my participants to express a more structural and political critique of their situation.

The last element of my analysis and the focus of this paper is the resistance that also occurs in the debt relation. Hardt and Negri's considerations around the possibility of resistance during the crisis are important in this context. The analysis shows that my participants made small attempts to resist the process of subjectivation, which mostly take the form of accusations against the banks, financial institutions, and politicians. Furthermore, some verbalized how the crisis represents a collective condition. It is important to note, however, that resistance is often expressed in very ambivalent terms.

The individualization of both guilt and responsibility, which becomes very clear in my analysis, should be seen in the context of the political and economic shifts following neoliberalism, shifts that are part of the reason for steadily rising private debt. I point to four factors crucial to the role of private debt in neoliberalism: transformations in the system of production and global monetary systems, changes in lending practices, and the need for persistent and increasing private consumption. Hence, while debt occupies a more central position on a structural and societal level in the neoliberal paradigm, during the current crisis debt becomes more of an individual responsibility and condition through a process where the individual is shaped as an indebted subject. On the other hand, the crisis also seems to lay the foundation of an incipient resistance in the debt relation. Thus the crisis plays a pivotal but also very ambivalent role in shaping the indebted subject.

Even though my participants only make relatively small attempts to resist the indebted neoliberal condition and these attempts are mostly verbalized rather than actions such as refusing to repay debt, their resistance can still play an important role in the sense of Hardt and Negri, since the formation of common concepts and thus a common reality is the first important step to bringing change to the world (Hardt & Negri 2000, 302–303).

References

AE Rådet. 2012. "Tal fra Eurostat viser stigende ulighed, Gennem 00'erne har Danmark haft Vesteuropas største stigning i ulighed." Analysis from *AE Rådet* August 22, 2012. Available at http://www.ae.dk/analyse/gennem-00-erne-har-danmark-haft-vesteuropas-storste-stigning-ulighed

Bernsen, Markus. 2010. "Ud af Luksusfælden." *Weekendavisen*, November 19.

Bræmer, Michael, and Overgaard, Anna Glent. 2011. "Mange vil bruge efterlønspenge til at betale gæld." *Ugebrevet A4*, September 13.

Christensen, Pil. 2013. "I gæld – En sociologisk undersøgelse af det forgældede individ i lyset af den aktuelle krise." Master's thesis, University of Copenhagen.

Christensen, Pil; Nielsen, Peter; and Poulsen, Lars. 2012. *Magt og Modstand, En introduktion til Michael Hardt og Antonio Negris tænkning*. Frederiksberg: Frydenlund.

Crouch, Colin. 2011. *The Strange Non-Death of Neoliberalism*. Cambridge: Polity Press.

Due, Henning. 2011. "Det ville være bedst, hvis folk selv tog ansvar." *Information*, June 21.

Epstein, Gerald A. 2005. *Financialization and the World Economy*. Massachusetts: Edward Elgar Publishing.

Foucault, Michel. 1982. "The subject and power." *Critical Inquiry* 8(4): 777–795.

Foucault, Michel. 1997. "The ethics of the concern of the self as a practice of freedom." In *Michel Foucault Ethics, Subjectivity and Truth (Essential Works of Foucault, 1954–1984, Vol. 1),* edited by Paul Rabinow. New York: New Press.

Foucault, Michel. 2006. *Viljen til Viden – seksualitetens historie 1*. Copenhagen: Det Lille Forlag.

Foucault, Michel. 2008. *The Birth of Biopolitics – Lectures at the Collège de France 1978–1979*. New York: Palgrave Macmillan.

Gordon, Colin. 1991. "Governmental rationality: an introduction." In *The Foucault Effect, Studies in Governmentality: With Two Lectures by and Interview with Michel Foucault,* edited by Graham Burchell, Colin Gordon, and Peter Miller. Chicago: University of Chicago Press.

Hardt, Michael, and Negri, Antonio. 2000. *Empire.* Cambridge: Harvard University Press.

Hardt, Michael, and Negri, Antonio. 2004. *Multitude – War and Democracy in the Age of Empire.* New York: Penguin Press.

Hardt, Michael, and Negri, Antonio. 2012. *Declaration.*

Harvey, David. 2005. *A Brief History of Neoliberalism.* New York: Oxford University Press.

Harvey, David. 2011. *The Enigma of Capital and the Crisis of Capitalism.* New York: Oxford University Press.

Kris. 2010. "Danskerne har verdens største gæld." *TV2 Finans*, February 25.

Larsen, Erling Røed, and Mjølhus, Jon. 2009. *Finanskrise! Lånefest, boligbobel – og dagen derpå.* Oslo: Gyldendal Akademisk.

Lauridsen, Lasse. 2012. "Kreditslaver i alle lande foren eder." *Agenda* (radioshow) on Program 1, Danish State Radio, April 9.

Lazzarato, Maurizio. 2009. "Neoliberalism in action, inequality, insecurity and the reconstitution of the social." *Theory, Culture and Society* 26(6): 109–133.

Lazzarato, Maurizio. 2012. "The making of indebted man, essay on the neoliberal condition." Unpublished manuscript, 2012 (When I first encountered Lazzarato and his ideas about the indebted individual, his book was not yet translated into English. Therefore I wrote to him, asking if he had a translated version I could use for my thesis. Luckily Lazzarato had one, which he sent me. Therefore I worked with a Word version of the book and the references are thus also from this version. The book is now published in English (Maurizio Lazzarato. 2012. *The Making of Indebted Man: An Essay on the Neoliberal Condition.* Los Angeles: Semiotext(e)).

Marazzi, Christian. 2011. *The Violence of Financial Capitalism.* London: Semiotext(e).

Milchman, Alan, and Rosenberg, Alan. 2009. "The final Foucault: government of others and government of the self." In *A Foucault for the 21st Century: Governmentality, Biopolitics and Discipline in the New Millennium,* edited by Sam Binkley and Jorge Capetillo. New Castle upon Tyne: Cambridge Scholars Publishing.

Nationalbanken (Danish National Bank). 2011. "*Danmarks Nationalbank, Kvartalsoversigt 1. kvartal del 1.*" Available at http://www.nationalbanken.dk/c1256be2005737d3/side/Kvartalsoversigt_2011_1_kvartal_Del_1/$file/kap04.htm

Nielsen, Peter. 2011. *Velstandssamfundet*. Frederiksberg: Frydenlund.

Organisation for Economic Co-operation and Development, national account database.

Pedersen, Ove K.. 2011. *Konkurrencestaten*. Copenhagen: Hans Reitzels Forlag.

Read, Jason. 2009. "A genealogy of homo-economicus: Foucault, neoliberalism and the production of subjectivity." In *A Foucault for the 21st Century: Governmentality, Biopolitics and Discipline in the New Millennium,* edited by Sam Binkley and Jorge Capetillo. New Castle upon Tyne: Cambridge Scholars Publishing.

Ritzau. 2011. "EU: Danskernes gæld er en trussel mod økonomi og vækst." *Politiken*, June 6 (Based on European Union Note 2011).

Rose, Nikolas. 2003. "At regere friheden – en analyse af politisk magt i avanceret liberale demokratier." In *Perspektiv, Magt og Styring – Luhmann og Foucault til discussion,* edited by Christian Borch and Lars Thorup Larsen. Copenhagen: Hans Reitzels Forlag.

Rossau, Katrine. 2010. "Gælden vokser os over hovedet." *Politiken*, March 13.

Skovgaard, Lars Erik. 2010. "Danske husholdninger er verdens mest gældsatte." *Berlingske Business,* February 24.

Torp Carlsen, Lene. 2009. "Roden til alt ondt." *Samvirke* 11: 58–60, 62.

United Nations Development Program (UNPD). 2011. "Human Development Report 2011 – Sustainability and Equity: A Better Future for All." Available at http://hdr.undp.org/en/reports/global/hdr2011/download/en

13. Political Attitude in the Age of Globalization

Kurt Dauer Keller

It is evident that Hardt and Negri's writings, from Empire (2000) to *Declaration* (2012), establish a new foundation for political philosophy and, in particular, for the left-wing political thinking, which is always oriented toward the notion of a civilized society beyond the regime of capitalism. In *Declaration* the authors make it clear that today – since the subjective figures of the neoliberal crisis are not only pervasive in the economic and social conditions of everyday life, but also of decisive importance to political and constitutional processes globally – the democratic alternative to imperial capitalism is a radical demand of 'the good life'. However, this seems to call for closer political reflection of our social existence at different levels and of subjective experience than Hardt and Negri offer: The political engagement is not simply a matter of spontaneous kinds of 'decision making' at de-centered levels of social life; the ethics and powers of our own everyday life is addressed and structured into politics only through experience of freedom: the lived coherence of attitude and comportment. So, while Hardt and Negri spell out that the crisis of imperial capitalism calls for explication of the political nature of social life, it must be elucidated in particular how everyday praxes of our time are constituted as well as challenged through the basic freedom that institutes any *habitus*, i.e. the experience and expression of social order that is *performed* by knowledgeable and accountable subjects[1].

We must examine, therefore, how the writings of Hardt and Negri render the continuous and ubiquitous structuring of 'the common' – in the sense of bare life and elementary human institutions – into the ethics and power of the social praxes. First, we have to look upon the notion of biopolitics that concerns the generative dimension of the human life. This leads to a discussion of the multitude and its constituent potential to change itself from a field of subjected praxes into a self-defining subject that can create the social relations and institutions of a new society. In continuation of that, we are led to focus on the understanding in Hardt and Negri of sociality as machinery and as lived experience which, finally, opens an elaboration of the phenomenology of flesh that they lean on, where contemporary ethical and political implications of this phenomenological perspective are indicated.

1 Cf. Bourdieu 1990 and Merleau-Ponty 2010.

Global biopolitics and generative human life

With the appearance of Empire*,* we are reminded that, regardless of how flexible and variable the forms of social life may be that global capitalism can exploit and endorse—and despite the fact that this regime of political economy is indeed turning into a global empire, which incorporates and subsumes the subjective as well as the objective aspects of human existence—it never could and never can stand on its own. The increase of profit or rent is a principle of social organization that can reach and mark every aspect of human life with modes of self-interest, but always only as the capture and exploitation of the overwhelming creativity that is the expressive and perceptual wealth, the spontaneous sociality of bare human life.

Empire is a cogent diagnosis of the contemporary global economy, where capital is becoming based less on physical labor and more on communicative, cooperative, intellectual, and affective forms of labor. Hardt and Negri (2000, xiii) describe this tendency through Foucault's notions of biopower and biopolitics: "The creation of wealth tends ever more toward what we will call biopolitical production, the production of social life itself, in which the economic, the political, and the cultural increasingly overlap and invest one another."

Though the authors will later, in *Declaration*, characterize debt rather than labor as the "general condition of social life", the political matter still concerns a biopower that seeks to rule over and exploit human nature in its global extension, as well as in its intensive being. But whereas the globalization is a mixture of many diverse processes, a spread of uncontrolled social networks with unpredictable events and changes, the controlling and intervening power of the empire remains abstract and only 'concluding'. It is a virtual "machine" that is embedded in the concrete productivity of the social bios that consists of nothing but the corporeity of human affects, communication, and intellect. Thus, the empire is itself exposed and vulnerable to the spontaneity and creativity of the incalculable social existence that it integrates and regulates through individualizing social technologies and through the marginalization of civil society.

This unmediated relationship between abstract biopolitical power and the concrete productivity of social bios, which is also understood with reference to Deleuze and Guattari as the immense diversity of singular human subjects in relation to the power of the empire, involves potentials of emancipative reinterpretation, reorganization and redirection of the basic creative forces that sustain the empire. However, Empire does not unfold this possibility of emancipation in much detail, and also ends up with a rather mystifying notion of how the scattered social and political initiatives around the globe are supposed to provide an alternative political and economic regime. 'Multitude', 'virtuality' and not least 'generation' are key terms by which struggle over the biopolitical fabric of the empire as well as the potential break down of imperial sovereignty are conceived.

> By the virtual we understand the set of powers to act (being, loving, transforming, creating) that reside in the multitude. We have already seen how the multitude's virtual set of powers is constructed by struggles and consolidated in desire. Now we have to investigate how the virtual can put pressure on the borders of the possible, and thus touch on the real. (Hardt & Negri 2000, 357)

With the vertical dimension of generation and consolidation follows an ontological notion of general social activity that unfolds from the pre-orderly, immeasurable sociality of desire and bare life, a continuous creation and innovation, which is already political and already includes notions of value and justice. This is an ontology of immanence: the constituent and self-valorizing power of collective capacities, corporeal as well as discursive, that Marx calls "general intellect" but which is subsumed under globalized capitalist rule as the biopower of production and reproduction: "The powers of science, knowledge, affect, and communication are the principal powers that constitute our anthropological virtuality and are deployed on the surfaces of Empire" (ibid. 365).

The imperial government is an essentially negative and coercive imposition that subsumes the powers of the multitude to exploit them, which implies the regulation of actions and events that risk descent into disorder (ibid. 360). However, the constituent power that is configured by common actions of labor, intelligence, emotion, and affect is really not explicated any further than as a reciprocity of community and activity, or of the common and the singular.

The multitude is, of course, the biopolitical battleground of its generative power versus the imperial domination, distortion and "corruption". It is also the "first fact of metaphysics, ontology, and anthropology" (ibid. 388), which is a collective apparatus of love and desire. Still, the entire dynamic of generation and power is insufficiently explicated in Empire. But this dynamic is crucial to the vertical dimension of events and transformations that structures the creative primacy of desire, the unfolding of virtual potentialities into social actualities, and the tendencies of the multitude to form itself into a political subject. In line with that shortcoming, the aims and aspirations of this subject, its teleology and mythology, are simply declared "theurgical" and a "material religion" (ibid. 396). As is pointed out by Laclau (2001), this is a poor political perspective that offers only little clarification of the articulation and constitution—the rights of global citizenship, social wage, and reappropriation—whereby the multitude is supposed to express itself as activity and consciousness.

Constituent bases of the multitude

In their next book, Multitude, Hardt and Negri (2004) explicate three different bases, or 'standpoints' of the multitude's constituent power whereby it becomes a subject defining itself as resistance and creating the social relations and institutions of a new society: an ontological, a social, and a political basis. Now, the question is whether this conceptual distinction between bases for the constituent power of the multitude actually clarifies the crucial topic of social transformation, that is, the entire dimension of generation, constitution, and articulation, and thus the vertical political dynamics of the multitude through which it can take over the structuring of its own being.

The ontological basis is a corporeal domain of social interplay in which biopolitical production constantly recreates the mutual relationships between the multitude and the common and thus constantly creates a new social being, a new historical formation of human nature: "The conditions of the production and reproduction of the social life of the multitude, from its most general and abstract aspects to the most concrete and subtle, are developed within the continuous encounters, communications, and concatenations of bodies" (ibid. 348).

The common is the natural, 'preliminary condition' as well as the artificial, 'final product' of this biopolitical production. Ontologically, the life of the multitude is thus a common life produced by an indefinite, diffuse set of corporeal singularities, "a kind of social flesh that organizes itself into a new social body" (ibid. 349). The ontologically constituent power of the multitude is to be understood as an expression running through the various levels of the biopolitical common, expressing it "ever more widely and effectively." In this ontological complexity, Hardt and Negri (ibid. 349) ascribe a particularly basic role to the common, whereas any singularity, communication, or production is established in the common and it "configures the mobile and flexible substance of the multitude."

The social or sociological basis of the multitude's constituent power is the cooperative and communicative social labor that is marked by knowledge, information, and emotion, which tends to expand into all forms of work. This creation of new social relationships in direct association with socioeconomic forms of biopolitical production inevitably includes political aspects. Economic production and political production coincide in collaborative networks that indicate the possibility of a new institutional structure of society. Thus, the social basis of constituent power consists in networks of social production that "provide an institutional logic capable of sustaining a new society" (ibid. 350).

Together the ontological and sociological perspectives articulate the "theoretical possibility" of the democracy of the multitude, which requires *a political basis* for its practical implementation. The political aim of the multitude is an "absolute democracy" that is contrary not only to war[2] but also to representation and sovereignty. So, the political perspective assembles in a determinate time and place the common power and 'decision making' capacity of the multitude as a constituent power. This power "emerges out of the ontological and social process of productive labor". It is also designated as "a deployment of force that defends the historical progression of emancipation and liberation" and—like the ontological notion of generation in Empire—as "an act of love" in a broad sense of love, namely "that our expansive encounters and continuous collaborations bring us joy" (ibid. 351).

The greater part of the book emphasizes the close coherence of economic and political production, which relates to the assertion that there is an inherent potential for resistance and liberation 'from below' at play in the productive unfolding of social relations: Resistance is not just a response, but "primary with respect to power" (ibid. 64). That is because the imperial biopower depends on and draws on recurrent actualization of the multitude's creative forces in the extensive utilization of global networks, as well as in the intensive utilization of social relations. In a brief genealogy of resistance since early modernity, Hardt and Negri again point it out that the intensive dimension of the global struggle has now become biopolitical, which is to say that it involves the bare life, or social flesh, of the human beings. In addition, the various forms of resistance are associated with a democratic tendency that is inherent to the multitude and which contrasts with any organization of the globally networked multitude into capitalist or modern forms of sovereignty. This is a huge mouthful: "The great production of subjectivity of the multitude, its biopolitical capacities, its struggle against poverty, its constant striving for democracy, all coincide (…) with the genealogy of these resistances stretching from the early modern era to our own" (ibid. 68).

Rather superficially, Hardt and Negri (ibid. 68) claim that this genealogy of resistance reveals some guiding principles "that are really embedded in history and determine its movement." One of these poses a correspondence between the most effective form of resistance of an era and its dominant form of economical and social production. With the current global recomposition of social classes, adequate resistance no longer takes the form of a people's army or guerrilla war-

2 Distinctions between war and politics have become increasingly blurred with notions of legitimate violence outside any framework of international law, with notions of war against evil or terror and war-like police actions. Hardt and Negri use terms such as "a permanent state of exception" and "a global state of war" to designate the contemporary context of ongoing struggles of insurgency and counterinsurgency.

fare but, instead, consists in network movements or 'swarms', and this is in accord with the hegemony of immaterial labor and network-based forms of decision making. In sectors central to the global economy, such as information, knowledge, and communication, innovation requires common resources, open access, and free interaction. In these productive realms—that tend to influence and dominate other realms of the global economy—innovation does not rely on the genius of any single individual, but emerges from the open networks of the multitude.

Thus, Hardt and Negri suggest that the network-based economic innovation is in analogy with the multitude's political decision making. This assertion is based on the important point that in addition to goods and services the multitude produces cooperation, communication, forms of life, and social relationships. But it also implies a surprising claim of analogy between innovation and decision making. This claim tends to downgrade social innovation into acts of political will and to devalue democracy into a matter of open-source collaboration (cf. ibid. 340). Democracy is not primarily—and not merely—the lucky outcome of networked collaboration, and it is not particularly by the power of will or decision making that social collaboration is innovative! Still, such notions turn out to be basic to Hardt and Negri's assertion that current forms of networked innovation and decision making constitute a kind of political economy or social technology that is essential to imperial suppression as well as to democratic liberation.

Another guiding principle of historical movement that appears from the genealogy of resistance seems entirely opposite to this notion of socio-technical correspondence between contemporary forms of suppression and liberation, though Hardt and Negri actually deny that (ibid. 87). The other principle refers to democracy and freedom in that each new form of resistance becomes ever more democratic, whereas it addresses the undemocratic qualities of the previous forms of resistance movements. Thus, "democracy and freedom constantly act as guiding principles in the development of organizational forms of resistance" (ibid. 87). This demand for more democracy and freedom has nothing to do with a social technology (or political-economical structure) that can be supplanted from one political regime to another but is, on the contrary, defined in opposition to and as surpassing the new, contemporary forms of sovereignty and tyranny:

> Sovereignty in all its forms inevitably poses power as the rule of the one and undermines the possibility of a full and absolute democracy. The project of democracy must today challenge all existing forms of sovereignty as a precondition for establishing democracy. (Hardt & Negri 2004, 353.)

Hardt and Negri insist that the current and emerging forms of biopolitical production are not just existing conditions from which today's democratic project must launch. The biopolitical networks are within the constituent powers of the multitude and offer the basic capacity—the constitutional mechanisms and institutional procedures—for the democratic project: "The institutions of democracy today must coincide with the communicative and collaborative networks that constantly produce and reproduce social life" (ibid. 355).

The authors distinguish *biopolitics*, the dominating contemporary structuring of economical production that includes the cultural production of social relationships and social order, from a notion of *biopower* as sovereignty that is ontologically limited and always dependent upon the productive forces of biopolitics. So, though biopower now tends to subsume the entire global production of social life, it remains a relational matter that depends "not only on the consent but also on the social productivity of the ruled" (ibid. 335). However, it is obscure how the social life of the multitude, which is through and through subsumed by imperial power, turns out—simply by a change of perspective—to be the unfolding of an autonomous productive source, guided by principles of freedom and democracy, and about to burst into the realization of an alternative social order that is entirely incompatible with sovereignty.

The problem is not really solved when, instead, Hardt and Negri render the changing perspectives at play as historical (political-economic) versus ontological or, what we have also seen, as practical (political) versus theoretical (ontological and social). For, clearly, the core of the problem is that the very topic of generation and dynamic change, the vertical dimension of human life, in which history, visions, will, and desire must be understood, is treated too superficially in Multitude. Certainly, important points are made about the notions of flesh, freedom, and democracy—the main concepts whereby the authors attempt to grasp the excessive productivity, force, and capability of the multitude—but through the application of these concepts, not much is clarified concerning actual matters of social generation and political change, such as how absolute democracy in an ontological, Spinozan sense relates to the contemporary, unprecedented "restlessness for freedom and democracy" throughout the world, why freedom remains essential to suppression, or the phenomenological notion of flesh that holds the ontological spontaneity and creativeness of social life.

Closely associated with this weak conception of the vertical dimension is the unsettled relationship between the different forms of constituent power. At times, Hardt and Negri present a circularity of social and historical production in which the multitude of singularities starts from the common and reproduces it in new ways. This perspective is compatible with the notions of social technology, political machinery, and global networks of social production, all of which are systems and functions that could be preserved from the capitalist empire and arranged within a democratic social order. On other occasions, the picture is rather one of social productivity and a common wealth that belongs to the multitude but which is subsumed under the imperial hegemony and exploited by it. From this perspective, the common, as the creative and democratic sources of the multitude, is external and opposite to the suppressive biopower of the empire that arranges everything in its own parasitic and corrupt way. Hardt and Negri can only be praised for holding on to both of these perspectives. What they are to be blamed for, however, is that in this context they do not distinguish between a theoretical perspective and an actual platform of being and becoming, that is, a real basis of constituent power. Therefore, their ontological and anthropological notions—everything pre-given about bare human life as well as profound cultural and historical conditions that frame and contextualize the contemporary social and political situations of the multitude versus the empire—are alarmingly blurred. This is the case, not least, when it comes to the concepts of the common and singularity.

Social machinery and lived experience

In *Commonwealth* (2009) and *Declaration* (2012), Hardt and Negri further unfold the lines of thinking along which the autonomy, creativity, resistance, insurrection, and democratic attitude of the multitude are formulated in Multitude. In particular, the topic of production of new social relations and ultimately a new social order comes to the fore as a question of the production of subjectivity, which is largely understood in extension of Deleuze and Foucault. But, perhaps because these pioneers offer mainly a conceptualization of the just mentioned 'mechanical' or socio-technical perspective of the social life, Hardt and Negri find it necessary to move on and include Spinozan and phenomenological approaches, both of which do indeed present a richness of generative and ontological thinking. This triangle of theoretical positions (Spinoza, phenomenology, and the 'post-structuralism' of Foucault together with Deleuze) indicates the new conceptual background for their thinking—Marxist, of course, at its core—of the common and singularity as the constituents through which the multitude always reproduces and renews itself.

In the preface of Commonwealth we are reminded that a new space for politics is opened, which is neither private nor 'public' (in the sense of state affairs), neither capitalistic nor socialistic, but the political project of instituting the common wealth of the material and the social world. Contemporary globalized society—dependent on information, knowledge, images, and affects distributed in decentralized networks—creates the possibility of a social and economic order grounded in the common, a biopolitical production in which the central matter is of an ethical kind: the production of subjectivity itself. This concept is to be understood as a *dispositif*, Hardt and Negri suggest:

> Gilles Deleuze, reflecting on Michel Foucault's notion of the *dispositif* (the material, social, affective, and cognitive mechanisms or apparatuses of the production of subjectivity), claims, "We belong to the *dispositifs* and act within them." (…) At issue "is not what we are but rather what we are in the process of becoming – that is the Other, our becoming-other." A key scene of political action today, seen from this vantage point, involves the struggle over the control or autonomy of the production of subjectivity. The multitude makes itself by composing in the common the singular subjectivities that result from this process. (Hardt and Negri 2009, X)

It is Hardt and Negri who comprehend the *dispositif* as a current matter of struggle over the control (or autonomy) of the production of subjectivity, which is quite different from other interpretations of Foucault's concept. They quote from Deleuze, who himself ends up pointing out that for Foucault, insofar as the *dispositif* invokes the present and creativity—a theme in some of his interviews but not in his major books—our 'becoming-other' in the 'process of becoming' is simply "the unknown which knocks on the door" (Deleuze 1992, 164–166). Agamben's discussion of Foucault's concept and its historical roots leads to a more pessimistic conclusion. The concept stems from a Christian distinction between being and praxis, in which the Greek *oikonomia* and the Latin *dispositio* refer to government that has to take place without any reference to being and therefore must include subjectification in the sense of production of its own subject (cf. Agamben 2008). This broader contextualization of the notion of the *dispositif* only underlines the relevance of its tight contemporary association with the governmentality and biopolitics that Foucault also uncovered. But, as Agamben sees it, the 'production' of subjectivity that the *dispositifs* of our days are sustaining is more like destruction: "The *dispositifs* we are dealing with at the current stage of capitalism, however, have less to do with bringing about the production of a subject; they stand out, rather, through processes of what we could call desubjectification" (Agamben 2008, 36; translated).

To what extent does the notion of dispositif actually illuminate the production of subjectivity? In Empire, following Foucault (1977), the notion is rendered as a strategic and general apparatus or mechanism of disciplinary power. In the early capitalistic society, such *dispositifs* were abstract, distinct, and external (or "transcendent") to the dominated social practices but, with the society of control that evolved in the 20th century, they became dispersed, floating, and internal (or "immanent") to new social practices marked by hybrid forms of self-disciplining of subjects. However, later when Foucault (1998) begins to analyze and understand the production of subjectivity as ethics and aesthetics of existence, not just as the *episteme* of an epoch or the hegemonic discourse and strategic orientation within an institutional field, the *dispositifs* are of sexuality rather than power and are associated with changing hermeneutics of the self rather than with changing disciplinary systems of control and subordination. In this analytical perspective, Foucault's themes and categories are designed to characterize the distinctions between entire culture-historical epochs in which freedom and power are allied in a general 'self-technology', which is, of course, very abstract in relation to any lived subjectivity.

So, in Foucault, the *dispositif* is found to denote a heterogeneous social structure that is suggested as the basis for the production of a specific form of subjectivity, without an explication of how this structure really functions as a strategy or how subjects experience their active or passive incorporation into the machinery of the *dispositif*. However, it is precisely these issues of strategy and subjective experience that are decisive to Hardt and Negri's idea of a social apparatus: the evolving circularity of a *dispositif* that always produces the subjectivity of social life along strategic political lines and thus is ready-made for this subjectivity itself to take over—with its own democratic strategies—the formation (or 'constitution') and the functioning of that operative social machinery. All in all, the conceptual and explanatory shift from Foucault (together with Deleuze and Agamben) is radical when the *dispositif* is to be conceived as a platform for the political action of the multitude, which really means that it is a lived unfolding of common power, that it is directly and explicitly experienced as a potential for social and political change.

Declaration, the culmination of Hardt and Negri's theoretical reflection on freedom, equality, and democracy, thematizes *dispositifs* in connection with political resistance and insurrection. Such political action and organization require the production of subjectivities who can foster and support free, equal, and democratic social relations and, ultimately, a multitude capable of self-management and the management of the common. The necessary *dispositifs* of the production of subjectivity are strategic processes that start from constituent power: "A constituent power is necessary to organize social production and social life in accordance with our principles of freedom, equality, and solidarity" (Hardt & Negri 2012). When the struggle of the movements stands out as indicating a remarkable political alternative, it is a *dispositif* that holds an autonomous temporality, a different organization of common time through which subjectivity is also changed (ibid.). If we ask how it is possible to think of transforming Foucault's concept so radically, we would have to look into Commonwealth to find the answer.

Commonwealth asserts that with new understandings of the forms of productivity, as well as of the corporeity of human life, a transformation took place in Marxist thinking throughout the 20th century: from the Marxist critique of property to the phenomenology of bodies (Hardt & Negri 2009, 22–38). Structuralism, critical theory, and political activism – together with the new conditions of immaterial labor that became separated from the control of capital and at the same time hegemonic over all the other forms of valorization processes – marked the "entry of a phenomenology of the bodies into Marxist theory" (ibid. 25):

> The result of these diverse interventions is a "phenomenologization" of critique, that is, a shift to consider the relationship between critique and its object as a material *dispositif*, within the collective dimension of bodies – a shift, in short, from the transcendental to the immanent. (Hardt & Negri 2009, 24)

In prolongation of this phenomenologization, the dispositif is understood as a dynamic of desire, an ethics of the free will that permeates everything and "elevates man to the threshold of transforming being itself" (ibid. 318). The *dispositif* is construed as an expression of life and a theory of value that exceeds or breaks away from determinism and creatively redefines time and space (ibid. 313–19). Furthermore, the *dispositif* is rendered as a learning mechanism for the desire as well as the capacity of democracy. It is the celebration of an ancient concept of happiness as a long-lasting political condition and an enlightening collective process of learning by doing, the institution of a multitude that governs itself (ibid. 376–77).

In a closer view, however, the phenomenology of bodies that Hardt and Negri embrace turns out to be half-hearted. Their notion of singularity is certainly far from the lived bodily experience of a human being, and neither is the common really understood as flesh in the phenomenological sense that they claim. When the metropolis is presented as production of the common and as encounters among singularities, it is not clarified how this engages people in passive or active ways and how their daily forms of praxes are thereby politically structured. When multitudes and institutions are composed of singularities and singularity is conceived of as a kind of social atom, although it is also reproduced by social apparatuses, we are offered only a superficial conceptualization that tightly associates social experience with the singularity of the body. In spite of the many harsh attacks that the authors make on concepts of identity and individuality in contemporary social philosophy[3], they seem themselves to fall back into a naïve ontology of our bodily being. If sociality is conceived of ontologically on the basis of entities defined by the singularity of the body, we are far away from the phenomenological understanding of the body and of the flesh of sociality; surely, we are already trapped by simplistic models of social tech-

3 See for example Hardt & Negri 2009, 124–25, 338–39, 358.

nology such as in the economic and juridical thinking of traditional liberalism (cf. Keller 2007).

Hardt and Negri remain fixed in a notion of social apparatus and distant from any serious phenomenology when the common is regarded only as a counterpart in the relationship to singularity, not as the ontological flesh of singularity. Their references to the phenomenological concept of flesh to explain their basic concept of the common and its wealth are hasty and eager to move on to Spinoza, Deleuze, or Foucault, who play a major part in the suggested phenomenology[4]. The inclusion of a largely Spinozan concept of the common implies a speculative approach that substitutes teleological and religious vitalism for phenomenology. When Spinoza is interpreted through Deleuze, matters are not necessarily clarified. In Hardt's (1993) own book on Deleuze it is particularly apparent that Deleuze's inventive interpretation of Spinoza brings us to a strange mixture of understanding social life as an apparatus and as a spontaneous unfolding of striving and desire.

Although Deleuze adopts important aspects of the phenomenology of the flesh, his rigorously anti-Hegelian and anti-dialectical thinking, which is largely taken over by Hardt and Negri, throws us far from not only Marxism but also the very idea of dynamic social generation and historicity that is crucial to their project. Thus, Deleuze turns phenomenology's ontological notion of elementary meaning as an experienced event into an effect of intervention or even of conceptual construction. He allows for no difference between virtual and real, between constructed image and perception. As Nancy (1996) precisely points out, Deleuze is not really occupied with being, process, history or even genesis:

> Deleuze's interest in the cinema is not just appended to his work: it is at the centre, in the projective principle of this thought. It is a cinema-thought, in the sense of having its own order and screen, a singular plane of presentation and construction, of displacements and dramatization of concepts. (Nancy 1996, 110.)

Thus, 'event' and 'becoming' are conceived of almost like the occurring and shifting pictures in a film: as appearance, disappearance, naming, and indexing in a universe with moments, durations, and sequences of forces, configurations, and stratifications. Indeed, this distributed and composed chaos that folds onto itself as it is named and reconfigured in a new moment is far from the lived experience of strivings and struggles.

4 See Hardt & Negri 2004, 100, 192–94; Hardt & Negri 2009, 29–31, 122.

Political implication of a phenomenology of the flesh

The weakness that Hardt and Negri inherit with their foothold in Deleuze and Foucault is the concept of subjectivity, which is either a produced effect or a political actor, not the lived experience and overwhelming wealth of meaning and significance that really defines human subjectivity. In spite of their clear attention to the growing importance of phenomenological perspectives in the Marxist thinking that unfolds during the 20th century—where particularly matters relating to the common, to 'flesh' (i.e. sense as corporeal meaning or bodily experience), and to freedom are understood through the phenomenology—Hardt and Negri always end up subsuming these issues under the categories of social machinery or speculative vitalism. Nevertheless, a coherent conceptualization of the common, flesh, and freedom is significant to the ethics of attitude, i.e. social character as a principle of the good life. Here "attitude" and "character" denote the integration of emotion, action and cognition—of pathos, ethos and logos—in a typical approach to sociocultural conditions and problems or a style of comportment in front of conflict and suppression.

To get a picture of the phenomenological notion of the common, we only have to take more seriously Arendt's (1998) discussion that Hardt and Negri themselves point to. Arendt renders the common as the public realm: the ethical and political community of communication and action. This is the political life of a civil society and democratic participation, which is marginalized today and about to vanish from its traditional fora. Actually, Arendt pinpoints what characterizes the democratic experience that is sought by Hardt and Negri: the ethics of a plurality of singular positions and the corresponding political interplay of a variety of perspectives. This is, however, social life in a horizontal perspective and at the vertical level of established praxes, where we exist as able individuals and groups with reflected, articulated, and negotiated political positions within a common social space. More than half a century ago did Arendt regret the tendency of politics in this early modern sense to disappear, but Hardt and Negri are not unhappy about the loss of this advanced—and historically unique—form of societal interplay and organization, whereas they find that democracy reemerges in other and stronger social forms including the new networked and more spontaneous movements in the age of globalization. When Hardt and Negri (2009, 174-75, 354), furthermore, blame Arendt for her sharp distinction between politics and economy, they seem to forget that her discourse of the common maintains focus on social praxes, the vertical level of human existence at which people can meet as knowledgeable and accountable groups or persons to negotiate politics or to take up another sort of praxis, while their point is about the new networked forms of work and collaboration in which cognitive and social innovation emerge and spread in de-centered ways. This brings them in danger of missing the very concept of politics, which starts from the attitude of groups and persons who have already the *political* freedom to articulate and defend their interests in the common (or 'public') social space (Arendt 1968). Hardt and Negri, thereby, tend to end up with a notion of the political only, which is the mere subjection to historically given power relations and involvement in processes of social change.

Like Foucault, Hardt and Negri are, however, well aware that freedom is the ubiquitous precondition for the entire unfolding of political and productive praxes. No historical and cultural framework of established power would work if people did not take it on, if they did not recurrently exist and act as able and responsible participants along the prescribed lines. It is not very well known, but in fact the concept of freedom that was clarified in existential phenomenology—not least by Merleau-Ponty (1962) together with Sartre—is largely accepted by Foucault and Bourdieu: Deeper than all questions of being 'able to do what we want' is the human condition that we are always 'able to want what we do'. If a social practice is to depend on knowledgeable social actors, it must pass through this gateway of thematization. The particular cases of freedom may be actualized in many different ways: anonymously or adhering to specific social identity, collectively or individually, recurrently or more rarely. But in all cases, freedom basically presents the ethical perspective on social life—and forms the power relations of social life—as a situated interpretation and 'valorization' (ascription of significance), which is something quite different from the theoretical scenery of determinism versus voluntarism, not to speak of the combination of mechanistic causality and speculative vitalism that Hardt and Negri suggest together with Deleuze.

Because the praxes are our 'second nature'—that have not to do with simple or random human behavior, but require our comportment and *habitus* in which we have actually taken on (with the imagined possibility of refusing to do so) our objective performance—the structure of the relevant social situation or context appears quite different before and after our choice to engage in it: open and contingent before the actualized freedom, settled and over-determined after it. Freedom in this basic sense is the passage for the vertical structuring of meaning where the experience of our own being is invested in a social order that is new to this experience. Equally important to the vertical structuring of human life is the oppositely directed sedimentation of practices that are taken on, which includes the very formation of institutions[5]. It is through the generative dynamics, that is, the unfolding of experience and cultivation of meaning, in these opposite direc-

5 Cf. Merleau-Ponty 2010, Keller 2010.

tions of verticality that the common, multitude, and singularity are experienced as coherent matters that can also be distinguished. Thus, the vertical structuring of social life through freedom and institution is interpretations of the surplus of wild, overwhelming expressive-perceptual meaning (which is in itself pre-practical or unpractical: sexual, aggressive, dramatic, imaginative, mythical, religious, etc.) into the over-determined order of social praxes. Because Hardt and Negri attempt to include the entire political structuring of social life in a Deleuzian machinery, they inevitably lose sight of this vertical depth in which the various forms of overdetermination are imbedded in the omnipresent surplus of aesthetic meaning and emotional experience. Their concept of 'the common' hardly captures the hermeneutic notion of overdetermination as the 'taken-for-grantedness' and presumed inevitability that upholds a regime of social order until it breaks down due to (or at least in close association with) its own lack of social reason and cultural value. The phenomenology in Merleau-Ponty together with the structuralism in Althusser took up this notion from not only Freud's understanding of the unconscious but also Gramsci's understanding of hegemony. Thus understood, the common is not simply a wealth of creative and productive resources but first and foremost an overwhelming mess of passions, orientations, reactions, and moods. It will always be necessary to lift up the various expressive-perceptual modes of the common into the practical fields of multitudes and singularities; the common flesh will always have to be formed into ethics, power, and politics through the structuring of social order in the creativity of freedom and in the sedimentation of institutions.

The flesh of human life is not what we are—in this Foucault disregards or misinterprets Merleau-Ponty (1968)—but what we are of. Flesh is elementary meaning (i.e. expressive and perceptual sense), which includes intertwinement of materiality and imagination and in which both nature and the human body appear as matters of expression and perception. So, the social common is primarily the de-centered forms of being in which we are absorbed in emotions, engagements, and fascinating or disgusting impressions. Surely this common is an overwhelming resource of productivity and creativity, like Hardt and Negri emphasize it, but the authors tend rather systematically to neglect that this source of human life is basically wild and free-floating, not necessarily promoting for any particular political project. The political significance of the flesh has to be conceived through distinction between politics and the political. Bare human life immediately confronts the political conditions under which we live. Our emotions, expressions, desires, and naïve beliefs are shaped as political myths through political dramas, but as compound and more or less unpredictable strivings, reactions, and effects, not as orientations and energies that can be calculated or directly monitored by political decisions. At these levels of 'dense sense' and corporeal existence, where the life lived remains more or less anonymous, there is hardly room or 'the fresh air' for the freedom of political reflection, discussion and action.

Therefore, the democratic project suggested in *Declaration* requires political reflection and interpretation of the various emerging forms of the common. Historical and cultural structuring of the good life is not just a spontaneous process. And the creativity of the common does not necessarily become more democratic when it assumes global and networked forms. On the contrary, there are global forms of suppression that should be met with global notions of a political alternative. This implies visions of a truly democratic order, as well as opposition and insurrection against the existing order. Undoubtedly, the four forms of praxes that evolved in Europe over several millennia—only to be increasingly shaped through the last centuries by the logic of the marked together with the logic of governmentality—are now present throughout the globe and call for democratic attitude: work, play, education, and consumption (Keller 2005). Necessarily, the very notion of a concrete democratic process differs considerably between these forms of sociality, whereas the matter is precisely of diverging types of praxis. They are all, however, suffering and degenerating from the lack of good life.

It is not new that work is alienated under the conditions of capitalism. But it is somewhat neglected that the new forms of work where knowledge, communication, and emotion have come to the fore imply their own forms of severe strain and stress. The intensity with which employees must ordinarily commit themselves to their work increases steadily at the cost of the time and energy with which they can engage in other aspects of life. Working stress is a social pathology that has been predominant and well-known since the 1960es. In addition, public governance has established programs and intensified measures to control and intervene in professional work since the 1980es. These developments influence the quality of work as well as working conditions. It is, indeed, getting difficult and rare to develop or maintain good work. Thus, the political task to preserve and elaborate notions of professionalism and competent work is of a civilizing significance.

Play, which is the opposite of work, is also alienated and downgraded or reduced to marginal activity and practices. The majority of a population is likely to be involved in arts and sports mostly as passive entertainment. The entire expressive side of the human existence remains undervalued, just like joyful captivation and time-forgetting social interplay. To really have fun or to be engaged in serious social praxes directed at imaginative or aesthetic matters rather than economic value or practical outcome is a vital field of democratic vision and politics.

Education, the upbringing and enlightening of adults as well as children and the young, is likewise a field of praxes that call for democratic perspectives. The qualifications and socialization that people acquire through ordinary or special education is largely nothing more than social integration into the systems of markets and bureaucracies. Though it is a widespread and growing objective to teach students to be self-determining and innovative, the bulk of educational praxes offer only little opportunity for critical reflection. Governmentality directs new generations into the dominant forms of individuality, just like courses in 'empowerment' are disciplining to social clients.

Consumption is the field of praxes directly opposite to education, whereas it relates to products and services rather than human relations and it consists in immediate fulfillment rather than strategic development. Though notions of 'the consumer society' and 'the political consumer' are well-known, consumption is still highly in need of political attention and refection. A lot of social pathologies are attached to the patterns and habits of consumption. The quality of products and services is only poorly secured through competition or by law, and this circumstance calls for the public attention, critique and sanction from the consumers. This does not relate solely to the singular product or service, but primarily to the general conditions of advertisement and declarations together with established standards that are designed to deceive the consumers and may expose them to extensive risks.

Political struggle over these praxes thematizes, of course, topics of the social order and everyday life in a horizontal perspective that rests on their shared vertical organization of historical and cultural flesh. Under entirely different conditions of freedom and institution the vertical formation of the praxes is build on another disciplining of the human body and another control of creativity and time, associated with its own power relations and ethics. In so far as praxes of work, play, education, and consumption can be found that are markedly different from the described picture dominating most of the world now, this points to the urgent problem of inequality. While inequality is hardly a problem to imperial power, it is undoubted the hardest challenge to democracy in the age of globalization, the crucial test of democratic attitude in our time.

References

Agamben, Giorgio. 2008. *Was ist ein Dispositiv?* Zürich: Diaphanes.

Arendt, Hannah. 1998. *The Human Condition*. Chicago: University of Chicago Press.

Arendt, Hannah. 2006. *On Revolution*. New York: Penguin Press.

Bourdieu, Pierre. 1990. *The Logic of Practice*. London: Polity Press.

Deleuze, Gilles. 1992. "What is a *Dispositif*?" In *Michel Foucault Philosopher*, edited by T.J. Armstrong, 159-166. New York: Routledge.

Foucault, Michel. 1977. *Discipline and Punish*. New York: Vintage Books.

Foucault, Michel. 1998. *The History of Sexuality Vol. 1: The Will to Knowledge*. London: Penguin.

Hardt, Michael. 1993. *Gilles Deleuze. An Apprenticeship in Philosophy*. Minneapolis: University of Minnesota Press.

Hardt, Michael & Negri, Antonio. 2000. *Empire*. Cambridge: Harvard University Press.

Hardt, Michael & Negri, Antonio. 2004. *Multitude*. London: Hamish Hamilton.

Hardt, Michael & Negri, Antonio. 2009. *Commonwealth*. Cambridge: Harvard University Press.

Hardt, Michael & Negri, Antonio. 2012. *Declaration*. Argo Navis Author Service, www.argonavisdigital.com.

Keller, Kurt Dauer. 2005. "The Corporeal Order of Things: The *Spiel* of Usability". *Human Studies* 28 (2): 173-204.

Keller, Kurt Dauer. 2007. "Pre-personal identity. A critique of Harré's notion of a singular self." In *Citizen City. Between Constructing Agent and Constructed Agency,* edited by V. Deventer, M. Blanche, E. Fourie, & P. Segalo, 294–300. North York: Captus University Publications.

Keller, Kurt Dauer. 2010. "Institution – A Generative Structuring of Meaning." In *Thinking in Dialogue with Humanities. Paths into the Phenomenology of Merleau-Ponty*, edited by K. Novotny, T.S. Hammer, A. Gléonec & P. Specián. Bucharest: Zeta Books.

Laclau, Ernesto. 2001. "Can Immanence Explain Social Struggles?" *Diacritics* 31(4): 3-10.

Merleau-Ponty, Maurice. 1962. *Phenomenology of Perception*. London: Routledge & Kegan Paul.

Merleau-Ponty, Maurice. 1968. *The Visible and the Invisible*. Evanston: Northwestern University Press.

Merleau-Ponty, Maurice. 2010. *Institution and Passivity*. Evanston: Northwestern University Press.

Nancy, Jean-Luc. 1996. "The Deleuzian Fold of Thought." In *Deleuze: A Critical Reader,* edited by P. Patton, 107-113. Blackwell Publishers.

Notes on editors and contributors

Editors

ÓSCAR GARCÍA AGUSTÍN is associate professor at the Department of Culture and Global Studies at Aalborg University, Denmark. He has published several articles on social movements, civil society, and political and discourse theory. With Martin Bak Jørgensen he has coedited the special issue 'Civil Society and Immigration: New Ways of Democratic Transformation' (*Migration Letters*, 2013). He is author of *Zapatista Communication: Counterpower and Political Action* (Manuscritos, 2006), *Discourse and Institutionalization* (Universidad de La Rioja, 2010) and *Discourse and Zapatista Autonomy* (Peter Lang, 2013).

CHRISTIAN YDESEN is assistant professor at Aalborg University, Denmark. He holds a ph.d degree in the history of education from Aarhus University. He has been a visiting scholar at the University of Edinburgh, UK, and the University of Birmingham, UK. He has published the book *The Rise of High-Stakes Testing in Denmark, 1920-1970* and "Fundamental Aspects of the Human Condition and Multiculturalism under the Reign of Neoliberalism" (in *Globalization and Transnational Capitalism.* edited by Li Xing, 2009). He has written several articles on topics such as the history of educational accountability, history of psychology, history of educational testing, intercultural philosophy, basic income, the political philosophy of Michael Hardt and Antonio Negri, and the disciplining effects of the contemporary work regime.

Contributors

PIL CHRISTENSEN holds a master degree in sociology from the University of Copenhagen (2013). Pil spent one year as a visiting student at UC Berkeley in 2010-11. Her academic interests include economy, money, power, precarious labor and labor organizing. Pil has given numerous lectures and taught workshops to various trade unions, students, and grassroots organizations. She maintains a political blog and regularly participates in television and radio debates and interviews. In addition to writing several articles and contributing to numerous research reports, Pil wrote a chapter in the book *Value Battles: Economy and Society* (2009) and co-authored an introduction to the collected works of the political philosophers Michael Hardt and Antonio Negri (2012).

GUISEPPE COCCO is associate professor at the Federal University of Rio de Janeiro (UFRJ). He holds a master degree in Political Sciences and a ph.d in social history. He is a founding member of the network Universidade Nômade. His main fields of research are tranformation processes of work, cognitive capitalism, and development. With Antonio Negri, he is author of *GlobAL: Biopower and Struggles in a Globalized Latin America* (Paidos, 2006). His most recent book is *Mundobraz: the becoming-Brazil of the world and the becoming-world of Brazil* (Record, 2009; translated into Spanish: Traficantes de Sueños, 2012).

BEN DORFMAN has a ph.d in history and is associate professor of intellectual and cultural history in the Department of Culture and Global Studies at Aalborg University. Ben is editor of the journal *Ideas in History: Journal of the Nordic Society for the History of Ideas* and is head of the Research Group in International Studies at Aalborg University. Ben has published on ranges of issues in cultural theory, philosophy of history, intellectual history and human rights in journals from *Critical Horizons* to *Culture, Theory & Critique* to *International Social Science Review*. His doctoral dissertation, *Repoenings: Georges Batailles and the Theorization of the Postmodern Age*, was completed at the University of Kansas in 2002.

ANDREA FUMAGALLI is associated professor of economics in the Department of Economics and management, at University of Pavia. He is member of UniNomade Network, founder member of Bin-Italy (Basic Income Network, Italy) and of BIEN (Basic Income Earth Network). He is active in the San Precario network. Among his recent publications, see *Bioeconomics and Cognitive Capitalism: Towards a New Accumulation Paradigm* (Carocci, 2007), *The Crisis of the Global Economy: Financial Markets, Social Struggles and New Political Scenarios* (Semiotext(e), 2010) (with S. Mezzadra), "Life Put to Work: Towards a Theory of Life-Value," *Ephemera*, vol. 10, (with C. Morini).

KURT DAUER KELLER is associate professor at the Department of Learning and Philosophy, Aalborg University. His primary fields of research are the phenomenology of Merleau-Ponty, social philosophy, social psychology, work organization, and professionalism. He is co-editor of a new book series in Danish on existential phenomenology. Among his works are "Intentionality in Perspectival Structure", *Chiasmi International. Trilingual studies concerning Merleau-Ponty's Thoughts* vol. 3, 2001; "The corporeal order of things", *Human Studies* vol. 28 (2), 2005; "Pre-personal Identity" (In *Citizen City*, edited by V. Deventer et al., Captus University Publications, 2007); "Institution – a generative structuring of meaning" (In *Thinking in dialogue with humanities*, edited by K. Novotny et al., Zeta Books, 2010).

MAURIZZIO LAZZARATO is a philosopher and sociologist. He is an independent researcher, working at the University of Paris I and a member of the International College of Philosophy of Paris. His areas of research include immaterial labour, cognitive capitalism, biopolitics, and production of subjectivities. He is one of the founding members of the editorial committee of the journal *Multitude*. He is the author of, among others, *Immaterial Labour: Forms of Life and the Production of Subjectivity* (Ombre Corte, 1997), *The Revolutions of Capitalism* (Les Empêcheurs de penser en rond, 2004), and most recently *The Making of the Indebted Man* (Semiotext(e), 2012).

CHRISTIAN MARAZZI, economist, is professor at the Scuola Universitaria Professionale della Svizzera Italiana, where he is director of the unit of social research. He is the author of numerous publications about the transformation of the systems of production and about the financiarization of capitalism. He is author of *Capital and Language* (Semiotext(e), 2008), *Capital and Affects* (Semiotext(e), 2011), and *The Violence of Financial Capitalism* (Semiotext(e), 2011).

SANDRO MEZZADRA teaches political theory at the University of Bologna and is adjunct fellow at the Institute for Culture and Society of the University of Western Sydney. In the last decade his work has particularly centred on the relations between globalization, migration and citizenship as well as on postcolonial theory and criticism. He is an active participant in the 'post-workerist' debate and one of the founders of the UniNomade network (http://uninomade.org/). With Brett Neilson he is the author of *Border as Method, or, the Multiplication of Labor* (Duke University Press 2013).

CRISTINA MORINI, graduated in political theory at University of Milan, is independent social researcher and journalist. She is member of UniNomade Network in Italy and active in social movements on migration and social insecurity. Her fields of research are working conditions of women and the transformation processes of work. Among her recent publications, see "The Feminization of Labour in Cognitive Capitalism" (in *Feminist Review*, 87(1), 2007; *Per amore e per forza. Femminilizzazione del lavoro e biopolitiche del corpo* (Ombre Corte, 2010), "Life Put to Work: Towards a tTheory of Life-value", *Ephemera*, 8, 2011 (with A. Fumagalli).

TIMOTHY S. MURPHY is Houston-Truax-Wentz Professor of English at Oklahoma State University. He is the author of *Wising Up the Marks: The Amodern William Burroughs* (California, 1998) and *Antonio Negri: Modernity and the Multitude* (Polity, 2012), co-editor of *The Philosophy of Antonio Negri* volumes 1 and 2 (Pluto, 2005-2007), and translator of Negri's books *Subversive Spinoza* (Manchester, 2004), *Books for Burning* (Verso, 2005) and *Trilogy of Resistance* (Minnesota, 2011). From 2000 to 2013 he edited the scholarly journal *Genre: Forms of Discourse and Culture*.

LARS POULSEN is MA in philosophy with psychology as minor subject. He periodically works as teaching assistant in the theory of science and ethics at the faculties of health science at the University of Southern Denmark and at the University of Copenhagen. Additionally, he has, through the years, worked as a teacher in psychology and philosophy at various preparatory courses. He is co-author of an introduction in Danish to the work of Michael Hardt and Antonio Negri. His special areas of interest are social philosophy, analyses of power, philosophical psychology, critique of society and related topics, and he has written articles on various of these topics.

www.ingramcontent.com/pod-product-compliance
Ingram Content Group UK Ltd.
Pitfield, Milton Keynes, MK11 3LW, UK
UKHW041826100926
8556IPUK00002B/41

9 783631 640388